PAVAROTTI
AND PANCAKES

AN ITALIAN-AMERICAN FAMILY TORN APART BY OLD
WORLD SECRETS. THEIR LIVES RAVAGED BY CRUELTY
AND YEARS OF SEXUAL ABUSE. THE TRUE STORY AND
LASTING IMPACT OF COVERING UP CHILDHOOD CHAOS.

FRANCESCO GRANIERI

A MEMOIR

Cover Artwork and Interior drawings by Michael Bell
www.MBELLART.com

Cover Design by G. Matthew Dixon
www.jestergraphix.net

Author Photo by Jordan Matter
www.jordanmatter.com

Editor: Amy Bonino

Text set in Georgia (11)

ISBN 978-1974399895

To connect with Francesco, visit his website:

www.francescogranieri.net

Second Edition: May 2018

Printed in the United States of America

for the little girl in the greenhouse...

~ Author's Note ~

This book reflects the author's personal experiences and recollections.

The events characterized as abusive or traumatic, have been retold as accurately as possible. Staying true to the conversations and memories shared with the author, by the victims.

Some names and identifiers have been changed. All dialogue has been recreated, so as to mimic the essence and nature of those speaking.

No medical records or police reports have been consulted in the writing of this book.

The author recognizes that certain members of his extended family may have different interpretations of their collective past. He respects their opinions, and honors them for the hardworking, loyal people they are.

No harm was intended by the publication or promotion of this book.

"I don't know what is it about this town, but it's always been my favorite place. I've worked all over the country, all over the world – London, Paris, Los Angeles, Chicago, you name it – but I get a special feeling when I'm here; maybe it's because I'm a Jersey Boy. But, I'll tell you something: there's something I get from an audience in Atlantic City that I don't get anywhere else."

~ Francis Albert Sinatra

PAVAROTTI
AND PANCAKES

AN ITALIAN-AMERICAN FAMILY TORN APART BY OLD
WORLD SECRETS. THEIR LIVES RAVAGED BY CRUELTY
AND YEARS OF SEXUAL ABUSE. THE TRUE STORY AND
LASTING IMPACT OF COVERING UP CHILDHOOD CHAOS.

FRANCESCO GRANIERI

A MEMOIR

"Sometimes, you are just happy to get through
an opera without trouble."

~ Luciano Pavarotti

Preface

I am a survivor; a descendant of abuse, and an heir to madness. I should be a derelict, a bum, or a drug addict living under the Atlantic City Boardwalk—but I'm not. Instead, I am a Jersey boy free of pretense and pedigree; a Garden State guinea armed with a story that **needs** to be told.

This is the story of my life, of my brothers' lives, of our parents' and grandparents' lives. An all American tale with Italian roots, planted firmly within the rocky soil of dysfunction. Ours is a real story, a true story; and this book is my humble attempt at bringing to light the many shadows of rage, despair and hope cast upon our path.

Like everyone else, I have memories that live within me, that are an essential part of who I am—but unlike so many, I felt compelled to collect those memories and share them with all who would listen. I wanted to recreate those moments and present them in such a way that others may benefit from studying the nuances of our "family portrait."

I wanted to use my experiences, and those of my relatives, as a way to forge a bond between reader and writer. It was that alchemy I sought. It was that connection and recognition of a joint crusade into the murky mystery of our past, that fostered my need to be heard.

—

There was a tradition practiced by many southern Italians who made the decision to leave their homeland, and make that journey to the New World. It was a simple tradition rooted in the 19th century, and it involved a simple ball of yarn.

Often times, entire families would accompany their one departing relative to the docks in Naples. As their loved one boarded the ship, the soon to be immigrant took a hold of one end of the yarn, and naturally, this ball of cloth began to unravel with each step across the gangplank.

When the departing family member took their spot along the ship's railing, the string would now be stretched from the dock to the deck. As the horn blasted, and the massive vessel slowly moved towards the sea, their ball of yarn completely came undone. The family members each held onto their end for as long as they could—until all at once—the string grew taunt and slipped from their fingers. It lingered in the air for a moment, then began its slow, regal descent into the deep, dark harbor.

That's how I think of this book—that ball of yarn. The last contact between an Italian mother and her loving son, an umbilical cord of sorts, a long look back on her tragic life. For *la mamma* is my muse, and my mother is the force behind our crusade. So, let's unravel the past together, allowing its texture and tension to slip between us like that regal reminder of all that once was of a time, a place, and a people I will forever call home....

1

My mother and her madness decided to kill us all one dark and gray winter morning. It was just after five a.m. and I was peacefully lying in bed. In a few short hours Dad and I were going to take Mom back up to Philadelphia. I knew that wasn't going to be easy. Many times over the last four or five years we've had to resort to this in order to buy ourselves a few weeks or months of sanity—an escape from living with her Dissociative Identity Personality Disorder.

Mom always fought the idea of going to stay with her family in Philly, but this time my father was adamant. Dad felt a heightened sense of urgency about getting her out of the house. He wanted my mother's oldest sister to watch her for a few days while he worked on making the necessary arrangements to have Mom readmitted to the Institute of Mental Health. Dad's desire, his need to make all of this happen *now*, was because of what he discovered yesterday morning. My father was in the master bathroom of our two-story, contemporary home, when he noticed that one of the fishing magazines he usually kept next to the toilet had a lump in it. It looked like something was stuck in between the pages. When he picked it up and opened to that page, what he found inside was a large pointed fillet knife. Unsure as to why the knife seemed to be hidden he brought it into the bedroom where he found my mother. "Ann," he said, showing her the blade, "what's this doing in the bathroom?"

Ann is my mother. She is fifty years old with olive skin, soft hazel eyes, and short salt-and-pepper hair. Sadly, Mom has the look and feel of a lost soul unable to move beyond her childhood, and incapable of admitting she needs help. Sitting on the edge of the bed, in clothes she has worn for the last three days, my mother became anxious when Dad showed her the knife, pushing for an answer as to why it was in the bathroom. Stammering at first, she blurted out, "I...was...using it to clean the tile in the shower. The grout needed to be scraped, so I brought it upstairs." Dad knew she was lying because Mom hadn't cleaned anything in years—but he decided to play along. "Then why was it hidden between the pages of the magazine?"

"Oh, I...um...."

"Ann, tell me the truth," he demanded. "Why was the knife in the magazine?"

His insistence on knowing the real reason for why it was hidden brought on crying. Mom soon agreed that the cleaning story wasn't true. She dropped her chin to her chest and tearfully told her husband of nearly twenty-two years, "I brought the knife upstairs to use on myself."

Upon hearing that, Dad lightened his tone and moved to comfort her. After all, it was just eighteen months ago when Mom attempted suicide. She drank half a bottle of liquid carpet cleaner, swallowed a handful of aspirin, and stabbed herself in the stomach with a butcher knife.

My father, Frank, is forty-seven years old and looks like he belongs in the middle of *The Godfather*. With his European hairline, pencil-thin mustache, broken nose, olive skin, and broad shoulders, he is a younger version of Marlon Brando's *Vito Corleone*. When we were growing up, our friends used to tease my brothers and me about having a father in the Mafia because he looked the part so well.

Dad was "old school," a man's man; full of confidence and swagger, loaded with integrity, poise, and gifted with a silky smooth singing voice. If we lived in a different part of the country our friends' needling wouldn't have meant much. But everyone knew the Mafia ran Atlantic City in the 1980's, and my father stood out in our small suburban town like an Italian sore thumb.

Frankie the Voice was the nickname my friends came up with to describe Dad's sinister Mob look. Though he was the most affectionate and supportive father any son could ask for, at times, he brandished a no-nonsense edge thanks to his ten years in the Army Reserves. When that edge was combined with his signature dark sunglasses, popped collar and black leather jacket, Dad looked like the Boss of Bosses, or *il capo di tutti capi.*

The Mafiosi who ran Atlantic City were really Philadelphia gangsters who had migrated southeast and lived on Georgia Avenue in the Little Italy section of the East Coast Gaming Capital. They were Italian. They were infamous. And just like my father, many of them were concrete contractors by day in the up and coming casino town. This only seemed to heighten the Mafia mystique Dad so often projected.

Even though he looked like a Made Man and was cavalier about hanging-out in the Mob's clubs and bars, Dad knew never to get involved with them—for his drive, his hunger, his *purpose* was his family.

My mother, my two brothers and I were why he worked so hard to become a success in the concrete business.

It was because of this bravado he embodied—this aura of southern Italian machismo—that I was so startled to hear him scream from his room down the hall. Lying half-awake in my bed under the covers on that dark and gray winter morning, three words pierced my soul as Dad screamed, "*Oh God, no!*" Each syllable laced with the terrorizing realization that *Frankie the Voice* was about to die.

At any other time, if my brothers or I screamed like that, Dad would come running to save the day. Once, when a burglar attempted to enter our house, my brother, Tony, saw him and shouted, "*Dad! Dad! Someone's tryin' to break in!*" My father leapt out of bed—completely naked—grabbed our Louisville Slugger, and chased the man through our massive backyard. Dad was hollering and screaming and scaring the shit out of the would-be intruder—but that was then.

On this day, my father awoke to find that my mother wasn't in bed. Often, she chose to sleep fully-clothed on the floor in the den downstairs, but this time was different. Dad knew Mom had been in bed with him last night, and that she was normally a late sleeper. This is why he was so surprised to wake-up and find that he was alone at five a.m.

From bed, he heard noises downstairs. It sounded like the opening and closing of drawers. The thought occurred to him that she might be searching for a knife in the kitchen, but he remained under the covers, half asleep.

Dad didn't fall asleep until three-thirty a.m. He was uneasy since finding the knife in the fishing magazine, and tried to stay awake until dawn, so as to keep a close eye on Mom, but fatigue got the best of him.

Shortly after he heard her rummaging through the drawers in the kitchen, Mom appeared at the top of the stairs. She was wearing what she always wore to bed—dirty panties, and a filthy button down dress shirt. But for some reason, my mother lingered at the top of the stairs mesmerized by a black and gold crucifix hanging on the wall outside my parents' bedroom.

From bed, my father could see her through the doorway. Not wanting to wake my brothers or me down the hallway, he softly called to her, "Ann, what are you doing?"

She didn't answer. Instead, Mom walked ever so slowly into their dark bedroom. Making her way across the foot of the bed, she stopped at the window overlooking the meadows, and glared at the glittering Atlantic City skyline in the distance.

"Frank," she said, "I don't wanna go back up to Philly."

My father took a deep breath, and tried to gather his thoughts. Before he could respond, Mom did an about-face and walked across the room. Stopping at the bureau, she eerily turned several framed baby pictures of my brothers and me face down; it was like she didn't want us to see what she was about to do. After finishing with the photos, Mom slowly made her way to her side of the bed. My father rolled to his right and slightly propped himself up onto his elbow. He softly said what he always said.

"Ann, you wouldn't have to go if you would just try to help yourself, but Philly seems to be the only answer right now."

All of this took place very calmly. Mom seemed like she knew what she was doing, and Dad was just too tired to make sense of what was going on; he could barely keep his eyes open. Yet, he noticed that Mom seemed to be holding a white, bunched up towel in front of her stomach. Struggling to focus his eyes in the dark, he soon realized that what he thought was a towel was actually one of Mom's sweaters. Thanks to the moonlight bleeding through the window behind him, Dad had a sense that Mom was using the sweater to hide something—but he didn't know what.

As the seconds ticked, in what seemed like slow motion, Mom leaned in towards him from across the bed. Dad thought she was coming closer in order to talk to him more intimately. Yet—in a flash—she dropped the sweater, causing the terrified sound of his ferocious scream to fill our house with those three fatal words, "*Oh God, no!*"

It was in that moment that I jumped out of my bed. I didn't even think; I just moved. I felt the adrenaline grow with each step as I raced down the hallway towards my parents' bedroom convinced of one thing—*Frankie the Voice* was about to die....

2

Long ago, decades before my mother dropped that white sweater at five in the morning, my parents were just two Italian kids from Philadelphia. They met in April of 1969; Mom was twenty-two, and Dad was nineteen. My parents worked in an office hardly noticing each other, until one day when Mom came into work with tears in her eyes. My father, ever the hero, moved to comfort her and learned that she was engaged to be married. However, Mom was becoming less and less enamored with her then fiancé, whom she saw as a weak momma's boy. Their relationship and pending marriage left her feeling trapped. In the summer of '69, Mom broke off her engagement and became Dad's girl.

On my parents' third date, my mother told my father something he would never forget. As they ate ice cream in the front seat of Dad's '66 Chevy, Mom said, without even a slight hint of remorse, that she couldn't wait for her own father to die. Dad stopped licking his ice cream cone and looked over at her.

"Yeah," she said, poking the spoon around in her sundae. "I swear, I'll wear a red dress and dance on his grave."

My father was confused, but Mom continued on very matter-of-factly.

"I'll never cry over him." She turned and looked at my father, "I can promise you that. When my dad dies, I'll never cry over him."

My mother's comments—and the nonchalant manner in which she delivered them—gave my father a sense of pause. But it didn't stop him from continuing to date this raven haired Italian beauty with the hazel eyes.

Over the next five years, my parents' relationship became serious as they began to dream and plan a life together. Every chance they had they headed down the shore, and drove the hour to Atlantic City where they spent time with Dad's huge, extended family whom adored my mother. Mom enjoyed the affection she received from Dad's relatives since most of her *famiglia* remained back in Italy.

My father came from a well-adjusted, Italian-American family. As the first grandchild born in this country, he was the prince who could do no wrong. All through his early years, summers were spent down the shore with an endless number of cousins. Love was everywhere, and he soaked it up.

When high school ended, and his first attempt at college didn't work out, an uncle arranged for my father to join the Army Reserves so as to avoid the Vietnam Draft. A year later, after he decided to try college again—only to drop out again—his mother, whom we called Grandmom, became concerned.

My grandmother didn't like the idea of her son floundering like he was. Her Neapolitan family always thought of themselves as being 'special.' They refined their Italian accents, and changed their names to sound more American. The last thing she wanted was to watch her oldest son squander away the opportunities available to him in The United States. So, she took Dad to a human engineering laboratory where my father took a test designed to determine a person's aptitudes and abilities.

The problem was—the test results came back to suggest that my father had too many aptitudes.

"Too many aptitudes?" my grandmother asked. "How is that a problem?"

The test administrators suggested that my father would spend the rest of his life struggling to be happy, let alone successful. They said he would never be able to follow anything through to completion. Not because he was lazy or untalented, but because other interests would always be pulling at him. The only advice they could offer was to suggest that he might want to become a writer—since writers could 'do' much on paper—but after two failed attempts at college, that idea seemed silly.

Someone else may have shrugged off such a hollow prediction, but Dad went out and proved it right. For the better part of a year he worked that office job where he met Mom, then abruptly gave that up to sell vacuum cleaners door to door, only to quit and deliver soda for a year. Creatively, he tried learning the guitar, the bass, the drums, the piano, the flute, the clarinet and the accordion—until finally giving them all up to study voice. In the meantime, he pursued acting opportunities in Center City Philadelphia, studied *bel canto* with classical voice teachers, and nearly passed an exam to become a Chinese linguist while a Sergeant First Class in the US Army. In the middle of all this, Dad found the time to start and front a jazz band with his younger brother, while changing jobs yet again, this time opting to work for a siding contractor.

After he quit the siding job he got into the construction business with his father, only to quickly *get out* of business with his father, and finally settle on becoming a concrete finisher for a friend of the family from Italy.

My father's early twenties were like one giant whirling dervish of endeavors tried and abandoned. The only constant in his life—was the young Italian girl he couldn't seem to figure out.

Dad didn't know what to make of Mom. They spent most of the first two years of their courtship apart, while my father fulfilled his obligation in the Reserves, and tried his hand at college. But, by the summer of 1971, he was back in Philadelphia full-time, spending nearly every evening with my mother. The more time he spent with her, Dad started to pick up on inconsistencies in Mom's demeanor. One minute, she'd be so charming and adorable in her old-fashioned way. Then, like someone flipped a switch, Mom would become cold, arrogant and distant. The more he watched this transformation take place, the more perplexed he became. No argument had precipitated the change, nothing traumatic had happened, but this routine would repeat itself again and again throughout their years as a couple. Whenever he tried to talk to her about it, Mom would either shut down or become belligerent.

Despite the feeling of confusion in my father's mind, he couldn't bring himself to leave my mother. The problem was, he also couldn't bring himself to marry her. He loved her, and considered her a part of his family, but something inside him remained concerned.

By early 1974, my mother started to complain to Dad that if they didn't get married soon, she was going to have an emotional breakdown. They had been together nearly five years; Mom was twenty-seven years old, and more than ready to be a wife and mother. "What are we waiting for?" She would ask. "What's the problem, Frank?" My father couldn't pinpoint what the problem was exactly. He just felt something about Mom didn't add up, and it started with what he saw of her family.

My mother came from a largely dysfunctional and closed-minded Italian immigrant family, where two phrases were never heard: 'I'm sorry' and 'I love you.' She was the youngest of six, and the third girl, a fact that would ultimately prove to be too much for her father to accept. Babbo, as we used to call him, was an alcoholic who embodied the worst of the Old World. He was barely five feet tall, but aggressively hated my mother, and her oldest sister.

My grandfather's drunken, and often times violent, abusive escapades were carried out behind closed doors—and *never* in front of his sole surviving son, whom he adored.

Babbo was devastated and depressed by the untimely deaths of his two other boys, both of whom became ill and died as babies. He held a grudge against the world, and a grudge against two of his three daughters. Babbo would never relinquish this anger; and would spend a lifetime punishing his oldest and youngest female children. For whatever reason his middle daughter was spared the years of abuse. Yet, this twisted and superstitious Old World mentality meant Mom and her family learned to excel at one thing: The Cover-Up.

In their close-knit Italian neighborhood, Babbo was viewed as a wonderful man, a model neighbor and deserving of the utmost respect. My grandfather routinely brought his homemade wine as a gift to strangers, and freshly picked vegetables from his garden always found their way to a friend. Babbo was always the charmer to those he thought he could impress, and people tended to gush over how cute he was. At barely five feet, with that olive skin, slightly receding white hair and adorable broken-English, he carried himself like a true *Signore*. In truth, Babbo had the remarkable talent of hiding his demented self-hatred from almost anyone he chose, which was in part thanks to my other grandmother, whom we called Nonna.

In addition to being husband and wife, Nonna and Babbo were first cousins who came from neighboring villages outside of Reggio di Calabria, located at the toe of the Italian boot. Life for my grandparents in Calabria during the first quarter of the twentieth century meant abject poverty as they lived in one of the poorest regions of Europe. This was not Rome or Florence, bustling with sophisticated businessmen and international tourists. Reggio di Calabria—and the rest of Italy's southern towns and provinces—were basically failed states that lacked any sort of industry. People like my grandparents, and their southern *paesani*, relied heavily on agriculture—primarily the growing of grapes and olives, and the exportation of wine and olive oil.

After centuries of foreign rule, the Calabrian people, or *Calabresi*, grew suspicious of authority and developed a legendary stubbornness referred to as *testa dura* in Italian—which literally means hard-head. Once a true *Calabrese* like Babbo made up his mind about something—that was it—game over. There was no chance of talking any sense into him; to try and do so would be like negotiating with a mule.

The presence of organized crime was another fact of life for my grandparents, as the local 'Ndrangheta, or Mafia families, controlled large segments of Calabrian territory, commerce and governance. I remember how Nonna used to tell me she was taught to be extra respectful towards those well-dressed men who wore their fedoras with a bit of a tilt. She said the tilt was always the 'give away,' the sign they were *malandrini*, and part of the secret society.

In Calabria, my grandparents were also introduced to a severely traditional approach towards relationships between men and women. For example, it was typical for a peasant woman like Nonna to carry a heavy basket full of olives on her head, and walk for miles behind Babbo, as he rode home on the family donkey. When they finally got back to their village, they would gather with other men and women, and sit by the road in front of their doorstep to enjoy the summer air. Men like Babbo and his friends would smoke their cigarettes and stogies, while women like Nonna would knit or sew. The men always looked out towards the street, so they could nod to the passersby—while the women talked amongst themselves facing the house.

This spoke to an old-fashioned, outdated tradition still practiced by some in the time my grandparents were coming of age. It was common, after some weddings during that period, for new husbands to produce bloody sheets as proof they had married a virgin, and consummated their union. If the sheets remained un-bloodied, the bride's family would be deeply dishonored. Charges may have even been brought forward of marital fraud. This being the case, many brides, often under the guidance of their own mothers, secretly carried pig's blood into the bedroom. Others would carefully file a fingernail to a sharp point, just in case they needed to cut themselves on the thigh and stain the sheets with droplets of blood.

Either way, women were used to going to great lengths to satisfy this ancient tradition. Women of my grandmother's generation were the last to proudly tie their bloody sheets to the railing of the balcony outside their bedroom. They wanted their family and friends to see they had bled after making love to their new husbands for the first time.

In my grandparents' world, Babbo was the undisputed champion of the household. Over the years, after they had immigrated to America, he liked to get drunk on his homemade wine, and regularly dismissed Nonna with a demeaning, "Go to hell'a *puttana*," the Italian word for whore. Nonna wouldn't do or say anything about it, for she understood that it was his right as the head of the family to treat her as he pleased. If she ever forgot her place, Babbo was right there to remind her, "I'ma da' boss," he liked to say in his heavy accent. "Dis isa my house, shut uppa, o' go'a to hella!"

But my grandmother was aware of her importance. She knew that without her, the entire façade would collapse. She knew that within the security of their close-knit society, sadness must be suffered in silence. No one spoke of sex. If her husband over-drank, that was considered a fact of life. Anything that happened, that could embarrass the family, would be swept under the rug. People didn't call the police on one another. Often when a problem arose, it was either denied to the point of being pretended away, or dealt with internally. The neighborhood was relatively strict, strong, church-going, and very family oriented, with a limited tolerance for laziness or disrespect.

Nonna worked diligently and incessantly in her efforts to keep up a certain appearance—devoting the same zeal and spirit to her family as a soldier would for his country. She made it her life's work to keep the shame hidden. My grandmother was such a convincing cover-up artist, that other women from the neighborhood would often tell her how lucky she was to be married to a man like Babbo.

13

3

It was the remnants of what Nonna had tried to keep hidden for so long that stirred up a sense of doubt in my father's mind about his future with my mother. As Dad struggled with his feelings towards Mom, Grandmom began to voice her concerns. My well-read, Neapolitan grandmother never liked my mother—or her Calabrese, peasant family. She picked up a bad vibe the first time she met Mom back in 1969, but Grandmom had bitten her tongue for years, in hopes the relationship would fizzle out. Now that she realized her son was seriously contemplating the idea of marrying this girl, she began to vehemently voice her opposition.

The year was 1974, and as Grandmom attempted to convince my father that Mom wasn't right for him, others in the family were telling him the exact opposite. My father was extremely close to his extended family, yet they only saw Mom from time to time. To them, she seemed sweet and innocent with a childlike charm. Because they did not spend much time with her—like Grandmom did—they did not pick up on the strange dynamic in Mom's disposition.

You see, my mother was the daughter of first cousins who were simple, Old World peasants. Babbo never received a single day of schooling in his life, while Nonna was only schooled as far as the Italian equivalent of second grade.

Even though my mother excelled at sports, and got decent grades all through school, there was something about her that could be construed as odd. She had a propensity to mispronounce simple words over and over again. No matter how many times my father corrected her, Mom used the term *traffic single* instead of *traffic signal*. When listening to music, she constantly called it a record *alblom* instead of a record *album*. My father couldn't get through to her.

Something else that baffled him was Mom's tendency to zone out in the middle of a conversation. He would be talking to her, waiting for Mom to respond to something he said, yet often she seemed to mentally vanish. Dad would have to say, "*Ann, Ann,*" several times before she snapped out of it, and returned to their chat. Then, there was an almost shocking naiveté that Mom seemed to regularly exhibit when taken out of her element.

Having spent her entire life in the Greater Philadelphia area, Mom traveled to nearby New Jersey for nearly thirty years. One would think Mom could have recognized where she was, especially after she herself started to drive the same route to and from these locations.

Yet, during the six plus years she spent as Dad's girlfriend traveling back and forth to Atlantic City, she would consistently and sincerely ask him, "Frank, are we in New Jersey yet?" Or, "Are we still in Pennsylvania?" My father would become exasperated and say, "Ann, what are you talkin' about? Of course, we're in New Jersey. We left Philadelphia and crossed the Delaware River, don't cha remember? That means we are in New Jersey now. You know that."

He would express shock that she couldn't recognize any of the landmarks they passed each and every time they traveled to and from the shore. It was almost like she was kidding, like she was trying to play a gag, but she wasn't. Mom was legitimately confused and disoriented. Once, after spending the weekend at her sister's summer cabin in northern Pennsylvania, Mom made a crucial mistake by going west instead of east on Interstate 80. She spent the next several hours driving in the wrong direction. She didn't realize her mistake until one of her nieces pointed at the huge WELCOME TO OHIO sign by the side of the road—causing them to spend many hours doubling back to Philadelphia. Along the way, Mom missed all the clues that she was off course. She paid no attention to the mile markers, or the fact that after a few hours, not a single highway sign mentioned anything about Philadelphia—her destination. She just continued to plow forward, without any clue she was lost.

This oblivious lack of common sense, or direction, spoke to something much deeper as far as Grandmom was concerned. Yet, based on their limited interaction, a few of Dad's aunts and female cousins offered to host an engagement party *against* Grandmom's wishes. When she discovered their plans, Grandmom was furious and stopped speaking to her sisters and several female cousins for a time. My grandmother was convinced that something troublesome was lurking beneath Mom's charming exterior. Yet, her sisters and cousins adored my mother and actively encouraged my father to propose. They thought

Mom would be a wonderful addition to the family, and their encouragement is what ultimately pushed Dad down the aisle. Like his aunts and girl cousins, he figured Grandmom had it all wrong, and that marrying Mom would smooth out whatever inconsistencies he saw in her personality.

To some of the more soft-spoken observers within my father's enormous Italian-American family, there existed the idea that Dad was marrying Mom—in part—to defy Grandmom. They recognized that my father didn't like being told what to do by his mother. His relatives felt Dad's motivation to marry was partially driven by his desire to show Grandmom that he could make his own decisions, separate from her approval.

Regardless of the reasons, my father was convinced the time had come to propose. Yet, he scoffed at the idea of having to get down on one knee and offer his girl an expensive diamond ring. *He* was the real prize, as far as he could tell.

So instead, Dad broke with tradition and bought Mom a ruby engagement ring, opting to sit next to her on the couch when he casually popped the question on Christmas Eve, 1974. These minor details illuminated the truth behind my parents' union—my father was going to ride the family donkey, and Mom was going to carry the heavy basket of olives behind him. They married that September, and my father soon found himself at a professional crossroads.

He and his brother had been performing with their band in the Greater Philadelphia area for years, but had yet to be discovered. Their musical style was anything but typical for the 1970's, as they mostly played standards specializing in Sinatra, Brazilian Bossa Nova and traditional Neapolitan songs.

In early 1976, the brothers began to discuss the possibility of taking their bandmates and their new wives to Las Vegas. They were hungry for exposure and big-time success.

The brothers wanted to put together a show celebrating America's Bicentennial in July, and felt like a casino showroom was the perfect venue. Their bicentennial aspirations quickly got squashed by their young wives, whom hated the idea, but it wasn't until Frank and

Ann realized they were expecting their first child, that the idea of moving to Las Vegas was forgotten.

With fatherhood looming, Dad scrambled to figure out what to do next. He had it in his mind to become a millionaire, but that was never going to happen if he remained a concrete finisher by day—and an Italian lounge singer by night. My twenty-seven year old father was in search of direction. He had an entrepreneur's spirit, but lacked focus.

That is until The State of New Jersey offered him an answer in late 1976.

My father had always been in love with Atlantic City, New Jersey. Nicknamed "America's Favorite Playground," his family owned property there since 1940, when his grandparents operated a boardinghouse on Arkansas Avenue, just steps from the sandy white beach.

Atlantic City had been the nation's premier seaside resort through much of the late nineteenth and early twentieth centuries with its sprawling supper clubs and back alley speakeasies. People came from hundreds of miles to parade down the Boardwalk, and dance their troubles away on Steel Pier, or take in a show at the famous 500 Club where Hollywood stars and Broadway acts performed nightly.

To my father, Atlantic City came to represent hope, optimism and family. Dad used to marvel at the massive Victorian-Era hotels that towered above the Boardwalk. He loved how Atlantic City had a *big city* feel, with a beach town's soul—sort of like a *Big Apple down the shore.*

Like the real Big Apple, Atlantic City never slept. All through his teenage years, Dad developed a love affair with the "Queen of Resorts," which may have blinded him to its split personality. Atlantic City was simultaneously the place to come for good, clean, family fun—complete with tacky souvenirs and games of chance, while also loaded with illicit temptation. It has always been a city filled with sex, drugs, illegal gambling, organized crime, and an inordinate number of bars and saloons.

In short, it was a twenty-four-hour city complete with a famous diving horse, expansive Fifth Avenue-style Easter parades, the one and only Miss America Pageant, and *loads* of urban misery. Tourism started to wane in the 1950's, thanks to improvements in the airline industry. Now, those same people who drove a few hours to spend a few days in Atlantic City could hop a cheap flight to Mexico or Hawaii causing

"America's Favorite Playground" to suffer a decline in popularity that slowly turned the once glorious town into a gigantic slum by-the-sea.

The ghetto that the city had become in the 1960's nearly fell into oblivion by the 1970's. When my parents got married, the Boardwalk Empire was a sad ghost town suspended in time, as its once majestic past was padlocked and boarded up. To my father, it remained a magically haunted place filled with such grandiose potential, but to the rest of the country, it was a forgotten city. The windswept isolation of her empty beaches and deserted streets caused the year-round population to plummet and summer tourists to stay away.

But all that was about to change....

On November 2, 1976, a referendum was passed in New Jersey that allowed casino gambling along the Boardwalk, and in the Marina District of Atlantic City. The dynamics of this new legislation immediately caused a *gold rush* mentality to sweep through the south Jersey/Philadelphia area, as Atlantic City seemed destined to make a return to glory. The hope was that this new legislation would revitalize the once proud resort, and allow it to take its place next to Las Vegas as the nation's other gambling Mecca.

Though my father enjoyed the singing he did with his brother and the band, he quickly changed his focus to getting in on the ground floor of what should have amounted to an explosion in the construction world—Atlantic City and the onset of legalized gambling.

With Dad's family-ties to Atlantic City, and the promise of work created by the casino frenzy, he decided to move his young family down the shore. He bought a small duplex in Atlantic City, without ever consulting Mom. To further complicate this sudden move to New Jersey, there was a squabble about the funds used to make the down payment for the purchase. Had Dad used money Mom had saved on her own prior to getting married? Or did he use his own personal money? My parents had only been married for three years by this point, they were still figuring out "how to be married." Was the money "theirs," or was this a "his and hers" type marriage?

Mom threatened divorce over the fact such a huge decision had been made without her being consulted. The idea that some of her own money may have been used to buy a home she didn't choose sparked outrage amongst her immediate family. Bottom-line, Mom had no intention of leaving her relatives and she did *not* want to move to Atlantic City, but eventually she backed down, and went along with the idea.

This decision to move down the shore illustrates how my parents' marriage would unfold—Dad was to lead and Mom was to follow.

It was May 1978, when Resorts International Casino opened its doors for business, and my parents took their young son, Francesco, to try their luck in Atlantic City.

After moving to Atlantic City, Dad put his singing aspirations on hold, and set his sights on starting his own concrete and masonry business. In less than one year, my parents nearly doubled their money on that small duplex as the gold rush that was Atlantic City drove real estate prices through the roof.

In 1980, with five casinos now operating in town, my parents decided to move out of Atlantic City and into a quiet little bedroom community fifteen minutes inland. There they purchased a cute three-bedroom rancher on a sleepy street across from an old-fashioned schoolhouse in a shadowy neighborhood full of tall maple trees, and elderly WASPs. It was shortly after we moved to the suburbs that Mom strapped me in a stroller, so we could take a walk through the neighborhood. Only, she proceeded to get so lost, it took us six hours to find our way back home. Our new house wasn't in some big, foreign city, full of complicated streets she never heard of; my thirty-two year old mother just couldn't retrace her steps.

Mom would spend her entire life getting 'lost.'

After the birth of my brother, Antonio, in early 1980, my mother became pregnant again almost right away, only to miscarry months later in the bathroom. Soon after the miscarriage, she became pregnant yet again with my youngest brother Michael. All this took place in less than twenty months, which caused Nonna to react. Rather than celebrate another pregnancy, Nonna verbalized her distorted and severe view of relationships as she decided to ridicule my mother for getting pregnant so many times so close together. She turned it into an attack on my parents' sex life. She claimed my mother must be having too much sex with her husband, evidenced by the successive pregnancies. This attack shocked my impressionable mother who had always revered Nonna. She said, "I thought you'd be happy for me, Ma? You know how much I want a little girl."

Only Nonna cut her off, and said she didn't want to hear it. In her thick Italian accent, she scolded my mother. "I no raise'a you be *puttana!* I no raise'a you be whore! You be lady and tell'a you husband leave you alone, he need learn'a respect!"

Nonna's angry disapproval pushed Mom into an even deeper fit of confusion and despair. She had been struggling since the miscarriage, but Nonna's accusations seemed to drive Mom out of the bedroom, and onto the living room couch—where she began sleeping on a regular basis. Whether trying to avoid another pregnancy or not, this habit of sleeping on the living room couch became so routine, that as a child, I knew that was where I could find her if ever I had a nightmare and got scared.

The truth was, despite the pregnancies, my parents struggled with intimacy ever since they got married. My parents' courtship was very formal which meant their honeymoon was truly about coming together for the first time as man and woman. Yet, something buried deep inside my mother came back to haunt her during my parents' honeymoon.

My folks spent their first few nights as husband and wife in Atlantic City where they could not consummate their union because of Mom's monthly "friend." It wasn't until three days after their wedding that Mom's body was ready to make love for the first time. After nearly six and a half years together, during which time they "never went all the way," Mom didn't know how to explain her discomfort after my parents' first sexual encounter. As she sat with her back against the headboard, feeling uneasy and confused, she looked up at her new husband and said, "Somethin's the matter, Frank."

"Whaddaya mean?" My father asked confused and concerned.

"I don't know, but somethin's wrong. It's like I've had this feeling before."

"What feeling?"

"Of being with a man...."

This mysterious moment of uneasiness and confusion between my newlywed parents set the tone for the rest of their lives. Soon after their honeymoon, even casual acts of affection on my father's part were met with disdain. If he draped his arm across Mom's shoulders while the couple sat together watching TV, my mother would turn to him and say, "Do you mind?" Dad would look over confused, only to have Mom continue, "Would you please remove that weight from my shoulders?"

Prior to having intercourse, my mother would never have said such a thing. She always welcomed my father's affection, but after consummation, something changed.

My young mother even confided in her sister-in-law, Bridgid, that the "smell of sex" reminded her of something, but Mom couldn't explain what that something was.

After being married for only six months, Dad sat down with his own mother.

In typical Italian fashion, their conversation took place around the kitchen table one afternoon, when in March of 1976 Dad said, "Ma, something's wrong with Ann."

He didn't tell Grandmom about their honeymoon confusion, but he shared with my grandmother how Mom was acting differently in private. How she avoided his romantic advances and seemed slightly annoyed by his mere presence.

Despite her fears about my father marrying my mother, Grandmom was a devout Catholic—her oldest son was **not** about to get divorced a mere 180 days after he said, *I do.* He took a vow for better or for worse, which meant he had entered into a covenant with my mother. Although she listened intently to his concerns, Grandmom softly insinuated that it was too late to do anything now—for Mom and Dad were going to be husband and wife in this life, and the next.

Looking back, I can't help but feel that this conversation was an act of capitulation on my father's behalf. By confessing the existence of issues so early into his marriage, Dad was inadvertently admitting to Grandmom that her instincts were right, and that his insistence on marrying Mom was wrong.

Grandmom may have been "right," but her oldest son already felt stuck. My parents didn't come from sophisticated American families, they were Old School Southern Europeans to the core. This private talk between mother and son would never be discussed again. No counselors or therapists or priests would be consulted. My father would have to deal with these circumstances as best he could, for this was the life and the wife he had chosen before God.

My mother's initial sexual discomfort in 1975—combined with Nonna's claim that she had turned into a *puttana* by 1981—was enough to force Mom out of the bedroom and onto the couch.

In addition to sleeping on the couch, Mom developed another habit that further frustrated my father. Even while pregnant, she started spending as many as four nights a week gambling in the new, posh casinos of Atlantic City. Many times, over the years, my father would call the police worried for her whereabouts, and often she would not return home until dawn.

Once, after one of her late-night gambling jaunts, Mom got mugged while walking back to our Cadillac with her sister, Colomba. My father had specifically asked her to park valet since he felt they were easy pickings—Aunt Colomba with her heavy limp, and Mom with her obviously pregnant stomach. But my mother chose to ignore his request, and park on the street in a notoriously dangerous section of Atlantic City.

The two women had just left Caesar's Palace and were startled by the muggers who snuck up on them from out of the shadows. Mom was dragged a few feet as her attacker knocked her to the ground, and struggled to rip the purse off her shoulder.

Thankfully, my unborn brother wasn't harmed. But the mugging, her mother's ridiculing and her bathroom miscarriage were nothing compared to the betrayal Mom would suffer next—during her fourth and final pregnancy.

It was 1981, and I was four years old, when Babbo kicked my mother in the stomach. We were in the living room at my grandparents' house in Philadelphia. Mom had just told her parents she was going to have another boy.

She was standing in front of Babbo, who was sitting in his favorite armchair. I was playing on the floor with my brother, Tony.

It was time to eat—Nonna had gone into the kitchen. I could smell her fried eggplant—lunch was almost ready. We were going to leave the living room for the kitchen table. Mom wanted to help twenty-month-old Tony to his feet. "Hey, Toe'nooch," that's what she calls him, "c'mon sweetheart."

She bent over, and reached for him. At that moment, Babbo took his right leg and swiftly kicked my mother in the stomach. He hit her with such force that she grunted and winced in pain. Her hands immediately moved to protect her womb. She closed her eyes; it seemed like she couldn't move.

Right then, Nonna came into the living room to tell us that lunch was on the table. When she found her daughter with her eyes closed, breathing deeply, wincing in pain, she said, "What happened? Ann, *chè successo?*"

Mom opened her eyes only slightly. She was still in shock, and she was still bent over. My mother turned her head towards Nonna, and tried to look up.

"Babbo kicked me in the stomach."

Nonna was confused—so Mom said it again.

"He kicked me, Ma." This time—she began to choke-up.

Once Nonna realized what had happened—that her husband/cousin had kicked her pregnant daughter in the stomach—she started screeching at Babbo in Italian—but he didn't care. My mother was his property. He was the boss. *Who the hell was she to have another son when he was cursed with three daughters, and the heartbreak of burying two baby boys of his own?*

When Mom graduated high school in 1965, she traveled to Italy where she met many of her cousins, aunts and uncles for the first time. It was during her summer in Calabria that she met an older, chain-smoking Italian named Alberto, who asked her to marry him.

Though Mom was flattered, she declined his proposal because she wanted to go to college back in America. But when she returned stateside, Babbo wouldn't hear of it. She thought to enroll in community college against his wishes, but in an effort to get away, decided to become an airline stewardess instead. Yet this time, Nonna didn't like the idea—too modern, too daring.

She finally settled into the office job where she met my father, and where she saved every penny she could, so as to help her big sister, my Aunt Colomba. Even though Mom was seventeen years younger than Aunt Colomba, she was the only one in the family to step in and attempt to save Colomba and her children from Babbo's abusive ways.

Mom's other sister, Renata, and her only living brother, Nick, were spared the years of abuse Babbo seemed to relish dishing out to Aunt Colomba. Having never finished high school, Aunt Colomba was always overweight and required special shoes to combat her heavy limp.

Had she been a part of Dad's family, Aunt Colomba would have been loved, cared for and made to feel special. But in Mom's family, following Babbo's lead, Aunt Colomba was seen as a second class citizen.

From the money she saved prior to getting married, Mom bought a small triplex down the street from Nonna's house. This triplex was so Aunt Colomba, who was raising four kids without any help from her estranged husband, could escape the barrage of abuse Babbo hurled at them.

Aunt Colomba's youngest child, my cousin Alex, was singled out and tormented by Babbo, even though he was a boy. They could be in the same room sitting together at the same table, but Babbo refused to speak to his grandson. His hatred was based on the fact that Alex looked like his father, my Uncle Larry, who was an Irish drunk. Babbo held a grudge against Uncle Larry, ever since he got Aunt Colomba pregnant out of wedlock. Babbo threw her out of the house, only to let her back in years later. Now that Uncle Larry has left his wife, and all but abandoned his four children, my grandfather starts torturing Alex on a regular basis.

Poor Alex shared a remarkable resemblance to his estranged father with the big eyes and the flat face. Mom said that Babbo loved to grab a handful of Alex's hair with both hands and pick him straight up off the floor. My cousin was only a toddler back then, but he would be on his tippy-toes, red-faced, screaming, with tears rolling down his cheeks begging for mercy. But Babbo would grit his teeth and growl as his grandson hollered in agony.

Other times, Mom said that Babbo amused himself by slapping Alex in the face over and over and over. He wasn't attempting to discipline his grandson for some perceived bad behavior, he was assaulting him. My grandfather would continue to slap Alex over and over and over even as his brother and sisters came running into the kitchen, begging him to stop.

It was traumatic for everyone to witness, a defenseless little boy being slapped with such violence and vigor that Babbo actually snarled. But Aunt Colomba was powerless to stand up to her father, and Nonna could only beg and plead, since Babbo wouldn't quit until he felt like it.

My mother said that Babbo seemed to derive pleasure from torturing Alex. I know from listening to family stories that Mom was the only one to step in and save him. On one occasion, Mom even shoved Babbo to the kitchen floor, so as to put an end to yet another chaotic and abusive episode.

My grandfather never forgave Mom for that act of defiance, but it wasn't until The Noose, that Mom knew she had to get her sister and the kids out of Babbo's house. Aunt Colomba could barely fend for herself after her husband left, let alone clothe, feed and house her four children—so they were forced to live with Nonna and Babbo.

On one summer afternoon in the early 1970's, as Babbo slowly got drunk on his homemade wine, between shots of whiskey, he started to pick on young Alex yet again. "You make'a me sick," he slurred in his heavy accent. "I hate'a look at'a you. I no wanna you here. *Disgraziato!*"

His insults and taunts grew worse and worse with each shot of whiskey. Aunt Colomba tried to intervene, "Hey Babbo, enough!" But that only enraged him. Soon my grandfather was out of his chair, Alex knew what was coming—more slaps, more hair pulling, more slurred insults. How much longer would this go on? How many more years would he have to endure such torment?

As Babbo moved towards him, Alex cowered, yet today Aunt Colomba grabbed her young son by the wrist. She yanked him away from her father, "Babbo," she screamed, "*stop it!*"

My aunt limped with her young son out onto the front porch where the sun was hot, and the humidity was thick. But the atmosphere inside the house was what she feared most; she could not allow her son to be tortured anymore—not today—but Babbo wasn't done.

With Alex in tears, he slowly descended the front steps, while holding his mother's hand, as Babbo scurried out the backdoor. He went into the garage and quickly found some rope. Knowing that Colomba couldn't drive, and that she didn't walk very well, he arrogantly strolled down his long driveway until he caught up to his worthless daughter, and her worthless son.

Babbo continued the verbal assault, as his slurred insults and drunken aggression accentuated what he was doing with his hands—my grandfather was tying a noose.

He swore up and down that he was going to end his grandson's life—today was the day. Babbo promised that Alex would not live to see tomorrow; he would swing from The Noose tonight.

Alex and Colomba were horrified. Babbo had gone mad. His eyes were as big as saucers; as mother and son tried to brush past him, Babbo kept snarling and cursing his grandchild. It was a two mile walk from my grandparents' house to Aunt Renata's home, which Colomba had decided would be their sanctuary.

Yet, Babbo kept on taunting them in his heavy accent, until he spotted a sturdy tree along the sidewalk. Stepping towards the tree he eyed up the distance overhead. Babbo then tossed the rope over a thick branch. With the stage set, he returned to demonically taunting his poor, little grandson as The Noose swung back and forth in the blistering summer breeze.

Aunt Colomba and my cousin made it past Babbo. They arrived safely at Aunt Renata's house, but when my mother heard about The Noose a short time later, she knew she had to get Colomba and the kids out of the house. It wasn't long after that sweltering summer afternoon, that Mom purchased the triplex.

Decades later, my cousin continues to insist that Mom saved his life. If he didn't swing at the end of The Noose, Alex believes our grandfather would have concocted some other way to kill him. "Frankie," Alex says, "your mother saved me from that madman."

Mom's family embodied an *Us against the World* mentality despite Babbo's selective abuse. They had more of a clan feel about them; very Old World in their view of outsiders. This made my mother even more desperate to love, and to be loved by Babbo. But by my mother's fourth pregnancy, sitting there in his comfortable armchair on that day in 1981—Babbo had only disdain for his youngest daughter.

Despite a lifetime of torture, and wanting to wear a red dress and dance on his grave, a part of my mother desperately held out hope that her father would one day give her a sign that he loved her. That's why his desperate and demented kick to her womb was doubly devastating. He knew she had just been mugged, and that she was relieved the baby hadn't been injured, but he didn't care. All he felt was a betrayal of fate—his worthless daughter was going to have another prince.

Nonna instinctively knew The Kick had to be swept under the rug as The Cover-Up continued. Both she and Mom understood that if Dad ever learned what had happened that day, he would forbid my mother from visiting her family in Philadelphia, and may even lash out at Babbo physically. So once again, Babbo was allowed to get away with whatever he wanted, as the women in his life were forced to suffer in silence.

When Mom finally gave birth to a healthy baby boy named Michele, or Michael, in November of 1981, my father decided to go fishing *immediately* after the baby was delivered. Fishing was my father's passion and something he did regularly back then. Once he realized my mother and newborn brother were physically okay, Dad and a buddy drove 9 hours to North Carolina for several days of fishing.

Although Mom didn't argue with him about it, her sisters thought it was wrong. They openly wondered what kind of a husband leaves his wife, newborn baby and toddler sons, to go off gallivanting.

They called him inconsiderate and arrogant, and labeled him an absentee-father. After Dad forced Mom to move to Atlantic City back in 1978, and decided to leave her and Michael in the hospital in 1981—many of my relatives on Mom's side of the family lost what little respect that ever had for my father.

"What a *stronzo*," they liked to call him—a real schmuck.

4

I'm six years old. I have light brown eyes, olive skin and long, curly brown hair. On Saturday mornings, when Dad doesn't go to work, he sits with me at the dining room table and teaches me Italian words. He drinks coffee out of a big green mug, and his hair is wild and messy. Dad is wearing his gray robe, and I am wearing my Spiderman pajamas. Turning to a page in *The Atlantic City Press*, he points at a picture and asks, "What's that, Chichi?"

I look and say, "That's a car, Dad."

He turns to me so that I can watch his lips form the Italian word for car.

"Ma-key-na," he says. "Can you say that, Chichi? Ma-*key*-na."

"Ma-*key*-na."

"Good, that's my boy. That's how you say car."

Dad and I go through the entire newspaper like this, and I like when he teaches me the Italian words and calls me Chichi. I like that he tousles my hair and tickles me, and offers me sips of coffee from his big green mug. He chuckles if I mispronounce a word in Italian, but that's okay because I know Saturday mornings belong to us.

Some summer mornings, Dad sneaks into my room and wakes me up. "Cheech," he whispers. "Hey Chichi—you wanna come to work?" He's whispering because my brother, Tony, is asleep in the bottom bunk, but I whisper back, "Yeah, Dad, I'll go."

When I go to work with him, Dad lets me shift the gears in his big green dump truck. He sits me next to him as he works the clutch and tells me when it's time to shift the truck from *first gear* to *second gear* and so on. Dad pays me fifty cents an hour, and when he passes out paychecks to his small crew of laborers on Friday afternoons, I get one too. I have my own set of trowels and work clothes, and Dad thinks nothing of letting me kneel beside a sidewalk of wet cement and get to work. Out of all the things I help Dad with: brick, block, stucco and stone—my favorite is pouring concrete. When we pour concrete, Dad comes alive and sings Italian songs. After all those years of studying voice and performing on stage, he sings loud and full. And as I drag my trowel back and forth across the top of the cement, I know nothing makes my father happier than taking me to work with him.

Dad lives to show me off to the other tradesmen on the crowded worksites. He especially wants me to showcase how skilled I am with that trowel in my hand. I'm only six years old, but I've been coming to work with him since I started to walk, and Dad is proud of me when the other men peek over my shoulder at the job I'm doing with that trowel and say, "Wow, he's a natural, Frankie!"

I look up and smile, because I love going to work with my father.

Dad was in for a rude awakening when he opened shop as a concrete contractor in 1978's Atlantic City. The gold rush that swept through south Jersey brought all sorts of shady characters to town in the hopes of striking it rich. And as a result, my father was forced to learn business the hard way. He got stiffed on his very first job. Dad installed five thousand dollars' worth of concrete work. Only when it came time to collect the money, the client claimed he didn't have the funds, and wouldn't be able to pay. At the time, I was only a baby and my father said, "I have a young son at home, and another on the way. Whaddaya mean you can't pay? I did the work as per our contract. I held up my end of the bargain." But he never saw a dime.

My father was at a loss for words. While he did the work thoroughly and with integrity as he was taught by his Old World mentors, he had a lot to learn. As a naïve young businessman who trusted people at their word, Dad couldn't believe that some men had no problem misleading him, or flat-out lying to his face.

In Ducktown, the historically Italian section of Atlantic City, my father quickly earned a name for himself by the manner in which he poured concrete, relying on his eyes and hands instead of a *screed*. A screed is a vital piece of equipment in the world of concrete. It's generally six to ten feet long and resembles a standard *two by four* made of wood or aluminum. Applicators use it to level wet concrete so as to ensure the freshly poured slab, sidewalk or driveway is perfectly flat. Any decent concrete man knows using a screed is the best way to avoid leaving any trip-spots behind, or low areas where water will gather in the form of puddles once the cement hardens.

Dad disliked using a screed because it required squatting or bending over each time you wished to move it. This tended to cause back pain, and was quite time-consuming. In addition, using a screed generally requires two men to shimmy it across the top of the wet cement, back and forth, back and forth—with each pass scraping and splashing the excess concrete all over the place. My father's reputation was based on pouring yards and yards of concrete with little or no help, and doing so by trusting his instincts. With a sturdy rake in his hands, Dad preferred to neatly push and pull the concrete from here to there and trust his eyes to tell him whether the surface was plumb.

The old timers who lived in Ducktown, the ones who had come over from Italy, said anyone who poured concrete like that was either totally incompetent, a real *citrul*, or a true master. And by 1982, my father was one of the best. He had been pouring concrete for almost ten years, four of them in his own business. Dad also laid brick, block, stone and did stucco work, but concrete remained his bread and butter.

My father's reputation as one of the best concrete guys in Atlantic City was only enhanced by the fact that he saw himself as an Old World artisan. His grandfather had been a stonemason in Italy, and from what he learned from the old timers, my father applied a sense of honor to his work.

The men who tended to work in the masonry field back then were often drifters who drank heavily with no education and dressed in the same filthy work clothes each day. Dad was different. He got his work clothes tailored, and wore his work boots only to the point they became slightly tattered before replacing them with a fresh pair. In the summer, he wore a crisp, clean white tee-shirt and prided himself on returning home from a long day pouring concrete with that same shirt still as white and clean as when he had left in the morning.

My father recognized that what he did for a living was different than being an accountant or an attorney, but he didn't think that meant he had to give-up his sense of dignity. Dad desperately wanted nothing to do with the American slobs he saw driving around in their beat-up pick-up trucks, bidding on the same projects in town. In a sense, my father wanted little to do with the American approach to life, which explains why some people called my parents Greenhorns.

A Greenhorn is slang for a newly arrived immigrant, someone who is unfamiliar with the ways of their new home. That term described my parents in the early 1980's, as Mom and Dad didn't vote or pay attention to American politics. Instead, they carried on like recent arrivals to the States busying themselves by making sopresatta each winter, and wine in the fall. When my brothers and I were baptized as infants, the priest who himself was from Italy, tried to talk my parents out of using the traditional Italian names of Francesco, Antonio or Michele.

He said, "We're in America now, they should be called Francis, Anthony and Michael."

But my parents refused his counsel.

They may have been American citizens born and raised in Pennsylvania, but internally Mom and Dad were hard-wired southern Italians.

This is why my father didn't bat an eye over what he saw in Ducktown each day. Atlantic City had long been an 'open town' where illegal gambling, prostitution, drugs and racketeering were common place. Now with six, huge, corporate casinos towering above the Boardwalk, the city was abuzz with showgirls and celebrities. By the time the Tropicana Casino opened in late 1981, a dispute had broken out between the Philadelphia and New York City crime families over control of the East Coast Gaming Capital.

The gangsters who lived and worked in Atlantic City were men my father knew, and worked for occasionally in the concrete industry. Dad understood who they 'really' were and what they 'really' did, but he was never afraid of them. He figured they were Italian, and if he didn't bother them, they wouldn't bother him. Yet, something of their brand of machismo began to rub off on my father.

Ever since getting stiffed on that concrete job back in 1978, Dad struggled to wear the many hats of a small business owner. He was excellent at pouring concrete, but the young man with too many aptitudes had spent the past few years bidding on the next project, while finishing the current project, and fighting to get paid for the last project. This constant battling to get paid for work that he rightfully completed, led to an evolution in my father's demeanor. It caused a hardening in the way he dealt with people, and the beginnings of that Mafia mystique he would come to project.

Throughout the 1980's, as Donald Trump, Steve Wynn and Hugh Hefner were vying to build the biggest, most elaborate casinos along the Boardwalk, Atlantic City became the single most visited resort in the country. Routinely attracting more than thirty million visitors a year, America's Favorite Playground was **back**—and regularly hosted more out-of-towners than Las Vegas or even Disneyland.

Yet, there remained a seedy element to much of the town. A ghetto-like atmosphere stood in contrast to the glitzy, multi-million-dollar gaming halls and hotels that dominated the Boardwalk and the Marina District. But that was Atlantic City in the 1980's, a place riddled with poverty and crime, where speculators, gangsters and degenerates mixed with weekend tourists and millionaire High Rollers. In the spring of 1984, the mayor of Atlantic City received a fifteen-year prison sentence for using his office to extort bribes from local businessmen. These bribes were meant to benefit the wiseguys from Georgia Avenue who really called the shots. It seemed like corruption and deceit were a part of the DNA of Atlantic City, and by 1985, my father had learned this lesson. He was no longer the naïve young man who came to town seven years ago. He was thirty-five years old and had been molded by the ways of America's Favorite Playground.

When he had completed all the concrete work on a building in Atlantic City and was having difficulty collecting his money, my father kept his poise and remained patient. Yet, the General Contractor, for whom my father was working, kept offering up all sorts of delays and excuses as to why he couldn't pay Dad. After several months of waiting for his money, my father became frustrated and decided he had been jerked around long enough.

Dad knew which bank in town was financing the project, he was friendly with the manager of this particular branch. So one day, after the bank manager tipped him off that the General Contractor would be in to collect a large check, Dad took our dark blue, two-door, 1977 Cadillac with the white leather interior and waited outside the bank until right before closing time. Minutes before closing for the day, the General Contractor walked into the building, just as the bank manager had predicted. This was Dad's cue; a moment later my father walked in with his dark sunglasses and black leather jacket, with the collar popped.

Just as one of the employees was locking the front door, Dad grabbed the keys dangling from the lock and locked the door behind him so no one could leave. Then, he put the keys in his pocket and calmly approached the General Contractor. Dad grabbed the man by the elbow and walked him into the bank manager's office where he closed the door.

Dad had already spoken to the General Contractor on several occasions, and was turned down when he politely and professionally requested his money. Now that months had passed, my father adopted a different tone. In that near empty bank with the employees confused and concerned, my father simply informed the General Contractor that neither one of them was going to leave until he got the $16,000.00 he was owed.

The bank manager was in Dad's corner, and held a check for $18,000.00 that was made out to the General Contractor's company. Understandably, the G.C. protested this seemingly calculated move. Who did my father think he was to pull a stunt like this? Only my father assured him this was no stunt. "You're gonna give me the money you owe me," he said, "or you won't be goin' home tonight."

Any other town in America—and the General Contractor would have called the police—but this was Atlantic City. It was the *Wild West*, and my father resembled those Italian cowboys from Georgia Avenue who held the strings.

Dad looked the guy right in the eye and told him, "I don't care what you gotta do, but neither one of us is leavin' until I get my money. My family has suffered long enough because of this shit! Now, the bank manager is gonna cash your check, and he's gonna give me my cut, and you're gonna deal with it. Otherwise, it's gonna be your turn to suffer, no questions asked."

As the General Contractor's protests continued, my father became even more relaxed. No less intimidating, but his body language spoke of a confident poise. In his core, my father knew he was going to win this battle. He was so calm, in-fact, that as each bank employee clamored to leave for the day, Dad got up, unlocked the door, and politely allowed them to exit, only to lock the door behind him, and return to the bank manager's office where he worked on changing the General Contractor's mind.

In those days, my father was a force to be reckoned with. All of those years pouring concrete had forged him into an impressive figure sitting before that babbling General Contractor. At 6'1" and 225 pounds, Dad embodied the sort of confidence that was both cool and intimidating, and after nearly an hour of pleading his case, the G. C. realized there was no way out. The man actually broke down in tears and started crying—*literally*.

He told my father that he was desperate for money himself, that he was going to get burned on this project, but my father was tired of the excuses. Dad had poured the concrete, his part was done; it had been months. "Pay me what you owe me," he barked, "or I can promise you, you won't be goin' home tonight...."

"The Queen of Resorts" was run by a lethal, Italian organized crime family. The one thing they virtually controlled was any and all concrete work done in the Greater Atlantic City area. As a matter of fact, they supplied *all* the reinforced concrete for the first six casino projects in town—and there was my father with his Mafia mystique.

The G.C. couldn't be sure if Dad was "connected" or not. All he saw was that my father was handsome, masculine, intimidating and determined. He was not going to be denied. After months of the General Contractor giving him the run around, and an hour of him crying and tripping over his words, Dad walked out that night with his $16,000.00.

Years later, when he told me that story, I asked Dad, "Didn't you think you were gonna get in trouble?"

"What could he do, it was *my* money? I wasn't robbin' him. This wasn't a stick-up, I was just tryin' to get paid. He eventually endorsed the check, turned it over to the bank manager, and I got what I was owed."

"Yeah, but Dad he still cudda called the cops or somethin'. You threatened him...."

At that my father cleared his throat, ran his right index finger across his pencil-thin mustache a few times, then calmly said, "Trust me Chichi, it wouldn't have been in his best interest."

5

The year is 1985, and I'm in second grade at the local Catholic school, where I am easily recognized for my role as the teacher's pet. I am also labeled the class storyteller, for my ability to hold my classmates spellbound in the playground or on the school bus, with the tales I create.

My mother volunteers each week to work Friday Night Bingo at the parish hall, so as to offset my tuition expenses. She also volunteers at school every other Tuesday, to help Sister Margaret in the library.

Mom is thirty-eight years old, with a nickel-sized, light brown birthmark on her left cheekbone and big, yellow teeth from twenty-five years of smoking. Despite four pregnancies, she fills out her 5'6" frame very nicely. Never a girly-girl, Mom shies away from manicures and pedicures. She rarely wears makeup or earrings, and is much more comfortable in front of a stove than discussing the latest gossip at some beauty salon with other housewives.

Mom's life is simple.

For the past several years, her days have revolved around the care of her three young boys, and weekly visits to her family in Philadelphia. And even though she prefers to sleep alone on the couch and spend her nights gambling in Atlantic City, my brothers and I love our mother very much.

With Dad always out working, Mom is the center of our world. That same childlike charm Dad's relatives picked up on years ago is what helps make her a great mother.

If it starts snowing, she gets as excited as we do. Mom will be the first one to suggest a snowball fight or a snowman building project. In the summer, she eagerly takes us to the beach or plays with us in our pool. Even discipline is a game to her. She has a birthmark the size of a pencil's eraser on the inner side of her left wrist. If we get too rowdy, Mom holds her right index finger over the birthmark, and swears she'll press the 'button'—as she calls it—and blow herself up. But we beg. "No! No, Mommy! We'll stop! We'll stop! Don't blow yourself up!"

Mom is such a good cook, that as I sat through my First Holy Communion—I remember looking up at Jesus, so sad and skinny on the cross, and thinking somebody should help him off that thing—so we could bring him back to our house—where my mother would have a field day stuffing him with meatballs and pasta fazule.

My brothers and I are *crazy* about Mom, and the four of us are inseparable. We make weekly trips to Philadelphia where we visit Nonna and Babbo and all our cousins. In the summer, Mom leads us on adventures to the beach and the Boardwalk; and in the winter, she excitedly bangs those pots and pans as loud as we do, out on the front porch, on New Year's Eve.

Whether playing together at home, running errands in the Cadillac, or attending Philadelphia Phillies' baseball games, Mom is always the ringleader, and we adore her.

Despite being a tomboy—and having grown up in an abusive, dysfunctional household, Mom has a genuine, compassionate outlook towards the world. She tries to impart that world view to us, every chance she gets.

In my second grade class at school, there is a boy named Sean Crost whom nobody likes. He has dirty blonde hair, and crystal blue eyes—but everybody makes fun of him, because he smells. Sean is teased so much that he hardly ever says a word. I feel so sorry for him, that when he brings in invitations for his birthday party, I ask Mom if I can go.

The day of the party, she walks me up the front steps of Sean's house. But when his mother opens the door to let us in, she is holding a tissue and dabbing her eyes.

Mom says, "Carol, what's wrong? Why you crying?"

"Nobody's coming."

"Whaddaya mean, nobody's coming?"

"There was only one other boy whose mother RSVP'd, and they just called to cancel." Mom nods her head for a second, "Okay. Frankie, why don't you go inside with Mrs. Crost?" Then she looks at Sean's mom and says, "Carol, I'll be right back." Mom walks back down the front steps, only to turn around and walk back inside a minute later with Tony and Michael saying, "We're gonna have a birthday party. Right boys?" Tony gets so excited when he hears that—that he starts to sing, "Happy Birthday to you, Happy Birthday to you...." Until I tell him you can't sing without any candles, as Sean's mother smiles through her tears. "Ann, you're too sweet."

Mom smiles back, "Oh, Carol. Now, where's the birthday boy?"

Sean comes over with a shy smile, and Mom motions for me to give him the gift we brought. I hand it to Sean, and he tears the wrapping off. He studies the collection of Matchbox Cars we got him. His shy smile becomes a big smile, as his mother says, "Now, whaddaya say to Frankie, honey?"

His eyes go from the cars to me when he says, "Thanks, Frankie."

Sean breaks out his Matchbox Cars, and the four of us play on the white linoleum floor in the kitchen, while Mom sits at the table drinking coffee, and talking to Sean's mother. After a little while, they ask us if we want to play, 'Pin the Tail on the Donkey,' and we all laugh at Tony when he pins the tail on the donkey's face.

Tony doesn't care that we laugh at him for pinning the tail on the donkey's face because when it's time to sing *Happy Birthday*, he keeps singing even after Sean blows out all the candles.

I tell him, "Tony, you can't be singing without candles."

But that only makes him sing even louder, until Sean's mother starts passing out cake and chocolate milk. Tony finally stops singing when we take our milk and cake, and sit on the floor, with our backs against the kitchen cabinets. He has stopped singing, but Mom laughs as she helps Mrs. Crost clean-up.

"That's my Tony, Carol. That's my Tony...."

After we finish our cake, we take our glasses of chocolate milk and go into the other room to watch *Tom and Jerry*. Mom clears her throat, as we walk out of the kitchen.

"Now boys, I don't wanna walk in on a concert in there."

My brothers and I roll our eyes when she says that, because we know what she means. Mom likes to joke around and call us *The Chocolate Milk Symphony*. She says one glass of chocolate milk, and we'll be shooting bunnies for the next two hours—her term for passing gas.

We drink our chocolate milk on the couch in front of the TV in the living room. During the first set of commercials, Sean turns to me with a smirk on his lips, lifts up his leg and toots. The smirk becomes a smile as he starts tooting like a boy gone mad. He lifts, toots and smiles—lifts, toots and smiles.

Soon, Michael is looking at Tony, and Tony is looking at me; we're not sure what to do. Do we act like nothing is happening? Do we say, *way to go Sean?* Or do we start tooting ourselves, and tell Mom that Sean started it?

Finally, Sean toots a toot that sounds like a trombone in a cavern, and we all get going. *The Chocolate Milk Symphony* builds to a powerful crescendo as we cover our noses and laugh at the composition we write.

Mom pokes her head into the living room to see if we're okay. When she does, she crinkles up her nose, "Oh, boys! Open one of the windows! *Open the windows!*"

She disappears back into the kitchen for the fresh air that's in it, and I know I'll never forget this day when my brothers and I helped Sean write a powerful piece for the birthday party nobody came to.

When it starts getting dark and the symphony has died down, Mom sticks her head back in and says, "Frankie, Tony, Michael, *andiamo....*"

We know when she says *andiamo* that it's time for us to go. Mrs. Crost walks us to the front door. She gives us all a kiss, and tells us we're sweet boys with a wonderful mother. But Mom blushes and says, "Oh, Carol, stop it...."

The winters in southern Jersey are cold; but since we are so close to the Atlantic Ocean, we rarely get *loads* of snow. However, when the snow *does* stick, and school gets cancelled, Mom routinely dresses us in our winter hats, gloves and boots. She smiles as we walk out into the winter wonderland, and says, "Let's build a snowman, boys," only Tony gets upset when we start rolling balls of snow to make the snowman's body. He says, "Mommy, we're ruining the snow."

Tony likes the look of untouched snow and doesn't want to see it vanish. "But how can you build a snowman without snow?" I ask.

"You can't," Michael says, and now Tony feels outnumbered. He shrugs his shoulders and hesitantly joins our project. We roll three balls of snow in total, one a little smaller than the last. Mom helps us place the balls of snow one on top of the other. Dad is working, or he would be here too, he plows driveways in the winter with his Suburban, but complains to Mom it ruins the transmission.

We all stand back and look at our creation; that's when Michael wants to know, "Where's the snowman's eyes, Mommy? He has no eyes."

So Mom goes back inside and grabs a carrot, two buttons and says we'll need a twig for the mouth. I'm in charge of finding the twig, "Near the bushes," she says, "look near the bushes."

She puts everything in place, and even after Mom tells him not to, Tony takes his scarf and wraps it around Frosty's neck.

"Toe'nooch, you're gonna catch pneumonia."

"Mommy, he's made of snow, he's colder than me."

"Good point, honey," she laughs, "but please put your hood up."

Again we step back and look at Frosty. Michael loves him, Tony thinks the scarf is fantastic, but Mom turns to me when the boys aren't looking and says, "Whaddaya think, Frankie?"

"Well Mom, the buttons are too small, he looks like he has pebble sized eyes."

"Oh I know, but don't tell your brothers he looks funny, I'm afraid Tony might take his eyes out and put them on Frosty, too." Mom chuckles after she says that, but in between taking pictures of us playing in the snow, Mom says, "Okay boys, snow angel time..."

Michael doesn't really know what she means, but he's hopping and skipping through the snowdrifts as we head over to the driveway near the Cadillac—where there is untouched snow. Mom carefully places her camera onto the hood of the Cadillac; then she lays down in the virgin snow. Michael looks puzzled. His expression asks me, *what the heck is she doing, Frankie? What is Mom doing?*

What Mom is doing is flailing her arms and legs around in the snow. She gets up and says, "That's a snow angel, boys."

Of course I already knew that, but Tony and Michael seem to need a refresher course every snowstorm we get. They flop down and try it. Tony's snow angel is lopsided because he says his angel is special, it has just one arm and one leg. Michael makes a pretty angel, but kind of smears his artwork when he stands up, and I decide just to shake my head at my brothers—the snow angel rookies.

Mom laughs at our innocence, and after an hour outside playing in the cold, she ushers us back to Frosty. She wants to take one last picture, before we head back inside. With the three of us surrounding our Jersey-born snowman, Mom holds her Polaroid camera in front of her face. With one eye closed, she peers at us through the view finder with her other eye and says, "Okay boys, on three say Frosty. One, two, three!" – "Frosty!"

In addition to being a great mother, Mom is firmly entrenched in her role as that *calabresella* with the heavy basket of olives on her head. Her daily routine is that of the Old World. She does everything from the traditional house chores to cutting the grass, weeding the beds, planting the flowers, organizing the garage, raking the leaves, pruning the trees, and trimming the hedges. In addition to *all* of that, my father expects her to prepare a home cooked meal each night.

It was an exhausting existence, and though it may have been the life she signed up for, by her late thirties—Mom was a lonesome figure with no real friends.

Even though she loved her three sons profoundly, Mom struggled with the lingering effects of that bathroom miscarriage. Every time she saw a little girl that looked Italian, she got upset. We would be on the beach or the Boardwalk, and she would get misty-eyed over Vanessa Marie—the name she chose for the baby she lost.

Whenever we were out with Nonna at the supermarket or the mall, Mom would point at a little girl and say, "Hey Ma, that's what Vanessa would'a looked like." Or, "Ma, whaddaya think, are those Vanessa's eyes?"

Once, when we were in church, there was a little girl in front of us. She was in her father's arms. He may have been facing the altar, but the little girl was facing us. Mom was playing with her and whispering, "Hey, cutie pie. Hey, pretty girl. What's your name sweetheart?"

The girl had curly dark hair, and diamond blue eyes. She smiled at Mom, as they played throughout Mass. When it came time for The Collection, my mother handed us each a dollar bill, and gave one to the little girl as well. Her father turned around, smiled—and mouthed—*thank you.*

But when the man with the collection basket was beyond us, my mother slid out of the pew and out of church without explanation. When

40

we followed her outside, we found Mom on the steps of the church, crying over how much she wished she had a daughter of her own.

During my childhood, there were many times when Mom seemed to be 'somewhere else' mentally. This was particularly true when seated Indian style on the floor in the living room, just feet from the TV set. There, with her eyeglasses on, chain-smoking and transfixed by the television—Mom would go into a trance.

She smoked and blinked, and even reacted to the events unfolding on the TV screen—but she was not "present" in the emotional sense. My brothers and I would have to call—*Mom*—several times, before she "heard" us. It was like she had left her body.

These dissociative fugues—as they're called—occurred regularly. We grew accustomed to watching our mother "disappear." It was a fact of life that we accepted as normal. But to outsiders, her "delayed reaction" or, "momentary amnesia" was shocking, and hard to believe.

Uncle Bruno is Dad's only brother. He is five years younger than my father, with the same receding hairline and brown eyes. When gambling came to town, Uncle Bruno and his young wife, Bridgid, followed my parents down the shore, and bought a house across town.

Uncle Bruno makes his living as a band leader in Atlantic City. He and his wife have three children. Aunt Bridgid is almost ten years younger than Mom, with brown hair, soft eyes and an even softer voice. She is Irish-American, and normally calls my mother to make plans to go shopping, or to arrange for us to spend time at the park with our cousins.

Only, it's becoming routine for Aunt Bridgid to arrive at our house with her children, ready to spend the day together, and find that Mom has completely forgotten they ever made plans.

Aunt Bridgid will say, "Ann, how could you have forgotten? We made these plans last night?"

But Mom will innocently shrug her shoulders. "I'm sorry Bridgid. Just give me a minute, and I'll get the boys ready."

There are days when Aunt Bridgid stops over, and Mom is in her trance. Once, Aunt Bridgid was standing on our small porch, outside the front door, with her baby daughter in her arms. Her other children were standing beside her as she called to Mom through the screen door.

"Ann," she said "Hey Ann, the door's locked. Let us in."

Mom was sitting in our living room. She was only a few feet from Aunt Bridgid, but it's like she had gone deaf. My aunt tried again. "Ann, c'mon, open the door."

But Mom still didn't move. Finally, Aunt Bridgid *bang bang banged* on the door. "Ann, I know you can hear me. I'm looking right at you. Open the door! *HELLO!*"

Yet, Mom still didn't move. Deep in her trance—her body may have been in the moment—but her mind was elsewhere. After Mom *still* didn't move, Aunt Bridgid was beside herself. She called to my brothers and me who were playing in the backroom. We came and opened the screen door. When she walked in, Aunt Bridgid marched right over to Mom. She bent down and said, "Ann, what are you doing? Why didn't you come to the door?" Mom seemed startled, and came out of her trance a bit disoriented, "Oh, hi Bridgid."

"Ann, I was bangin' on the door for like two minutes!"

"I'm sorry, guess I didn't hear the doorbell."

"Doorbell? What doorbell? I didn't ring the doorbell."

"Oh, I mean I didn't hear you knock."

"Ann, c'mon, that's impossible. How could you not have heard me?"

"I don't know. I just didn't hear you."

"Ann, don't play dumb with me."

"I'm not playin' dumb."

"Well, how do you explain it?"

"Explain what?"

"The fact I was lookin' right at you—standin' five feet away—but you were in a different world."

This wasn't the first time my aunt had seen Mom in her trance. Weeks prior, my parents went on a double-date with Uncle Bruno and

Aunt Bridgid. The four of them were standing in the lobby at Resorts International Casino, on their way to see Bill Cosby perform. They were early, so my father asked my mother if she would like a cocktail before they went into the showroom.

But, Mom said nothing.

"Ann," my father tried again, thinking she hadn't heard him. "Do you want somethin' to drink?"

Still, Mom remained silent.

"Ann...." my father repeated. Only, when she turned to look at him, his wife could only blink and sigh.

Aunt Bridgid, who had always viewed my father as an arrogant brute, thought she knew what was happening—my parents must have had a fight during the car ride into Atlantic City. My mother was probably just giving Dad the cold shoulder—something he more than likely deserved. So, she took Mom by the arm, and walked her into the ladies' room, figuring they could talk it out, and salvage the night. Only, when they got into the bathroom, Mom seemed unable to speak. It was weird. My aunt didn't know what to do, or say. She kept asking my mother if everything was alright. Had she and my father been arguing? But Mom could only sigh and blink. It seemed like something was troubling her, like she was cornered by fear. Every time my aunt tried to prompt her to speak, my mother could only resort to more sighing and blinking. Mom wasn't being rude; she couldn't talk.

It went on this way for fifteen minutes, my mother seemingly trapped inside herself; unable to communicate and struggling with "something" that was lurking right below the surface of her psyche.

6

My father was in love with being a father. Nothing made him happier than when he came home from work and my brothers and I raced to greet him at the front door. The moment he walked in, we all screamed, "Daddy's home! Daddy's home!" We reached for his arms and legs as he kissed us hello.

Sometimes Dad will kneel down and let us climb all over him so we can play Bronco. Dad will go around on all fours, bucking up and down like a Bronco, and we will ride him for as long as we can.

I'm usually in the back so I can hold Tony in place, and he then holds Michael in place—but when we fall off, *look out!*

Dad likes to tickle us when we fall off, he holds us down and takes his hands or his mouth and goes after our bellies, arms pits and necks. We laugh so hard we can hardly catch our breath. We love playing Bronco with Dad.

There are other nights though, when Dad would have his arms full of my brothers and me, and he would say hello to Mom, who was sitting on the long, brown couch in front of the TV. But she wouldn't move or say a word. Dad would say it a second time, "Hey Ann, how you doin' sweetheart? How was your day?"

But again, Mom would completely ignore him. Dad would drag us over to her, Michael hanging onto his leg, "Daddy's home! Daddy's home!" Tony and I clinging to each of his arms, as he asked, "Ann, what's the matter?"

But she wouldn't look up until he was forced to bend down and stick his face in hers.

"Ann, I'm talkin' to you. Are you okay?"

At that point, Mom would finally look up.

"Am I bothering you, Frank?"

"What?"

"I said, am I *bothering* you?"

"C'mon Ann, I'm just tryin' to say hello...."

"Fine," she would say curtly. "Hello."

44

"Ann, I just walked in from work, my arms are full of kids, everybody's happy, and the only thing you can say is, 'Am I bothering you?'"

"Well, am I?"

"Christ Ann, you sure know how to ruin a night...."

"That's a nice thing to say to your wife."

"Ann, I don't get it. What's the matter?"

"Nothin'."

"If nothin's the matter, then why do you ignore me when I walk in the door? How come I have to say hello five times before you even recognize the fact I'm home?"

"Oh, Frank—can't you just leave me alone?"

"Ann, I just want an answer. And what's with that look in your eyes?"

"What look?"

"*That* look."

Dad points at my mother's face—she is glaring at him, with hate in her eyes.

"I don't know what else to call it except the hate look."

"Frank, what are you talking about?"

"Ann, you're looking at me like you hate me. Like I'm the devil or something...."

"That's another fine thing to say to your wife...."

"I don't care what kinda thing it is to say to your wife. You're lookin' at me like you hate me."

"I am not."

"You are, too."

"Frank...."

"Lissename, Ann. I'm not your father."

"What's that supposed to mean?"

"It means I'm not your father. You always told me you hated him, but I'm not him. I don't deserve that look, I'm Frank. If I've said it once, I've said it a thousand times; I'm not your father. I've never done anything to you. I think you're confusin' me with him or something...."

Mom shakes her head in disbelief, and starts to look away from him, turning back to the TV. But Dad steps closer.

"Look at me Ann, I'm serious. I'm Frank, I'm your husband. I'm *not* your father."

"Yeah, and...?"

"Stop lookin' at me that way. Stop lookin' at me like you hate me."

"Oh, Frank, please...."

"Ann, I think we should see somebody, a marriage counselor, a priest, somebody. I can't come home to this anymore. It makes no sense."

"Then don't come home...."

"What?"

"You heard me, don't come home. Go find somebody else."

"Ann!"

"No, go find somebody else! If you're so unhappy, then go find some young fluff because I don't have a problem, and I'm not talkin' to anybody. If you wanna go, then go yourself, I don't care. But don't come home if you're only gonna jump down my throat about greetin' you at the door."

"This isn't about greetin' me at the door, Ann. It's about normal things people do. They don't sit in front of the TV ignorin' their husband or wife, makin' them say hello five times, before startin' an argument over nothin'."

"Who's arguing Frank? Just leave me alone...."

This was my parents' relationship, a sustained state of confusion. Whatever happened on their honeymoon; whatever memories my mother stumbled upon the night they consummated their union, remained unresolved. Those repressed feelings only served to mix with my mother's predisposition for confusion, thus driving their marriage into the ground.

By the early 1980's, Dad started locking their bedroom door, so Mom *couldn't* sleep in bed, even if she wanted to. He was angry at her and heartbroken over the state of their marriage. My father was convinced Mom was confusing him with Babbo, and begged her to "talk to someone," but she continuously refused to do so. Disappearing into those dissociative fugues, as she was apt to do, Mom resembled a time traveler in a dysfunctional version of *Quantum Leap*. She never knew who she was, and struggled to recognize her surroundings.

The same woman who saved Sean Crost's birthday party—and happily volunteered at my school—found herself unwittingly trapped in a marriage with a man she identified as the father she both desperately wanted to love, yet hated with every ounce of her soul.

Sometimes, Mom calls Aunt Bridgid and asks her to come over and watch my brothers and me. My aunt says, "Sure Ann, whatever you need," and appears at our door with my cousins.

When she returns home hours later, Aunt Bridgid asks, "So is everything alright? What was it you had to do, that I had to rush over to watch the boys?"

"Oh, I just had to run some errands."

But my aunt knows better—she studies Mom's eyes.

"Ann, you went gambling again didn't you?"

"Oh, Bridgid...."

"Ann, you and Frank don't have the money."

"Just cut me a break alright, it was only a couple hours."

"You can't do this anymore."

"Bridgid, look, thanks for watchin' the kids, but leave me alone. I'll do what I want."

"Fine, but I told you I couldn't watch the boys—if you're only gonna go to the casinos."

"Then I won't call you anymore."

When Dad gets home from work, and finds the refrigerator nearly empty, he calls to Mom, who is in the living room.

"Ann, I thought you were gonna go food shoppin' today?"

Mom doesn't say anything. Dad closes the refrigerator door, and sticks his head into the living room where Mom is sitting Indian style on the floor, staring at the TV.

"Ann, didja hear what I said? I thought you went shoppin'."

Mom keeps looking straight ahead at the TV, and doesn't move or say a word. Dad walks into the living room and gets a little closer to her.

"Ann, didja go shopping or not?"

47

Finally, she looks up.

"Uh? Whaddya say, Frank?"

"I asked you now three times. Why didn't ya go food shoppin'?"

"I didn't have any money."

"What happened to the cash I gave you this mornin'?"

"I spent it."

"On what?"

"I went to the casinos."

"You did what?"

"I went to Resorts."

"You went to Resorts with the *grocery* money?"

"Yeah."

"Ann!"

"So what?"

"*So what?*"

"Yeah, what are you gonna do about it?"

"What am I gonna do about it? What kinda question is that?"

"Just what I thought—you're not gonna do anythin' about it."

"Ann, are you outta your mind? That's all you can say? What am I gonna do about it? Jesus, if it's not you sleepin' on the couch every night of the week, it's this gamblin' shit!"

Mom looks up at him, "Oh, and I guess you can go fishin' anytime you want?"

Dad sighs and shakes his head.

"Ann, I don't get it. We have three beautiful boys, a nice house, our own business. What? What is it? What's the matter?"

"Frank, just leave me alone, alright...."

My father looks up at the ceiling. He is exasperated.

"You know what? I'm outta here. I don't have the stomach for this tonight...."

He heads for the front door, but Mom scrambles to get off the floor.

"No, don't go Frank!"

Dad is already out the door, but Mom grabs me and my brothers, and shoves us out after him.

"Frank," she shouts, "here take *these* with you!"

My father's eyes grow wide when he turns around and sees us on the porch. He blows back through the door, brushes us aside, and knocks

Mom to the living room floor. I start to cry. Tony starts to cry, and Michael is screaming.

Dad is on top of Mom. His hands are around her neck; he is choking her.

"You're makin' me crazy, Ann!"

Mom is beating him with her fists. Tony starts to scream. I start to scream. Now, all three of us are screaming. A moment later, Dad let's go of Mom's throat. She rolls over onto her side, and starts rubbing her neck.

"I can't believe you, Frank!"

"Ann, you're pushin' me to the edge!"

"I can't believe you—*in front of the kids!*"

"Jesus, Ann! You can't keep doin' this!"

Mom gets up off the floor. Her chest is rising and falling; her shirt is un-tucked. Tony reaches for her, but she storms out the front door.

Angry and in tears, Mom walks two miles to Aunt Bridgid and Uncle Bruno's house where she proceeds to spend the weekend.

Desperate for help, Dad reaches out to Mom's sister, Renata, or Rena. Aunt Renata is sixteen years older than Mom, and is the mother of five adult children. She has always been extremely skinny, and generally walks around with a scowl on her face. Aunt Renata is "harder" than Mom or Aunt Colomba, but when it comes to my brothers and me, she can be charming.

Anytime she comes down the shore, Aunt Renata always stops at Gino's Italian Market in Hammonton, and walks into our house with bags full of capicola, mortadella, provolone, mozzarella, Italian bread, olives, sweet peppers, hot peppers, pepperoni and sun dried tomatoes. She and Mom spread everything out on the dining room table, and pick at the capicola, as they delight in making us sandwiches and saying, *"Mangia! Mangia!"* We love when Aunt Renata comes down with the Italian food, but we also love how she likes to surprise us with gifts.

When I was little, Aunt Renata bought me a beautiful red wagon, but there was one problem—the handle was very short. Every time an adult bent over to grasp the handle, the moment they stood up to pull me around, I would tumble out the back of the wagon and crack my head on the patio. Dad grabbed the wagon to inspect it, and told everyone to be careful.

"Look, you can't stand all the way up, or the front tires come off the ground, and Frankie falls out the back and cracks his head on the concrete."

A few days later, it happened again. One of my big cousins picked up the handle, ready to pull me around the patio, and I suddenly tumbled out the back.

"Wah, wah..." I cried, when my head hit the concrete.

Dad grabbed the wagon again, and told Mom to put it away.

"Ann, put it in the attic," he said. "Keep it as a memento or somethin', but don't let Frankie keep fallin' out and gettin' hurt."

When it happened a third time—Dad snapped.

"Ann, I thought I asked you to put that away so Frankie wouldn't get hurt?"

"But it was a gift from Rena," she said. "If you're careful, he won't fall out. Nobody is doing it on purpose. It's just they don't realize you can't stand up all the way. It's surprising how quickly he falls out."

"I don't care if it's an accident, Ann. Frankie has fallen out three times, and *I'm tired of it! He's gonna hurt his head!*"

Dad marched out the front door, opened the back gate of his blue Suburban, reached in through the clanging of tools and trowels, and grabbed a sledgehammer. He slammed the door, *bang*, marched back into the house, through the front door and quickly out the back.

Mom asked, "Frank, what are you doing?"

She moved to the kitchen window where she could see Dad in the backyard. He grabbed the wagon, held it up and shouted.

"*It was a gift from your sister?*"

Mom shouted back, "*Frank!*"

Dad tossed the wagon to the ground. He stood over it, picked up the sledgehammer and began to smash it.

"Your sister," he said between swings of the sledgehammer. "Maybe if you listened to me," another swing, "my son wouldn't be fallin' out," swing again, "every time you turned around, and crackin' his head on the concrete!"

When he was finished beating the wagon, Dad looked up at her in the window and pointed to the mangled mess at his feet.

"Here, maybe now he won't fall out anymore. How 'bout now? Whaddaya think, Ann? Maybe your sister'll like it now!"

Dad threw the sledgehammer down, and walked back inside where he got in Mom's face about how he had asked her three times to put it away. If Renata didn't like it—too bad!

When Mom told her sister what Dad did to the wagon, she called him a brute.

"You're a brute," she said. "You know that, Frank."

The same thing happened when Aunt Renata bought Tony a rocking horse for Christmas. This particular type of rocking horse was suspended a few feet off the ground by four springs attached to four metal legs; so it was more of a bouncy horse, than anything, but Tony loved it. When my brother fell off the bouncy horse one too many times, and scraped his cheeks along the metal springs; Dad destroyed it with his sledgehammer.

When my parents first started dating back in 1969, my mother asked her sisters to watch their language whenever they spent time around Dad. She would say, "Look, Frank and his family don't curse like we do, so just watch what you say, alright?"

This caused resentment in my aunts, especially Aunt Renata. From then on, she always said, "Frank thinks his shit don't stink."

The truth is, she and Dad never saw eye-to-eye. The two of them had even gotten into a heated argument once at a family barbecue, resulting in Aunt Renata dumping a pitcher of water on my father's head. Only to have him retaliate by throwing her fully clothed into the swimming pool. They weren't fooling around; they just about hated each other.

By the time they sat down "to talk" in mid-1985, Aunt Renata had no sympathy for my father. She never forgave him for leaving Mom in the hospital hours after Michael was born, and was constantly upset that he chose to go away on fishing and hunting trips, leaving her sister alone for days at a time.

To her, Dad was a pompous, arrogant, Neanderthal, and it wasn't long into their conversation before Aunt Renata raised her voice and became accusatory.

"Oh, Frank, the only reason you're not happy with my sister is 'cause she won't sleep with you, just admit it."

"Look, Rena, it's not just sex; there is no love in this house. It's like Ann doesn't want to be married."

"That's absurd...."

"No, let me finish. She's out gamblin' so much; I feel like I don't have a wife."

"Yeah, but Frank, she can enjoy herself, right? I mean if she wants to gamble a little bit, what's wrong with that?"

"Not every night, Renata. That's not normal."

"Oh Frank, give me a break. When you wanna go fishin' there's nothin' Ann can say that's gonna stop you. So why don't you just let her have her fun? I mean she's a good mother; it just sounds to me like this whole thing is about sex, and that disgusts me. I mean, what is this sex thing with you men anyway? I haven't had sex with my husband in two years, and we're fine. Maybe you just need to learn to control yourself. You ever think of that?"

"Renata, I don't care what happens between you and John. This isn't the girl I married. Now, I've been askin' her to see a marriage counselor, or a priest, or—"

"For what?"

"To see if we can figure out what's goin' on. To get some help...."

"Why? She doesn't need any help...."

"*Yes she does!*

"No Frank, it's like I said. You need to learn to control yourself; that's what it comes down to. She's a good mother, and a good wife. So what if she goes out, and enjoys herself at the casinos? She deserves at least that much. So, don't tell me this isn't about sex."

"Okay, fine. Then let me make one thing clear. If you guys wanna keep pretendin' everything's fine, and Ann refuses to talk to someone, then don't be surprised when I find someone else."

"*What?*"

"You heard me. I won't leave my family; I won't leave the boys, but this is ridiculous...."

"No, Frank. You're ridiculous!"

"Yeah, great Rena, I'm the one that's ridiculous! *It's your sister that's ridiculous!* But I'm tellin' you right now, I'm not goin' on like this. She just stares at the television, and ignores me half the time, never wants to make love, doesn't want to talk and gambles away the grocery money. So, I'm tellin' you, things gotta change around here, or I'm gonna find someone else."

Dad rushes out after that, but what he doesn't share with his sister-in-law are the nights he paces in front of our house worried about Mom's whereabouts, and wondering aloud to himself about the future.

My brothers and I will be asleep in bed, his wife will be at the casinos until 3, 4 or 5 in the morning, and Dad will talk to himself on the front walk about his marriage. He is lonely, in particular he is starving for affection, and although Dad is staunchly against divorce, he starts keeping a log of how many nights Mom goes out to gamble, and noting what time she returns home.

My father is unsure how much longer he can go on this way, yet he can't even begin to imagine living away from his sons. On many of the nights when he tires of awaiting Mom's return from Atlantic City, Dad will quietly slip into our bedrooms and fall asleep on the floor. He just wants to be near us. His three boys are the only reason he continues to stay in the hollow shell his marriage has become.

Yet, the anger and frustration he showed Aunt Renata is all she can use to gauge how bad things have gotten between my parents, for Dad never opens up and shares his intimate struggles with anyone. He doesn't want to come off as a complainer. His code as a "man" won't allow it. This heated discussion with Aunt Renata only served to reinforce her low opinion of him. After Dad rushed out, my aunt turned to Mom and said, "I don't know how you do it, Ann. Ten years married to that barbarian; I just don't know how you do it...."

If the women in our family were convinced my father was an arrogant brute, he certainly didn't do much to dissuade them or deflect that image. Some nights, after long days of pouring concrete, my father would stop and have a drink at a bar in Ducktown with some of his friends. On one of those nights, he nearly got killed.

When Dad was on a pay phone, telling Mom he was going to be late and not to worry about having dinner waiting, this young man taps my father on the shoulder, and tells him to hang up. Dad turns around and recognizes the face, so he calmly says, "I'm on the phone with my wife; just gimme a second."

But the young man doesn't want to wait. He tells Dad to get off the phone immediately—but my father blows him off, and keeps on talking. This young man is barely 20 years old, but he is the son of a Made Man, which he thinks gives him the right to push my father around.

When Dad finally sits back down at the bar, this young man and his friends get in my father's face and threaten to stab him. Who did my father think he was for blowing off the son of a Made Man?

"If I tell you to hang up," the young man shouts, "*you hang up the fuckin' phone!*"

But Dad still doesn't back down, and Uncle Sal has to step in.

Uncle Sal isn't really our uncle. We call him that out of respect. He's from Catania, in Sicily, and talks with a heavy Italian accent. He has a pencil thin gray mustache, and always wears this hat that looks like something a newsboy would use. Under the cap, Uncle Sal likes to hide a tiny twenty-two caliber pistol.

When his sister's jewelry store was robbed the summer before last, Uncle Sal chased the thieves down the Boardwalk with a machete. He tackled one, and tore the man's shirt open with the blade, demanding he return the jewelry—causing an unforgettable scene for any innocent tourist down the shore that day.

Uncle Sal was nearly twenty years older than my father. He knew the wiseguys of Georgia Avenue very well, and even though this young man was *not* officially a gangster, Uncle Sal knew this was a no-no. You don't disobey someone connected to the Mafia, especially in a crowded bar, and think you're going to walk away without a scratch. So, Uncle Sal used his Sicilian credibility to vouch for my father. He told the young man that Dad was just talking to his wife, and meant nothing by the slight. Now that he knows better, Uncle Sal assured the gangster's son and his friends that my father won't disrespect them again.

There were countless other nights when Dad and Uncle Sal would be at a bar in Ducktown, having a drink together, when one of his buddies, a fellow named Lorenzo, would subtly poke my father in the rib cage a few times with his elbow. Then he would quietly say, "Hey Cheech, look who just walked in, *La Famiglia.*"

Dad would look up from his drink and before him would be several well-known members of the Philadelphia/Atlantic City Crime Family: the boss, the underboss, several capos and soldiers regularly wandered in off the streets for dinner or a drink, and each time they did the entire joint would come alive with this masculine electricity.

My father never feared these men, despite the fact they controlled the Delaware Valley—everything from Philadelphia, to the southern shores of New Jersey and northern Delaware. As a matter of fact, not only wasn't Dad afraid of them, he naturally knew his place amongst them and as a result *La Famiglia* knew my father by name, and always said hello to him and Uncle Sal. These nights in Ducktown were a connection to the Old Country for my father. Here, he was a proud Greenhorn, for this same scene, this same parade of honor, was taking place in the bars of Naples and Palermo, right across the sea.

Shortly after Uncle Sal intervened on my father's behalf that night with the gangster's angry son, Dad got in some legal trouble for beating up one of his tenants. The man had fallen months behind on his rent, and at first, Dad tried to work out a payment plan so the tenant could catch up, but that didn't work. Next, the man changed the locks to the apartment, and stopped paying any rent at all. After eight months of no rent, Dad went over and knocked on this man's door and demanded he get out, but the fella hollered at Dad through the chained-door, and told him to *"Fuck off!"*

My father struggled with other tenants over the years, sometimes even knocking on their doors with a sledgehammer, ready to break in if they didn't come up with the rent money. But this time, Dad decided he had no other choice but to literally throw this guy, his wife and their baby out on the street. So, one night, Dad parked our dark blue Cadillac outside the man's apartment, waiting for him to come home. When the man pulled up and got out of his car with his wife and baby, Dad approached them on the sidewalk. In no uncertain terms, he said they had to get out of his apartment that night.

Only the man arrogantly looked my father in the eye, and said, "Fuck you, you fuckin' dago. I can stay here as long as I want. I know my rights."

At that moment, *Frankie the Voice* lost touch with reality.

Dad grabbed the guy around the neck with both hands, and tackled him to the ground where he started to beat on him in the gutter between the sidewalk and the street.

Weeks later Dad had to appear in court—but this is where his Made Man looks came in handy.

The day of their scheduled appearance before the judge, my father was dressed in his work clothes—those clean work boots, pressed and tailored work pants, and signature crisp white tee-shirt.

He looked like the imposing Italian alpha-male he had become.

As the court dealt with another matter, my father slyly sat behind his tenant, and leaned forward ever so slightly. Like something out of a movie, he softly whispered in the man's ear.

"Lissename you jerk-off. If I end up goin' to jail because of your stupid ass, and my sons have to deal with their father bein' locked-up, you're a dead man. You hear me? I'm tellin' ya right now. If you go through with this, and press charges, and they lead me outta here in handcuffs—you're dead—that much I can promise."

When their case was called before the judge, the man suddenly had a change of heart. He stammered a bit, but said he had changed his mind, and wanted to drop all charges. The judge was surprised. He asked whether the tenant had been coerced, or intimidated into changing his story.

But the man said, "Oh no, your Honor, absolutely not," and so the case was dismissed, and the tenants moved out.

The FBI also picked up on my father's Mafia mystique, as Dad learned from one of the real wiseguys who had a 'man' on the inside. He said the FBI had pictures of my father—even pictures of him at our house.

Dad was told the Feds were watching him, and that he was under surveillance, and may be the target of an investigation. Though Dad had a clear conscience, and never saw any proof these photos actually existed, I think he secretly *loved* being mistaken for the Real Thing.

Despite the dangers and difficulties of doing business in Atlantic City, my father decided to take a chance at financially backing his younger brother, my Uncle Bruno, in the music business.

Their deal involved my uncle continuing to gig and work as a bandleader in Atlantic City, but to spend the rest of his work week writing and composing an album of original music, while my father paid Uncle Bruno's mortgage and other household expenses.

Dad had landed a few profitable contracts recently and was doing well financially. His plan was to sponsor Uncle Bruno for one year, and see what his efforts could produce. The thought was that one hit song could change both of their lives forever. In addition, Dad occasionally sang with Uncle Bruno and his band when there was a need for someone to sing Italian songs. It was during this time that he and Uncle Bruno performed at a dinner in Atlantic City for High Rollers where the Italian tenor, Luciano Pavarotti, was one of the guests of honor.

Dad was on stage, in a casino ballroom, in the middle of singing *Vogliamoci Tanto Bene*, when a door off to the side opened, and in walked Pavarotti. "It was just that simple," Dad said. "There was no announcement or anything. He just came walking in with this big smile on his face. He had just gotten off the plane wearing a simple scarf and a hat. He came right up on stage. He was huge, bigger than I thought he'd be, but came right over and shook my hand. I gave him my microphone and he apologized to the crowd. See—it was supposed to be he and Joan Sutherland together. But he said that they had just gotten in from the airport, and that she was too tired to make it. He looked tired too, but hung around and said hello to all the High Rollers. I'm tellin' ya, the crowd just couldn't get enough of him, talk about commanding a room. He got down off the stage after that, and made his way around, shaking hands and taking photos. It was pure joy, people smilin', everybody happy. A true superstar."

The night *Frankie the Voice* met Luciano Pavarotti would live in my father's memory forever.

He would never forget how proud he felt serenading those High Rollers, as the King of the High C's embraced his adoring fans....

7

My brothers and I *love* pasta. It is our favorite food in the whole wide world. We go bonkers for fettucine, linguini, farfalle, ravioli and lasagna—but our first love, our true love—is rigatoni.

Mom is quite possibly the greatest cook in all of New Jersey, which is saying a lot because New Jersey is the most densely populated state in the union. Not to mention, it is home to more Italian-Americans than anywhere else in the United States; so Mom has plenty of culinary competition here in the Garden State. But when I say she can cook, I mean Mom can *cook*. It doesn't matter if she's making chicken cutlets, pork chops, meatloaf, stuffed shells or homemade ravioli, Mom has no equal. And when I say my brothers and I love rigatoni, I really mean we love *Mom's* rigatoni with the homemade sauce, the perfectly browned sausage and the lovely ease she possesses in the kitchen.

When we went to Hershey Park over the summer, with our cousins, aunt and uncle, we had a fantastic time enjoying the amusement rides, the chocolate factory and the warm weather. There was only one issue—we missed Mom's cooking. Our hotel room didn't have a kitchen, which meant we had to eat out every single meal, and this disgusted me and my brothers.

We are spoiled by Mom's food and when she boils a pot of water, adds the salt and drops in a pound of rigatoni for dinner, Tony gets all excited. He marches around the kitchen, pounding his chest, repeating, "Rigatoni toni toni! Rigatoni toni toni! Rigatoni toni toni!"

He thinks the pasta is named in his honor, and he keeps professing his pride so much that Mom has to roll her eyes and say, "Okay Tonnooch, we get it, riga-tony. That's cute, honey, but *basta*, eh?" Only Tony keeps going, "Rigatoni toni toni! Rigatoni toni toni! Rigatoni toni toni," until Mom raises her voice and says, "Antonio Paolo!"

Whenever Mom uses our full Italian names, we know she means business, and Tony knows to stop. Michael's real name is Michele Giuseppe, but he's too young to know that and too young to know not to smear the red spaghetti sauce all over his face like he does at dinner every night. Mom smashes up a few rigatoni so Michael can pick at them with his hands, but he wipes the sauce all over his cheeks and Dad says, "Migalooch," that's what he calls him, "Migalooch, whaddaya doin'?"

Dad is only teasing, because he smiles as he takes Michael onto his lap and wipes the sauce from his cheeks. This is how our happy nights go; Mom will make a fabulous dinner, my parents *won't* get into an argument about The Hate Look—and the five of us will eat and laugh and giggle until it's time for bed.

We may love pasta—but there are three things Dad goes on and on about at dinner, and the first one is salad. Even though we eat it *after* everything else, Dad mixes our salad first in a big metal bowl with olive oil and vinegar and sprinkles of salt and pepper. He goes on and on about how important salad is for our "system," and says it's one of the reasons why the Mediterranean people are as healthy as they are. My brothers and I nod our heads in agreement, because we know Dad is only getting started—after salad, Dad talks about wine.

My father loves wine, he keeps a big bottle of red wine next to him on the floor, and during dinner he normally asks us if we want to try a little *vino*. Dad will pour a few drops in our own glass, or let us drink out of his, since he drinks wine from a small juice glass. Sometimes, if Dad is peeling an apple after dinner, he will dip little pieces of the apple into his wine for flavor, which I love.

Mom tells him she's worried he's setting a bad example, but I like to drink the wine because I feel so grown-up, especially when we have guests over and they watch me drink it. They all say the same thing though, "Wow, who's a big boy, but not too much, eh?"

I smile when they say that because I already know too much is no good. Dad says it all the time, "Chichi, remember this, drink too much wine and it's like poison—drink just enough, and it's like medicine."

The last thing Dad tends to discuss at dinner—is something he calls The Staff of Life.

The Staff of Life is Dad's word for bread, but not just any bread—Italian bread. To Dad, Italian bread is the greatest thing in the world. It doesn't matter how hard and stale the bread gets, Dad has even stood over our kitchen sink and cut a brick-hard loaf of Italian bread with a saw—an actual saw from the garage—because he *loves* Italian bread and couldn't fathom throwing it away. His favorite part of the bread is the *culo*.

Culo is the Italian word for *ass* or *butt*, which explains why when we go to the beach in Atlantic City Mom playfully smacks our backsides and says, "Oh, what a cute little *culo* you have!" But *culo* is also the word Dad uses for the end of the Italian bread, the hard part that everybody fights over. Dad uses the *culo* to clean his plate of spaghetti. He mops up the tomato sauce so well that he holds up his dish to show us just how clean it is. Dad says, "You see that, boys? That's how your plates are supposed to look, like they were never used."

These are the days we are the happiest—the nights our family dinners are cloaked and soaked in abundance and love.

It's April 1986, and I'm nine years old. Mom is wearing a black dress with a bright red scarf tied around her neck. She is sitting alone, and refuses to go over to Babbo.

My grandfather is lying in an open casket, with rosaries clutched in his hands, and flowers all around. He looks peaceful. Babbo slipped into a coma and passed away a few days ago.

Dad says, "Ann, c'mon, let's go over and see your father. It's almost time to go."

Mom doesn't answer.

"Ann, I know it's tough, but for your mother, for your sisters, c'mon...."

Dad reaches for her arm, as if to help her to stand, but she says, "Look at them, Frank. Look at the way they're crying over him. Don't they remember what a bastard he was?"

"Ann, now isn't the time."

"Frank, I will not go over there."

"Ann...."

Mom shakes her arm free from Dad's grasp. Her eyes focus on the floor. A moment later, the Funeral Director comes out, clears his throat, and asks everyone to leave so the family can have one last moment with the departed.

Dad tries again to coax Mom over to Babbo's casket, but she refuses him a third time. My father sighs, shakes his head and looks up at the ceiling. My mother stays true to the promise she made on my parents' third date, seventeen years prior.

She may not have worn a red dress, and danced on his grave, but Mom certainly didn't cry over Babbo. And, she steadfastly refused to say goodbye.

Babbo's passing marked the end of an era for Mom's family—their patriarch was dead. For Mom and Aunt Colomba, whom had spent a lifetime suffering under his abuse, Babbo's passing was both sad and suffocating. It allowed no reconciliation, no redemption, and little peace. They had to watch as their other sister, Renata, and their only living brother, Nick, mourned the loss of a hero. Babbo never mistreated them, it was truly the tale of two fathers: one a villainous dictator, the other a benevolent Old World papa.

This divide caused a slight schism amongst the siblings, but Nonna was there to set things straight. Despite having suffered under his wrath for decades, Nonna made it clear—Babbo would be remembered as a figure of respect and the champion of their hearts.

My grandmother's revisionist history was in stark contrast to the fact that the last few years of Babbo's life were spent in a constant state of misery, and drunken stupors. He eventually lost his driver's license after getting plastered on homemade wine and whiskey. A chaotic argument erupted between him and Mom one night at our house, which was typical of their relationship. He was drunk, and she tried everything in her power to get the car keys from him, only to have Babbo bully his way past her, and speed off with one of his adult granddaughters hanging out the passenger's side door.

My cousins started calling him 'Mad Grandpop' after that because he was always so miserable. He hardly said a word to us as we watched TV with him. He just sat there unshaven, white stubble covering his face and neck, his white hair sticking up in all directions, and with a hint of body odor in the air

Not long before he died, he got so drunk that while standing in front of the toilet trying to urinate, he fell backwards into the bathtub and cracked his head. His pants were down around his ankles; there was blood and piss everywhere.

In his later years, alcohol was also the cause for his inappropriate behavior around women—including my father's mother, whom we called Grandmom. One night we were all sitting in the dining room. Mom had just put a big bowl of rigatoni in the center of the table, covered with bright red spaghetti sauce, and a big white scoop of ricotta cheese resting on top.

Tony was halfway into his, *rigatoni toni toni* routine as Nonna mixed the ricotta in with the sauce, and Babbo put his hand on Grandmom's thigh, then winked at her suggestively. Mom saw him do this and yelped, *"Babbo, what are you doin'?"*

But Grandmom was quick to grab his hand and say, "Would you mind keeping your hands to yourself?" She took his hand, and put it back in his own lap. Nonna screeched at him in Italian, and asked Grandmom to excuse him—saying that he didn't know what he was doing, that it must have been the wine's fault.

Nonna always covered for him. She did the same thing at a cookout when he was introduced to one of my cousin's adult friends—a woman in her twenties, wearing a tight blouse. Babbo was so drunk all he could do was stare at the woman's chest—swaying back and forth. Finally, overcome with drunken desire, he lunged for her and grabbed her breasts.

Babbo had a boob in each hand, and wouldn't let go until his eyes rolled back in his head, and he yelled, *"Yippee!"* He slumped to the ground a moment later, and stayed there until Dad and Uncle John picked him up and carried him inside. Mom was mortified, and even though she fought the idea of moving down the shore back in 1978, she regularly thanked my father for getting her away from the sort of chaos Babbo thrived on in Philadelphia.

Upon my grandfather's death, Mom began to experience emotions she had kept bottled up for years. These were feelings of worthlessness lodged in the core of her identity—sentiments that worsened and pushed her towards the edge; ultimately defining who she would become as a person, a mother and a wife.

Sometime after Babbo passed—Mom was sitting alone in our Cadillac—parked outside a convenience store. A woman named Claudia, with whom my mother was beginning to develop a friendship, pulled her crimson, Pontiac Trans-Am, into the same parking lot. She wanted to run in, and buy a pack of cigarettes, but when Claudia saw my mother's car, she decided to say hello.

She walked over and tapped on the passenger's window like, *hey, Ann, it's me, Claudia.* But Mom gave no reaction. Claudia tapped on the window again, this time Mom half-turned, so Claudia opened the passenger door, and let herself in.

As soon as she sat down, Claudia realized something was wrong.

"Ann," she said, "what's the matter? Is everything alright?"

Mom kept staring out the windshield.

"Ann, it's me, Claudia. You okay?"

Again, my mother said nothing.

"Ann? What's goin' on?"

When my mother finally looked over, she started to cry. Again, Claudia asked, "Ann, what is it?"

"Why didn't he love me? Why didn't he love me?"

"Who? You mean Frank? Why doesn't Frank love you?"

"No. *My father*, why didn't my father love me?"

"Whaddaya mean, Ann?"

Mom started to cry some more. Claudia had never met Babbo; she had no idea he and Mom had such a strained and complex relationship. This was all new to her.

"It's alright, Ann," Claudia said. "Get it out. I'm here. But, whaddaya mean, he didn't love you?"

My mother turned her head back towards the windshield, and got quiet. Claudia pushed for an answer. "Ann, whaddaya mean he didn't love you?" As she kept pressing for a response, Mom finally snapped, and started slamming her hands on the steering wheel, shouting, "He just didn't love me! He hated me because I was a girl! Ok? Is that what you wanna hear? He hated me, Claudia. God, he hated me."

At that, Mom started to hyperventilate, and all at once, she opened the car door, and began dry heaving. Her eyes became bloodshot, and she had drool hanging from her lips as Claudia tried to comfort her the best she could.

Babbo's death marked a turning point in my mother's life. She would never again be the same....

8

Now that Babbo is dead, Nonna only wears black, and decides to go to Italy for a period of mourning. She stays with a great-aunt of ours who lives in Reggio di Calabria.

It's funny to hear Nonna talk when she calls from Italy because she forgets her English, and will say things that make us laugh, and leave us scratching our heads.

She sends postcards home that Dad has to translate for my brothers, though I like to attempt to read them aloud without his help.

Some nights at dinner, Mom and Dad will say little things in Italian, thinking we don't understand them. But I understand some, and they know I understand some, which makes me feel special—like I'm an adult.

Between those Saturday mornings when Dad teaches me vocabulary words, and the way Nonna will sometimes just speak to me in Italian, my "ear" is getting better and better.

But tonight, my parents are speaking English.

Mom says Dad has been making great money for a while now, and can't understand why we don't buy a new house.

Dad says we own apartment buildings in Atlantic City, only owe seven thousand dollars on our home, have all our vehicles paid off *and* have one hundred thousand dollars cash in the bank.

"Why," he wants to know, "do we have to move and spend a whole bunch of money on a big mortgage? Didn't I just spend thirty grand on a new Cadillac for you? Didn't I just give you a mink for your birthday, a diamond bracelet for Christmas? That's all possible because we don't have a huge monthly nut. If we buy something big, we're gonna be stuck with it and...hey...Ann...why you cryin'?"

Mom is crying because she hasn't wanted to bring it up, but Vanessa Marie has been on her mind more than ever, now that Babbo is dead.

She says that every time she walks into the bathroom, she thinks of how she lost the baby in there.

"It's not fair Frank, that little girl should be sitting here with us right now, but she's not. I can't walk into that bathroom anymore without thinking about her. You hear me, Frank? I can't do it...."

Dad softens his eyes, and puts his fork down, "Okay, Ann," he says. "Let's see what's out there."

For months after that, Mom brings Dad real estate listings, only to have my father shake his head and say, "*Four hundred thousand dollars?* Ann, we could never afford somethin' like that."

"Oh, Frank....."

"No Ann, if we're gonna do this, then you gotta find somethin' realistic."

"What's realistic?"

"Two, two fifty at the most...."

In January 1987—the month Mom turns forty years old—she finds a house for two hundred and thirty-five thousand dollars, and wants to know if that's too much money.

She tells Dad it's everything she has ever wanted, and though he says the price is pushing it, he decides to take a look. More than anything, my father wanted to make Mom happy.

The house is only at the other end of town, but during the ride over Dad says, "Now, Ann, if you like what you see, don't let on. Okay? Don't show any emotion. It'll only give the realtor leverage when she goes back to the sellers."

"Okay Frank, I won't."

"Ann, I'm serious."

"I won't say a word, don't worry."

The real estate agent walks my parents through the spacious, two year old, two-story contemporary home. It has gray, wooden siding, a two-car garage, a large foyer, an impressive master bedroom—with its own Jacuzzi, heat lamps and a skylight.

Mom is wowed by the large kitchen, the gigantic den with a cathedral ceiling, the sauna just down the hall from the powder room, and the *enormous* backyard with a view of the Atlantic City skyline.

To top it all off, the house is equipped with a central vacuum system. There are outlets all throughout the home that tie into a massive vacuum cleaner in the garage. Mom is in heaven, and equally as taken with the neighborhood.

The house sits on a quiet cul-de-sac, across the street from a villa for Catholic priests. Our would-be neighbors are all doctors, lawyers and successful business people whose beautiful homes leave my mother speechless.

She gets so excited she literally starts jumping up and down in the foyer. "This is it! This is my dream house! Frank, can I have it? Can I have it? Oh, Frank, *please!*"

"Ann! *Ann!*"

My father tries to calm her down, but Mom keeps shouting.

"No, this is it! This is it!"

Dad can only shake his head in disbelief, as the realtor smiles, and shrugs her shoulders. When they get back in the Cadillac, Dad says, "*Ann, what was that?*"

"It's my dream house."

"Yeah, I saw that. But didn't I ask you not to say anything?"

"Oh, Frank, c'mon. So what if they know I like it? That's my dream. Make it happen, won't cha Frank? *Please! Pretty, please!*"

Dad does try to make it happen, but says Mom's reaction is the reason why the owners won't budge on the price, and the deal falls through.

He says, "Ann, had you just controlled yourself like I asked, maybe they would'a been willin' to negotiate, and we cudda gotten the house. But not now, not after they saw how much you loved it."

"But Frank, I couldn't help it; that's my dream house...."

"Yeah, well now it's somebody else's dream house."

My parents spend the next year looking for something to buy, so Mom can move on from the pain of losing Vanessa Marie, and be happy again. But they don't find anything that comes close to that house on the cul-de-sac. Mom finally gives-up, and tells her sisters it's never going to happen—Dad is never going to buy her a new house.

Every August we go on vacation as a family. We've been to Cape Cod in Massachusetts and saw a replica of the Pilgrims' boat: *The Mayflower*, in Plymouth Harbor. The following year we went to Virginia and witnessed what colonial life was like in Williamsburg and Jamestown. Of course there was also that week of fun in Hershey Park with our cousins, albeit without Mom's cooking—but when we're not on vacation, we enjoy everything there is to love about living down the shore.

The beaches, the ocean, the pizza parlors, the miniature golf courses, the amusement park rides and all the fishing spots Dad knows make up our world.

Surf fishing is our family's favorite pastime, and it's one of our father's passions. There are wonderful days when the five of us pile into his big, blue Suburban and drive the 25 minutes from our house on the mainland, until we reach the town of Brigantine, which is the island just north of Atlantic City. There, Dad puts his Suburban into 4-wheel drive and takes us out onto the sandy white beach where we park near the water's edge and surf fish. We use these real long fishing rods that are twice as tall as Dad, and snack on the mortadella and provolone sandwiches Mom packs us for lunch.

On chilly afternoons we love when she wraps us in a big blanket, and pours us hot chocolate from the thermos, as we linger by the shoreline laughing, chatting and taking turns reeling in the fish.

If the Bluefish and Stripers are *not* biting, and we spend all afternoon without even a nibble, Dad will turn to us, shrug his shoulders and say, "Well, boys, whaddawesay...?"

My brothers and I know that's our cue to break out our "fishing song."

So there, tucked within the rhythmic crash of the waves, and hidden by the tall, grassy dunes, three Jersey boys and their parents can be heard serenading the Atlantic Ocean; their voices a harmony, their melody a march:

Sometimes you catch them
Sometimes you don't
Sometimes you catch them
Sometimes you don't

In August of 1987, we take our "fishing song" north of the border, as Mom and Dad take us to Canada where we'll spend a week together on a houseboat. We make the 400 mile drive from southern New Jersey, through upstate New York, stopping at Niagara Falls along the way, until we finally reach Ontario.

There we find our home for the next seven days: a forty foot long, two-story high, aqua colored houseboat with a fiberglass white rooftop deck. The dwelling itself sits atop two huge aluminum pontoons. Attached to the back of the house is a long sliding board, and inside there is a full kitchen, a motorhome-style bathroom and plenty of sleeping space for the 5 of us *plus* Aunt Colomba, who has come along for the trip.

We are all excited about our week of leisure upon Lake Ontario— only—Dad is worried about Tony. For the past few years my seven year old brother has developed the odd and unique habit of sleepwalking *and* urinating in random places throughout the house, *while* sleepwalking. "That's right," Mom says, "my Tony doesn't do anything halfway. Lots of people sleepwalk, but only my Tony Baloney can wander out of bed in the middle of the night and go pee-pee while he's sound asleep."

Mom can joke about it now, but over the past six months Tony has woken up several times and urinated all over her sneakers, peed in a drawer full of clean clothes, *and* pissed all over our cousin Vinny. We had a sleepover with Vinny and his sisters, all of us in sleeping bags, knocked out cold, on the living room floor. At some point, in the middle of the night, Tony got up, pulled his pants down and peed all over Vinny. The next day when Mom woke us up, Vince smelled like urine and Mom chuckled, shook her head and said, "Tony!"

My brother's sleepwalking and zombie like pissing habit, has Dad worried that Tony might wander off the houseboat in the middle of the night and drown in Lake Ontario. So he locks my brothers and me in the upstairs bedroom, and even barricades the door to our room, so Tony can't find his way out. But on this trip, Tony is the least of Dad's concerns.

Dad's first summer job was at a marina in Brigantine, when he was 15 years old. He has owned several small fishing boats throughout his life, so it is easy to see that Dad is more than comfortable on the water.

He rolls his eyes when the company from whom we are renting the houseboat requires him to take an instructional course on how to properly operate the vessel. Dad is exasperated and says, "Ann, this is silly. I know how to drive a boat. What a waste of time."

Yet, he sits through the two-hour required class, albeit under protest. This may explain why twenty minutes after we take command of the houseboat, we have our first of several, comedic calamities.

After Dad finished the class, my brothers and I helped him and Mom unload the Suburban, and of course we helped Aunt Colomba with her luggage, too.

Aunt Colomba is our favorite aunt on Mom's side of the family, she is so funny, and *always* excited to play card games and board games with us. She loves us like we are her own children, which I know makes my mother very happy.

After we carried the luggage onto the houseboat, and took the grand tour of our new digs, Dad carefully backs the 40 footer out of the marina. We are slowly cruising through the harbor, enjoying the brilliant August weather, when my parents decide we should go ashore and do some food shopping. "What use is it to have a full kitchen, if we don't have any food?" Mom asks. Dad agrees, and points the boat towards the shoreline. I can see the dock and boat slips ahead of us. There are dozens of different types of boats anchored and docked near the shore, and lots of people in shorts and bathing suits upon the dock.

Everything is so smooth upon the water, so effortless, but the moment Dad tries to slow the boat down, panic sets in. The engine won't respond to him. He tries again, and it still won't respond. Even I know we are going too fast. "Dad," Michael says, "the land."

"I know, Migalooch."

"Yeah, Dad," Tony says, "watch out for the land."

"Toe'nooch, I know."

Our eyes grow big as we approach the dock.

"We're gonna pretty fast." Aunt Colomba says.

"I know! Listen, I know! She won't back off. I don't know what's goin' on." It's too late for Dad to turn around, or veer in a different direction. We're too close to the shore at this point, we are heading straight towards the dock at a healthy speed. We can see the people gathered on the dock. They spot us approaching, and we're close enough to notice the puzzled look on their faces. They're not sure what's happening, and Mom isn't sure either because she is in the bathroom.

"Christ!" Dad hollers. "Colomba, boys, hold on! Ann!" he shouts towards the bathroom door, "We're gonna hit the dock! Everyone hold on!" The people on the dock finally realize we can't stop and start scattering for cover. "We're gonna slam into 'em!" I shout.

"Jesus, Frank!" yells Aunt Colomba.

"Boys, get down! Get down!"

We strike the dock with such force that Mom comes tumbling out of the tiny bathroom with her pants down around her ankles. My brothers and I crash into the front wall like cartoon characters, and Aunt Colomba does a complete 360, tiptoes like a drunken ballerina with a limp, and wipes out, face up on the floor. The only one left standing is Dad. As soon as we come to a stop, he scrambles to check on the five of us, then jumps onto the dock where he starts apologizing to the crowd. "She wouldn't stop. I'm so sorry. I mean, I had no control of her. Oh my God, is everybody alright?"

We damaged the dock pretty severely, and did quite a number on the front of our boat as well. Dad is embarrassed when a representative from the houseboat company is called to assess the situation. As our father tries to explain what happened, Mom turns to us and says, "Our maiden voyage, boys. Only us. This would only happen to us."

This is Day 1—20 minutes into our Canadian vacation.

The next day, we stop to fish in the middle of the lake. Aunt Colomba decides to go up to the rooftop deck and read a book, since fishing was never her thing. But my brothers and I are beyond excited to catch some Canadian fish.

Dad picks out the perfect fishing hole. He is standing at the wheel and calls to Mom. "Ann, grab the anchor, will ya? Toss it overboard. This spot looks good." Only when Mom throws the anchor into the water, she didn't think about the waste high iron railing surrounding the tiny front deck. This means that when the anchor takes hold, and the line grows taunt, it sits upon the iron railing. As the pressure increases, the railing gets ripped from the deck and goes tumbling into the water. Mom and Dad scurry to grab what they can, as the sections of railing break away, but they can't save them all. One piece of railing escapes their grasp and sinks to the bottom of Lake Ontario, never to be seen or heard from again.

This is Day 2 of our Canadian vacation.

Our poor boat now has a damaged front end, from the dock collision, and looks like she is missing several front teeth, as the entire left side of our front porch is rail-less. Dad got some rope and tied the pieces of railing he could save together, then he tied those pieces to the other, still intact railing, on the right side of the porch. "We look like pirates." Tony says.

"Yeah, Jersey pirates," Mom chuckles.

After two peaceful and relaxing days, with no crashes or equipment damage, we anchor again, this time to go swimming. Mom makes us all wear lifejackets, which is fine because it is hard to swim the way we are so distracted by the smell. We take turns sliding down the sliding board near the back of the boat. But as we slip into the water we are overwhelmed by a terrible stench.

Mom pinches her nostrils together, as if to ward off the bad smell and asks Dad, *"Frank, chè puzza?"*

"Ann, I think it's the sewage tank."

"Well, why does it stink like that?"

"I dunno."

"Yeah, Dad. It smells really bad." Tony says.

"I know, boys."

"Lemme guess," Mom quips, "you didn't pay attention to that part of the class, either?"

Dad says nothing, but I can only imagine that black water tank packed with our piss and shit to the point where it needs to be dumped. But we soon forget all about the stench when Aunt Colomba shouts down from the deck, "Frank, Ann, look at that...."

We crane our necks towards the sky and see this massive line of black clouds moving our way. "Boys," Mom says, "c'mon, let's go. Out of the water." We do as we're told as Dad quickly pulls up the anchor. We spend the night riding out the thunderous Canadian storm, tied to a huge tree near the shoreline of a tiny island. The boat rocks back and forth all night, none of us get any sleep and we still have to do battle with the odor of sewage that wafts into the living quarters. Aunt Colomba mumbles, "*Mamma mia, che puzza,*" as the boat rocks to and fro, and she crinkles up her nose in disgust.

This is Day 5 of our Canadian vacation.

A few mornings after Mom wrecked the railing, and Dad rammed into the dock, he pokes his head into the room where my brothers and I are sleeping, "Cheech," he whispers, "hey Chichi, you awake?"

"Yeah, Dad. I'm awake." I whisper back.

"Why don't cha come downstairs and help me drive the boat?"

"Really?"

"Yeah, c'mon...."

Dad is drinking a cup of coffee as he instructs me on the dos and don'ts of navigation. The entire houseboat is quiet, since everyone is still asleep. It reminds me of those Saturday mornings when Dad used to sit me on his lap and teach me the Italian words, except now we are standing behind the steering console where he continues to whisper at me, showing me how to use the throttle, and telling me to aim the boat at a certain landmark along the shoreline.

"Just keep her pointed at that cluster of trees, ok, Chichi?"

"Ok, Dad."

My father has the camcorder out and is busy recording the peaceful and pristine Canadian morning. I feel so good, so important— the ten year old captain of the ship. Every so often Dad glances ahead to make sure I'm still on course, then he goes back to recording the stillness and the beauty. We are gliding and I feel grown-up. As we approach a buoy I turn to Dad. He looks down at me, I point out the front window and ask, "Dad, the buoy. What do we do?"

"First of all, don't panic, Chichi. You always stay to the right, when you come to a buoy. *Capisce?*"

"Stay to the right, ok, Dad."

I nod my head and throttle the engine down to a few knots as I steer our massive home to the right of the buoy just like Dad said, but that's when I hear the Italian word he told me never to use—*minchia*. I know *minchia* is pronounced "mink-ya" and that it is a bad word that means "dick," but that's the word Dad shouts when our boat violently shutters to a halt. The two large aluminum pontoons make a tremendous rumbling sound as we come to a sudden stop. The engine is still engaged, but we're stuck. Dad shouts, "*Minchia!* Did, we run aground?" He drops the camcorder onto the couch where it continues to record our dilemma upside down. "Chichi," he shouts, "what happened?"

"I don't know, Dad. I stayed to the right of the buoy like you said."

He looks and says, "Yeah, you did. What the hell? I don't get it."

The rumble and the sudden manner of how we stopped wakes up the rest of the family. Soon Mom and my brothers are standing beside me. Aunt Colomba is still half asleep when she asks, "What happened?"

Dad explains that we are lodged atop the pebbled bed of the lake. He tries backing the boat off the rocks, but no matter how hard he revs the engine, it won't budge. Mom has picked up the camcorder and continues recording. My father is half embarrassed and unsure what to do. It is early in the morning, so no one else is around to help, or laugh at our predicament. We are in very shallow water, I can see the bottom of the lake only a few feet below the surface. But the real sight are the five Italians from New Jersey, and their lovely aunt from Philadelphia, shipwrecked on the rocks.

Michael is worried. He can be heard on the video asking, "Mommy, are we gonna sink?"

"No, honey, we're not gonna sink. But we're definitely stuck, right Frank?" Not only are we stuck, we are missing half of our front railing, our front bumper is wrecked, our vessel smells to high heaven and the man in the dark sunglasses, with his collar popped, jumping down off the front deck into the water is too much for Mom to take. She is laughing hysterically on the video as Dad is waste high in the water, he is barking directions at me as I stand at the wheel, revving the engine in reverse.

Dad is *literally* pushing the boat off the rocks as Mom laughs so hard she says, "Frank, I can't! I can't! I'm gonna pee myself!" Dad is trying not to laugh himself. He is shoving the boat off the rocks as I crank the engine backwards. It only takes us a few minutes to shimmy the houseboat off the rocks, but as Mom continues to point the camera at my father, still waist high in the water, she says, "There he is, my hero. Mister I don't need no boating lessons...."

And this was our Canadian vacation—August, 1987.

Nearly a month later, on the weekend of their twelfth wedding anniversary, my father surprises Mom with the deed to that same house she fell in love with. Even though it is their anniversary, Dad is in Cape Cod, surf fishing with friends when he purchases the home over the phone. The owners were willing to negotiate after several deals had fallen through, so Dad made them an offer they were desperate to take, they accepted his offer of $219,000. Mom is so happy at the news, we immediately start packing, and move into her dream house just days before Christmas, 1987.

In the summer of 1988, if we're not surf fishing in Brigantine, then we are on the beach in Atlantic City where my brothers and I marvel at the huge casinos hovering above the Boardwalk. Every time we go to the beach in Atlantic City, we visit our aunts, uncles and cousins on Dad's side of the family who are *always* gathered in a circle of beach chairs playing Pinochle, and listening to Frank Sinatra on a little transistor radio.

Behind us stands the massive Tropicana Casino, as Dad unfolds a big white blanket next to the circle of beach chairs and tells us to kiss everybody hello. We say hello to Dad's family, even though it can take us fifteen minutes the way they all want to pinch our cheeks and say, "*quanto bello*," which means they think we're cute.

When Mom comes with us, she will lie on the white blanket and visit with our relatives, while Dad stands along the shoreline in cut-off dungarees tossing a tennis ball high into the air. He tosses the tennis ball to the three of us who are standing waist deep in the surf—we are taking turns trying to get the, *At'a boy!*

My brothers and I try to time our dives just right so we leap for the tennis ball at the exact moment a wave comes crashing over our backs. If we're able to catch the ball, despite the sea slamming down upon us, Dad will holler, "*At'a boy!*" He first waits for us to stick our arms out of the water and show him we were able to hold on, before he gives us the, *At'a boy*—but when he does—Dad smiles and claps his hands together, pride etched upon his face.

We love making Dad proud, but our favorite time to play is when Mom takes a break from reading her paperback novel, and watches us chase the *At'a boy*. We love showing off for Mom, and she loves cheering us on. She stands beside our father along the waterline, wearing a one-piece, white bathing suit and raises her fists in the air each time she shouts, "Go get'em, boys! Way to go, Tony! Great job, Michael!"

The five of us stay out on the beach playing *At'a boy* as the sky turns orange then pink and the sun disappears behind the casinos. We stay out on the beach long after Dad's family has folded up their beach chairs and taken their Pinochle game home to be finished on the front porch. We stay out on the beach because we are happy, and nothing is better than that.

9

By the late 1980's, those Italian gangsters who ran Atlantic City had been rounded up, and either sent to prison, or forced to turn Government's Witness. Some said the loss of Mob rule in Atlantic City was bad for business, while others claimed it was long overdue. Either way, this transformation of the city's make up caused a change in my father's tiny world. Gone were the old-timers and the romance of pouring concrete like they did in the Old Country. Ducktown had changed, and so had my father.

In late 1988, after ten years in business, Dad decides to stop being a concrete contractor. Even though he has done very well for himself, he doesn't want to pour driveways and sidewalks for the rest of his life. He wants to be an entrepreneur; he wants to be a home builder.

Not long after we move into our new house, and on the eve of his fortieth birthday, Dad takes out a *massive* business loan, and buys one hundred acres of land for a considerable amount of money. The land is in Cumberland County, about an hour's drive inland from Atlantic City.

It is in Cumberland County where Dad partners with his best friend, a successful businessman who emigrated from Italy years before, to start a neighborhood development project. Since his partner lives out of state, Dad is the project lead, and oversees every detail as plans are drawn up, and names are chosen for the streets of the community they are creating.

Even though I'm only twelve years old, I know this is a big step. Dad has stopped bidding new concrete work, which means we are living off my parents' savings. My father now spends all of his time out at the development where there is an endless amount of work to be done.

He even sells his big green dump truck, and leases a brand new, charcoal colored GMC Jimmy. Dad starts carrying a briefcase, and wears a necktie to work. I can't help but think how much has changed.

He used to be a Greenhorn. He used to come home from work with those boots on, and that crisp, white, tailored tee-shirt.

But now that he's a developer—now that he's an American Businessman—Dad walks in the door looking like an architect, with blueprints tucked under his arm, and a mobile phone pressed against his ear.

After some initial excitement, life in Mom's dream house isn't much different than life at our old house. All through 1988 and into 1989, my parents' marriage continues to deteriorate behind closed doors. In public, and amongst our family, they are seen as a solid, old fashioned couple. Yet privately, their relationship is haunted by Babbo—both figuratively and literally.

Figuratively—in the sense that Dad repeatedly has to remind Mom not to give him the 'hate look.' He is still convinced that she is confusing him with her dead father, thus projecting their 'unfinished business' upon my parents' marriage.

And literally—in that Mom develops a real fear of Babbo's dead spirit.

In my parents' master bedroom, there is a big walk-in closet that Mom is afraid of. She isn't afraid of the closet exactly, but who might be hiding inside.

Mom says she can't sleep if the closet doors are closed, because she's worried Babbo might be hiding inside—waiting to kill her—once she nods off. And the sad part is, she isn't joking.

Babbo has been dead for almost four years. Still, she asks Dad to check the closet for her on nights she sleeps upstairs in bed. Dad normally tries to tell her, "Ann, your father's dead. He's not hiding in the closet, listen to what you're sayin'...."

But Mom insists, so Dad gets out of bed, with only a towel wrapped around his waist, walks over to the closet, opens the doors, turns on the lights, walks around the closet, checks behind the clothes hanging on the hangers, sticks his head back into the bedroom, and tells Mom the coast is clear.

She will have the covers pulled up to her chin, just in case.

"You sure, Frank? Are you sure my father's not in there?"

"I'm sure," Dad says, as he shuts-off the closet lights, and climbs back into bed.

When Dad goes away for two weeks with his buddies, checking the closet becomes my job as The Man of the House. Every night, when Mom tells us to head upstairs and get ready for bed, she calls me down to her room, where I know I'll find her with the covers pulled up to her chin—afraid to make a move.

I'll be in my pajamas, standing in the doorway to her bedroom, looking at her tanned face, and salt-and-pepper hair as she motions me towards the closet. I'll walk over and open the doors, turn on the lights, and check everything like Dad always does. When I'm through looking for Babbo, I'll stick my head into the bedroom, turn the lights off and tell her I don't see anything. "You sure, Frankie?"

"Yeah, I'm sure Mom."

"Babbo's not in there?"

"No, Babbo's not in there."

"Okay then, just leave the doors open and get to bed sweetheart."

That's what's most important to Mom—leaving the closet doors open. That way she'll know whether Babbo snuck in or not during the middle of the night. I know it's weird to be checking the closet for my dead grandfather, but as I wander over to her bed to kiss her goodnight, I can't help but think I like when Dad is away, and I get to be The Man of the House who protects Mom.

At our old house, Mom routinely slept on the couch in the living room. It's where I knew I'd find her if ever I had a nightmare and needed to be reassured everything was alright. But at our new house, she divides her nights between the master bedroom and sleeping in the den without a pillow or a blanket. When she sleeps downstairs, we normally find her sprawled out on the floor fully clothed; sometimes she'll even have her green winter jacket on, which tells us she went to the casinos the night before, and came home so late that all she could do was "collapse" on the floor with the keys to the Cadillac still clutched in her right hand.

Maybe it's because Mom is afraid of Babbo hiding in her closet that she sleeps in the den so much. On those mornings, my brothers and

I get up for school and find her sprawled out on the floor; one of us literally steps over her in order to reach the TV, and turn it on, so we can watch cartoons as we eat our cereal. The sound of the TV normally wakes Mom, though she stays motionless on the floor—with one exception. Mom always sleeps face down, and the first thing she does when she hears the TV is change cheeks. She will keep her body still, but switch which side of her face is lying on the carpet. When she does that, we can see the side of her face that she has been sleeping on with its pink color, and little pock marks from the carpet. Mom's hair will be messy and lopsided from the way she has been sleeping, but that doesn't stop us from telling her to hurry up.

"Mom," we say. "C'mon you have to make us lunch. Get up, let's go!" Our tiny Catholic school doesn't have a cafeteria, so if we don't bring lunch, we don't eat lunch. None of us have any idea how to make anything ourselves, so we need to get Mom up and into the kitchen before our bus reaches the corner at five of eight.

No matter how much we plead with her, Mom goes through the same routine every morning. After changing cheeks, she will lie there another minute just breathing, before moving her arms under her body, and pushing herself back onto her legs. Then she will sit there another minute on her legs, looking at the three of us with her sleepy eyes moving from face to face, like she is trying to figure out where she is, and who we are. Next, Mom will take a big, deep yawn, stretch her arms to the sky, let out a bit of a yelp at the top of the stretch, smile, blink once, then twice, stand up and do a trunk twist, before slowly moving into the kitchen to pack our lunches.

Sometimes before she does the trunk twist, Mom will burp or fart, and that always makes us laugh. But my brothers and I don't think much of Mom sleeping on the floor. We know we are going to find her there most mornings; it's not a surprise to us. Similar to her dissociative fugues, it is another fact of life that we have accepted as normal.

The thing is—we also know we *won't* find Mom on the floor in the den when someone is down visiting from her family. When we have company, Mom sleeps with Dad in bed, continuing those Cover-Up skills she learned as a child. It's like something inside her instinctively knows that no one outside our immediate household must be allowed to witness even the *slightest* sign of dysfunction. And sleeping on the floor, like a passed out drunk, is just that sort of dysfunction.

81

10

Ever since Nonna got back from her period of mourning in Italy, she has been coming down to stay with us for months at a time. Either Mom will go up to Philadelphia and pick her up, or Aunt Renata will drive down to drop her off. Although Mom says, "Boys, Nonna is coming down to visit for a while," it really seems like she comes down to work.

Nonna is seventy-five years old, but Nonna isn't *old* at all. When she comes down, she makes it her job to busy herself with all of the cooking and cleaning Mom normally does. There is always something in the air when Nonna is down. It's usually the smell of basil or meatballs frying in olive oil. The smell is so strong that we don't even have to see her. Aunt Renata could have dropped Nonna off during the day, while we were at school, but the minute we walk in the front door, we can tell she's here just by the way our house smells.

When Nonna is down our kitchen is transformed into a Jersey Shore version of Calabria. Mom is a fabulous cook in her own right, but Nonna is *Michelangelo*, she is *Da Vinci*, she is *Mozart* in a culinary sense. My brothers and I sit and pant like Italian dogs as Mom and Nonna make ravioli and lasagna, pizza and gnocchi from scratch.

They both buzz around the kitchen, Nonna with her apron on, smiling and taunting us with the smell of Calabrian cuisine in the air.

Nonna starts each day by making all the beds in the house. Then, she washes all the laundry, cleans all the bathrooms, and does all the vacuuming before setting off to find another project to complete, whether it's tending to the tomato plants or making iced tea from scratch.

Mom does these same chores when Nonna isn't around; but, somehow it's different when Nonna does them. It's different, I tell myself, because when Mom does the housework, she does just that—the housework. It's a chore. However, when Nonna does it, it's like watching Dad pour concrete; she *loves* it.

She sings old Calabrese songs, as she scours the toilets and scrubs the floors, humming through the parts of the songs she doesn't remember. In between the singing, she talks to herself in Italian and laughs out loud, tossing her hands up in the air with a "*mamma mia*," if our bedrooms are messy.

Nonna never complains, and she *never* asks us to help—neither does Mom. If there are chores to be done and Nonna isn't around, then Mom does them all, everything from cutting the grass to folding the clothes. It's easy to see the one thing Mom learned from Nonna is how to be that good *calabresella* with the heavy basket of olives on her head.

The only time Dad ever cooks is when Mom volunteers to work Friday Night Bingo, or spends the night in Philadelphia visiting Nonna and her sisters. On those nights, my brothers and I know exactly what Dad will make for dinner—his Blue Collar Carbonara.

When Nonna makes carbonara, she uses her homemade fettuccine, the best pancetta she can find, freshly ground black pepper and farm fresh eggs. She fries the pancetta in olive oil then drops the hot fettuccine into the frying pan to finish cooking for a second with the pork fat, before mixing in the raw eggs and Romano cheese. Once in a while, she'll add green peas or mushrooms.

But when Dad makes it, he uses store-bought spaghetti, store-bought eggs and regular breakfast bacon. He mixes everything together in a pot, normally with the phone wedged between his shoulder and ear, talking business about his development out in Cumberland County. My brothers and I love Dad's Blue Collar Carbonara, even though that's all he ever makes—and the reason for that is—Dad can't make sauce.

I'm twelve going on thirteen and can honestly say we've never eaten sauce out of a jar. Mom and Nonna both make their own tomato sauce from scratch. This is why Dad says, "Never! Not in my house! My boys will never eat sauce out of a jar!" As he breaks the eggs into the pot full of steaming spaghetti and fried bacon, he reiterates what his father always used to say, "Boys, just remember this. If you marry an Irish girl, you'll always eat out of a can, and if you marry a Jewish girl, you'll always eat out."

The only other thing Nonna does, besides cook and clean when she visits, is watch 'her show'—*The Wheel of Fortune*. She'll be in the kitchen doing the dishes after dinner, when she will come to the steps leading into the den and say, "Boys, can'a you put'a my show?"

83

Even if Tony, Michael or I are in the middle of watching a ballgame, or playing videogames, we know that Nonna will stay by the steps with a dish towel over her left shoulder, and a puppy dog look on her face, until one of us says, "Okay Nonna, we'll put on your show." At that, she'll smile, clap her hands together one time, and thank us in Italian, "*Grazie, ragazzi.*"

With her feet resting on the ottoman in the den, we can see the two huge bunions she has, as Nonna peels pears and apples, without taking her eyes off the TV screen.

Her bunions are so big; they cause her big toes to point out to the side so bad they're almost laying on top of her other toes. Yet, there she sits and watches her show, talking to the screen half in English, and half in Italian. Even though she is talking to the screen, we know she is really talking to the contestants. Nonna always picks one player to root for.

However, if her "favorite player" solves a few puzzles, and gets a big money lead, Nonna will reverse course and cheer against him, even going so far as to put the *malocchio* on him—The Evil Eye. Despite the fact those contestants on the TV screen are thousands of miles away, Nonna curses them with the *malocchio*; and if her "favorite player" happens to lose a puzzle, or lands on BANKRUPT, Nonna cheers and laughs—her body rocking back and forth on the couch.

"Cheech," she'll chuckle, as she turns to me, "you see this'a chooch? I get'a him good'a *con il malocchio.*"

Nonna never stays with us for more than a few months at a time, and this is because she gets worried about her house, the same rowhome she and Babbo bought in Philadelphia back in the 1930's. Even though she lives in a safe neighborhood, after a long visit with us, Nonna gets antsy and says she wants to go home because, "Nobody watch'a 'da house."

We never understood why she had to go *watch'a 'da house*, but every time she left the shore, something sad and secretive seemed to surface inside my mother's psyche.

Ever since I was little, watching my mother and Nonna say goodbye to one another was an agonizing, almost traumatizing event to witness. It didn't matter if we were leaving Nonna's in Philadelphia, or if someone was taking her home from our house in Jersey, the sentiment was always the same.

Of course, they cried. But it wasn't "normal" crying, where each shed a few tears and a couple, *I'll miss you's*. No—they cried profusely— as if they would never see each other again—as if someone had been kidnapped. Also, it was always a silent goodbye; they never spoke. There was no, *I'll miss you, Ma*, or, *Ciao, Antonietta*. No—the sadness they seemed to share was something they couldn't put into words. Instead, they spoke with their eyes.

Looking back—I can remember feeling like something tragic was hidden right below the surface of those moments. Something that had haunted them for decades....

When Mom was eight years old, Nonna went back to Italy for several months. My grandmother desperately wanted to see her parents, and spend some time with them before they died. The year was 1955. Nonna had left her village at sixteen, and was returning as a forty-two year old mother of four with a few grandchildren of her own.

She always got teary eyed when she talked about that trip, for her arrival in Calabria was storybook. Nonna got off the train in Reggio and saw her father, Domenico, through the crowded platform of the station. He was facing the opposite direction, but his fedora gave him away; she recognized him instantly. My grandmother hopped down off the train and smiled her way over to him. They embraced, but he quickly pulled away, pointed at her with the index finger of his right hand and said, "You have been gone for twenty-five years, three months and eight days."

That was all she needed to hear before the tears began, as they did each time she told that story. Her father had *literally* counted the days since his daughter had left for America. Nonna had been in the United States for so long, that she had to introduce herself to siblings born after she left for the New World. A wave of nostalgia washed over my grandmother as she was finally a daughter again—back in Calabria for the first time in a quarter century.

But on the other side of the ocean, this trip was having an equally lasting impact on Mom. Even though she was left in the "care" of her father, it was really her older, married sisters who tried to look out for her. The thing is—they had children of their own, and households to run. They weren't there to watch my eight year old mother, or keep her company, on a daily basis.

Her twelve year old brother, Nick, was beloved by Babbo and seemed to naturally have more confidence about himself. He wasn't heartbroken by Nonna's absence, like Mom was. My mother felt completely abandoned.

Mom said the day Nonna left, the entire family drove from Philadelphia to New York. There they *all* boarded this big beautiful ship. My mother was mesmerized by the long, dark red, velvet curtains dangling from the ceiling to the floor. She liked the way they felt against her tiny hands. Mom became distracted by the curtains, because the next thing she knew she, her siblings and Babbo were climbing back into her father's car. Once they began to pull away, my eight year old mother became confused and concerned. *Where was her mother?* Nonna was not riding with the rest of the family. Nobody seemed to want to give her a straight answer. Mom turned around and tried to look out the rear view window but there was no sight of Nonna—no sight of her beloved mother.

She couldn't understand why Nonna had left, and it was this sense of abandonment that surfaced each and every time the two of them parted ways.

Decades later, if Aunt Renata came down to cart Nonna home, the tears and the silent look of agony on their faces would start as soon as they walked out the front door. Aunt Renata, who never cried at such partings, would climb behind the wheel of her gray Chrysler LeBaron, as my grandmother settled into the passenger seat, and lowered her window.

Mom and Nonna would look at each other longingly, as Aunt Renata slowly backed out of the driveway. My mother would walk beside them on Nonna's side—both of them crying heavily—Mom's right hand covering her mouth.

When Aunt Renata reached the end of the driveway, Mom would follow them out into the street, where she always moved to Nonna's window so they could touch hands one last time. Their fingertips only separated when Aunt Renata's LeBaron slowly accelerated forward towards the corner. My mother would remain in the middle of the street sobbing, as my aunt's car made a right at the stop sign, and disappeared out of sight.

Long after the LeBaron had vanished, Mom would stay in the middle of the street. The sobbing would subside, but this sad trance seemed to carry her away. Dad would call to her from the front porch, "Ann, come back inside! They're gone." But Mom would remain motionless in the street—sometimes for a half an hour. Frustrated, and worried for her safety, my father would go out into the street and *literally* walk her back inside. Mom was that traumatized, that deeply affected by Nonna's departure, that again—looking back—there seemed to be something tragic hidden right below the surface of those moments.

Something more than just memories of Nonna's 1955 return to Italy. Something we wouldn't fully understand for years.

11

Despite the deadlines and demands of his housing development, my father finds time to volunteer as a football coach for our neighborhood team. Since I'm twelve years old, I'm on the varsity squad; Tony, nine, is a pee-wee; and seven year old Michael plays for the taxi squad. We are all quarterbacks.

My father is always telling us, "There's nothing like playing quarterback. You're the understood leader of thirty or forty guys your age. You have to know the plays better than anybody else, and when there's adversity, you must find a way to overcome it."

Dad goes on to say we ought to be thankful for the opportunity we're getting to learn about leadership, especially since he had to go into the army to learn all that as a Sergeant First Class. Just like in the army though, Dad insists we call him and the rest of the coaching staff 'Sir.' He tells us players that if we're asked a question, we're not allowed to say, *yeah*, we are expected to respond, "Yes, sir."

Football season begins in late August and runs until early November, and we have practice four nights a week, with a game every weekend. It's Mom who gets us fed, dressed and down to the field by six p.m., Tuesday through Friday. Dad leaves his development out in Cumberland County and meets us at practice right at six. There he leads us through calisthenics between bites of the meatball sandwich and sips from the tiny bottle of wine, Mom routinely brings him for dinner.

With his new pencil-thin mustache, and signature dark sunglasses, wearing a white polo shirt with the collar up, Dad will pace back and forth in a pair of black spandex biker shorts and socks pulled up to his knees. After we finish warming up, Dad pushes his baseball cap back a little bit so we can see his whole face, but the sunglasses stay on. He just turned forty in September, but when the head coach blows his whistle, Dad turns back into that twenty-one year old Sergeant First Class.

My teammates and I take our helmets off, and lay them beside us, as we kneel on one knee and form a semi-circle around Dad. The other coaches stand in the back as my father goes on and on about discipline, strength and desire. He moves his hands a lot, and his voice is full, as he proclaims success comes from playing like a team and believing in one another. But above all, he says, success comes from perseverance. That seems to be Dad's favorite word—perseverance. He says nothing can be accomplished without it, and that nothing is impossible with it. Dad studies our eyes, going from face to face as he says, "If we just persevere and stick together, great things will happen, not only in football, but in life."

He calls us men—not boys—and always wraps up his speech by looking around at all of us and asking one simple question, "How far we gonna go, men?" We're expected to respond in unison, "All the way, sir!" The next time he asks us, Dad is a little more aggressive, "I said, how far we gonna go, men?"

Again, we respond, slightly louder, "All the way, sir!"

Until finally the third time he bellows out, *"I said, how far we gonna go, men?"*

"All the way, sir!"

We spend the rest of practice going through tackling and passing drills. If somebody drops a ball that he should have caught, that player knows he has to stop and do ten push-ups right away. If an offensive lineman jumps offside, he'll drop and do the same without Dad having to say a word.

After two seasons of having him on the sidelines, we get it. Dad doesn't make us do push-ups as a punishment; he does it so we will learn that there are consequences for our actions.

On game day to get us pumped up, Dad has all thirty of us line up for our *pre-game shots*. He'll stand with his legs shoulder-width-apart and both hands covering his crotch. With his stomach muscles pulled tight, every player is allowed to haul off and give him one punch in the gut as hard as they can. It's always quite a scene—30 ten year old boys beating their coach like savages in the wild, as he eggs them on.

Though it may have worked to instill fear in our opponent, it didn't work for the suburban, white-collar parents—especially the mothers. They said this was only youth football, that we were only boys, and didn't he think he may have been going a little too far with all this machismo? But Dad said they were missing the point. That he was only trying to show us what we were capable of by teaching us perseverance through strength and discipline.

Looking back, I realize Dad was only trying to teach us how to be men. Ever since he got out of the army, he always talked about wanting to start a Hero School. He says there are no more heroes, but I know that when he says that, he means there are no more men.

Dad says men have become extinct and that they need a place to go to learn how to be strong and respectful. For him, he says, that was the army. But for my brothers and me, he says, that place is going to be football.

During our games, Mom either volunteers to work the snack bar, or stands off on the sidelines at the fence and smokes and cheers with the other mothers and coaches' wives. It's there she makes the first friends I ever remember her having; two women we start to see so much that we call them 'aunt' out of respect.

Aunt Ellen and Aunt Teresa are sisters, but look nothing alike. Aunt Ellen has short dirty blonde hair with brown eyes, while Aunt Teresa has long brown hair, with dark circles under her big, round, brown eyes. The sisters both smoke like Mom, "stay at home" like Mom, and identify themselves as being Italian—even though they're half German. Their kids become like cousins, and their husbands like uncles, but it's the ladies Dad holds spellbound in the kitchen.

Through our involvement with football in the fall, youth basketball in the winter, and Little League baseball in the spring, my parents become friendly with nearly all our teammates' parents. Before my brothers and I started playing sports, my parents hardly ever did anything with anybody who wasn't family. Dad took his two week vacations with friends of his, but as a "couple," they rarely socialized with outsiders.

Now, no matter the season, Aunt Ellen and Aunt Teresa are always coming over our house with two or three other mothers to sit around the kitchen table, with a cigarette and a coffee, to visit and watch Dad put on his show. He may look like a Mafioso, with abs of steel, and a gift for giving speeches—but on stage is where Dad belongs.

My brothers and I stay in the den, crowded around the television set, playing videogames with the mothers' kids, while Dad pulls out a bottle of Sambuca, pours drinks for the ladies, and works the room.

From the kitchen, we hear two things all night—women's laughter, and Dad doing his Kitchen Table Act. He sits at the head of the table with his collar up, rocks his chair back on its hind legs, and holds court as smoke fills the kitchen, and the women scramble to catch their breaths.

Dad makes them laugh so hard with his impressions, accents and stories that they slap their hands on the table and laugh until they cry. When they finally catch their breath, they tell him he missed his calling; that he should be in Atlantic City playing some showroom, making millions in movies, with his picture on the wall of the White House Sub Shop. Dad smiles and says, "You know what? You might be on to something there."

No matter how much fun they have on those nights Dad puts on his Kitchen Table Act—there is no denying my parents' marriage is in trouble. They seem to bicker all the time and when they fight, they yell at each other with their hands and arms waving wildly in the air.

"*I've had it!*" Dad shouts.

"Don't you threaten me, Frank!"

"No, I'm not threatening, Ann, I'm promising! *We're through!* I'm tired of you sleeping on the floor every fuckin' night, after spending so much money at the casinos!"

"Oh, so now it's about the money? Whaddaya expect me to do? The way you go away whenever you damn well please!"

"Oh, for the love of Christ!"

"No, let's see, North Carolina, Idaho, Montana, Florida...where else? What I miss?"

"Yeah, you know why I go away? — To get away from your stupid ass!"

"Fine then, go! And while you're at it, find somebody else to take care of your kids and be your slave, because that's all you want, you asshole!"

When Mom and Dad scream like this, I always end up crying and my brothers end up hiding. They hide behind the curtains in the living room, or behind the couch in the den because nothing makes any sense when Mom and Dad fight.

"You're oblivious, Ann. Fuckin' oblivious! I bought you that Cadillac sittin' out front, the jewelry, the mink, this house, but you're so fuckin' arrogant, you don't appreciate any of it! All I get is that look, that hate look, but I'm not your father and *I don't deserve it!*"

"Frank!"

"Enough! Fourteen years we been married and it's the same old shit...."

"Oh, yeah?"

"Yeah! I tell you *we* need to talk to somebody and you blow me off. I say maybe *you* ought to talk to somebody, and you don't wanna hear it."

"Yeah, that's right Frank, and you know why that's right? Because, *I don't need help!* You hear me? *I don't need help!*"

"Please Ann, you're afraid to fall asleep in your own bed because of your damn father. I told your sister years ago that you needed help, and now you won't be happy until I find somebody else."

"Oh, you don't have the guts."

"Yeah, we'll see Ann. We'll see...."

12

It is the autumn of 1989, and I'm in seventh grade. A girl named Peggy likes me, and I only know because two of her friends, Clara Johnson and Elizabeth Davidson, cornered me at recess to break the news.

"Frankie," they said, "Peggy Williams likes you."

I was with my buddies, so I had to look like I wasn't interested—yet they continue.

"Peggy thinks you're gorgeous. She says she loves Italians, and told us to tell you that when she looks at you, she sees Italy in your eyes."

I'm not sure what that means having Italy in my eyes. Mom always used to say that she didn't know she was pregnant with me until she was in Italy visiting our cousins, and because of that, I could always say Italy was my home; but, I don't think that's what Peggy means.

When I tell Mom that Peggy Williams says I have Italy in my eyes, she says, "What? What kind of a girl says that to a boy in seventh grade?"

I have to remind her that Peggy didn't say anything, her messenger girls did, but Mom doesn't care. She goes blind, "Frankie, I don't care who told you she said what, you're not to go near that Peggy, any girl who says that is a harlot."

"A what?"

"A harlot."

Dad overhears us in the kitchen.

"Ann, don't cha think you're overreacting?"

"Frank, she said he had Italy in his eyes...what's next, Spain in his spandex?"

Dad rolls his eyes.

"Cheech, do you like this girl?"

I don't know what to say; I never thought about whether I liked her or not. So Dad says, "*Could* you like this girl?"

I shrug my shoulders.

"Just listen Frank, it's not a big deal. If you like her, tell her, or tell the girls she's sending over. If you don't, then it doesn't matter what she says, because in the end, she's just a girl."

Even though Dad says she is just a girl, and Mom swears she's a harlot, I don't know what to do about Peggy—until Andy Boderski overhears me talking to Ron Montgomery.

Ron is one of my best friends from school. He is short, with a perpetual crew cut, and that means he's the opposite of Andy Boderski—who is tall, with stringy blonde hair, a crooked nose and freckles that don't match his skin.

Everybody calls Andy 'Boogs,' because on top of his nose being crooked, he always has a stray booger or two hanging from his nostrils. If you tell him to wipe his nose, he'll only pick it out of spite, and eat the boogers right there in front of you, which is odd, because when you go over his house, you're required to take off your shoes—his parents are that obsessed with cleanliness.

Boogs says, "Forget Peggy, what you want is right here."

He opens his book bag, and shows me a small magazine, with a pretty girl in red underwear on the cover.

"What's that?"

"The Victoria's Secret Catalog."

"The what?"

"The Victoria's Secret Catalog. Here, take a look for yourself."

He passes it to me, and my eyes want to jump out of my head. The pages are loaded with pretty girls in their underwear. Boogs says it's his mother's. That he swiped it out of the mailbox one day—and that if I have any brains—I'll check my own mailbox, and do the same myself.

Ron and Boogs come over almost every day to play after school. They live so close, they can ride their bikes. The same goes for many of Tony's and Michael's friends. Between the three of us, we never have a problem getting a big football or baseball game going in our backyard. Mom says we can have over whomever we want, whenever we want. We don't even have to ask permission, since it's the same cast of characters every day. Our parents like the fact that we play here at our own house, as opposed to somebody else's—that way they can keep an eye on us, and get to know who we're hanging with.

Our backyard is part of the reason why Dad says he decided to buy the house—part of why he kept his eye on it after the original deal fell through. He says that because our backyard is huge, and perfect for all sorts of sports.

In the fall and winter, we play football. In the spring and summer, we play baseball.

It backs right up against the meadows, which means we have a sea of cattails waving at us on windy days, with Atlantic City sparkling right across the bay. Our backyard is so popular, that it acts as a sort of "Community Park," where everybody is welcome, and anybody can play.

When we come home from school, my brothers and I are in the habit of racing from the bus stop, down the half block to our house, down the long driveway, walking in the front door, getting two steps inside and shouting, "*We're home!*"

When Aunt Colomba is down, she'll say, "There they are. There are my three princes."

But today when we do it—all we hear is a little bit of sniffling coming from the living room. Mom is normally in front of the TV when we get home from school, playing videogames, wearing the same clothes she had on when we found her on the floor in the morning. But today, she's lying on the couch in the living room with the shades drawn, and tears in her eyes. I walk over to her, put my book bag down and say, "Mom, what's the matter? What is it?"

She just looks at me, and starts to cry again, while Tony and Michael move into the living room behind me. I'm sure they're thinking the same thing, *why is Mom crying?*

We've only seen Mom cry when Nonna leaves with Aunt Renata, and she follows the car out into the street. But now she is crying and Nonna left weeks ago. So, I ask her again what's wrong, and all she says is, "He said he had to tell me about them, Frankie...."

"About who, Mom?"

"He said he had pictures of them...."

"Of who?"

"Of my husband and his wife, Frankie...of your father and *his wife*...that's who called me, Frankie. Her husband...."

95

"Whose husband, Mom? What are you talking about?"

"He said they were together, Frankie...*together!*"

"Mom...."

"I told him he must have had the wrong number, because my husband would never do something like that...he's a married man...we have a family...."

"Mom, you're not making any sense. Who's he?"

"...the pictures must be fakes, right Frankie? Tell me they're fakes. Tell me he cut your father's head off to match it to them pictures. Tell me it's all a lie, Frankie...."

"Mom, answer me, who are you talking about?"

"Her husband, Frankie...."

"Whose husband?"

"Oh Frankie, oh boys...it can't be true...."

"Mom?"

"...he can't be doing this to me...your father can't be doing this to me...."

"Doing what?" Michael moves next to me and says, "What, Mommy? Tell Frankie what...."

"Yeah," Tony says. "What is it, Mom?"

But she just turns away from us, and buries her face into the back of the couch to cry some more. Her body shakes as she sobs, and I'm not sure what to do, as my brothers and I stand motionless in the living room with the shades drawn.

Should I call Aunt Bridgid? Try Dad on his mobile phone? Call Grandmom? I don't know what to do because I've never seen Mom like this before. I don't understand what she's talking about. *Whose husband? What pictures?*

Before I can make a decision, she unburies her face from the back of the couch, swings her legs around and sits up straight. She hangs her head, and takes a deep breath.

"Boys, just go out and play."

"But Mom...."

"Frankie, take your brothers and go and play."

I take my brothers and we go out and play, but we start to find Mom crying on the couch so much that I know something is really wrong. She never cried like this before, and little by little, things start to change over the next few weeks.

96

There are nights when Mom forgets to make dinner. And if she does make dinner, she just sits there and pushes her rigatoni from one side of the plate to the other, not eating a thing, not making a sound. There are other nights when she sits in the corner crying while we try to watch the Philadelphia 76ers play basketball on TV. If we have friends over watching the game with us, Mom cries in front of them, and we don't know what to say. She tries to apologize, but that only makes it more uncomfortable because almost nothing makes her stop, and our friends don't know what to say either.

I'm her oldest son, and I should know what to say, but I don't. I can only shake my head, and wonder why she's like this. I want to know what happened to make her so sad. And I want to know what pictures she is talking about.

Now that school is out—the summer of 1990—Mom lets me ride my bike to Grandmom's house, so Grandpop and I can watch baseball together. We both love the Philadelphia Phillies. We watch as many games as we can, in my grandparents' living room, where Grandmom serves us dinner on big, red metal trays.

Grandpop and I are best friends.

He fought in World War II as a member of the United States Army, where he was routinely ordered to guard the Italian soldiers— since he could speak to them. But it's hard for me to imagine Grandpop guarding anybody because he is so laid back. Anytime anything goes wrong, he just shrugs his shoulders and says, "Eh, whatta ya gonna do?" But when he says that, he always sounds like he's whispering and that's because if people say my father looks like a younger version of Marlon Brando's *Vito Corleone*, then Grandpop *sounds* like *Vito Corleone*. My father's father speaks with this masculine whisper—just like Brando's character in *The Godfather*—it's literally how he talks.

In the summer, we play golf every Thursday afternoon. Grandpop paid for my lessons with the club pro, so I'm pretty good for my age. I know all the rules, and the etiquette, and can play with adults without embarrassing my grandfather—which he is very proud of.

During tonight's Phillies' game—as she sometimes does—Grandmom softly calls to me from the kitchen, "Frankie," she says. "Hey Frankie, will you come in here a minute, sweetheart?"

"Okay, Grandmom. I'm comin'."

When I walk into the kitchen, I find my grandmother sitting at the table, looking at some papers. Standing beside her, on the kitchen table, atop some open pages of the newspaper is a three foot tall statue of the Holy Virgin Mary. Grandmom regularly volunteers to refinish old statues for our home parish.

Grandmom is different than Nonna. If Nonna was born to cook and clean—then Grandmom was born to paint, and sculpt, and write. She is always working on something creative like a portrait, or a story. Even though the paint on the clothes, and on the skin of the statue of Mary is flaking off, and her left arm has all but been broken off—I know Grandmom will have Jesus' mother looking good as new in no time.

I know this because every time I come over to watch the Phillies' games with Grandpop, she is putting a piece of clay in my hand or teaching me how to draw. Even her daughter—my Aunt Sofia—teaches my brothers and I how to play piano through formal weekly lessons. Art is a part of Grandmom's family and tonight my grandmother has called me into the kitchen because she wants my help with a story she's writing.

"It's a children's story," she says. "Something I've been working on for a little while. It's about a purple rabbit and his friend, the raccoon."

Grandmom says she wants to submit the story to a children's magazine for publication. But when she asks me to help her I say, "I'm no good at writing, Grandmom."

"Nonsense! You're Italian, you're my grandson, and you're a very good storyteller. You seem to have a knack for it. So, what kinda thing is that to say? Of course, you can write."

Grandmom says we're Neapolitan, and that means we're artists—not slow and backwards like Grandpop, who is Calabrese. I don't know why Grandmom says Grandpop is slow and backwards, when he can fix anything you put in front of him. And I don't know how to react because I'm ¾ Calabrese and ¼ Neapolitan, but I know Grandmom feels this way because she has always said that our family is special—that we have talent.

Special, special, special—that's all I've ever heard since I was little. And though all she wants is my help with her story, I'm not feeling all that special when Grandmom slides the papers in front of me.

"Frankie," she says, "could you read it aloud to me?"

"But Grandmom, it's probably really good, you don't need my help. Can't I go back into the living room, and watch the game with Grandpop?"

"Sure, you can. But it's only a short-story. It won't take that long. Besides, it'll be good for you to help me because you're gonna be a great writer someday. I would love to hear you read it."

"But I don't want to...."

"Oh, c'mon honey, there's nothin' to it."

"But...."

"C'mon, Frankie."

She keeps insisting—and I get fed-up. "I said I don't want to read your *stupid story!*" I take the papers, and I shove them across the table, where the pages reach the edge, and trickle off onto the floor one-by-one. When I look back at Grandmom, her eyes are big and furious.

"*Excuse me, young man?* Who do you think you're talking to? You're lucky I don't reach across this table and brain you! Get over here!"

But in the second it takes Grandmom to explode, I start to cry. My tears have nothing to do with the story, or her yelling—they have to do with Mom and Dad. *If we're so special*—I want to ask her—*then how come my parents fight like they do? And how come it feels like they're going to get a divorce? What's so special about that?*

But before I can say anything—Grandmom realizes something is the matter and forgets all about how I was short with her, and tossed her story onto the floor. She says for me to relax, and take a deep breath. Grandmom gets up from her chair and takes me into her arms. She kisses my forehead and wipes away my tears.

"Now, Frankie," she says. "What is it, honey? What's the matter?"

I take a few deep breaths and tell her about the fights Mom and Dad have where there is screaming and hiding and crying. I tell her about the nights I check the closet when Dad's away to look for Babbo, who has been dead and buried for years. I confess about finding Mom on the couch, crying over pictures she won't explain, and how I'm worried my parents are going to get divorced. Grandmom says, "Now, Frankie, now, Frankie...."

She looks up at the ceiling, looks back down at me and says, "There's something I want to tell you, honey, something you ought to know. Marriage is a very difficult thing, and sometimes people who get married have a hard time getting along. Now, Mom and Dad have been married a long time, but they've been fighting, like you said, and neither one of them is happy. Now, Frankie, what I want to tell you is that Dad has met a lady, and they've started having coffee together. I've met her myself, and she seems very nice. Her name is Gail and she gets along very well with your father and makes him happy. And we all want your father to be happy. Don't we, Frankie?"

"Yes, Grandmom."

"So, don't worry about Mom and Dad so much. Whatever is supposed to happen is in God's hands anyway. Just remember that they both love you and your brothers very much, and would never do anything to hurt you. Okay sweetheart?"

"Okay, Grandmom."

"Promise?"

I nod my head. Grandmom says, "Good," and smiles. But a voice in my head wants to ask if Gail is a friend like Aunt Ellen or Aunt Teresa, because I've seen Dad have coffee with them, too. I want to ask whether he puts on his Kitchen Table Act for Gail. But something in what Grandmom said tells me Gail is nothing like Aunt Ellen or Aunt Teresa. Something tells me Gail is different—that Gail is Dad's girlfriend.

I take what Grandmom says about Gail, and I bring it to Mom. She is crying again on the couch. Instead of comforting her, I ask if she is sad because Dad has a girlfriend. She sniffles and says, "What did you say?" Now, I'm not sure if I should have said anything—but I need to know. "Mom, does Dad have a girlfriend?"

"Who told you that?"

"Grandmom."

"She told you that your father has a girlfriend?"

"Well, she said he met somebody, and that they have coffee...."

"How dare she!"

"Mom...."

"How dare she! Who does she think she is?"

She sits up straight in anger, but before I get a chance to ask whether it's true—she's bent over again, crying even harder than before. It's times like this when I get the most scared because she's angry, sad and crying, and I don't know what to do.

Part of me says I could ask Father Gordon at weekly confession. *Bless me Father for I have sinned, but what do I do when my father has a girlfriend, and my mother cries all the time?* I'm sure I could ask Father and he would tell me, but school is out for the summer, and I could never say, *Mom I'm gonna ride my bike down to school, and have confession with Father Gordon.* Even though I should confess my sins in the worst way because of how I've been jerking off so much with the Victoria's Secret Catalog.

I should go see Father Gordon at once—but I can't; I won't—because there are more important things right now than me and the Victoria's Secret Catalog. Then a thought comes to me, I could walk across the street to the Villa—the retreat house for priests—right next door to Aunt Bridgid and Uncle Bruno's house. I could knock on the door, and ask to see Father Leonard—Nonna's favorite priest. He's her favorite because he's from Italy. He would understand if I went over and said, *Father Leonard, my Neapolitan grandmother says her son has a girlfriend. This is making my Calabrese mother very sad, even though my Neapolitan Grandmother would probably say she's slow and backwards, like she does her Calabrese husband. I'm really confused. Could you ask Our Lord—who was neither Neapolitan or Calabrese— what he thinks I should do? I know His father was a tradesman like mine—maybe He could help me out—because I have no one else to turn to.*

But I never cross the street, and I never seek out Father Leonard for advice. I just shake my head over the fact that what I felt the day of the Phillies' game with Grandmom was right; Dad has a girlfriend.

I don't need Mom to confirm it; I just need Dad to pay for making her sad.

13

When Aunt Colomba and Aunt Renata come down, they sit around the kitchen table and talk badly about Dad. They tell Mom she should leave him. That he is no good, and how they are appalled at how little he cares about keeping his affair secret.

My aunts are beside themselves when they learn that Dad rents an apartment over in Ocean City, so he and Gail can sneak off together whenever they want. Mom's sisters can't believe how bold and brazen he is.

Their anger escalates when they find out Gail came to the Memorial Day Parade we had during baseball season, so she could watch me and my brothers march in our Little League uniforms. But, when Mom tells her sisters that Dad's penis bleeds—both their chins drop to the floor.

"*It what?*" Aunt Renata asks with a sharp tone.

"It bleeds, Rena."

"Jesus Christ! And how do you know that?"

Before Mom can answer, Aunt Colomba interrupts, "Tell us you're not sleepin' with him, Ann! Can't you see that's exactly what he wants?"

"Yeah," Aunt Renata adds, "let me guess—his dick is raw 'cause he's doin' that *puttana* and you in the same day. Oh, Ann will you stop bein' a fool, and leave that man for the love of Christ! You'll get the house; you'll get the kids."

"What are you waitin' for?" Aunt Colomba wants to know. "He's an arrogant bastard who doesn't deserve you."

"He's an asshole," Aunt Renata adds. "Frank has shown no remorse throughout this whole ordeal. It's time you divorced that son of a bitch. Now, do us all a favor, and be the one to end this nonsense!"

"Yeah," Aunt Colomba says. "When is enough, *enough?*"

14

My brothers and I are watching a new TV show called *The Simpsons*. When there's a commercial, I get up and run my empty ice cream bowl into the kitchen, where I find Dad standing at the counter eating cheese and drinking wine. He is so focused on the newspaper, lying open on the counter, that he doesn't turn to me when I come dashing in and drop my bowl in the sink. With him quietly reading to himself, I want to reach over and dump the glass of wine on his head and scream, *cheater!*

Ever since I learned of his affair, I haven't been able to look him in the eye because he is not who I thought he was. He is a liar and a hypocrite. I want him to suffer the way Mom suffers there on the couch in tears. I want him to be sad. When I toss my spoon into the sink, and watch it land in a dirty salad bowl, bits of lettuce and drizzles of vinegar splash all over Dad and his cheese. This makes him turn towards me.

"Hey Cheech, watch what you're doin', huh!"

"Why," I say, "you got a problem?"

His face grows hard when I say that, and he stops chewing.

"What did you say?"

"I said if you got a problem, you should ask Gail to clean it up!"

Everything in me wants to fall on the floor and cry, because I don't want to be saying this to my father, and I can feel the tears swelling in my eyes—but I won't do it; won't give him my tears. I won't cry in front of him. He has all these rules we have to follow. We can't curse. We can't be rude. We can't get in trouble at school. We can't mouth off to our coaches—always can't, can't, can't. So, how come he can have a girlfriend and make Mom cry? I wish I could reach into the sink and throw the whole dirty salad bowl into his face, then stuff the cheese into his ears. No one should be allowed to make my mother cry like she does. But what I said about Gail cleaning up the mess—drains the hard look from his face. He is not sure what to do. He didn't know I knew about her, and that means he doesn't know I wish he was dead. I want to tell him that I wish he went away all the time, because I'm a better Man of the House than he'll ever be. I would never make Mom cry over a girlfriend I had, who was married with two kids, whose husband called Mom saying he had photos of the two of them together. I would never do that. I wish I could call the FBI to come get my father, because we don't need him or his stupid Hero School around here anymore! But Dad comes over to me from the counter, and points his finger in my face. He says nothing about the tone I used with him or the anger in my eyes. He looks down at me, wags his finger and says, "You go back in that room with your brothers, and don't let me ever hear you bring up that woman's name again!"

When Dad sells a house out at his development—his parents—Grandmom and Grandpop, are the ones he relies on to tie up any loose ends before settlement. Sometimes I ride with them out to Cumberland County, and assist Grandmom with the final cleaning, or help Grandpop double-check all the workmanship, making sure the faucets, sinks, and doors, are set properly.

Today, my grandparents and I are in a house my father just finished building. It is already under contract, and Grandmom is going from room to room, vacuuming and sweeping, while Grandpop is fixing one of the cabinet doors in the kitchen that just won't close right.

My job is simple; I am cleaning the windows. Dad gives me a razor blade, and tells me to take all the stickers off the new panes, then go around and wipe them down with Windex. He tries to pat my head after explaining what he wants, but I pull away, and wouldn't let him.

As I'm wiping the windows in the front of the house, I see Dad in the driveway talking to a blonde lady in a gray business skirt-suit. I don't know how I know—but something inside me says—*that lady is Gail.*

It would make sense, since she works for the County's building department—but when I see them standing there, I want to rush right out and say, *Hey, Gail! Yeah, you! My mother is a mess 'cause of this stupid affair. So, knock it off, before I show you a thing or two with my razor blade!*

104

But I never say anything like that. It's all I can do to try and conceal the fact I am studying their every move as I stare at them through the window. When Dad reaches for his mobile phone, and starts walking away to answer the call, I watch Gail turn and head towards the front door. When she walks inside a moment later, Grandmom greets her with a kiss on the cheek, and I listen to them chit-chat about how great the house looks. I don't know how Grandmom can behave this way when she knows this is Dad's girlfriend—but that's what she does. I peek into the kitchen, to see what Grandpop is doing, but he keeps his head down, working on that cabinet door. That is what I decide to do. I try to stay focused on my window cleaning, until I hear Gail's voice behind me.

"You must be Frankie?"

I turn around, and seven years of Catholic schooling takes over. I force a smile and say, "Yes, ma'am, I'm Frankie."

With big brown eyes, bending slightly at the waist, she extends her hand and says, "I'm Gail; it's nice to meet you, honey."

I blush when she calls me honey, and say it's nice to meet her too because I'm not sure what else to say. I peek back at Grandpop again, when she asks me if I'd like a Coke. But he's still busy with the cabinets, so my eyes wander over to Grandmom who gives me a nod that says *be nice.*

So I say, "Sure, a Coke sounds good." The next thing I know, Gail is handing me an ice cold can of Coca-Cola and I say, "Thank you."

But what I really want to say is, *who do you think you are? And what do you think you're doing? You're married! My father is married! The two of you have no right to be doing whatever you're doing at that apartment over in Ocean City!*

I want to tell her that she isn't being fair. That she has her own family, with two kids, and a husband that calls my mother about pictures.

I want to ask her how she can sit there and chit-chat with my grandmother like nothing is wrong, like I'm not standing right here, with the can of Coke sweating in my hands and the image of my father's penis bleeding in my head. I want to know how someone can lie, cheat, and smile all at the same time.

On the ride home with Grandmom and Grandpop, I think about Gail—the dark circles around her eyes, the blonde hair with the dark

105

roots and that peculiar smile that told me she knew she was doing something wrong. Yet, as I drank the cola, I wondered if I was doing something wrong, too. Did I cheat on Mom because I took the soda from Gail? Should I have shaken it up, popped the top, and sprayed her in the face? Would that have been better? Would that have shown her I was mad at her for ruining my family?

A few days after I meet Gail, I walk in the front door to find Mom crying on the couch in the living room with the blinds drawn, and her blouse wet from the tears. I kneel next to her, and immediately feel older than she is. Even though Mom is forty-three, and I'm only thirteen—I have started feeling like I'm the adult, and she's the child. I feel that way because I change when I talk to her. I slow down, I listen intently to what she says, and today, she wants to know why Dad doesn't love her.

"Mom, of course he loves you, you know that."

"No, he doesn't...."

"Yes, he does."

"No, Frankie, he told Aunt Rena that he loves Gail."

Now, I don't know what to tell her. If Dad said he loves Gail, then should I tell Mom that I met her? Will that make things worse? Will she feel like I cheated on her because I didn't spray the Coke in Gail's face? Before I even know what I'm saying, I blurt out, "Mom, Dad can't love Gail, she isn't as pretty as you."

"You don't know that, Frankie."

"Yeah, I do. I met Gail the other day when I was working out at the development with Grandmom and Grandpop."

"You what?"

"I met Gail."

"You *met* her, Frankie?"

"Yeah, with Grandmom."

"That bitch!"

"What?"

"That bitch!"

"Mom...."

She sits up straight and says, "Get your brothers."

"Why?"

"Because we're goin' over your grandmother's!"

"But, Mom...."

"Frankie, get your brothers!"

We pile into the Cadillac, and on the ride to Grandmom's house Mom talks to herself.

"He wants to bring her around my family? He wants to bring his *puttana around my boys?* Fine! *So be it!*"

Tony and Michael are in the backseat. They look at each other like, *what is she talking about?* Tony finally feels the need to say something.

"Mom, you okay? What's the matter?"

"Gail! That's what's the matter!"

"Who's Gail, Mom?"

"Why don't you ask your father? She's *his* girlfriend!"

"Dad doesn't have a girlfriend."

"Yes, he does Tony!"

"No, he doesn't."

Mom half turns around and looks Tony right in the eyes.

"Yes, he does, *now shut up!*"

Michael can't stay quiet.

"No, he doesn't. You're making that up Mommy!"

"Will the both of you shut up? He does too have a girlfriend! Now SHUT UP!"

When we get to Grandmom's, Mom tells us to get out of the car. We follow her as she marches up the front steps, and bang, bang, bangs on the door. Grandmom answers a moment later, with her hair wet, and a towel around her neck. She has a jar in her left hand, and looks surprised to see us.

"Oh, hi boys. Hi, Ann."

We try to say hello, but Mom starts yelling over top of us.

"I can't believe you would play nice with that whore in front of my son!"

"Ann, why don't you watch your mouth in front of the children?"

"Why? That's what she is. Isn't she? She's married. Two kids she has, two kids!"

"Ann, this isn't the time, or the place for this...."

"No! No! He's married f'Chrissakes; your son is married!"

"Oh, Ann, you asked for this..."

"Asked for what?"

"What did you think was gonna happen? Year after year sleeping on the couch—then the floor. *He's a man.* My son can't be expected to put up with that. Just let Frank have his fun, or you're gonna lose your family."

"Let him have his fun? How can you say that?"

"Just let him have his fun, and take your medicine like a lady for God's sake...."

"Oh, you crazy old bitch! I can't believe you're gonna stand there and take his side! He took a vow! He made a promise!"

"And so did you, Ann. Now, take the boys and go on home."

Mom throws back her head, turns on her heel, and storms down the steps. She climbs into the Cadillac, and speeds away. My brothers and I stay the night at Grandmom's, but I have a hard time sleeping. A voice in my head keeps me awake. It says I'm to blame for all this. The voice says I should have just shaken up the Coke and sprayed it in Gail's face. If I had just done that, my brothers wouldn't know their father has a girlfriend who their mother thinks is a *puttana*.

After watching her son struggle through 15 years of marriage—to a girl she never approved of—Grandmom softens her Catholic views on divorce and develops a friendship with Gail. The two women chat over the phone several times a month and forge a bond based on their mutual desire to see my father happy.

Grandmom always knew something was "off" about my mother, and her about-face regarding divorce emboldens my father, he takes it as a sign of approval to continue seeing Gail. My grandmother may be partially motivated by guilt. She so vehemently opposed the idea of my parents getting married, that she privately feels she "shoved" my father down the aisle by daring him to "go against her wishes."

This time around, she will side with her son. If he wants to carry on a messy public affair, or take the necessary legal steps towards divorce, Grandmom will support him—no matter what.

15

When school starts back, my eighth grade teacher is a young nun named Sister Ruth. She looks different than the other sisters in school because she doesn't wear a habit. Instead, Sister Ruth wears gray, blue and charcoal colored business suits, and instead of saying God is a He, she says God is a She.

Sister says God is a loving, forgiving, all knowing spirit, and that those characteristics can only be attributed to a female deity. To drive home her point, she makes us add an 'S' in front of all the He's in our religion textbooks, and cross out all the His, and replace them with Hers.

It's strange to hear Sister call God *She* or *Her*, especially because we're in eighth grade, and getting ready for Confirmation. We study our catechism, day and night, so we can respond promptly and properly to the Bishop when he asks us questions about our Faith. I wonder how the Bishop would react if he knew Sister Ruth was teaching us to think of God as a woman and not a man.

I wonder what the Bishop would say if he knew Sister says, "Yes, it's true. Jesus came to earth as a man some two thousand years ago, but that's only because it was a male dominated society. No one would have listened to God had She come to earth in her true form—which is that of a woman."

As word of Dad's affair spreads through the family—from Philadelphia to the shore—my brothers and I struggle with what to make of Mom's daily ups and downs. It's hard to know what to make of her when we come home from school and find her crying on the couch one day, while the next day, she's busy cleaning the house with Diana Ross blaring on the stereo. We like the days when Diana Ross greets us at the front door because Mom makes us tomato sandwiches, with thick slices of mozzarella, before we go out to play with our friends.

But it's raining today, and that means no friends, no tomatoes and no Diana Ross. Dad is away on vacation, and won't be home until next week. My brothers already crossed the street to spend the afternoon at our aunt and uncle's house to play Nintendo with our cousins. Mom hardly says a word to me as I change out of my school uniform, and plop in front of the television to watch TV.

Lying on the couch, watching TV, my mind wanders upstairs to the Victoria's Secret Catalog under my bed. I feel a streak of excitement race through my soul, even though I know it's wrong to look at the Victoria's Secret Catalog like I do, and go mad with myself all alone in the bathroom.

Sometimes, I wish Boogs Boderski never turned me on to the idea of swiping Mom's copy of the Victoria's Secret Catalog, but I can't very well give it back to her now. I won't dare throw it away for fear she might find it in the trash and say, *Frankie, what's this?*

With my mind divided between guilt and excitement over the catalog I'm not supposed to have, Mom walks into the den and shuts off the TV. When she turns to face me a second later, I say, "Mom, why did you turn it off? I was watching that." But her eyes are dark, and I notice a belt in her hand. She takes a few steps towards me and I know something is wrong.

"How many times do I have to tell you boys I don't want to walk upstairs and find your rooms a mess? How many times?"

She stands over me on the couch.

"*I'm asking you a question goddammit!* I'm not a slave, you know; I'm not here to be walked over."

Before I can get a word out, she raises the belt above her shoulder, and hits me across the legs. The strike of the belt stings my shins and I scream, "*Mom! Wait! I'm sorry, I'll clean it up!*"

But she hits me again as I scramble to get off the couch. She chases me through the living room where I slip and fall on the hardwood floor of the foyer. She's over me by now, and the belt is wicked against my skin. It's all I can do to cover up as she shouts, "*I am so tired of your shit! Tired of your shit, Frankie!*"

After a moment, I'm able to squirm free and sprint up the stairs, yet I fall again—but this time so does Mom. She's still flailing the belt around, but I'm able to get up and get going faster than she can. I race down the hall to my bedroom, rush in and slam the door, locking it behind me. A moment later Mom bang, bang, bangs on the door. "*Let me in, Frankie! Let me in! I demand you open this door!*"

But I holler back, "*Mom knock it off! I'm not opening the door! Go away!*" My heart is racing a mile a minute. I'm not sure what to do. I look around and remember that there is no phone in my room—so I can't call Aunt Bridgid or Grandmom. I can't climb out the window, being on the second floor and it pouring rain outside. So, what do I do, with Mom banging on the door, and my skin fresh with the sting of leather?

Mom bangs on the door a few more times until there's a loud thud, and a lot of crying. I can't see through the door, but I think the loud thud was Mom collapsing on the floor. She is crying and saying, "I know he went away with that *puttana*...I just know he did...oh Jesus, oh God...."

She lets out a scream, and starts banging her head against the door to the rhythm of, "*Why? Why? Why?*"

With my heart still pounding, I wonder if I should open the door and say, *it's alright Mom, I know you only hit me because you're mad Dad went to Florida with Gail. Don't worry, I understand.*

While another part of me wonders why I shouldn't take the baseball bat propped up next to my bed, open the door and crack Mom across the head. The truth is I am so confused; I don't know what just happened. A minute ago, I was lounging in front of the TV dreaming of girls in lingerie, and now I'm standing in my room, with the rain pelting against the window pane, and my chest rising and falling. With my skin still stinging from the belt, my mind wonders out the window to Sister Ruth and God. I tell myself that I'd like to pray to God and ask Her for help—and that's just what I do.

I ask Her to take the belt out of my mother's hand, so I can walk back out into the world. I ask Her to grant me strength to protect my brothers, and be the best Man of the House while my father is on vacation with Gail. I ask Her to grant my mother peace.

The Lady God must have heard me because when I open the door two hours later, Mom is asleep—slumped on the floor, and the belt is by her side.

16

When Dad gets back from his vacation to Florida with Gail, my parents start seeing a marriage counselor, recommended to them by Uncle Bruno and Aunt Bridgid. After their initial session, where the counselor interviewed each of my parents separately, he suggests that their marital issues are secondary to what Mom shared with him regarding her childhood. He is quite concerned and suggests that my mother begin to see a psychologist as soon as possible.

It isn't long after Mom starts psychotherapy, that we learn she has secrets. Secrets buried deep inside.

We are in Philadelphia, sitting at the kitchen table, eating escarole soup at Nonna's house. My parents have come to talk to my grandmother about Mom's secrets. Dad turns to her and says, "Ann, I think it's time you tell your mother, what you told the doctor."

"What'a doc'a'tor?" Nonna says in her heavy accent.

Mom sits there fumbling over her words.

"C'mon, Ann," Dad says. "You've gotta come to terms with this. Tell your mother what happened."

Michael is in the living room, in Babbo's old armchair, watching TV. Tony and I sit at the table finishing our soup, when Dad turns to Nonna and says, "Ma...look...Ann and I have been seein' a marriage counselor. At his suggestion, Ann has also been talkin' to a psychologist. They have uncovered a few things from her childhood."

"What'a you talk'a 'bout, Frank?"

"Something happened to Ann when she was young...."

"I no unda'stand'a, Frank. What'a you say me?"

"Something happened to Ann, when you went back to Italy...."

"*It*-a-lee? What'a you talk about?"

"Didn't you go to Italy when Ann was small?"

"Yes, you know'a that. I go for see'a my parents."

"Right, that's what I thought."

Mom is taking heavy sighs. She looks at Nonna and weakly interrupts my father, "Don't you remember, Ma?"

"Remember what'a, Ann?"

"I came to you, after you got back from Italy. You told me to keep it a secret—said Babbo would kill them..."

"Kill'a who?"

Mom starts to cry. Tony gets up from his chair, and begins rubbing her shoulders. Dad turns to my mother.

"Ann, you can do it. C'mon, finish tellin' your mother what happened...."

Mom looks back up at Nonna, and takes another deep breath. It is hard for me to watch my mother cry. I feel the tears coming in my own eyes. When I look at Nonna, she is crying, too.

"Ann, *chè sucede?*" Nonna pleads. My grandmother is confused.

Since my mother can't speak, Dad asks Nonna, "Ma, who watched Ann all those years ago when you went to Italy?"

"Renata an'a Colomba, they watch'a her, she was'a little girl."

"I know she was only a little girl, but something happened...."

"*What'a happen Frank? Gesù Cristo, dimmi chè successo!*"

Nonna is tired of this. She wants answers—she wants to know why Mom is so upset. But the more she tries to speak, the harder Mom cries. Her face is in her hands. Tony is crying as he rubs her shoulders.

"C'mon, Ann," Dad says. "You can do it. I can't say it for you...."

Mom is crying too hard to speak. She gets up from the table, shaking her head. She takes a few steps, only to pause at the entrance to the dining room. Her back is toward us. Mom leans against the wall to her left. There are two small pictures—one of Jesus, and another of President Kennedy—stuffed behind the telephone. They fall to the floor, as Mom brushes past them. Her face is still in her hands. She moves into the dining room. Mom sits and sobs in one of the chairs around the table.

Nonna is ahead of Dad as they follow Mom into the dining room. Tony and I are standing in the kitchen, looking at Dad, who is standing behind Nonna. My grandmother is bonding over—softly trying to pry Mom's hands from her face.

Michael is standing in the other entrance way with the living room behind him. He must have heard the commotion. He looks innocent and confused. Michael looks at Dad, "Why is Mommy crying?"

But Dad doesn't answer him. He is focused on Nonna who is softly speaking to Mom.

"Antonietta," she says. "What'sa wrong? What'a is'a?"

My grandmother is holding her daughter's hands, but Mom keeps her eyes down. Through her tears, she says, "I can't, Frank. I'm sorry, I can't...."

When Aunt Renata and Aunt Colomba find out what happened at Nonna's house, they come down the shore looking for answers. They sit in our kitchen, drinking coffee and smoking cigarettes, when Aunt Renata says, "Ann, what's this Ma was sayin' about her trip to Italy when you were young?"

"Remember when I was a kid, how I was close to that boy from up the street?"

"Yeah...so?"

"Well, do you remember his grandfather?"

"Yeah, he was a nice man, always looked out for everybody. What about him?"

"Well, when Ma was in Italy, he...ah...he started takin' me into the greenhouse behind his garden. He told me it was a secret, that I was special...."

"And?"

"...at first I didn't know what was happenin'. He used to sit me on his lap, and we would talk. I liked him a lot, and he was very nice with me. But then he started touchin' me, and before I knew what was happenin', he started pullin' my panties aside and puttin' himself inside of me."

"Inside of you—what does that mean?"

"You know what it means, Renata."

"No, I don't."

"Sex. Intercourse."

"*Sex! Are you outta your mind?* He was one of the nicest men in the neighborhood!"

"Rena, I know, but...."

"That's nonsense! Did Frank tell you to say this? Because I'm not buyin' it! Colomba and I looked out for you and Nick when Ma went away. Nothin' happened. You're makin' this shit up."

"Now wait a second," Aunt Colomba says. "Wait a second...."

"Oh, Lardass, c'mon...." Aunt Renata snaps.

"No, Rena," Aunt Colomba continues, "just wait a second. That boy's grandfather was always touchin' me—grabbin' me. He never took me to any greenhouse, but he was always tryin' to get me alone."

"Oh, Colomba, that's ridiculous! Do you know how ridiculous that sounds? He was married f'Chrissakes. He was friends with Babbo!"

"No, Rena, it's true. He didn't stop foolin' with me until I married Larry. I even had to use my cane once to swat his hand away when he was tryin' to feel me up. So, what Ann is sayin' could have happened if you ask me."

"Well, who's askin' you? Ann, I'm tellin' you this is absurd. He was a good man."

"Rena...there was someone else, too...."

"Ann...careful what you say...."

"Remember Ma's friend from around the corner?"

"Yeah...."

"Well, her husband used to take me down into his basement, and put himself in my mouth."

"*Put himself in your mouth!*"

"Renata, I was only eight years old. I didn't know what was happenin'...."

"That does it!"

"Renata...."

"That does it! You're outta your mind. C'mon Lardass, we're leavin'!"

"No Rena, don't go."

"Annie, this is the most preposterous load of shit I've ever heard in my life. Ma went back to Italy to see her parents before they died. Me and Colomba watched out for you and Nick. That's what happened. That's the truth. End of story!"

"But Renata...."

"You expect me to believe this shit? I mean, where was the blood, huh? Little girl, with a grown man—where was the blood f'Chrissakes? I would'a noticed if somethin' was goin' on. You think I'm blind? You think

I'm dumb? As far as I'm concerned, this is nonsense and somethin' you are never to tell Ma...."

"I told Ma...."

"What?"

"I told her when I was a kid, when she got back from Italy. She was at the stove one day when I walked over to her, I pointed between my legs because I didn't know the word for vagina, but I told Ma I was in pain. I told her about the man down the street, and how he would sit me on his lap in the greenhouse and pull my underwear aside. That he was hurting me by putting himself inside of me—but Ma refused to believe it. She became agitated and animated and told me I was never to mention it again. I think she was afraid that if I told Babbo, he'd kill the guy. So, I kept it a secret. I never told her about the basement, and what happened down there. But those afternoons in the greenhouse went on for years until I realized what was happenin'. I never brought it up again because I didn't want the blame to fall back on Ma; life was hard enough with Babbo."

"What's that supposed to mean? If there's any blame to go around—it's *yours*. Now, we're out of here! Colomba c'mon...."

If my mother cried a lot when she found out about Dad and Gail, she cries in a harsher way now that her secrets have come back to haunt her.

Mom says she has been carrying around pictures in her head for years. Pictures of memories she could never understand. She would see a flash of an image—sunlight breaking through a greenhouse, the damp darkness of a basement—but there was always a feeling attached to those images she could never explain. She couldn't get the pictures to slow down long enough to understand what they meant. But, thanks to the fact she has been seeing a psychologist—someone trained to know what to ask and *how* to ask it—those images finally make sense to her.

She claims that her childhood best friend's grandfather lured her into his greenhouse over a four-year span, starting when Nonna went to Italy in 1955, and Mom was eight years old. She says their contact ended only when my twelve year old mother took it upon herself to stop frequenting his backyard. Mom said she finally realized what they were doing together was wrong, but her decision made this man very sad. He always asked her why she no longer came to see him. He said he missed those afternoons in the greenhouse, and tried to guilt my mother into returning.

But Nonna's friend's husband was different. He was more forward. Though their physical involvement was more intermittent, he kept aggressively pestering Mom until the day she got married. He was never one to accept 'no' easily. Sometimes, even in my grandparents' kitchen, while Nonna had her back turned working at the stove—this man would rub Mom's leg—hoping to excite her and entice her into setting up a rendezvous later that day.

In both cases, after years of innocently succumbing to their filthy advances and ploys, Mom was able to resist them, and move on with her life as best as she could.

Even though her sisters don't want to hear it, uncovering these memories of abuse sheds a whole new light on my parents' marriage. Now, my father feels like he better understands what happened on their honeymoon. He has a different perspective on all those years when Mom ignored him when he came home from work, the not sleeping in bed, the late-night gambling—Dad fully accepts the fact that Mom was abused as a little girl. It makes sense to him. He doesn't doubt her claims. In fact, he empathizes with her, and wants her sisters to come together and support his wife as she tries to overcome the grief. However, anytime Mom tries to call her sister Renata, and talk about the sexual abuse she suffered, my aunt becomes impatient and hangs up. If Mom thought she could count on Aunt Colomba to support her allegations to the rest of the family, she probably shouldn't have told her about Uncle Larry.

Uncle Larry was Aunt Colomba's husband. He was an Irish drunk and Babbo hated him. He died when I was a toddler, run over by a car as he stumbled home in a drunken stupor.

On top of his alcoholism, he privately entertained a sexual desire for his much younger sister-in-law, my mother. Uncle Larry would sometimes hide in my mother's bedroom closet, only to crawl over to her bed late at night. He liked to fondle her under the covers. Mom was going through puberty—and naturally, her body was showing signs of maturity. If my mother was half-awake, she would swipe his hand away as he reached up to caress her. But many times, his touching would go unnoticed until she woke-up the next morning to find the blouse to her pajamas unbuttoned, or her panties down around her thighs; these were the clues that told Mom her brother-in-law had made a late-night visit.

Even in broad day light, Uncle Larry wouldn't hesitate to stand in the doorway of Mom's bedroom as she got undressed. He loved watching her remove her Catholic school uniform. But Mom was older now; she knew his voyeurism wasn't right.

She stopped frequenting the greenhouse for the exact same reason—she knew she was being taken advantage of.

So, alone, half-naked and tired of her "Peeping-Tom-in-law," Mom took a stand and told Uncle Larry that if he didn't stop spying on her, and sneaking into her room, she would tell Nonna and Babbo.

Standing in the doorway, watching her undress, my uncle laughed and allowed his eyes to wander all over my mother's body, until Mom threatened him again.

The day he finally backed down, my Uncle Larry sheepishly dropped his chin to his chest, turned away from Mom's doorway, and stomped his feet all the way down the stairs like a petulant child.

Decades later, when Mom decides to come clean and tell Aunt Colomba what went on between her little sister and her late husband, my aunt says, *"Ann, that's ridiculous!"*

"Colomba, I never said anything about it because I didn't want Babbo to throw you guys out of the house, but...."

"Annie, Larry was my husband...."

"I know, and that's why it's hard for me to share...."

"The other men I can see, but not Larry, we had a family!"

"But Colomba, it's true, I'm telling the truth...."

"It isn't fair to bring it up after he's been dead all these years. He isn't here to defend himself...besides, I was his wife f'Chrissakes, what would he have wanted with a little girl? You're almost 20 years younger than me...."

Even though Uncle Larry had abandoned his family in the early 1970's, Aunt Colomba cries over my mother's allegations, and this causes Mom to feel guilty for having shared the truth. The cruel reality is that my mother would have to face these memories alone.

No one from her side of the family wants to hear any more about her alleged "abusive childhood." They blame her for sharing these tales, and are suspicious of my father and question his role in all of this.

It is the autumn of 1990.

17

Even though Dad has a girlfriend, and no one believes Mom's secrets, there are some days when everything is perfect. On Sunday mornings, Mom makes pancakes and Dad plays The Three Tenors on the stereo in his office. He sets the volume so high, that our house shakes with the sound of arias and Neapolitan songs, as Dad sings just like he does when he is pouring concrete.

Mom looks pretty as she stands at the stove in her long green housecoat, while Dad is dashing in his dark gray robe, going back and forth between his office and the kitchen, smiling, singing and flirting with Mom.

I smile too, because Sunday morning means no mention of Mom's abusive childhood, or Dad's extramarital affair. For a few hours, there is only happiness.

The five of us sit at the kitchen table smothering our pancakes with butter and all-natural maple syrup—the only kind Dad lets us use. He and Mom sip coffee out of big, thick mugs, while my brothers and I drink orange juice from tall, slender glasses. My brothers complain they want chocolate milk, but Mom says, "No, no, no, one concert at a time, if you please."

She still likes to call us—*The Chocolate Milk Symphony*—for the way we tend to toot when our bellies are full of Nestle Quick. Mom smirks and says, "Dad's records are just fine by me. I'd much rather listen to The Three Tenors, than The Three Tooters, thank you very much."

Her line makes Dad laugh so hard, he nearly spits out his coffee. He slaps his open palm against the table, and struggles to put his mug down without spilling coffee everywhere.

"Ann," he chokes out, between fits of laughter, "that was funny." Cough cough cough. "Our sons, the three tooters...how proud we should be!"

Mom starts laughing, too. She grabs Dad's forearm and soon they're both holding their stomachs, rocking in hysterics. My brothers sit there confused, as our parents wipe tears from their eyes while struggling to catch their breaths. Tony and Michael don't get the joke; they don't know The Three Tenors. The name given to opera singers: José Carreras, Plácido Domingo and Luciano Pavarotti, when they performed together this past summer at the 1990 World Cup in Italy.

Since my brothers don't know The Three Tenors, I'm sure they don't remember when Dad sang for those High Rollers at the Luciano Pavarotti welcoming party, years ago in Atlantic City. My father has always admired the work of Jimmy Durante, Antonio Carlos Jobim and Frank Sinatra, but ever since that night he and his brother performed at the gala for the King of the High C's, my father has felt a special connection to the larger-than-life Italian tenor.

He likes to whistle along with Carreras, when he sings *La Donna è Mobile*, or listen intently when Plácido Domingo interprets *Nessun Dorma,* but when Pavarotti sings 'O Sole Mio, Dad is center stage at La Scala.

Seated at the head of the table, he raises a hand to the sky, and belts out the first three dramatic words as loud and clearly as Pavarotti. Mom uses her spatula like a conductor, as my brothers and I sway with Dad and Pavarotti—their voices full—our kitchen their sound stage.

When their duet is over, Dad always sends one of us into his office to play it again. He says, 'O Sole Mio is the greatest song ever written. He says everything you need to know about Italy can be found in its lyrics and melody.

As the song starts again, the only thing I know for certain is that I always feel sad when breakfast is over. Something in me knows that if it wasn't for Sunday mornings with Pavarotti and pancakes, our world would be totally shattered.

'O Sole Mio becomes the soundtrack of our joy.

Even though Mom's full name is Antonietta—Lester and Darryl call her, 'Miss Ann.' Lester and Darryl are two of the men that have worked for Dad since I was little. They are a regular part of his construction crew and despite the fact they're black, and from the ghetto in Atlantic City, we treat them like family.

Dad says Lester and Darryl both have hearts of gold, despite the fact that they both spent time in prison—Darryl for homicide—albeit in self-defense. My father says he trusts them completely, and that they'll work from dawn till dusk without a single word edgewise.

Lester and Darryl are brothers-in-law, and on most mornings they ride together to work in Lester's old beat-up van. Normally, they stop by our house at 7 a.m. to get some tools out of the garage, before Dad sends them to his development in Cumberland County.

Sometimes, Lester and Darryl wait outside on our front porch for Dad to greet them with the day's instructions. But most mornings, he invites them in, and they have coffee at the kitchen table while my brothers and I wake Mom up from the floor in the den, so she can make us lunch for school.

Lester and Darryl are only a few years older than Dad, which means they're more like Mom's age. Yet, they tip their caps to her out of respect, and say things like, "Good day, Miss Ann," or, "Fine to see you, Miss Ann."

Dad says they grew up in North Carolina, which explains that funny accent, and why they are so formal around women. On Friday afternoons, when they stop by to collect their pay, Mom invites them in, while Dad finishes up in his office. If it's one of those days when Mom and Nonna have turned our kitchen into Calabria, they go crazy. "That sure smell good, Miss Ann! Is you makin' some eye-talian food?"

That's what they call us—not Italian—but eye-talian. They say from where they're from down south, they never met any real eye-talians. "Only seen'em in movies, Frankie," but that doesn't stop them from trying the peppers and sausage Nonna offers.

Lester and Darryl are fun. Whenever I go to work with Dad they do nothing but sing, or laugh, or cut-up on each other in their southern way. They never tease me, but always try to show me how to make the work we're doing easier. Lester and Darryl are laborers, and if we're carrying bricks or block from one spot to another, they show me how to load the wheelbarrow just right so we can *push* the bricks, instead of killing ourselves with the carrying. They have a workman's knowledge and pride and look at my father with respect.

The highest praise they can offer is a simple one. Whenever Dad steps up and delivers on a promise or task, they always say, "Your daddy know what time it is." Their way of saying Dad is nobody's fool.

One of the ways my father delivers is with the weekly paycheck. For years now Dad has employed a small crew of laborers, masons and concrete finishers. Many of whom are uneducated drifters, a few are skilled artisans from Italy, and some are ex-cons, like Lester and Darryl.

To ensure that he makes payroll each week, Dad has cultivated a personal relationship with a few of the bank managers in our area. Because of their friendship, these bank managers help Dad out from time to time, when he is in a fiscal bind.

The bank managers agree to cash Dad's often times large corporate checks—which is generally frowned upon in the banking world. If for some reason they can't do it, Dad drives up to South Philadelphia and cashes the check at those shady check cashing establishments run by the Philly Mob. He knows he'll have to pay them "a few points," but Dad will do whatever he has to in-order to make payroll each week. He can't let his crew down.

My father knows his men rely on him for their livelihood, and in turn, he relies on them. In addition to their weekly pay, sometimes Dad's employees will ask him for a loan, or help with their child support, occasionally they will even call from jail, looking for Dad to bail them out.

Dad has long been impressed with strength, and when one of his employees is a particularly hard worker he calls that man a bull. That's when you know Dad admires you, and that's what he calls Darryl—a bull. Yet, Lester and Darryl have long had their suspicions about my father and his Mafia mystique, and it started the first time they ever laid eyes on him.

Before Dad hired Lester and Darryl, they were working for an excavating contractor, so they only saw my father from afar. Dad was pouring the concrete and partnering with an asphalt firm to install all the streets, curbs and sidewalks of this brand new housing development.

The first time Lester and Darryl ever saw my father was in 1987 when he pulled onto that jobsite in our brand new, fire engine red,

Cadillac Roadster. He parked near the construction trailer offices and nodded to his future employees as he walked into the trailer for a meeting. Dad was wearing black dress slacks, black slip-on Italian loafers, a white polo shirt, with the collar popped, his dark sunglasses, a simple gold watch, matching bracelet and chain around his neck.

The moment he disappeared into the trailer, Lester excitedly turned to Darryl, "Sonny boy, sonny boy, you done seen that man?"

"You mean 'dat fella with 'da Cadillac?"

"Good gosh I reckonin' that boy's in 'da *Mah-fee-ah*."

"Da *Mah-fee-ah?*"

"Yes, Lord!"

"*Wooooo weeeee!*"

They had only seen men like Dad in Mob movies. The brothers-in-law had recently moved north from the hills of rural North Carolina, and to them, Dad was a revelation.

Before the three men ever exchanged a single word, Lester and Darryl witnessed *Frankie the Voice* in action, forever cementing the suspicion in their minds that my father was indeed, in the *Mah-fee-ah*.

Dad, and the asphalt firm he had partnered with, were owed $130,000—$80k of which belonged to my father. The builders they were working for were actually corporate lawyers, brand new to the development business. Before this project was complete, one of them would go to jail, and the other would suffer a heart attack and die from the stress.

Yet, they were being honest when they told my father and his partner that they couldn't pay them the money they owed. The money was due *months* ago, but the lawyers claimed to be broke. To prove their point, they literally allowed the asphalt contractor's brother, a licensed CPA, to take a look at their books—thus confirming the situation. These novice homebuilders were in *way* over their head, and did not have the funds to pay my father and his asphalt partner.

All they could do was promise that upon installation of the street scheduled to be paved, the city would release a bond to the builders worth $250k, from which the men could then pay my father and the asphalt firm.

My father didn't trust their promise. He knew that if they owed him eighty thousand dollars, they must also owe the plumbers, the painters, the carpenters, the electricians, the landscapers—basically every other trade on the job. Dad didn't believe that they would be able to pay—or even *want* to pay, once the street was installed. He was convinced they would make up another excuse; Dad had seen this all before.

My father contemplated walking off the job, but instead he proposed a compromise the builders agreed to. Dad said he and the asphalt firm would proceed with paving the new street, but **only** if the lawyers hand delivered two "good faith checks," by noon the next day.

The lawyers had the money to cover these "good faith checks," which were for half the amount owed. Dad would get a check for $40,000 and the asphalt contractor would get one for $25,000. This was enough to satisfy both men for the moment, and meant the all important street would be paved. It was wintertime and a stretch of below freezing temperature was in the forecast, so the street had to be installed ASAP.

But Dad felt the need to clarify. He said, "Let me make myself clear. We're gonna start layin' the blacktop first thing in the mornin'. We gotta break in the weather and tomorrow is the only clear day for a while, so we'll hold up our end of the agreement and pave the street. But let me say this, if you're not here by noon tomorrow with our checks, I'm gonna knock out one corner of each house under construction. By my count you have 17 homes underway, ain't that right?"

The lawyers were confused, but nodded in agreement—17 homes were under construction at the moment.

"So, I'm tellin' ya, if you're not here by noon, your houses are comin' down. It won't take me very long. And don't think the cops are gonna stop me, they're not gonna shoot an unarmed guy in a bulldozer. As a matter of fact," Dad continues, "I kinda hope you *don't* bring the checks tomorrow. I'm kinda excited. I'll never buy another drink in New Jersey for the rest of my life. I'll be a hero and may even make the news. Maybe even the national news."

The lawyers were bewildered, but *Frankie the Voice* meant every. Single. Word. My father knew that once you started talking like this—your body language, your tonality, your eye contact—all had to be genuine, and in-line with your message. He told me years later, "Once you say you're gonna cross that line, you've gotta be prepared to cross it all the way."

Sure enough the next morning Dad and his men, the asphalt firm and their men, begin installing the new street. Lester and Darryl have picked up a few days' work with the asphalt team and stay focused through morning coffee break.

Everyone on the job had heard about Dad's promise to knock down the houses under construction. Coffee break is generally around nine in the morning—still there were no "good faith checks." Soon, it was 10 a.m., then 11:15, by lunchtime the jobsite is alive with anticipation and *Frankie the Voice* does not disappoint.

The noon deadline has arrived.

As the men break for lunch. Dad keeps his word and climbs up into the massive bulldozer. He turns over the engine and revs the gas pedal causing the black diesel smoke to escape from the tall rusty exhaust pipe. Dad revs it again as the men unwrap their hoagies and sandwiches for lunch. The jobsite is still, there is a weariness in the air. *Is he really going to do it?*

One of the lawyers is present, standing on the wooden deck outside the door of the construction trailer. He keeps checking his watch. He's trying to reason with my father, but Dad keeps revving the engine of the bulldozer so aggressively that he drowns out the lawyer's pleas.

After allowing the engine to warm-up, Dad puts the bulldozer into reverse and the lawyer panics, "Jesus Christ, this lunatic is outta his fuckin' mind!" He bolts back inside in a desperate attempt to call his partner, who is the one in charge of bringing the checks to the jobsite at noon.

Lester and Daryl are amongst the 30 or so men observing all this. My father puts the bulldozer into drive, he pulls up parallel to the construction trailer. The lawyer steps back out onto the deck.

"Frank, c'mon, Bernie is on his way!"

"I told you, Harvey! I told you noon! Its 12:05, where are my fuckin' checks?"

"They're comin'! Jesus, they're comin'!"

"Too late, Harvey! You had your chance!"

The lawyer panics as Dad reengages the engine and proceeds out towards the first house that he plans to knock down. All he wants to do is knock down one corner of the building, that will force everything out of plumb—and if not the entire structure—at least part of the structure will need to be rebuilt. Which is what he wants, he wants the lawyers to incur more expense, more headache; more heartache. The $80k they owe my father in 1987, is equivalent to $175,000 in 2018. It isn't Dad's fault they can't pay. He has a family to feed, and so does the asphalt contractor.

My father is focused, he is possessed and as he made clear to me many years later, when you say you're going to "cross the line." you have to cross it with every ounce of your soul.

Lester and Darryl cannot believe what they are about to witness. My father has his black sunglasses on, he is dressed in his winter work clothes, with his collar popped—this is the moment of truth. The lawyer shouts in vain from the deck, "Frank! Frank! Bernie's on his way! Just give us a few more minutes!"

It's easy for Dad to ignore him, since the bulldozer is so loud. My father is approaching the first house he plans to semi-demolish. He knows it will take nothing to knock down a corner of each house. Literally, as he engages the front plow, a tiny silver Mercedes comes speeding around the corner. The other lawyer has arrived with the "good faith checks." He pulls nose to nose with the bulldozer. The attorney throws open his car door, he is waving the checks in the air. "Frank! Frank! Don't do it! Here's your money! We got your money! Stop! Stop!"

My father peers down at the lawyer. The man scrambles over to the bulldozer, he extends his arm and hands my father two envelopes. Dad peeks inside, the checks have arrived, and the houses will survive.

Whenever he would tell me this story Dad would always say, "I was a little disappointed he showed up. I was prepared, I had made up my mind. I was gonna destroy their entire project. I could see the news that night: *Jersey Contractor Loses Mind, Bulldozes a Dozen Homes....*"

For as long as Lester and Darryl worked for my father, they always referred to this day, always said, "Good golly, ain't nobody like your daddy, Frankie. We was in shock, here was this man, this gangster lookin' eye-talian fella 'bout to terrorize them buildings. I mean, I turned to Darryl and said, we's gotta work for that man. I ain't know nothin' 'bout no concrete, but I sure 'nough knew your daddy was no joke."

At that Darryl would *always* add, "Frankie, your daddy know what time it is...."

18

Mom has been having the same nightmare for many months now. Sometimes, she'll be sound asleep on the couch in the den, when she will suddenly sit straight up like a board, and scare us half to death. In the nightmare, Mom commits suicide. Not the forty-three year old mother that I know, but the eight year old little girl who was lured into the greenhouse.

In the nightmare, my adorable, hazel-eyed, raven haired, little girl of a mother hangs herself. She is standing atop a table with a noose around her neck when the little girl kicks the table out from under her, and Mom is left to dangle from the rafters. She tells Dad that eight year old is a bad girl—and the reason why the forty-three year old is having all these problems.

We're in the Cadillac, driving home from Nonna's house. It's nighttime, and Michael is squeezed between Mom and Dad in the front seat, while Tony and I have our grandmother hemmed in the middle of the backseat. Dad's behind the wheel, guiding us down the Atlantic City Expressway—the fifty-mile-long highway that connects Philadelphia to Atlantic City.

On the radio, Don McLean slowly starts to sing one of our favorite songs, 'American Pie.' As the tempo picks up, Dad starts to play the drums on the dashboard; he's driving with his elbows. My brothers and I strain to see who can sing louder than the other, and just as we're at the fullest, fastest part of the song, Dad looks over at Mom, and shouts, "Ann, what's the matter?"

He stops playing the drums, frantically reaches to lower the radio, and shouts again, "*Ann! Ann!*"

Tony and I are still singing, but Nonna screeches for us to "Stop'a you sing!" That only makes us sing even louder, until Dad hollers back, "Frankie, Tony, *state zitt!*"

He doesn't have to tell Michael to shut up, since he couldn't sing even if he wanted to. Dad is leaning across him, smushing my kid brother into the seat, trying to stop Mom from swaying like she is. He's driving with one hand and leaning over at the same time. When he turns Mom towards him, I can see that her mouth is open, and that her eyes are in the back of her head.

Nonna screams, "Ann, *chè sucede? Chè sucede?*"

Dad shouts, "I think she's passing out! Christ! Ann! *Ann!*"

It is bedlam. The Cadillac is slowing down. Dad pulls over onto the shoulder. He jumps out and rushes around the front of the car. He gets to Mom's side, and opens her door.

"Ann," he says, "c'mon, what's the matter?"

He's helping her out, leaning her up against the car. Then *boom*, the door is closed and the Cadillac is dark and quiet. Even though my brothers and I crane our necks to see what's going on, we can't hear what Dad is saying. Nonna tells Michael to lower the window, and she starts hollering at them in Italian.

I'm scared; I don't know what just happened to Mom. A minute ago, we were singing and laughing, Dad was playing the drums, driving with his elbows, and now, Mom is passing out. Nonna keeps hollering in Italian, wanting to know what's going on, but my father ignores her. I feel helpless in the backseat. I could *scream* because Mom must have had her nightmare again. I wish I could turn to Nonna, and ask her to sing *'O Sole Mio* with me, so that Mom would feel better, but Nonna is too busy rambling on and on in Italian.

After twenty minutes by the side of the road, Dad tells us Mom is coming out of it, as he eases her into the front seat. Before he closes her door, he asks us to be quiet and to let Mom rest. Nonna keeps peppering him in Italian, but he closes the door without answering. My grandmother starts talking to Mom, but my mother looks like she just went ten rounds with Clubber Lang. She is perspiring, exhausted and speechless. I watch my father walk around the front of the Cadillac, and get in on the driver's side.

As we merge into traffic, and head back down the Expressway, the radio stays off. We ride in silence, as the image of Mom with her mouth open, and her eyes in the back of her head haunts me.

For the first time ever, I find myself afraid for her. Afraid that maybe Mom's secrets are too much for her to handle, after all.

After she passed out in the Cadillac, Mom's psychologist recommends that my mother see a psychiatrist for a diagnostic evaluation. She feels Mom may need to start taking medication, and possibly even be hospitalized. Dad doesn't like the sound of the word *hospitalized*, and says he wants to find an alternative to medication. He does, however, agree to take Mom to see a psychiatrist.

The doctor is in New York City, so Dad arranges for Grandmom and Grandpop to watch my brothers and me, while he takes Mom to the Big Apple, for three full days of analysis. When they get home, they say the New York doctor agrees with Mom's weekly psychologist—she needs to be medicated immediately and possibly hospitalized for a time.

For weeks after that, our kitchen is alive with conversation among friends and family—should Mom be hospitalized, or not?

Anybody, and everybody, who comes over is a part of the conversation. They sit around drinking coffee and smoking cigarettes, wondering aloud about Mom's future, and the doctors' recommendations. The thing is—these conversations occur without any of my cousins, aunts, or uncles from Mom's side of the family. They have made it very clear that they think the idea of medication or hospitalization is ridiculous. In their opinion, whatever is going on with Mom, is Dad's fault for being with Gail, and for carrying on like an oppressive, male chauvinist husband.

Even though Dad is nervous about medication and fearful of hospitalization, over the next few months, he takes Mom to Methodist Hospital, Jefferson Hospital, and the Princeton Biological Brain Center.

Tests are conducted including a chemical analysis, a brain imaging study, and a complete physical work-up. My father hopes these institutions may uncover the reason for Mom's latest issue, severe stomach pains.

Since the episode in the Cadillac, Mom has been saying it feels like something is eating at her from the inside. Sometimes, this sensation of being eaten alive is so bad that she rolls around on the floor, clutching her stomach, shouting, "Frank, help me! Frank! *Frank!*"

When she cries for help, my brothers or I instantly go running towards the sound of her voice. Tonight, when I hear her cries, I race into Mom and Dad's room where I find her rolling around on the floor in the dress shirt she wears as a nightgown. She is writhing in pain, lying between the foot of the bed, and the bureau. Her knees are pulled tight to her chest, with both of her hands on her stomach. Her neck is stretched back as far as it can go, like she's trying to get as far away from the pain in her gut. Mom rolls from side to side, calling for my father, who is kneeling right beside her, looking helpless.

I'm not used to seeing my father look helpless. All he can say is, "I'm here Ann...I'm here."

As Mom keeps rolling around and calling his name, he glances up at me in the doorway, "Frankie is here, Ann. Come on honey, calm down, everything's alright."

I'm scared and say, "What's wrong with Mom?"

But Dad says, "She's just scared, Chichi...."

"Scared of what?"

Dad doesn't answer.

I stay silent in the doorway, as he moves closer to Mom, and takes her into his lap. She is still writhing about, but when she feels his body, she moves her hands from her stomach to his arms and shoulders. Mom is holding on for dear life. I get that same feeling I got in the Cadillac; I find myself afraid for Mom.

Dad holds her, and soothes her, and soon her breathing slows down. Her legs relax and she seems more tired than scared. My father helps her into bed before walking me down the hallway to my room.

I want to ask him what just happened. How come Mom was rolling around? But I have a feeling he doesn't know. I have a feeling my father is just as confused as his thirteen year old son.

The doctors at Methodist Hospital, Jefferson Hospital, and the Princeton Biological Brain Center, run a battery of tests on Mom, only to conclude that she is in good health. They say she is free of tumors, calcifications, hemorrhaging or bone trauma. As far as her gastro-intestinal abnormalities, and that burning she complains of, it isn't an ulcer, or the even the beginning of menopause. When my parents share this with Mom's weekly psychologist, they learn a new term—guilt pains.

The psychologist says Mom's stomach issues are most likely the result of having harbored feelings of guilt since she was a little girl. The doctor says these sorts of gastro-intestinal issues are common for ACoA's, and that it makes sense; her guilt pains are just surfacing now that she's talking about her past so much.

When Dad asks the doctor to explain the term ACoA, he's told it means Adult Child of Alcoholic. Soon, Mom starts attending meetings for Children of Alcoholics Anonymous, as Dad begins going to ALANON meetings—for spouses and children of alcoholics.

Mom's psychologist says it might be beneficial for my father to attend these ALANON meetings since Mom exhibits many of the traits of a dry alcoholic.

My parents bring home pamphlets from their weekly meetings that describe life growing up in a home with an active alcoholic, and how it can affect how a child looks at life. They learn that Mom has "repressed emotions," and that she needs to learn how to "let go," and "be free." They also read about the rigid rules of an alcoholic household, and how they produce silence, denial and isolation. My parents learn that most children who grow up in families affected by alcoholism never really grow up, which may explain *Swing-Set Annie*.

Swing-Set Annie is my mother, my eight year old mother. It is who Aunt Ellen found on the swings at the ballpark. When football practice ends at eight in the evening, there's always a few dozen mothers smoking and chatting as they wait for their sons. They start gathering by the fence, near the home team's sideline, about twenty to eight. That's just what they were doing the night Aunt Ellen found *Swing-Set Annie*.

Mom was talking to a few of the other mothers. She was laughing, telling them how Dad won't allow my brothers or me to use our microwave because he's afraid we'll be hurt by the radiation. Yet, he encourages our teammates, at risk of not making weight, to use the sauna at our house, to sweat off a couple pounds the night before a game.

Aunt Ellen laughed right along with Mom. She thought Dad was funny for his contradiction, and walked away for a few minutes to say hello to another group of mothers. When she came back, my mother was nowhere to be found. With practice winding down, Aunt Ellen, and Mom's other friend, Claudia, went looking for her. At first, they thought maybe Mom had gone back to the Cadillac for another cigarette. But they checked, and she wasn't there. Next, they tried the ladies' room, but again, Mom wasn't there.

The ballpark where we have football practice is a huge, all-sports complex. The entire park is open. You can stand at either end of the property and see everything; there is no place to hide.

By the time practice ends, the entire complex is dark, except for the lights shining down on the football field. This is why it was so hard for Ellen and Claudia to make out the figure swinging on the swing-set half-way across the park. Whoever was playing on the swings was doing so in virtual blackness. Aunt Ellen thought it could be Mom. She and Claudia trotted across the field calling to the figure.

"Ann, is that you? Ann!"

But the figure seemed to be deaf.

"Ann!" they called again—still, no answer.

When they got close enough to recognize my mother, Mom stopped playing on the swings, stumbled, fell down and started to giggle. Aunt Ellen and Claudia rushed over.

"Ann," Claudia said, "what happened? Are you okay? One minute you were there, and the next you were gone?"

Mom kept giggling as the two women helped her to her feet. Aunt Ellen kept pushing for an answer. "Why were you playing on the swings? Your children are done with practice, and ready to go home."

"My name is Annie," my mother responded, in a childlike tone.

"Ann, c'mon, why are you talking like that? We were worried sick."

"My name is Annie. I was just playing on the swings." Mom insisted innocently. Aunt Ellen looked at Claudia, and both women instinctively knew something was wrong. They knew not to rile up my mother, in lieu of her recent emotional struggles. Aunt Ellen decided to play it safe, and talk my father into letting us go with her and her sons for a pizza while Dad drove Mom home.

Later, when Aunt Ellen had a chance to tell Dad about *Swing-Set Annie*, he finally gave in, and agreed it was time for Mom to start taking medication. So, in addition to her weekly therapist visits, and Children of Alcoholics Anonymous meetings—in late 1990—Mom begins a psychopharmacological treatment plan.

Little by little, thanks to her weekly therapist, attendance of those meetings for Children of Alcoholics Anonymous, and the taking of her daily psychiatric medication, Mom stops crying so much. She seems happier. Her gambling slows down. The sleeping on the floor becomes less frequent. She even decides to go to school to obtain a real estate license. Mom also starts to coach Michael's third and fourth grade basketball team, while working part time as a nurse's aide, at the nursing home around the corner. Through the nursing home, Mom starts volunteering at ARC—the Association for Retarded Citizens.

She also begins to take pride in her appearance for the first time in years. Mom starts getting her hair and nails done regularly. Dad is so happy she is putting more interest into the way she looks that he fills her side of their walk-in closet with a whole new wardrobe full of skirts, heels, blouses and dress pants.

Now, the small window of happiness we only used to find on those Sunday mornings with Pavarotti and pancakes bleeds into the other days of our lives. Mom's resurgent makeover causes Dad to tell everyone, "After fifteen years, Ann is finally starting to remind me of the girl I married."

In addition to her new grooming and clothing style, Mom seems friendlier, and more outgoing than ever before. At home, the changes in her demeanor serve to energize and stabilize our lives while causing my forty-one year old father to fall in love with her all over again.

Ever since their honeymoon confusion, my parents have been growing apart. For years, Dad had to endure an indifferent wife. If he brought her flowers, Mom would give no reaction—nothing; not a, *thank you, Frank,* or, *why don't you go to hell?* —nothing.

She did the same thing one Christmas when Dad hid a diamond necklace in the Christmas tree. Once she found it, Mom gave no reaction. She simply took it off the branches, and clasped it around her neck, without saying a word.

It wasn't until later in the day, that Mom confessed to my father that she felt unworthy whenever he gave her a gift. She explained that it was because she had watched Nonna suffer for years with Babbo, and felt equally bad about Aunt Colomba, who married a drunk, only to be abandoned by her husband in her mid-forties with four kids.

My mother says she feels guilty receiving presents from her husband, when her own sister and mother got nothing but abuse from theirs. But all that seems like ancient history now. Now, when Dad brings her flowers, Mom treats him like a hero. Now, when he comes home from work, she greets him at the door with a smile, a glass of wine and a, "How was your day, honey?"

Even though Dad's thrilled about Mom's new look and demeanor, many of the women on both sides of the family quietly take offense to it. They find it disgusting that he could brazenly sleep with another woman, in turn, forcing his wife to become someone, or something she isn't. They shake their heads in disapproval at Mom's sudden attempt at glamour, and style. My aunts, and older female cousins resent Dad for his affair with Gail. They resent him for another reason too, Mom's past.

Though he had nothing to do with her childhood, some of Dad's *own* relatives find it hard to believe Mom's "past" is the only reason for her emotional struggles. They have always felt sorry for my mother since they saw Dad as a Neanderthal with outdated views on women and marriage. They view the discovery of Mom's childhood secrets and scars as a "convenient out" for my father. It takes him and his affair off the hook to an extent, and that irks them. They say, "He would make love to his wife in the morning, then go fuck that *puttana* in the afternoon. Who does he think he is?"

Everyone has an opinion on my parents' marriage, and rumors are spread from Philadelphia to Atlantic City. Some say my father has *always* had a woman on the side, but has only recently gotten caught. Others claim Mom is concealing the fact that Babbo is truly the one who sexually abused her as a child—that they had an incestuous relationship.

My parents may be falling back in love—but they are doing so amidst the winds of gossip. Their marriage is a regular topic of conversation among our extended family throughout the Delaware Valley.

Aunt Sofia—Dad's much younger, only sister—often says that my father reminds her of Frank Sinatra. I know that when she says that, my aunt is not comparing their musicality, but their masculinity.

Just like my father, Ol' Blue Eyes has that Mafia mystique, that *My Way* outlook on life, and an east coast Italian's affinity for the Old Country. Dad has long admired Mr. Sinatra, religiously tuning into the weekly radio program hosted by legendary Philadelphia disc jockey Sid Mark that features nothing but music, stories and interviews of all things Sinatra. But I know that Aunt Sofia is truly referring to the fact that Dad most resembles the Chairman of the Board in one particular way—they are both the tender tough guy.

Dad and Aunt Sofia have long had a distant relationship, in part because of their 15 year age difference. When Dad was a young man he loved to tickle his baby sister, but often times ignored her pleas for mercy. My father is famous family-wide for his particular brand of tickling: aggressive and painful. He digs into one's rib cage, he needles you deep into the armpit. It is done out of affection, but you squeal in hysterical agony. Aunt Sofia felt trapped within his grasp and used to bite him, so the tickling would stop. As she grew into adulthood, my aunt struggled with her weight. Out of genuine concern, Dad took her to task over the weight gain, but he often did so in front of others, and in an abrasive manner, like a sergeant might dress down a private.

Aunt Sofia was keenly aware of Dad's tender tough guy approach, but with us boys he was the perfect mixture of both ends of the spectrum. Throughout the 1980's we went to Mass every Sunday, not because Dad truly believed in the teachings of the Church, but because that's what a good Italian family does. When he checked our homework, Dad always took his pencil and drew a tiny cross at the top of the page, as if to bless our work. If we ever get scared, Dad told us we should make the Sign of the Cross, and everything would be okay.

Whenever my brothers or I misbehaved, or got into a fight, Dad was stern with us and we knew to fall in line. He handled most of the discipline; my brothers and I used to shudder when Mom would say, "Just wait till your father gets home."

After voicing his displeasure at our behavior, he would make us stand in the corner at attention. Now that I'm older, he makes me write an essay about my poor behavior and how I can do better next time, but with my brothers, Dad still makes them stand at military attention in the corner for "half an hour." He says 30 minutes, but I know that he secretly sets the timer for only 15 minutes and softly greets them when the timer runs out. He will kneel down on one knee so he is at eye level with them; then Dad orchestrates the peace accord. Our father will make Tony and Michael apologize to each other, or to him, then give each other a hug, and a kiss on the cheek.

Dad has always been stern, but fair, yet Michael is the one that tests Dad's tender guy patience the most. Migalooch, as Dad likes to call him, is the most *testa dura* of the three of us. Although Tony and I love to taunt him about "being adopted," my little brother fights back. He knows we're being dishonest and takes his revenge with saliva. Tony and I will tease him about being a Gypsy that Mom found on the front porch years ago. Michael will first cry over the allegations saying, "That's not true! You're lying! We're real brothers!" But Tony and I will double down and say, "Oh, it certainly is true. You're not our real brother. You're adopted!"

Our insistence on pushing the envelope, causes Michael to snap. He gets angry and charges us. Since we overpower him physically, Michael resorts to spitting in our faces, and typical brother tussling ensures.

Only when he gets in trouble for the spitting, Michael routinely refuses to apologize and often proudly serves his entire punishment in the corner, out of spite. Dad will say, "Michael, your brothers are gonna get in trouble for teasin' you, believe me. But are you gonna apologize to Frankie for spittin' on him?" Michael will be tightlipped and stone-faced, offering no response. When Dad approaches him after the "30 minutes" in the corner, he tries again. "Migalooch, if you just apologize you won't have to stand in the corner anymore. Just say you're sorry to your brother and you can go back to playing Nintendo."

But Michael will look right through our father and shake his head no, he is *not* going to apologize, which always amazes Dad. Tony and I will have already said *we're sorry*, so as to get on with our lives, but Michael always proudly returns to the corner to serve out the remainder of his sentence. Dad can only chuckle to himself, impressed by his youngest's commitment and refusal to give-in.

For Thanksgiving, 1990—Dad planned to take me and my brothers surf fishing in Cape Hatteras, North Carolina. I say "planned" because after the four of us piled into Dad's GMC Jimmy and made the nine hour drive south, we learned that the Bonner Bridge, leading into Cape Hatteras, had been severely damaged a month prior. A large dredge had drifted into the structure and literally wiped out the midsection of the causeway. This caused us to adjust our travel plans slightly and we wound up spending a long weekend in Kitty Hawk, and the other quaint, sleepy fishing villages of the Outer Banks.

Mom couldn't come with us on this trip because she was scheduled to work at the nursing home, so it's Dad that gets us dressed, fed and showered each night at the tiny motel we call home. It's Dad that makes sure we're warm enough and comfortable despite the wicked winds we encounter out on the beach; and it's Dad that orchestrates the most unforgettable Thanksgiving Dinner the four of us have ever had.

Typically, our Thanksgiving Dinner is celebrated at Grandmom's house where *literally* 40 to 50 cousins, aunts and uncles gather around an enormous makeshift table Grandpop builds just for the day. Grandmom and her sisters spend days preparing the escarole soup, antipasto, manicotti, turkey, stuffing, potatoes, yams, gravy, biscuits, muffins, pastries and cookies. It is a feast to say the least. Afterwards, we'll move down into the basement where we'll play pool and ping-pong until the wee hours of the morning. Thanksgiving is truly one of the highlights of our year.

But since we are several states away, Thanksgiving Dinner takes on a much different culinary meaning this year. There will be none of Grandmom's, and her sisters' delicacies. Instead, we raid a local convenience store and purchase turkey loaf lunchmeat, Velveeta cheese and soft, white hotdog rolls.

We smother the rolls in mustard and eat our makeshift turkey dinner in Dad's truck, parked by the Oregon Inlet. We take turns passing around his car phone as we speak to Mom and wish her a Happy Thanksgiving. She sounds tired, just having come home from work. We tell her we miss her, and that we love her—and she says the same. Dad takes the phone back from us and tells Mom that he took some wonderful photographs with his camera, pictures of us boys on the beach that he will enlarge and hang on the walls of our house, when we return to New Jersey.

After we say goodbye to Mom, the four of us laugh and joke and sing as the moonlight dances upon the Atlantic Ocean. This brief trip to Kitty Hawk, this Thanksgiving evening on the Outer Banks, with our singing and our sandwiches, will live in our collective memories forever. For it marks the first time *Frankie the Voice* and The Three Tooters have taken their act on the road....

19

Before he got married, Dad made a half-hearted, short-lived attempt at becoming an actor. He auditioned for various casting directors and talent agencies in Center City Philadelphia, but nothing panned out. Decades later, he decides my brothers and I are going to give it a shot.

Informally, we've been acting for years in our annual Family Christmas Play, written, produced and directed by Aunt Sofia—Dad's much younger, only sister. In addition to performing in Aunt Sofia's yearly piano recitals—now that we all take weekly lessons from her—our aunt writes parts for the three of us, and Uncle Bruno's three children, in an adaptation of the biblical nativity scene. It is a somewhat serious little production complete with costumes, weeks of rehearsal and memorized lines. Since I'm the oldest of us six kids, Aunt Sofia normally casts me as the "narrator" of our play, which suits me just fine.

Christmas Eve was always the night of our performance, and of course we always got "rave reviews," from our parents and grandparents. We even put up a Thanksgiving Play one year for the *entire* extended family, and it was a big hit.

So when we sit for headshots, and sign with a talent agent, we're more than ready for the casting calls we answer throughout the Greater Philadelphia area. On one of the calls, the director running the audition notices Mom standing off to the side. He tells her that she is striking with that olive skin, and salt-and-pepper hair. The man says she has a wonderfully distinctive European look, and asks if she has ever done any modeling.

Soon, Mom is sitting for her own headshots, and then signs with our agent. Now, the four of us—me, Tony, Michael and Mom, continuously answer casting calls throughout the tristate area for print work, industrial films and TV commercials.

With his three sons and his wife making a foray into the acting business, *Frankie the Voice* decides to write a book.

With his housing development underway, my parents still comfortably living off their savings, and Mom reminding him of the girl he married, Dad begins dictating his thoughts into a small micro-tape recorder. He does most of his dictation during his daily hour commute between our house and his development in Cumberland County. Soon, he hires a woman to transcribe his dictated notes, and organizes them into the form and flow of a book.

He calls this manuscript—*Thoughts of a Common Man.*

When school lets out for the summer, Dad takes us to the beach in Atlantic City. He sits by the water's edge in a beach chair with his clipboard, a yellow legal notepad, and a copy of his *Thoughts of a Common Man.* Dad works on his revisions as we play on the beach until sunset.

Dad has always taken after Grandmom's side of the family—the talented Neapolitans who paint and sculpt and write—which is why he doesn't hesitate if somebody asks him what the book is about.

Confidently, Dad says, "It's about my blue-collar take on life. A common man's view of the business world, and the perseverance needed to succeed." Perseverance has long been Dad's favorite word. I've known that since those first pep-talks he used to give when I started playing football. Now that I'm older, Dad says it differently.

"Chichi, perseverance is what separates the men from the boys."

It's very important to Dad—this idea of being a man. I think that's why he loved the army so much, and explains why he runs football practice the way he does.

Even though we're only kids, laziness, disrespect or even the hint of *I can't do it* are forbidden. Discipline, confidence and hard work are embraced. But above all else, we are not allowed to quit. If Dad didn't learn that *never say die* attitude in the army, he most certainly learned it from *Rocky*. When Dad first saw *Rocky* back in 1976, it was like he had met a long lost cousin. After all, Sylvester Stallone's *Rocky Balboa* was Dad's age, lived and trained in Philadelphia—and most importantly—was Italian.

After seeing the film, my then twenty-seven year old father, went home and tried reenacting the famous scene where *Rocky* breaks several raw eggs into a tall drinking glass, and gulps them down for breakfast.

Mom laughs and says, "Boys, your father tried doing that, but he couldn't get the eggs down. He kept gagging on the yolks, and finally had to give-up."

Though he couldn't swallow the eggs, Dad seems to have swallowed everything else *Rocky* had to offer. Even Aunt Sofia says, "Every time I see any of those *Rocky* movies on TV, I think of your father."

Instinctively, I know what she means. Mom's story about Dad not being able to down the eggs is the only time I ever remember the words *give-up* being used in reference to him. Just like *Rocky*, Dad never quits.

Sometimes, late at night, just as I'm about to fall asleep, Dad comes into my room, sits on the edge of my bed, and talks to me about perseverance. I don't know if he does the same thing with my brothers, but those chats are always pure Hero School.

I just graduated eighth grade, and Dad says, "Chichi, you're gonna be in high school in a few weeks, and a lot of things are gonna be thrown at you when you get up there. I want you to remember that perseverance makes the difference—perseverance and self-discipline."

Dad sits on the edge of my bed, and gives me the same speech he always gives me, going on and on about self-discipline, and how that is just another word for willpower. He says willpower means doing the things you should do, when you *should* do them, whether you feel like it or not.

"That's character, Chichi. That's what allows you to follow through when everything inside you wants to quit. That's what *Rocky* has. It is not what you know, or how talented you are, it is whether or not you can put your head down, and discipline yourself to pay the price over and over and over. Don't forget that, Chichi."

"I won't, Dad. I won't...."

Tony's Baltimore Grill—an Atlantic City landmark, on the corner of Iowa and Atlantic Avenues—is like our extended family's headquarters. It's the one place our cousins, aunts and uncles go whenever they come down the shore. The restaurant and bar is old school. With its 1960's atmosphere, decor, and dim lighting—it's more like visiting a basement supper club than a first class pizzeria, but we love Tony's. Since there are always fifteen to twenty of us, the waitresses don't mind if we push together a few tables to devour our pizza and antipasto as we laugh, joke, and reminisce.

Tonight, as we gather around the tables inside Tony's Baltimore Grill, everybody is trying to make Michael feel better because of Randall, our pet rabbit. We got Randall on Easter, and decided to name him in honor of our favorite athlete—Randall Cunningham—the quarterback for the Philadelphia Eagles. The thing is, we found Randall dead in his cage this morning, and that set Michael off crying. He was heartbroken, carrying on and sobbing hysterically as Dad buried Randall in the backyard.

When Mom was a kid, she was given two bunnies as a gift from her godmother. They were the first pets she ever had, and she adored them. One was light gray, and the other was all black. She spent many afternoons playing with them after school.

Then one day, Mom came home and found their cage empty. She asked Nonna what happened, but my grandmother never gave her a straight answer. For days after that, Mom moped home from school as she missed her bunnies a lot. A short time later, while getting undressed after school, she noticed a shoebox in the trunk she kept in her closet.

She didn't recognize the shoebox. Mom removed the top, and looked inside. Lying in the shoebox, she found gray and black fur. Mom wasn't sure what she was looking at—until a light bulb went off in her head—*her bunnies!*

Mom ran downstairs frantically looking for her mother, but Nonna wasn't home, so she showed Babbo what she found. Only, he chuckled and told her what she ate for dinner the other night—that looked like chicken—well, that wasn't chicken at all.

Mom wanted to throw-up; Babbo killed her bunnies, and she ate them. Though it was typical for some immigrant families to eat farm animals the kids had adopted as pseudo-pets, these bunnies were given to Mom as a gift.

Babbo didn't have to kill them, and he didn't have to feed them to his unsuspecting daughter. The fact their hides were placed in a shoebox for Mom to find shows how little regard he had for her.

If Michael had eaten Randall the rabbit, and stumbled upon his fur weeks later, he would have been scarred for the rest of his life. But this was just another day in Mom's chaotic and turbulent childhood, as Babbo's youngest daughter.

Not long after the death of Randall the rabbit, we welcome a new addition to the family—Dimitri the ballet dancer. On Grandmom's side of the family—the talented Neapolitans—we have an uncle who is involved with a well-known Russian ballet company. Our uncle is helping to promote this ballet company's U.S. tour. The thing is—Russia is literally falling apart. I'm only thirteen years old, but even I have seen the news—the Soviet Union is turning into the Russian Federation. Mikhail Gorbachev is out, and Boris Yeltsin is in and all this change and uncertainty makes Dimitri the ballet dancer very uneasy.

He is in his early twenties, but he does not want to go home at the end of the ballet tour; he wants to stay here in America, despite not having the legal paperwork to do so. Dad agrees to take in Dimitri as a favor to our uncle. The plan is for Dimitri to stay with us until a more permanent place for him to live can be found.

So, there we are, five Jersey Italians trying to teach Dimitri the ballet dancer how to play Nintendo and throw a baseball, when he speaks not one word of English. Mom and Dad are very warm and welcoming to Dimitri as they show us how to make him feel at home.

After only three months, our uncle calls and says he found another home for Dimitri, closer to New York City. On the night before his departure, Mom prepares a special lasagna dinner in Dimitri's honor.

We laugh and giggle and practice the Russian words he taught us over the past few months as Mom clears the table after dinner and Dad raises his glass of grappa to offer an informal toast of sorts. With Dad's glass in the air, Mom sets a plate of cannoli down in the center of the table, just as my brothers and I raise our glasses of chocolate milk. Dad looks out at all of us and says, "Boys, let's wish Dimitri *buona fortuna* here in America, the greatest country in the world...."

20

In September of 1991, I'm the starting quarterback for the freshman team at the local public high school. After only three weeks of practice, my coach tells me that I'm the "future."

He is impressed with my natural leadership ability, strong throwing arm, pocket poise, and overall athleticism. Coach says, "Frankie, there hasn't been a quarterback here with as much potential as you in over a decade, and that kid went on to play at Penn State."

I'm flattered by the comparison and anxious to prove Coach right—but during our first scrimmage of the year—I break my right collarbone. My season is over before it even starts. But, my injury only serves to heighten the buzz regarding my future.

I am labeled 'the next big thing.' As a result, even though I can't play, Dad encourages me to attend practice every day. He particularly wants me to impress Coach Coffey, the varsity head coach, by showcasing my commitment to football.

All throughout the fall of 1991, I stand on the sidelines, and watch the varsity players prepare for each week's opponent. I am fourteen years old.

Over Christmas break, we take a family trip to Key West. It takes us nearly twenty-five hours to drive from south Jersey, to south Florida in Dad's GMC Jimmy. The entire ride Mom *literally* plays, and replays Whitney Houston's *I Wanna Dance with Somebody* on the tape player.

She listens to it so much, that we commit the lyrics to memory, and understand that Dad is the man she wants to dance with *and how*.

In Key West, as we fish and sightsee, I look back over our last few years and smile because things with Mom and Dad are better than ever—

starting with the fact that Gail is out of our lives. She and Dad broke up in July, nearly six months ago.

Mom seems happier and prettier than ever. Thanks to the new wardrobe Dad bought her, there are days she looks like she stepped out of a European fashion magazine. I'm not used to seeing her with earrings and makeup on every day, and I'm not used to the fact that she seems so cheery all the time. My parents don't fight like they used to.

Thanks to Mom's new outlook she becomes engaged in our day to day lives like never before. Now she will plan Family Movie Nights, where the five of us gather around the TV, and warm ourselves in front of the fireplace, as we watch films on our VCR. Other times, it's Family Game Night, where we all play UNO or Monopoly until *way* past our bedtime.

We spent a week camping in Algonquin Park this past summer, and Mom was constantly leading the way on our hiking and canoeing expeditions. It's like she has a new energy about her, and in addition, Mom doesn't gamble as much either.

We hardly find her sleeping downstairs with her jacket on—car keys in hand—as had become her routine. She volunteers at the ARC two afternoons a week, acts as Tony's and Michael's room mother at school, and seems so thrilled in her relationship with Dad—my old worries of divorce are long gone. In short, my mother seems like a well-balanced, happily married woman. The only thing that remains from her 'dark days,' is the fact that Mom is still terrified of Babbo. Even on vacation in Florida, she is concerned that he could be hiding in the closet—waiting to kill her.

21

Babbo was a huckster, which means he used to go around his Philadelphia neighborhood selling fruits and vegetables on an old bus he converted into a produce stand on wheels.

While making his rounds in the summer, he would sometimes take along his twelve year old daughter, Antonietta. As they went street-to-street, Mom—with her short, black hair and eyeglasses—would hand out bubble gum to the kids along the route. When my grandfather saw her doing this, he would snap, "Ann, don'ta do that. The gum'a no is'a free."

Whenever the bus was parked outside their house, Mom knew she could always wander out and grab an apple or a few grapes to snack on.

One day, when Mom went out to the bus looking for a piece of fruit, she heard something going on in the back. Curious, she walked down the narrow center aisle, and found Babbo on the floor with a woman. His pants were down around his ankles, and the woman's dress was up around her waist.

My twelve year old mother yelped at the sight of them in the act. Babbo shouted at her. He scrambled to his feet pulling at his pants.

He grabbed Mom by the wrist, and dragged her off the bus.

As he yanked her up the concrete steps, Mom complained, "You're hurting me!" But Babbo didn't care. He opened the front door, and shoved her inside, but not before he got in her face. "Ann," he snarled, in his heavy accent. "If'a you tell'a somebody what'a you see, I kill'a you. You hear'a me? *Morta!*"

The Cover-Up was in full effect—but Mom felt she *had* to tell Nonna what she saw. After initially getting angry, and calling him a *bastardo*, Nonna told Mom, "Don'ta you tell'a nobody."

More important than righting the wrong—than taking her husband to task, Nonna's primary concern was making sure the neighborhood didn't find out about his affair.

When Babbo discovered that Mom had disobeyed him, he was furious. He had specifically warned my mother not to say anything about the woman on the bus; Mom needed to be punished—but Babbo had to make sure his son Nick was not around to witness it. That was always of paramount importance to Babbo, Uncle Nick was his prince, his sole surviving son, and as a result he must never be allowed to see the dark side—that was reserved for his daughters and his cousin of a wife.

On the evening of Mom's punishment, Babbo grabbed one of his big butcher knives, and started to taunt my mother. They were in the kitchen. Nonna was at the stove frying meatballs, and Mom was seated at the table.

Only when her father began taunting her with the blade, Mom sprung to her feet, and began backpedaling. She was terrified at the sight of her father, swearing up and down that when he caught her, she was dead.

"Stop'a this'a!" Nonna shouted from the stove. But Babbo ignored her, as my twelve year old mother started crying. She begged Babbo to stop; Nonna had to do something. She moved to protect her daughter. She got between the two of them, and quickly corralled Mom behind her. Next, the two of them moved around the table where they mirrored Babbo. If he went left, they went left. If he went right, they went right. My grandmother pleaded in Italian with him to stop this madness.

The curtains were blowing in the breeze, and the meatballs on the stove needed to be turned, but Babbo kept taunting them with his blade. "I kill'a you, *disgraziata!*" He shouted at Mom.

These were the moments that traumatized my mother. She was powerless and afraid. It wasn't until Babbo lost interest, and got tired of chasing them around the kitchen, that he finally threw his knife onto the table—daring one of them to pick it up.

"Dis'sa my house'a," he proudly boasted, "I'ma da' boss."

22

After his many years of laboring in the sun, and a decade of discipline in the Army Reserves, there is no mistaking my father is a "man." Dad wears his masculinity just as brazenly as he wears those dark sunglasses and black leather jacket. His obsession with machismo may explain why he has such a problem with Ge-nip-ge-nods.

Ge-nip-ge-nods is a game my brothers and I created; it is very similar to playing Tag—with one exception. When you're "IT," the only way you can 'tag' someone else, is to slap him in the testicles. None of the players are permitted to cover their balls—they must leave their groins completely unobstructed—so whoever is "IT" can make a clean strike.

My brothers and I introduce Ge-nip-ge-nods to our friends, and it quickly catches on. Soon, we're not playing football or baseball in our huge backyard anymore, but hosting giant games of Ge-nip-ge-nods with fifteen or twenty guys running around trying to slap each other in the nuts.

Without fail—every time we play Ge-nip-ge-nods—somebody suffers a direct hit to his family jewels. They immediately collapse, cup their cock and balls with both hands, and roll around on the ground in excruciating pain. Despite these occasions of suffering, we laugh our way through endless rounds of Ge-nip-ge-nods—until one day Dad comes out onto the back deck.

He must have seen us through the windows in his office for when he comes out, he hollers, "*Ohhh!* What are you meatballs doin? You're gonna get hurt. You shouldn't be hittin' each other like that. Besides," he adds, his voice softening so the neighbors won't hear, "don't cha think that's kinda gay? I mean wouldn't you rather play basketball or somethin'?"

All fifteen of us stand there in an embarrassed, silent shock. We never thought of Ge-nip-ge-nods as a "gay-game." We just looked at it as a way to inflict pain in a humorous fashion. But now that Dad has made it sound like a "gay-game," akin to fondling each other's dicks, we agree right then and there never to play again. In 1992 New Jersey, being a teenaged jock, means shunning anything that borders on being gay—and we all think of ourselves as jocks.

Only my brothers and I are hooked; after all we invented the game. Even though we don't play Ge-nip-ge-nods anymore in the backyard with our buddies, we play it anytime and anyplace we can, just the three of us, even in the Cadillac on our way to visit Nonna in Philadelphia.

The three of us are in the backseat, as Dad drives up Route 73 towards Philadelphia. Mom is beside him in the passenger seat. Like always, she is completely disoriented and wants to know where we are.

"Frank, are we still in New Jersey?"

"Yes, Ann, we're still in New Jersey. We haven't crossed the bridge yet, have we?"

"No," she says, "I guess we haven't."

My father softly shakes his head, and smirks to himself over Mom's innocent amnesia as the three of us quietly play Ge-nip-ge-nods in the backseat. I'm in the middle, Tony is to my right, and Michael is to my left. We know to be quiet because Dad doesn't like when we horse around on the road. He says it distracts him from driving, and makes it hard for him to hear the sports talk-radio he listens to on the AM station 610 WIP.

Even though we know to be quiet, we're used to Dad hollering at us over his shoulder, or occasionally pulling the Cadillac to the side of the road, turning around, and threatening us with how we better stop horsing around or else.

Only today, when he realizes we're playing Ge-nip-ge-nods, Dad loses his mind. He quickly pulls off the road into an empty parking lot, feverishly lowers the sports talk-radio, spins around from the front seat and shouts, *"I told you I don't want you playin' that fuckin' game anymore!"* We stop cold in our tracks, but Dad isn't done. With his sunglasses on, collar popped, and his face full of fury, he shouts, *"My sons are gonna be men! So, if you wanna be a faggot, then go live with faggots! Is that understood? If you wanna touch each other's balls like a bunch of fairies, then go live with fairies. But as long as you're livin' under my roof, you will knock this shit off right now! Do you hear me boys?"*

23

When my parents drop me off at school—I always lean over and give them a kiss goodbye. It doesn't matter if it's Mom or Pop—which is what I've started calling my father now that I'm older. I no longer use the term "Dad;" but instead refer to him as "Pop," and I think he likes it.

Regardless of what I call him, I kiss both of my parents on the cheek when I greet them, or when we say goodbye. But when Patrick O'Reilly sees me kiss my father—he starts ragging on me about being gay. We're in the locker room after working out.

"You a faggot, Frankie?"

"What? What are you talkin' about?"

"Didn't I see you kiss your father this morning?"

"Yeah, so?"

"So, you must be a faggot."

"Why's that?"

"You're fourteen, right? Ain't you a little old for that sissy shit? I mean, unless you and your old man are a little funny. Ha, ha, ha...."

There are a bunch of guys around, getting dressed. They crack up at that.

"Hey, Frankie's a fag. Ha, ha, ha...."

"He kisses his father. Ha, ha, ha...."

"Do you suck his dick, too?"

"Ha, ha, ha...."

My face turns red, as everything inside me wants to stuff Patrick into a locker, but I know I could never do that. He is an offensive lineman, and could easily destroy me with one arm tied behind his back.

Still, I want to know what's wrong with me kissing my father; I've been doing it all my life. But the next few times Pop drops me off, I make sure to look around and see if anybody is watching.

A few days later, Patrick and some guys are standing by the curb when Pop drops me off at school. The moment I spot them, I try to quickly slide out of the Cadillac without giving my father a kiss.

But, he notices right away.

"Hey, Cheech," he says. "Whatta ya' doin'? *Dammi un bacio.*"

I don't lean in. Instead, I say, "Pop, is it okay if I don't kiss you this morning?"

He cocks his head, and looks at me funny.

"Why, what's the matter?"

My eyes must give away the fact that I'm worried about Patrick and the guys because Pop glances out the windshield, and gets it right away. "Okay, Chichi. That's alright, no sweat," and he shakes my hand.

All through the school day, I think about the look of confusion on Pop's face, when I told him I wasn't going to kiss him. It's like he was wounded. He couldn't believe it, and I feel badly.

Later that day, when Pop comes to pick me up in his GMC Jimmy, we sit in the driveway in front of our house, and I know he wants to talk. He pushes his baseball cap back onto his forehead, and stares out the windshield.

"Cheech," he says. "I want you to think about something."

"Alright, Pop."

"We're Italian, right?"

"Yeah."

"I mean what did I name you? Not Francis—but Francesco. Why?"

"I don't know, Pop."

"Because you and your brothers are thoroughbreds; you're just as Italian as any boy in Italy. So, when it comes to you and me, or you and your brothers, kissing each other, it's something our people have done for centuries. It's a tradition. But there are going to be those who think that this tradition is a weakness. Don't forget Chichi, even though we love America, sometimes the way things are done over here isn't always right. In Italy, men kiss men hello, and they kiss men goodbye. It's just the way it is. Now, I understand; you're fourteen, and maybe you feel like you're too old for it. Or maybe...."

"No Pop, Patrick O'Reilly saw me kiss you the other morning, and he tore me up...."

"Well, just think about what you're sayin'. You're makin' a choice based on what somebody else thinks is right."

"But, Pop...."

152

"Cheech, hold on a second. You ever think this kid Patrick doesn't know how to kiss his father? Or that maybe his father secretly wishes that Patrick would give him a kiss, but is too afraid to say anything? All I want you to take from this, Cheech, is that changin' who you are, because of somebody else, is almost never the right thing. I'll give you an example, back when I was singin' full-time with Uncle Bruno, I would sometimes apologize from stage if I had confused the lyrics to a song, or if I felt like I hadn't done the tune justice. Can you imagine standing on stage, and apologizing to the audience? I was too worried about what everybody else thought, instead of just focusing on being in the moment and being myself. The audience was there to be entertained; half of them weren't even really listening to me. Yet, I gave away my legitimacy. I gave away my confidence because I thought it mattered, when in fact it didn't matter at all. As long as I was being true to who I was, and what I knew how to do, that's all I could ever expect from myself. Now, when it comes to this kid Patrick, you do what you think is right, but just make sure it's what *you* want, and not him. I know he's bigger than you and all that, but sometimes you gotta stand up for yourself, Chichi. Sometimes you gotta be a man. If you think it's the right thing to kiss me hello, and to kiss me goodbye, then just do it. But don't do what I did years ago on stage, don't give away who you are. Put your shoulders back, stand up straight, and let the chips fall where they may."

Tony is only twelve years old, but Tony is a god. Girls call our house almost every night, and I find myself jealous of him, and of his easy manner with them. Peggy Williams may have told me I had Italy in my eyes, but that was years ago. I'm a freshman now, and nobody says I have anything in my eyes anymore.

Tony is two and a half years younger than me, but he's cool, and talks to pretty girls my age with such charm that I wonder why I'm not that way too. If I see a pretty girl, I feel my temperature rise, and my mouth go dry. My words escape me, and I end up stumbling through a conversation, only to have the girl smile, and politely walk away.

I wish I had more of what Tony has—but I don't—and I can't figure out why.

After I get home from the gym on a weeknight, Mom takes me and Michael down to my old Catholic school to watch Tony play basketball. Tony is only in sixth grade, but he is the starting point guard on the seventh and eighth grade team, and I know that makes Mom proud.

She used to be a star in sports when she was younger. Back in school, Mom played softball and participated in track and field. From listening to her talk, I know Tony is the sort of player she was, scrappy and aggressive.

During the game, there are gaggles of girls who scream his name like they are his own personal cheerleading squad.

"Yeah, Tony!"

"Go get'em, Tony!"

"Tony! Tony! Tony!"

In the middle of the third quarter of today's game against St. Peter's, I catch sight of a blonde girl looking in my direction. I think she must be looking past me at the game, but she holds my gaze, and I realize she is staring at me.

She smiles, and I don't know what to do. I act like I don't see anything which is easy to do with all the, "Come on Tony, you can do it Tony," going on.

I ask Mom for a dollar, to buy something from the snack bar. When I turn around from the counter, the girl is right behind me. She smiles again, and says, "Hi, my name's Sandy."

When she says that, my mouth suddenly goes dry, and I stand motionless for what feels like an eternity.

"Aren't you Tony's brother?"

I nod and mumble, "Yes, yes I am."

"I thought so. You're Frank, aren't you?"

"Yeah."

"Wow, that's so cool. You're a freshman, right?"

"Yeah."

"I thought I saw you at a couple of the games this year."

To avoid all the noise going on behind us, Sandy takes my arm and walks me out into the hallway. There, I find that after a little while, I can talk to her with ease. When she says that maybe we could get together and do something, I find myself writing down her phone number.

When I walk back into the gym, Mom wants to know where I went, and who that girl was, but Tony makes a great play and she gets distracted before I can answer.

Sandy and I talk on the phone every night for a week. Then one night, during another of Tony's basketball games, she takes my hand and walks me out of the gymnasium. Instead of stopping in the hallway, we go outside to the front of the school. Her sister will be here soon to pick her up. We are alone in the parking lot.

There she tells me it's time for us to set-up a real date to go to the movies.

Just then her sister pulls up, and Sandy leans in and kisses me on the lips. All at once it feels like Mike Tyson is in my chest, using my heart like a speed bag. I've never kissed a girl before, and when Sandy climbs into her sister's car, and pulls away, I float back into Tony's game, dizzy from the feeling of her lips against mine.

The next night, I tell my mother that Sandy asked me to the movies. But all Mom can say is, "Frankie, it's supposed to be the other way around. You're supposed to ask the girl."

I act like I didn't hear what she said.

"Mom, can I go to the movies, or what?"

"Sure you can, but only to a matinee show."

"A matinee show, what's that?"

"When they show a movie in the afternoon."

"Afternoon! Mom, I can't tell Sandy we're going to a movie Friday afternoon!"

"Frankie, if you want to go out with her, it's a matinee or nothing. You're only fourteen."

When Pop gets home, I tell him all about Sandy and how she'll never agree to go to a matinee; she's too cool, too pretty, and will certainly laugh at me if I say I can't go to an evening show.

Pop sits in the green chair behind the desk in his office; clasps his hands behind his head and makes sounds that tell me he's listening.

When I've finished pleading my case he says, "Chichi, I have no problem with you going to a night show with this girl, as long as you're home by ten."

"Alright."

"But I mean it, *ten*. Pick a movie that starts around seven, so that way you'll be home in time."

"Okay, Pop."

"Now—you need a ride?"

"No, I think her sister is gonna take us."

"Okay. Now, what's this girl's name again?"

"Sandy."

"What she like? She Italian?"

"No, she's not Italian, but she's nice. She wants to be a doctor...."

"A doctor?"

"Yeah, her father works down at the hospital, and she wants to be a baby doctor like him. She says that if we get married, I could stay home and take care of the kids."

When I say that, Pop unclasps his hands, and sits up straight in his chair.

"Chichi, first of all, you're too young to be thinkin' 'bout gettin' married. Secondly, you're not stayin' home with any kids. Takin' care of kids is for women. You follow me? Doing the wash is for women; loading the dishwasher is for women; ironing clothes is for women. You don't see me doin' any of that, do you?"

"Well, you make your Blue Collar Carbonara sometimes...."

"What? I'm not talkin' about that, Cheech. I'm talkin' about bein' a man. Now, I don't wanna hear you ever say you're gonna stay home, and let your wife work."

"But Pop, she was just...."

"No! You're Italian, and *we don't do that!*"

The night of our big date, in the winter of 1992, Sandy and I decide to see a comedy film but only catch the first few minutes because she is all over me. We only had that one kiss last week, but tonight Sandy is guiding my hands all over her body, and sticking her tongue in my ear. She says I'm the best kisser in the world, even though tonight is the first time I've ever made-out.

A week after our make-out session, I'm left wondering what went wrong and why Sandy stopped answering my calls. When I see her at one of Tony's games holding hands and talking to an eighth-grade boy, Mom sees them too. "Frankie," she says, "isn't that your girlfriend?" But I don't say anything because I feel so dejected and embarrassed.

"See," Mom continues, "that's why you should never date a girl who asks you out. It's supposed to be the other way around."

24

It's early 1992, and the bank has 'called' my father's business loan—he isn't sure what to do. Pop owes them nearly eight hundred and seventy-five thousand dollars. The bank is only going to give him six months to liquidate everything—after that—they are going to require the money immediately.

Never one to panic—Pop approaches a wealthy friend of his, and secures a personal loan of seven hundred and fifty thousand dollars to pay his business loan down to one hundred and eighteen thousand—but the bank isn't satisfied. They want the balance of the money in six months' time. Unable to raise the rest of the cash, Pop sells off some of his land.

Now, the problem is the economy. Each night at dinner, my brothers and I listen to my parents talk about 'The Recession.' Pop complains that interest rates have risen to the point where no one can qualify for a new home. He says it's almost impossible to sell any new houses, even though he has taken steps to become a VA, and FHA Home Builder.

My father says not long ago a buyer didn't need any money down at closing, but with the way the housing market is going—unless the person has a lot of cash—the sale fails to go through. As a result, his 'development' remains largely undeveloped, and the land he still owns out in Cumberland County just sits there like a stone tied around his neck.

Since the housing market has all but crashed, my father begins scrambling to look for work as a general contractor. No longer does he focus simply on masonry work, and specialize in concrete like he did when I was a little boy. His experience as a developer allows him to work on different projects. Now, he might manage an entire construction site for a few months while a store gets built, or simply supply the manpower for a renovation project.

Pop still pours concrete, and has his guys lay brick or block when a job comes along that requires it, but no longer is he comfortable living off his savings. Now, not only have my father's dreams of becoming a home builder been vanquished by 'The Recession,' but we stop acting.

No longer do we take off from school, or spend summer days running around the Delaware Valley to answer casting calls. Pop even stops working on *Thoughts of a Common Man.* The manuscript gets stuffed behind some bills in the bottom drawer of his filing cabinet, as my father's normally light-hearted spirit becomes bogged down by the monthly struggle to make ends meet.

My brothers are lying on their stomachs in the den, taking turns playing *Mike Tyson's Punch-Out* on the Nintendo. Pop sits in the connecting room at the kitchen table. He has dozens of papers spread out in front of him. Mom is out with Aunt Ellen, and I'm eating a bowl of cereal—standing at the counter—behind my father.

From where I am, I can easily see into the den. I watch as Tony does everything in his power to distract Michael from focusing on the videogame. Tony takes his hands and comes as close as he can to Michael's face without touching it.

Even though he's *not* actually being touched, Michael shouts, "Tony, stop touching me," as he fights to remain focused on the TV screen—bobbing and weaving around Tony's hands.

Pop calls to them from the kitchen, "Toe'nooch, leave your brother alone, will ya? I'm tryin' to work in here."

Tony ignores my father.

Michael keeps shouting, "Stop touching me!"

"I'm not touching you. I'm *almost* touching you," Tony says.

It goes on this way for ten minutes.

"Stop touching me!"

"I'm not touching you. I'm *almost* touching you."

"Stop touching me!"

"I'm not touching you. I'm *almost* touching you."

Pop calls to them again.

"Boys, I don't mind if you play. But I need you to keep it down in there, alright?"

They both ignore him.

"Stop touching me!"

"I'm not touching you. I'm *almost* touching you."

"Stop touching me!"

"I'm not touching you. I'm *almost* touching you."

Finally, Tony causes Michael to lose his cool. My brothers begin to tussle a bit on the floor—that's when *Frankie the Voice* walks onto the stage. I hear the scratch of Pop's chair against the kitchen floor, as he aggressively pushes back from the table. He strides into the den. From the counter, I watch him charge over to my brothers. He squats a bit, bends at the waist, turns my brothers over onto their backs, and grabs each of them by their shirts. Pop then lifts them each up off the floor, and sticks his face in theirs.

"I said knock it the fuck off!"

My father has each of them in a separate hand. He looks like a WWF wrestler. In one move, he throws both Tony and Michael over the loveseat. Their feet catch the back of it, as they and the loveseat go tumbling backwards. My brothers land on their backs, staring up at the ceiling. They are blinking; they are in shock.

Pop stands over them and shouts, *"Are ya happy now? Well, are ya?"*

Nonna is always so happy and full of energy, that except for her silver hair and massive bunions, you would never know she's seventy-eight years old. In a way, she reminds me of Sophia Petrillo, from the *Golden Girls*—only without the eyeglasses, or the attitude.

Just like always, whenever Nonna comes down, she sprinkles a little bit of love into every room. It's in the kitchen where she sprinkles the most love since that's where she spends most of her time.

La cucina is Nonna's passion, and it's where she pickles everything from eggplant and cauliflower to hot peppers and green tomatoes. It's where she makes her broccoli polenta, and homemade pastina. The kitchen is where she finds joy in breading a chicken cutlet or preparing her delicious string bean and potato salad with extra virgin olive oil, fresh garlic, and a pinch of salt and pepper.

But above all, my brothers and I go *crazy* for Nonna's meatballs.

The mere sound of them sizzling in the frying pan makes our mouths water. But Nonna doesn't just 'give' them to us—*no, no, no*—she has to play with us first.

Sometimes she carries on like a drug smuggler—literally tip-toeing out of the kitchen, and bringing us two meatballs on the sly. The meatballs will always be wrapped in a white paper towel—and always delivered with a wink and a smile—as if they were some sort of forbidden fruit, or illegal contraband.

Other times, she plays angry. Nonna will call us into the kitchen, *"Francesco, Antonio, Michele...venite qua!"* From the 'sound' of it—you would think she is furious. But when we walk into the kitchen, Nonna will be at the stove, pointing her wooden spoon at us with a big smile on her face—our meatballs ready and waiting.

Nonna *loves* feeding us. Literally *nothing* makes her happier than watching us enjoy something she has prepared from scratch. It is her *ragion d'essere*.

Today is Palm Sunday, and Nonna is back and forth between the kitchen table and the stove. We have just come home from church, and I know this is how she'll spend the rest of the afternoon—rendering fresh tomatoes down till they get soft for the sauce we'll have with dinner, while making crosses out of the palm that was blessed at Mass.

I keep Nonna company as she goes back and forth between the table and the tomatoes, softly humming old Calabrese songs, in between talking to me in Italian. The funny thing about Nonna—despite having lived in the United States for the past sixty years—she has never learned to become 'American.' Aside from *Wheel of Fortune*, or the *Golden Girls*, Nonna couldn't tell you a single thing about American culture.

Her neighborhood is full of Italians; many of whom are from her village back in Italy, so she has never really *had* to become American. She never learned to drive, speaks English well enough to get by, and worked as a seamstress all her life with other Italian women. Aside from raising her kids, she has spent all of her time cooking, cleaning and working in the garden.

As I watch her make another cross, I have to ask myself if she is the same woman Mom turned to for help years ago. My mother said she went to Nonna after she got back from Italy in 1955. Mom told her about the greenhouse, and all that had started happening in there, but Nonna told her to keep it a secret.

She did nothing, and I don't know how that can be. I want to ask her how she could have done that to her daughter because I know Nonna would do anything for me and my brothers. I can't imagine her allowing someone to hurt Michael, and he's not much older than Mom was when the greenhouse abuse started.

But then, I remember how things were for Nonna, and how she was married to her first cousin, who was an abusive drunk in private. I tell myself that if I was a woman back then, living with a husband like that, in an Old World neighborhood—I'm not sure I could have done any better.

As I think these thoughts, Nonna begins carrying the crosses into the dining room. She says she wants to set the kitchen table for dinner. She summons me to the stove where she holds her wooden spoon to my lips, and tells me to blow on the dark red sauce, before I give it a taste test.

"It's good," I say—running my tongue over my lips.

"*È buona?*" She asks. I smile and say, "*Si, è buona, Nonna.*" She reaches up to pinch my cheek with a "*Quanto bello!*"

Nonna starts setting the table. She is singing. She doesn't want my help. In her heavy accent she says, "Chichi, why you no go relax'a in'a the den?"

Minutes later, she brings me a glass of milk, and some of her homemade *biscotti*. I thank her, and she smiles. As she walks back into the kitchen, I can't help but think there is nothing like having a grandmother who never learned to become American.

25

My brothers and I are excellent baseball players, which makes sense, since both our parents were fine athletes themselves. Mom was a stellar softball player in high school, and Pop was such a natural outfielder that he was personally scouted by Granny Hamner, of the Philadelphia Phillies organization.

Two summers ago we took a family trip to Cooperstown, New York and spent several days at the National Baseball Hall of Fame. We loved every second of that vacation, and even though we are fans of the Phillies, Mom and Pop have taken us to the old Memorial Stadium and brand new Camden Yards ballpark, to watch the Baltimore Orioles.

We certainly love baseball, and as a result we routinely beg our parents to take us to the local batting cages, where we square off against pitching machines to work on our hitting strokes for hours at a time. All throughout the spring and half the summer we have practices and baseball games nearly every afternoon. Pop coaches Tony's and Michael's team, while Mom volunteers as a girls' softball coach, despite the fact we don't have any sisters. The five of us are so busy with our baseball and softball schedules, Sunday is the only day we have together as a family.

That means Mom will be at the stove in her green robe making pancakes, while Pop goes back and forth between his office and the kitchen, singing along with Sergio Mendes, Frank Sinatra and The Three Tenors.

Today is no different—with one exception—the phone is ringing.

We are expecting a call from Nonna. She went to Italy shortly after Easter. Aunt Colomba and Aunt Renata are planning to go over for ten days in May. Before she left, I asked if I could come over once school let out for the summer. Nonna said she would have to check with our family in Reggio di Calabria, but that the idea seemed wonderful to her.

As the phone rings a second time, Pop shouts over the music, "Can somebody grab that?"

Due to the "echo" of his voice, I can tell my father is in the foyer. Since I know it must be Nonna calling from Calabria, I shout, "I got it, Pop!" I decide to answer the phone the Italian way.

"*Pronto!*" I say. I know Nonna will get a kick out of it. I'm excited about finding out whether I can go to Italy in June. But all I hear after I say *pronto* is silence. A moment passes before there is the faint sound of a woman's voice.

"Is Frank there?"

This isn't Nonna. This lady sounds groggy. I almost have to shout over the music. "May I ask who's calling?"

"Just give the phone to your father, honey."

I can barely make out the sound of her voice. I smother the phone against my chest. "Pop, it's for you!"

"Who is it?" He shouts back.

"I don't know, some lady!"

Mom does a half-turn from the stove, and calls to me. "Frankie, who is it?" I shrug my shoulders as if to say, *I don't know.*

Pop comes into the kitchen with his eyebrows scrunched together like he does when something seems out of the ordinary. It's Sunday morning, business people know better than to call the house. He asks Tony to grab him the portable phone, instead of using the one on the wall in the kitchen. I hang up as he tucks the portable phone between his shoulder and right ear.

When he says hello, his expression goes blank. "What are you doing calling me on this number?" He asks the caller.

Tony is walking back into the kitchen, but before he sits down to eat his breakfast, Mom sends him into the office to lower the music. She wants to know who Pop is talking to. Her eyes study him as he drifts from the kitchen into the foyer.

Tony comes back from lowering the music, just as we hear Pop shout, "No! Now, Gail don't you do anything. *I'll be right there! I'll be right there!*"

Mom moves from the stove out into the foyer. My brothers and I follow her. We watch Pop charge up the stairs. In a matter of seconds, he comes back down with a pair of jeans on, halfway into a white polo shirt, his hair a mess, and his gray, New Balance sneakers in his right hand. Pop stops to slip on his sneakers at the bottom of the stairs.

Mom asks him, "Frank, where you going? What's wrong?" My father has panic written all over his face. He brushes past us without a word. We watch him quickly back out of the driveway, and speed off in his truck.

The four of us are quiet and motionless in the foyer, listening to the soft sound of Frank Sinatra's voice in the background. We all know that was Gail on the phone. We heard Pop say her name. I wonder how that can be. They're supposed to be broken up. Why would she call him on a Sunday morning? Why would he run out like that? I know Mom is thinking the same thing.

Hours later, when Pop comes home, he tells my mother that Gail had a gun to her head. She was going to kill herself.

"Ann, I had to drop everything. I had no choice...."

"Frank, I don't care about her."

"Ann, we're talking about somebody's life here. She left her kids. She left her husband."

"Well, that never concerned you before."

"Jesus, Ann! We're through—but she's not over it. She thought I would leave you, and the boys. She's a mess. It's not even a year we're apart, so take it easy."

"*Take it easy?* Frank, I'm not the one who had an affair!"

"Ann, are we gonna do this again? She thinks you're makin' up all that stuff about your childhood."

"You told her that?"

"I had to."

"You *had* to? What are you talking about?"

"Ann, didn't I just say she left her kids? She left her husband? We were in love. She deserved an explanation."

"An explanation? Jesus, Frank! Are you outta your mind? She doesn't deserve shit! That *faccia brutta!*"

"Ann, you don't get it, do you? You drove me to this. You pushed me to go out and find somebody else. Don't you remember all those nights you slept on the goddamn couch? What did you expect me to do? You're the one who used to tell me to go out and find a young fluff. Remember that? So stop acting so surprised."

"Frank, my sisters are right, you're nothin' but a selfish brute."

"I'm selfish?"

"Yeah, you're selfish! Oh, and tell that bitch she better not come around my family again."

"What are you talking about?"

"*A managia*, I saw her."

"Where?"

"She came to the ballpark."

"You mean the parade?"

"No, I already know about that. She was there one night when I was coaching softball. Wasn't she? Don't think I didn't know it was her. She's a blonde, isn't she? Some dirty ass blonde with bags around her eyes? She came to the ballpark, Frank. She kept staring at me the whole game. That's when I realized it was her. Fuckin' woman has a lot of nerve!"

"Okay, yeah. That was her. I saw her that night, too, but she didn't speak to me."

"Well, she better stay away from us."

"Ann, she's heartbroken."

"And what am I supposed to feel? Am I supposed to feel sorry for her? Freakin' *poveretta* needs to move on with her goddamn life. It's no one else's fault she left her family, but her own."

The day Pop ran out on Pavarotti and pancakes, Gail fired two shots from her handgun. The bullets traveled through the window of the house across the street from her home. Although nobody was injured, my father found her lying in bed—hysterically crying—with that loaded gun by her side.

Not long after the shooting, my brothers had a visitor. They were home alone when the doorbell rang. Michael went to answer the door, with Tony trailing close behind. When Michael opened the door, my brothers found a blonde lady they had never seen before. She sort of let herself inside. This lady stood in the foyer and smiled. All she said was, "I'm your daddy's friend," though neither of my brothers recognized her. Before either one of them could say a word, this lady moved towards the staircase. The thing is—she and Tony locked eyes.

As she climbed the stairs, she looked back over her shoulder. That's when Tony knew she was Dad's girlfriend. They locked eyes the entire time she climbed the stairs. There was something about her expression that let him know she was up to no good. Tony says he was going to go up and see what she was doing in our parents' bedroom, but Gail came back down very quickly.

"She must have been watching the house," Tony tells me. "Mom had just left to pick you up after baseball practice. Michael and I were only home alone for about twenty minutes, so she must have known she had to get in and out."

"Did she say anything?" I ask.

"Nothing—except, 'I'm your daddy's friend.'"

"That's it?"

"Yeah, when she finally came back downstairs, she walked right past us out the front door. She didn't say 'goodbye' or 'thank you,' or anything. Michael and I just stood there and watched her walk up the driveway."

"Did you go upstairs and check Mom and Pop's room after she left?"

"No."

"Well, why didn't you say anything when Mom and I got home?"

"I didn't think it was a good idea. I know how upset Mom has been since that day Dad ran out on breakfast."

Even though Tony is only twelve years old, he's right. Telling Mom and Pop that Gail had been in our house—that she had been in their *bedroom*—would have been a disaster.

The day Gail came to our house will be buried along with that time Mom came after me with the belt. My brothers and I are learning that some things are better left unsaid. We seem to have developed our own version of The Cover-Up.

It's just—I want to know why Gail came to the house. I want to know what she did during the minute she was in my parents' bedroom. I'm angry that she would come to our house like that. I'm angry she would let herself in.

If she owns a gun, she could have done anything to my brothers that day. She could have kidnapped them or could have left them for dead right there in the foyer.

The fact that Gail hasn't let go of my father is concerning.

26

In the summer of 1992, my friends and I like to go to the Boardwalk to hangout and look for girls. Our parents all know each other, so they take turns picking us up and dropping us off since my buddies and I can't drive yet.

My friend, Brian, is much more experienced than I am when it comes to girls. As a matter of fact, I haven't even talked to a chick since that date I had with Sandy over six months ago. Brian is confident and doesn't hesitate when approaching the pretty young ladies, so I normally stay back and let him do all the work.

Tonight, we're talking to a pair of girls from Fort Washington, Pennsylvania, a suburb of Philadelphia. Their names are Karen and Stephanie, and they're cousins. Right away, I realize that Brian is into Karen, so that means Stephanie is mine. She is cute with her long brown hair, and soft eyes. The thing is, she has a cast on her left leg, and can't walk very well. So, she and I stay on one of the benches where the street connects with the Boardwalk, while Brian and Karen go off to make-out on the beach.

After talking to Stephanie for a little bit—it turns out we've both been horseback riding in the Poconos with our families—so we establish a bit of common ground. The horseback riding conversation eases my nerves, and before too long I look into her eyes and lean in for a kiss. She responds, and we end up making out for a few minutes. But I forgot that tonight Pop is coming to pick us up at ten o'clock. Before I know it, I hear the sound of his horn behind us, announcing his arrival, and catching me red handed.

He has a big, silly grin on his face when Brian and I climb into his GMC Jimmy. I feel embarrassed over the fact Pop caught me making out with Stephanie. After we drop Brian off at his house, my father and I walk in the front door, and sit in the den, where we find Mom smoking a cigarette and watching TV.

My father is still chuckling over having caught me with Stephanie. He speaks to Mom in broken-Italian, thinking I won't understand what they're saying. Though I understand two words very clearly—*bacio*—which means kiss, and—*ragazza*—which means girl. My father is telling Mom how he caught me making out with a girl. My mother lets out a bit of a yelp, only to start giggling and smirking, as Pop mumbles out a few more lines in his broken-Italian. I can feel the redness in my face, and wish I could bury my head in the sand like an ostrich.

Days after my make-out session with Stephanie, Mom wants me to make a promise. We're standing in the kitchen, with the windows open, as the summer breeze softly plays with the curtains swaying in the air. "Mom," I ask. "What sorta promise?"

"I want you to promise, that you won't have sex until you get married."

"*What?*"

"You heard me."

"What sorta promise is that?"

"A serious one."

"But that's ridiculous!"

"Why is that ridiculous?"

"Because I don't even have a girlfriend!"

"Yeah, not right now, but you will, someday. And I want you to promise that when that day comes—you'll wait until you're married."

I shake my head, and sigh in disbelief. Yet, something strange happens when my mother mentions me having sex—and getting married. I simultaneously become embarrassed and aroused. Her words send a throb of excitement through me. It seems like all I ever think about anymore is girls. If I'm not studying those eighteen year old seniors in their short, plaid, field hockey skirts—then I'm fantasizing about the models in the Victoria's Secret Catalog.

There is the sound of my mother dropping several ice cubes, into a pair of drinking glasses as she says, "Frankie, I'm serious. This is important to me." She pours us both a glass of iced tea before returning the pitcher to the top shelf in the fridge. Mom then takes the glasses, one in each hand, and asks me to follow her out onto the back deck. When we get outside, we sit at the glass-top table, shielded from the sun by the huge umbrella. There is the smell of barbecues in the air, as Mom takes a sip of her iced tea, and leans back in her patio chair. She looks out over the meadows for a moment, rests her glass on the table-top, looks over at me and says, "Frankie, when I was seventeen, my best girlfriend and I went on a double date with these two college guys."

I nod my head, and listen. "They seemed nice, took us out to dinner, and showed us a good time. But when it was time to head home, they talked us into stopping at a motel. The next thing I know, my girlfriend is getting out of the car and going off with her date into one of the rooms. I was like, *what's goin' on here?* She left me alone with this guy I had only just met. Now, he was cute, and had been very polite. So, I didn't suspect anything when he said we should get our own room, because who knew how long we'd have to wait for my girlfriend and his buddy to finish what they were up to. So, I said, 'Okay.' Only, when we got into the room, he started taking his clothes off. I said, 'Hey, what are you doin'?' But, he didn't answer right away. All he did was take out his wallet, place it on the nightstand, and say, 'If you sleep with me tonight, the money and the credit cards are yours.' I looked at him like *are you crazy?* He tried to make nice, but I stormed out, and pounded on my girlfriend's door until they opened up, and we left. You have to understand, Frankie—sex is meant to take place between a husband and a wife. It's not supposed to be casual. Now, I know some of your friends may be experimenting, but I want you to promise me that you'll wait 'til you get married."

"But Mom, I'm not gonna take my wallet out and do that."

"I know honey, my point is as you get older, you may meet someone and fall in love, but that doesn't mean you have to sleep together. We are supposed to wait till we're husband and wife—that's all I'm saying. Sex is only special when it's with someone special—you know what I'm saying?"

I nod my head, yes. "So," Mom says. "Will you promise to wait until you're married?" I nod and say, "Okay Mom, I promise." My mother smiles and adds, "That's my boy. That's my Frankie. You made your mother very happy today."

My father doesn't know about The Promise—but he says I have to watch myself—because I'm too nice to girls. Whenever we go out to eat as a family, my brothers and I know Pop will flirt with our waitress if she is even remotely attractive. Before we're done placing our orders, he will have her eating out of the palm of his hand. The waitress may not even realize it, but she will be tossing her hair over her shoulder, and grinning from ear to ear, defenseless against my father's seductive charm. Now that I'm getting older, Pop wants the same for me. He wants me to tease and flirt.

In the summer, when we go to the tiny, touristy breakfast spots, where the waitresses tend to be my age, Pop says I'm being too formal when I say, *yes, please*, and *thank you*. If our waitress asks me if I would like sausage with my eggs, and I say, "yes, please," Pop waits until she walks away, then says, "Chichi, whaddaya doin'?"

"Whaddaya mean?"

"Whaddaya doin' talkin' to her like that?"

"The waitress?"

"Yeah. Whaddaya doin' fallin' all over her?"

"I wasn't fallin' all over her."

"Yeah, you were. You gotta watch the way you talk to girls, Chichi. You can't be too polite. You follow me? You can't put them on a pedestal. They'll lose respect for you. They want *you* to be on the pedestal."

"But Pop, I was just answerin' her question about my sausage...."

"Lissename Cheech, next time one of these girls asks you a question, say, *yeah*, instead of *yes, please*. Or *thanks*, instead of *thank you*. Being too polite makes you look weak. Even though she's only serving us breakfast, she's eyeing you up. Maybe you don't see it— because you're a little naïve—but I see it. And I'm tellin' you, you have to stop being so nice. You have to stop fallin' all over them. Women respond to a *man*; they don't want a priest. They want someone to put them in their place. I'm not sayin' to be disrespectful; I'm not sayin' to be rude. I want you to be a gentleman, but you gotta watch your tone. Sometimes you come off apologetic, as if you're burdening her with your order, and that's never gonna get you anywhere. You must never allow a woman to think they're doin' you a favor. This girl here—our waitress—is just doin' her job. Don't make her out to be a saint. I guess that's what I'm sayin', Chichi. She's only a girl—that's all she is. She needs you; she wants you.

So stop actin' like you're the luckiest guy in the world. The trick is to make her feel like *she's* the fortunate one. *Capisce?*"

"Not really, Pop...."

To drive home his point and to clarify my confusion, my father tells me about these two brothers from Italy. Pop says, "There were these two brothers who got along very well. They delivered milk for a living; that's what they did for work. You know, they had their horses, and a couple of wagons. The thing is, these brothers never argued and got along like a hot knife through butter. Then one day, they met these two sisters, and wouldn't you know it—they fell in love. The brothers married the sisters. They ended up moving away from each other; their villages separated by some mountains. They lost track of each other. You know how it goes. The truth is, the sisters didn't like each other very much, and couldn't wait to split up. So, they kinda forced the issue. Anyway, after a few years had gone by, the brothers bump into each other. And you know—they can't believe it. They jump off their wagons, and they hug, and they kiss. And they're like, 'I haven't seen you in so long; I can't believe it.'"

"They're crying. It's the sorta reunion they had both dreamt about. So, the one brother says, 'Look, you gotta come back to my house for dinner. We gotta celebrate.'"

"I mean this is before telephones and all that. You know what I'm sayin'? So, the brother accepts the invitation, and back they go to the house. Now, Chichi, their houses back then were different. The livestock lived on the ground floor, and the people lived above them. You follow me? That's how it was."

I nod my head to show I understand.

"So, they get back to the village, and they put their horses in the stable to feed. They walk into the kitchen, and the host brother says to his wife, 'My brother is here, bring us a bottle of wine, and a couple glasses.' She brings them a bottle of wine, and the glasses and goes back to whatever she's doin'. A little while later, the brother calls to his wife again."

"'We're both hungry; bring us some spaghetti.'"

"So, the wife stops whatever she's doing, and begins preparing dinner. Not long after that, she brings over two hot plates of spaghetti. But what's missing? Bread. So, the brother calls to his wife."

"'Bring us some bread.'"

"And she brings them a loaf of bread. Now, the visiting brother is in awe of the way his sister-in-law waits on them."

"He says, 'How'd you do that? How'd you get your wife to be this way?'"

"But the other brother asks, 'Doesn't your wife do that?'"

"'No,' he says. 'She's arrogant and nasty.'"

"'Well, it's too late now,' the first brother says."

"'Whaddaya mean it's too late?'"

"'It's too late. You gotta do it when you're first married.'"

"But the visiting brother doesn't get it. He wants to know how he can get his wife to treat him like this. So, the host brother says, 'When we first got married, the horse I used to keep downstairs was ornery, and would act up a lot. She would make noise all hours of the night. So, this one night after we just got married, I called down to the stable, and I told the horse to shut up, and the horse would get quiet for a while. But then she would start up again. So, I called down a second time and told the horse to shut up, and she would get quiet again, but the third time she started acting up, I lost it. I slammed my fist down on the table. I called to my wife, and told her to get me the lamp, and my pistol. Then, I went downstairs and shot the horse.'"

Pop says, "Chichi, the other brother is on the edge of his seat. He's soaking it all in, and says he wants to try the same thing with his wife, even though his brother insists it's not gonna work. He says it only would have worked right when they first got married. But the visiting brother has a newfound courage about himself, and when he gets back to his own village, he walks in the door with his chest puffed out. In a very demanding voice, he calls to his wife."

"'Bring me some wine.'"

"The wife is in the corner mending some clothes. She calls back to him. 'Get it yourself.'"

"Defeated, he goes over and pours himself some wine. But then he turns from the counter, and calls to his wife again."

"'You know, I'm hungry. A good wife—a nice wife—would bring her husband some spaghetti.'"

"But the wife just looks up at him like he has lost his mind. So, he makes himself dinner, and sits down at the table with his plate. Defeated, yet determined, he decides he is going to have his wife bring him some bread, and calls over his shoulder. 'Wife, bring me some bread.'"

"But the woman tells him to go fuck himself. Humiliated, he gets up, and slices himself some bread. He has lost all respect for himself. He doesn't know what to do, but then his horse downstairs in the stable starts to make some noise. This is his last chance. He calls down to the stable, and tells the horse to shut up, but the horse keeps making noise. So, he calls down again."

"'Horse, I said *shut up!*'"

"But the horse keeps making noise. So, he grabs his lamp, and his pistol, and goes downstairs. His wife is curious, and follows him downstairs. When he shoots the horse, she screams at him."

"'Now, how are you gonna deliver the milk?'"

"He looks at her dumbfounded. So, she angrily swipes the lamp from her husband's hand, and *clocks* him in the back of the head. Down he goes like a ton of bricks. I mean he's out cold, lying on top of the dead horse."

My father stops talking; he searches my expression.

"You get it, Chichi?"

I look at him confused.

"Get what, Pop?"

"The moral of the story."

"The moral? What's the moral?"

"If you let the woman call the shots, you'll end up passed out in the dark with a dead horse."

27

Going into my sophomore year—the fall of 1992—I'm expected to earn the varsity quarterback position on the football team. Coach Coffey has spread the word to the upperclassmen that I'm supposed to be as good as anyone who has ever played at my high school.

He tells them not to worry about my age—just fifteen—but to focus on my arm strength, and 6' 2" frame. Thanks to Coach's confidence, and a summer of baseball and lifting weights, I feel like I'm ready to live up to the hype, and take the reins as the starting quarterback. But, whenever Coach Coffey puts me in with the first-string offense, I make bonehead play after bonehead play. After practice, he pulls me aside and tells me to relax. He says I should remember football is supposed to be fun, but throughout the entire two week summer camp, fun is the last thing on my mind.

I can feel all the coaches' and players' eyes watching me—waiting to see a hint of the hype they've all heard about. But I'm so nervous, I look bad. If it's a running play, I take the snap from center, turn the wrong way, and miss the hand-off with the running back. If it's a pass play, I drop back into the pocket, but overthrow the wide-open wide receiver, and wind up yelling—*fuck*—because that's the only word that makes any sense to me when I'm performing like this. But that's also the one word Coach Coffey won't tolerate.

I may be the future but when I scream *fuck*, Coach reams me out in front of the whole team, with chewing tobacco spewing from his mouth, and veins popping in his neck.

When camp is over and school begins, I find myself third on the depth charts, intimidated by the upperclassmen, and banished to the bench.

It's tough being banished to the bench, when you're supposed to be the "future." But I can't seem to get out of my own way. Based solely on ability, I'm not only more talented than the other quarterbacks on my own team, I'm more talented than most quarterbacks in south Jersey. One of the coaches on our coaching staff played for nine years in the

NFL. He says I have the talent to play big time college football. He says I'm tall, with a strong, accurate arm, loaded with poise, and very coachable.

The problem is—the difference between my *talent* and my *performance* leaves me haunted by the word 'potential.' In the dictionary, potential is defined as: *a latent excellence, or ability, that may or may not be developed*. It's that phrase—*may or may not be developed*—that has me feeling like the most talented bench warmer in the Garden State. Whenever I'm given the chance to showcase my skills, I get so nervous, I overthink the situation to the point that I stumble around like a fool.

Despite being relegated to third-string on the depth chart, and the fact I am starting to struggle a bit socially thanks to a severe case of acne, the real challenge is the sudden change in Mom.

Although she tried real estate school, Mom didn't complete the class work. Pop thought if she got her real estate license, she could sell the houses he was building out in Cumberland County. But with the economy in the dumps, and the housing market still stagnant, the idea of Mom, 'the real estate agent,' is no more. That said; her part-time position as a nurse's aide at the nursing home, had been going well. It was the first time she worked outside of the home since I was born. Mom seemed happy with the few days she picked up here and there.

One day she came home from work with a golf ball sized bump above her right eye. When he saw it, Pop said, "Ann, what happened to you?"

"Oh, I bumped my head gettin' out of the Cadillac."

"Bumped your head? That's no bump. What happened?"

"I told you Frank, I bumped my head."

Even though he doesn't believe her, my mother sticks to her story. Not long after her mysterious bump appears, Pop gets a call from Mom's supervisor to inform him that she has been fired. The supervisor felt she had to call Pop to let him know how serious the allegations were against my mother. The woman explained that Mom was being fired because she had been overheard in the employee bathroom talking about suicide. When my father asks her about it, my mother says nothing at first. It isn't until he pushes for an answer that she finally blurts out, "Frank, I couldn't deal with the patients."

"Whaddaya mean you couldn't deal with the patients? I thought you liked it over there?"

"I did. It's just that they die."

"What are you talking about? Who dies?"

"The old folks, I mean, it's a nursing home, and I know it's only natural. But, I would get close to some of them, and come in the next day to find their bed was empty because they died during the night and," she starts to cry, "it just reminded me of my father. And...I couldn't take it. I couldn't take thinking of him like that. I didn't even say goodbye to him. Can you believe that, Frank? I wouldn't say goodbye to my own father? What kind of a daughter am I? Oh Jesus, oh God...."

Without a job to get up and shower for, without the need to be somewhere and look nice, Mom falls into a deep depression. It's late September 1992—just days after my parents' seventeenth wedding anniversary—and my mother is too afraid to be home alone. She says she can't escape the guilt she feels over not saying goodbye to Babbo at his funeral. Mom swears her father is going to find her and murder her.

Almost immediately after getting fired, Mom goes back to sleeping on the floor in the den most of the time. She fears Babbo will find his way into the walk-in closet, and kill her after she falls asleep. My father tries to reassure her, "Ann, no one is hiding in the closet. Your father is dead. He died in April of 1986, that's six and a half years ago. So please believe me, he can't hurt you."

But Mom is unable to let go of her fear.

Ever since the bank 'called' his business loan, Pop has been hiding from creditors, and struggling to make payroll for his small band of employees each week. Lester and Darryl are now the only consistent members of Pop's crew, as he lays off many of the other men working for him. In addition, folks who initially agreed to build homes on his land change their minds after they learn he has lost the bank's backing. They want Pop to return their deposits, but he won't give it to them. In reality—he can't give it to them, because it's gone—along with most of my parents' savings.

The once prospective homebuyers file a lien against my father's land, which just sits there half-developed—a reminder of what *could* have been. Between 'The Recession,' which makes it nearly impossible to find work as a general contractor, dealing with Mom's worsening behavior, and the stagnant housing market, Pop's eyes start to twitch from the stress.

The money is so tight, he is occasionally late with the mortgage on our house; it is a 'rob Peter to pay Paul' lifestyle. Collection agencies phone the house all the time. And even though he might be standing right next to us—Pop says, "If somebody calls looking for money, tell them you don't know where I am, or when I'll be back—and just hang up."

"Hang up?"

"Hang up."

He says we're to keep it short, and to the point.

"Don't get into a long, drawn out conversation."

But it's hard for me to hang up on men who talk so professional they call me "sir."

I am in the kitchen, when the phone rings. My father is at the counter eating prosciutto straight from the paper packaging. Since I am closer to the telephone, I answer after the second ring; it is another debt collector. I am polite, and tell him I don't know where my father is, but the caller matches my politeness.

"Do you know when he will be home, sir?"

"No, I don't know when he'll be home."

"Well, does he have a cellular number I could reach him at, sir?"

"Ah...yes, he does, but...."

I don't want to betray my father, but I can't escape the guilt I feel over being rude and lying. So, I try to let the caller off easy.

"How 'bout if I take a message?"

When he realizes who I'm speaking with, my father jumps all over me. "*Cheech, what are you doin'? Hang up the phone!*"

The caller hears Pop's voice.

"Who was that, sir?"

"Oh, that was my father."

"So, he is home?"

"Ah...he just walked in. Let me see if he can come to the phone."

"Great. Thank you, sir."

Pop's eyes are as big as saucers when he charges towards me from the counter. He swipes the receiver out of my hand, and slams it down.

"*What did I tell you, Cheech?*"

"I know, but...."

"*What did I tell you?* If anybody calls lookin' for me, just say you don't know where I am, or when I'll be back, and hang up. *That's it!* Nothing more, and nothing less. Now, c'mon Cheech—is that clear?"

28

It is Christmas Eve 1992, and my mother has disappeared. We are over Grandmom's house, but Mom is nowhere to be found. It's like she vanished. The Cadillac isn't outside, and no one knows where she went. Aunt Bridgid says, "Maybe she had to run home to wrap a few last minute presents."

But when we call, there's no answer.

Pop gets worried. He tells the adults how Mom hasn't been acting right since she got fired from the nursing home. As a precaution—he, Uncle Bruno, and Aunt Sofia's husband—my Uncle Bobby—decide to go out and look for her.

They come back—two hours later—after having checked all the lonely roads, and empty bridges, but Mom is nowhere to be found. I overhear Uncle Bobby say he peered into our garage window, half expecting to find Mom hanging from the rafters. That image scares me because I know it could happen. The deterioration Mom has gone through in the last three months has been *excruciating* to watch.

She has gone from happy and healthy to scared and depressed. It isn't until after one in the morning that we hear anything about Mom. Aunt Ellen calls Grandmom in a panic. She says she and her children had just arrived home from Midnight Mass, when Mom stopped by unannounced. The thing is—my mother was drunk, and my mother is *never* drunk.

Aunt Ellen says Mom told her she had just come from the beach, where she stood at the water's edge, and wanted nothing more than to walk out into the ocean until the water swallowed her up. Aunt Ellen says Mom started to cry after that, and left in a hurry through the backdoor. She left too quickly for her to guess where Mom may have headed.

Hours later, Pop finds her at home, passed out, face down, lying next to our Christmas tree....

Mom's fear of Babbo takes over her life. Since she no longer has a job, or anything to keep her occupied all day, my father begins taking Mom to work with him. He doesn't want her home alone especially after that Christmas Eve disappearance. With my brothers and me at school, he is worried Mom may follow through with what she started thinking about that night on the beach. Going to work with my father means Mom sits in his GMC Jimmy for eight hours each day while he tries to find work, submits job estimates, and supervises his men. Pop darts around to check on the progress of different projects, while Mom sits quietly in the passenger seat, reading those paperback novels she gets in the checkout line at Acme. Pop tells Aunt Ellen, "Some people may think it sounds charming, husband and wife traveling around together, mixing business with pleasure, but Ann just sits there, either staring off into space, or reading her books and not saying a word to me all day long."

At home, Mom is no better. She is back to sleeping on the floor most nights, even though the carpet in the den is covered with all sorts of stains from where all sorts of things have been spilled, or dripped.

In addition to the cat puke, there are stains from spilled milk, spilled wine, spilled soup, spilled soda, spilled juice, and drops of olive oil that lead to and from the kitchen, and around the couch where my mother likes to lay. There is always an ashtray, those cups of empty, stale coffee, and toenail clippings sprinkled around the loveseat.

Our house feels empty. It's not like my friends' homes where their mothers have taken the time to decorate, by hanging drapes that match the carpets, accentuating their living room furniture with throw pillows. They have knick-knacks, pictures on their walls, and statuettes, while our house is more like a barren, cold building with only a few photographs and paintings.

It seems to me that the condition of our house mirrors Mom's own appearance. She starts wearing the same sweatshirt *every single day*. A light pink sweatshirt, with a smiling teddy bear in the center that is surrounded by all sorts of stains that Mom must not "see," because when Pop asks her about it she says, "Oh Frank, why are you always doing this to me? It's only a sweatshirt f'Chrissakes, leave me alone."

"But Ann, it's dirty. You have a walk-in closet full of clothes upstairs. Go up, take a shower, and put something clean on."

Mom never does. She even stops showering regularly, and starts to smell so bad that Pop has to beg her to use a washcloth under her arms. Mom likes to wear her sneakers without a pair of socks, which means there is nothing to absorb the perspiration caused by her sweaty feet. After not showering for four or five days, her foot stench is strong, to put it mildly.

When she plops down on the red velvet loveseat to watch TV, she slips off her sneakers to reveal crusty, gray toenails. She never gets pedicures or bothers to paint her toes. However, Mom does like to clip her toenails while sitting on the loveseat, watching TV. She thinks nothing of wiping the clippings off the red velvet couch onto the filthy lavender carpet where they will then spend eternity.

If she tires of *Jerry Springer* or *The Maury Povich Show*, Mom will stop watching television, and start playing Nintendo. When she plays Nintendo, Mom sits Indian Style, in the middle of the filthy, lavender carpet, smoking, and drinking her coffee.

After hours in front of the TV and playing Nintendo, Mom likes to call her family in Philadelphia and complain to them about us, or badger Aunt Ellen and Aunt Teresa with nonsense. Because Mom is barely functional, we're forced to eat pizza every night of the week. I say *forced* because Mom has seemingly forgotten how to cook.

It all started about a month ago when Mom made the Salty Spaghetti. She put so much salt in the water that we nearly gagged after only one bite.

"Mom," Tony asked, "what's *this?*"

"Yeah," asked Michael, "what happened?"

"Ann, how much salt did you put in the water?"

"I don't know Frank, as much as I always put."

"Ann, c'mon, that's ridiculous, it tastes like you dumped the whole box in there. *Jesus!* Boys, don't take another bite, give your plates to me, c'mon, pass'em down."

We passed our plates down to Pop and watched as he dumped them in the trash and I couldn't help but think this never would have happened a few years ago. Mom always used to be an American-born version of Nonna; the good *calabresella* with that heavy basket of olives on her head, but now she is a domestic mess, and even for three Italian boys, pizza six nights a week gets old.

On the seventh night, we eat Pop's Blue Collar Carbonara, but now that Mom seems to have "checked-out" my father starts encouraging Michael to go to Aunt Teresa's for the weekends.

While Michael begins to regularly spend the weekends at Aunt Teresa's house, Aunt Ellen starts calling Mom about taking her meds. Nearly every morning, even after Pop tapes her prescription regiment to the inside of each kitchen cabinet—Aunt Ellen will call and remind Mom to take her medicine.

We're all concerned because sometimes Mom will binge on her meds causing enormous mood swings. For a while she'll take her medication as prescribed, then, for no apparent reason—won't take a single pill for days. She then figures she should double, or triple the dosage to make up for the days she missed, causing Pop to say, "Ann, if you're not careful, you're gonna ruin your stomach."

But Mom doesn't care. Even though Aunt Ellen tries to guide her through it over the phone, Mom continues to over and under medicate, thus worsening her stomach problems. Soon, she starts complaining of those burning pains again eating at her from the inside. Pop takes her back to the doctors, but the tests conclude, once again, that she has no gastro-intestinal issues, even though she has more episodes where she "holds onto the floor" begging for help.

In the months since she got fired, Mom doesn't seem to care about anything anymore, and Pop isn't sure what to do. She is a mess. My father understands her trauma about the nursing home, and not wanting to continue working with old people, so he does an about face, and asks Mom if she'd like to play golf regularly with a few female friends from town. The friends he is referring to are stay at home moms from well-to-do families that have memberships to several local country clubs. They invite Mom to play golf with them for free, then have lunch afterwards where she may possibly make some new friends.

Pop says, "Ann, if you're uncomfortable working right now, why don't you play golf with Tracy and a few of her friends at Atlantic City

Country Club? I ran into her the other day, and she said they have room in their ladies' league if you wanna play. Whaddya think? Would you like to play golf a couple days a week? I think it'd be good for you to get out in the air, and socialize a little bit. Coming with me to work isn't doing anything for you. So, whaddya think?"

Mom ignores him.

"Ann, whaddaya think?"

Mom ignores him.

"Ann!"

Mom finally turns towards him.

"What'd you say, Frank?"

"The golf. Do you wanna play golf with Tracy and a few of her girlfriends?"

"What? Why would I wanna do that?"

"Jesus, weren't you listening to a word I just said?"

"Frank, I only asked you a question. Why are you always doing this to me?"

"Doing what, Ann? *Doing what?* I asked you if you wanted to play golf a few days a week so you can get outta the house, make some friends, have some fun...."

"Frank, I don't wanna do that."

"Why not?"

"Because I don't."

"So, you're just gonna sit around all day and watch TV, pick at your toenails, and play Nintendo?"

"No, I go to work with you sometimes."

"Yeah, I know, and that's not realistic, Ann. You need to get back on your feet. Sitting in my truck all day isn't a life; it isn't living. You just ignore me, read your books, or stare off into space."

"Oh, you know what Frank, you're an ass. You do nothing but pick on me. I'm fine, just leave me alone. Okay? Just leave me alone!"

Even though Mom wants Pop to leave her alone—she doesn't look right—and stands out in a crowd for all the wrong reasons. It wasn't long ago that she could turn heads, garnering attention from that casting director with her distinctive European look, but now, it is her dirty hair, her disheveled clothes, and thick, red, clown lipstick that brings on the attention.

184

Other times, her slurred speech causes her to stand out—or—when she's on a med binge—her leg will hop up and down so much that it looks like she's from a different planet. If it isn't her leg, or the distant look in her eyes that makes her stand out—it is the fact that whomever she's sitting with will have to repeat themselves over and over and over.

"Ann, didja hear what I said?"

No answer. No look. No nothing.

"Ann, didja hear what I just said?"

No answer. No look. No nothing.

"Ann, didja hear what I just said?"

No answer. No look. No nothing.

After this happens several times, it makes people stare especially because Mom always comes back with, "Look, I'm fine. Just leave me alone."

No matter what is going on, or what has just happened, she either claims to be 'fine' or becomes the victim and blames everybody else for what is troubling her. "Stop doing this to *me,*" she says. "Why are you always doing this to *me*?" It is like she needs sympathy, even if she is the one causing the chaos.

By early 1993, my father begins to develop his own theory as to why Mom is back to struggling; Gail is out of the picture.

The way he sees it, Mom no longer has to "hold herself together" because her 'competition' is gone.

When she was going to lose her family, Mom became *Super Woman*—meaning that she was dressing nicely, constantly after Dad to have sex, volunteering, and working outside of the house.

But now that he and Gail have been apart for eighteen months, my father quietly begins to resent what he labels an "inherent laziness" in Mom's make up. He feels like Mom wouldn't allow herself to "fall this far" if Gail was still in the picture.

It's as if the proverbial rug has been pulled out from underneath him. He thought he had his wife back, the girl he married. But, his reality is much different.

The boy with too many aptitudes is married to a dirty, depressed, pill-popping *testa dura* who likes to gamble and lead people to believe she would be just fine—if her damn husband, and three ungrateful sons—just showed her a little appreciation.

29

When I walk the halls at school, I keep my head down, so as to avoid making eye contact with any of the pretty field hockey girls in their short plaid skirts. I know that if I caught their attention, they would only giggle and nudge each other, *awe, look at the poor pimple faced Puerto Rican kid.*

Everybody mistakes me for being Puerto Rican, with my thick hair and olive skin. People have even started calling me *Paco*, which is the nickname for Francisco in Spanish. Pop has always said because we're Italian, we're from the "Latin Family," so being recognized as a *Latino* only seems natural; it's just my zits that have me down. I don't have the occasional blemish; I have *severe* acne. My face is infested with craters from old pimples, as reddish mounds of puss boil up between my eyes, and protrude from my cheek bones.

I am the definition of a *Pepperoni Pizza Face*, and am forced to hide my *faccia* from all the pretty girls in school, even the lowly freshmen.

There are many days I wish I could go back in time and stop Mom from going into that greenhouse when she was a little girl. There are days I wish I could go back and stop Babbo from drinking so much, and saying all of those nasty things to her. There are days I wish I could go back and stop my father from ever meeting Gail. And then there are days, I wish I was dead.

The only thing that makes me feel better about life is the Victoria's Secret lingerie catalog. I get "lost" when I look at those models. Their beauty seems to dull the pain I feel inside, and I long for the day I'll have a girl like that of my own.

But, as a sophomore in high school, I don't feel like I matter. I don't feel like I fit in. I don't feel comfortable in my own skin, and I am confounded by Mom's recent struggles. She has become a constant embarrassment, and her lack of desire to get better, combined with my inability to live up to my potential has me worn-out.

I am worried about my father, and all the stress in his life. I'm upset by the anger directed at him from our family in Philadelphia, who points the finger at Pop for Mom's return to chaos. I struggle with my studies. I go through the motions on the football and baseball fields, and for the life of me, I can't find a girlfriend. In short, I am sad, and I feel hopeless.

These emotions overpower me, and in February of 1993, I confess to my parents that I want to commit suicide. We're sitting in the living room; the blinds are drawn and it's dark. I'm on the big couch, by myself, with my leg elevated because I just had knee surgery. It was only an arthroscopic procedure, to correct a meniscus tear, but it adds to my overall sense of worthlessness.

Mom is sitting in the pink chair in the corner of the living room, and Pop is on the love seat alone. He is leaning forward, banging his hand on the coffee table, trying to make a point.

"So, you're gonna take the easy way out, is that it? You're gonna kill yourself?"

"Maybe...."

"That's fuckin' ridiculous, Frank."

"Why is it ridiculous?"

"Because you have everything...."

"No, I don't...."

"Yes, you do. Now, lissename. You play quarterback, you're tall, you're healthy, you're from a good family. The knee will get better in time, and you'll be back on your feet. The doctor said you should be okay by baseball season."

"I know."

"Then what is it, Cheech? Is it the acne? If it is—I understand. I had acne too, so did Uncle Bruno, so did Aunt Sofia. Unfortunately, it's just something our family has, but it's no reason to kill yourself. We've tried to take care of it, Frank, but it hasn't been easy."

"Yeah, but I'm just sick of it."

"So, you're gonna kill yourself over pimples?"

187

"I don't know."

"Well, I'll tell you right now, you kill yourself—I won't come to the funeral."

At that, Mom finally speaks up.

"What did you say, Frank?"

He turns to her and says, "You heard me. If Frankie kills himself, I will not go to the funeral. Did you hear me, Cheech? Is that clear? Suicide is a fuckin' selfish act, and you're just sayin' this shit for attention, so I'm tellin' you right now, if you want to hang yourself, slit your wrists, or jump off some fuckin' bridge, I will *not* go to the funeral! Now, if you're confused about things, I understand. If you wanna talk to somebody about it, I think it's a good idea. But I think you're just feelin' sorry for yourself, you're over analyzin' things and not thinkin' straight. You're a teenager, and all teenagers get confused; that's not an excuse to go out and kill yourself. There are kids your age that are lyin' in hospital beds, or stuck in trenches fightin' for their lives. So, knock it off, sit up straight, and act like a man because I don't want to hear this shit again!"

When Mom's family hears what Pop said about not going to my funeral, they call him cold and arrogant. They want to know how he could say that to his own son. They want him to apologize to me which snowballs into them wanting him to apologize to Mom for his two-year affair with Gail.

Pop says when it comes to me he was just trying to make a point. He knows I'm confused, but is confident I'll come out of it. When it comes to apologizing for his relationship with Gail, the answer is clear; he is not sorry for the affair, and will *never* apologize to Mom for as long as he lives.

It goes on this way for months. Whenever her family comes down for a visit, or when we go up on holidays, it's always the same. They attack Pop, and he in turn, defends himself. This conversation has become a routine at every family gathering.

"Look," he says, "there was always a little bit of doubt in my mind about whether marrying Ann was the right decision or not; but that's not uncommon. Many people get married who aren't really sure about their partner, so I put it aside and took my vows. But I'm telling you, something happened to Ann on our honeymoon; and from that day on, she became a different person. Now, I think I've been doing the best I can in terms of trying to cope with, and understand her past. But for *years*, I had no idea what I was dealing with. She would gamble, she would sleep on the couch, she would ignore me when I came home from work. I mean, she acted like she didn't want to be married. I couldn't even say hello when I walked in the door half'a the time, without getting some sort of bizarre reaction out of her. She would never agree to see a counselor or anything because she always said she didn't have a problem. So, I mean, what did you expect from me? I told her, I said, 'Ann, don't be surprised when I find somebody else.' I wasn't going to leave my kids, but what I was putting up with was ridiculous. Men have had affairs since the beginning of time—presidents, popes, kings—it's not an excuse for someone to lose their mind. Ann had problems long before I met Gail. She has had problems since she was a little girl. But you people don't want to accept that! So whatever apology you think she deserves is *never* gonna happen. If anything—she owes me one."

30

Today is March 4, 1993. My mother and I are in the den watching television together. It's nighttime, and we are home alone. Mom is lounging on the loveseat, chain-smoking and drinking coffee. I'm lying on the couch staring at the TV.

We are watching a new awards show called the *ESPY's*. It is sort of like the *Academy Awards,* but for athletes.

The program is being hosted by the comedian Dennis Miller at Madison Square Garden in New York City. The awards are handed out for individual excellence in the different sports.

As I lay on the couch, watching my heroes parade across that stage two hours north of us, I can still feel that sadness inside. The sadness Pop called, 'feeling sorry for myself.'

Pop says, my 'feeling sorry for myself,' comes from overanalyzing everything. He says I'm a teenager, and that everybody gets confused when they're a teenager.

But my real problem is—I take things too seriously. My father says I overanalyze to the point where I end up feeling overwhelmed, which leads to self-pity and despair. Most of the time, the despair causes me to feel like no matter what I do, nothing is ever going to change.

Inside, I feel destined to be an unhappy underachiever.

I'll be sixteen in three months, and I don't see the point of living like this anymore. I wish I could just disappear. I've been struggling most of sophomore year with what it means to be me. Football season was a difficult blur, due to all of the expectations I left unfulfilled.

Now, with my knee surgery, and baseball season around the corner, I don't know how I can turn things around—especially since no girl will talk to me the way these zits have taken over my face.

Yet, a part of me knows Pop is right. I *am* feeling sorry for myself, but I don't know how to stop. It's what makes sense to me—it is all I know.

Right at the point when I feel the most susceptible to sadness and self-pity, I hear a man give an impromptu speech that changes my life. As the *ESPY's* continue, an announcement is made that it is time to present the *Arthur Ashe Award for Courage* to former Division I basketball coach Jim Valvano.

I'm familiar with Jimmy Valvano because he used to coach North Carolina State, and was a commentator on ESPN for years. I always felt a connection to Coach Valvano because he is an east coast Italian who could easily fit into my extended family. The sad part is—Coach Valvano is dying of cancer. He doesn't have much time to live. He looks weak and frail as he makes his way to the podium.

During his acceptance speech, he talks about the preciousness of life, and how no matter how bad things look—we should never give-up. He continues by stating that life should be lived enthusiastically. Coach Valvano is at times poignant, funny, thought-provoking and charismatic.

He references Vince Lombardi and Ralph Waldo Emerson as he urges the audience to enjoy their lives to the fullest. When he announces the motto for his newly formed foundation for cancer research, I feel like he is talking directly to me. The motto is simple and straightforward, "Don't give up, don't ever give up."

After he leaves the stage to a tearful standing ovation, I leave the couch for the powder room. I don't want Mom to see me cry. Looking at my reflection in the powder room mirror, I cry because everything Coach Valvano said is true. I need to stop feeling so sorry for myself. I need to figure out a way to break out of this self-imposed prison I live in.

Days later, I'm rummaging through the downstairs coat closet looking for one of my sweatshirts, when I stumble upon a cardboard box full of cassette tapes. I study the cassettes for a moment. It looks like they are part of an audio program called *Personal Power*. On the back of each cassette box is a picture of a young man with lots of hair and dressed in a gray business suit. The man's name is Anthony Robbins.

From what I can tell, by perusing the rhetoric and titles on the front and back of each box, *Personal Power* is a self-help program. It seems designed to assist people in unleashing their potential. Instantly, I know *Personal Power* is something my father must have bought in hopes of snapping Mom out of her funk. It sounds like something straight out of his Hero School, and something I desperately need.

Since hearing Coach Valvano speak at the *ESPY's,* I've been trying to find some way to persevere. I don't want to give up. I don't want to give in, and thanks to my accidental discovery of *Personal Power*, I'm introduced to a new outlook on life—a realization that things don't change; people change.

On his tapes, Anthony Robbins talks about the power of focus, and how our values and beliefs are the source of our successes or failures. He teaches me how to take control of my life by enlightening me on the power of *'why,'* and by encouraging me to create a compelling future through goal setting, and the understanding of the power of rituals.

The program my father purchased in hopes of helping Mom turn things around becomes my new best friend. Anthony Robbins' enthusiastic audio presentation touches me. It teaches me how to anchor myself to success while eliminating the self-sabotage I've struggled with so far in life.

It isn't a magic bullet. I don't completely "rewire myself," but listening to Anthony Robbins' *Personal Power* becomes an obsession. While other kids my age spend hours in front of the television set playing video games, I come home from practice each day, go up to my room, pop in the next cassette of *Personal Power,* and *literally* transcribe every word. I want so badly to turn myself around. I'm tired of being the underachieving, pimple faced quarterback with the weird mother.

It's the spring of 1993—and I want to change.

31

My brothers and I are sitting on the steps, listening to Mom and Pop up in their bedroom. They just came back from Philadelphia where they saw a new doctor, a man Pop trusts, his name is Dr. Wydell. This doctor told Pop that Mom needs to be hospitalized right away, and after years of worrying about what that means, my father is finally in agreement.

Dr. Wydell recommends the Institute of Mental Health at the University of Pennsylvania because he believes it to be the best at treating Mom's symptoms. He told Pop that if they act right away, he can arrange to have most of the cost of her care paid for by various agencies and insurance plans.

This is what my brothers and I have been listening to for the last twenty minutes—my parents discussing whether Mom should be hospitalized or not. Pop says, "Ann, how can we let this opportunity pass? I trust this doctor. I think he has a pretty good read on things. Let's give it a shot."

"But Frank, I don't want to do it."

"I know you don't want to do it. But what choice do we have? He can get the cost taken care of. He can get you the best doctors. He can get you in right away. What else could we ask for?"

After Pop says that, there's a long silence, and I can just imagine Mom sitting on the bed, looking at the floor, contemplating my father's words. She'll probably say what she always says, *I don't want help. I don't need help. I don't have a problem.*

I wish I could get inside her head, and make things click. I wish I could make her see that things need to change, that she has to change them, and that she has to change them *now*. But she would never agree to any of that. Only today, for the first time ever, she says, "Alright Frank, maybe you're right. Let's give the hospital a try."

My brothers and I look at each other in disbelief, and are encouraged when we hear Pop say, "Ann, we're gonna do this. We're gonna beat this thing."

The only thing left to do is call Philadelphia and tell Nonna and everybody up there that Mom has agreed to go into the hospital.

Only, when Pop gets Nonna on the phone, she doesn't like the idea. My father tries to explain to her that it's the best thing, but she says no daughter of hers is going into a mental hospital.

Pop starts yelling into the phone, "Ann has to deal with her past! Yes she does! I'm not trying to hurt your daughter. I'm trying to help her! If she doesn't do this right now, things are only going to get worse. I want what's best for her, and this doctor says this is the place. Why can't you accept that? *Why can't you see that?*"

My father slams down the phone.

"She hung up, goddammit! Ann, let's get you packed. I don't care what she says, you're goin' into that hospital tomorrow. *Frankie!*"

"Yeah, Pop?"

"Get your mother's pills together and bring them up here. Tony, Michael, go downstairs and get one of the suitcases in the hallway closet. Let's help your mother pack."

Early the next morning, Nonna and my godmother, Edith, show up ready to stop any trip to the hospital. They park their car behind the Cadillac, so Mom and Pop can't leave. They march into our house looking for a fight.

Grandmom and Grandpop are already here to help with things, but that doesn't stop Nonna from getting in Pop's face and screaming at him.

"My daughter no go'a hospital!" She says in her heavy accent.

"She is too!" Pop fires back.

"No! She no go'a! She no need'a go'a and that'sa final!"

"Listen to yourself. She does too need to go!"

"Frank, she been bunch'a doctor. Why she go'a so many *dottori*?"

"Because they get frustrated with her and...."

"No, you make'a her go, you make'a her change *dottore* on'a purpose, so she stay sick!"

"So, you admit she's sick?"

"You make'a her sick!"

"Oh, *va fan culo!*"

"No, you wanna hurt'a my daughter! You always wanna hurt'a my daughter!"

"I don't wanna hurt your daughter. I'm the only one here tryin' to *help* your daughter. You people keep doin' the same thing you've been doin' for the last forty years."

"*Managia la miseria!* You jus wanna put'a Ann away!"

"What are you talkin' about?"

"You jus wanna put'a my daughter away, and go'a back'a to you *puttana!*"

Grandmom gets in the middle of them, and starts screaming at Nonna, "How dare you! This has nothing to do with that! Ann needs help! Frank has found the right place for her, the right doctors!"

"Oh, *state zitt!*" Nonna shouts, meaning she wants Grandmom to shut up.

"No, you shut up! Frank has bent over backwards to help your daughter, but she has refused. Finally, she agrees to get some help and now you idiots come down here like this!"

"I say, *state zitt!* My daughter no go'a hospital! I no'a care what'a nobody say!"

Pop tells me and Tony to put Mom's stuff in the Cadillac, and to get Edith to move her car, but Edith won't do it.

"I'm not moving it, boys. Your mother does not deserve to be put away like this."

"Who's putting her away?" Tony asks. "She needs help."

"How do you know? You'll believe anything your father spoon feeds you. Where's your loyalty to your mother?"

Edith storms off to separate Nonna from Grandmom, as we go around and around like this for another hour. I wish I could make Edith and Nonna see that we need to do this; we need to get Mom help.

But after *literally* screaming himself hoarse, Pop finally gives in.

"You know what? Forget the whole fuckin' thing! I'm callin' the hospital right now, and cancelin' the visit!"

Then he points at Nonna and Edith, "I hope you two understand, whatever happens from here on out is on you. She's *your* problem now! You caused this mess to begin with by sweeping things under the rug forty years ago, so whatever happens, whatever she does, is on *you!*"

Weeks after Nonna and Edith came down to block Mom's entrance into the Institute of Mental Health, my mother disappeared on Easter Sunday.

We were over Aunt Bridgid and Uncle Bruno's house, where Mom had been quiet all afternoon, as she half-heartedly helped my aunt to prepare dinner. The only sounds she made were the deep sighs she took. As they set the table—it struck my aunt that Mom was bothered by something.

It wasn't out of character for my mother to behave this way in front of Aunt Bridgid. My aunt was accustomed to seeing her like this, for Mom had gotten into the habit of walking across the street, and ringing my aunt's doorbell at two in the morning, or calling at four in the morning wanting to "talk." It was always frustrating for Aunt Bridgid to be woken up at that hour. She had three children of her own, in addition to working outside the home. But, she wanted to "be there" for my mother, even though all Mom normally did during their "talks" was sit in silence, absorbing almost none of the advice her sister-in-law had to offer.

It wasn't until we were about to sit down and eat dinner that we realized Mom had vanished.

At first, the adults tried to look unconcerned, even though something didn't add up. Our Cadillac was still parked in the driveway across the street. Mom was either hiding somewhere in my aunt and uncle's house—or she had taken off on foot.

After they checked the entire property, Pop and Uncle Bruno went out looking for my mother. It was just like Christmas Eve when Mom disappeared, and they went to all the lonely roads and bridges in search of her.

How did we end up back here? Why did my grandmother and godmother have to get in the way? Can't they see that Mom is confused? That she needs help?

Mom finally turns up hours later with the vague, innocent excuse that indeed, she simply went for a walk. Even if that's all it was, my father asks, "For seven hours? You went for a walk on Easter Sunday for seven hours, and didn't say anything to anybody? Don't you think that's a little strange, Ann?"

Mom doesn't respond.

"Ann, answer me. We were about to sit down for dinner. Why didn't you say anything? We were worried sick. Bruno and I went out lookin' for you."

"Oh, Frank," she says dismissively. "I went for a walk, and I came back, and now I'm home. Whaddaya want from me?"

"How 'bout an explanation...."

"You know what, Frank...."

"What, Ann? What? How 'bout a simple explanation? Like, where did you go?"

"I told you, I went for a walk."

"Where?"

"Down the bike path."

"Why?"

"Jesus, Frank. Can't you just leave me alone?"

"Ann, can't I ask my wife why she decided to go for a walk when a house full of people were ready to sit down for Easter dinner? Isn't that a fair request? I mean, you ruined the day for everybody."

"Okay. Great, Frank. I ruined the day for everybody, whatta ya gonna do about it, huh?"

Pop shakes his head, and doesn't say anything in response.

"That's what I thought—nothin'. You're not gonna do anything about it. So, do me a favor Frank, leave me alone, okay? Is that clear? Is that a fair request?"

When I hear Mom like this, dismissive and arrogant, I think how she sometimes refers to the ex-husband of a cousin of ours who was crude and loud. In Italian, Dad called him a *gavone*, meaning he was low-class.

Throughout their marriage, rumors spread amongst our family about his physically abusive ways—word was that this *gavone* used to beat our cousin. My mother picked up on this, and used him as an example to my father when she would say, "I bet *he* wouldn't put up with my shit."

Mom used to say the same about Pop's "tough-guy" friends from Ducktown. This confused my father. If the rumors were true, and our cousin's marriage was full of domestic violence, why would Mom use them as an example of how Pop should handle things within their relationship?

It was as if Mom was insinuating that if she was married to someone physically abusive, her not sleeping in bed, her late-night gambling, or her Easter dinner disappearance, would not be tolerated—but instead met with force and violence. Was my father supposed to beat his wife, so Mom would behave herself?

There is a story my father once told me about an insurance man who came to our house. Pop said the insurance man wanted to sell him a new policy, and started his sales pitch by asking my father how long he had been in the construction/development business to which Pop answered, "About twenty years."

"Have you ever been bankrupt?"

"No," Pop said.

"Really?"

"No, never bankrupt."

"Wow, what a success story. Twenty years in the construction and development field and never been bankrupt, that's great."

"I don't think so," Pop said. "I just think I suffer from excessive optimism and a very high threshold for pain." Pop said the insurance man looked perplexed and chuckled a little, not knowing what to say to that. So, my father went on, "If I were a little smarter I might know when to quit, but I was taught to fight to the end, and that we can do anything if we put our minds to it. The problem is, this sometimes causes me to miss the obvious."

The insurance man sat there speechless, yet I think this is what my mother meant when she said our cousin's abusive husband wouldn't put up with her "shit."

Pop's self-proclaimed high threshold for pain caused him to miss the obvious; Mom wanted *Frankie the Voice* to lay down the law. She wanted to be "put in her place." She didn't want optimism. Mom didn't want my father to give her the benefit of the doubt, as he continued to suffer with her bizarre behavior.

He may have been mistaken for a Mafioso by the FBI and seen as a "brute" by all the women in our family, but the same man who told me I was being too nice to girls didn't follow his own advice. He was being *extremely* patient with his highly dysfunctional wife.

Some would even say he was an enabler.

The little bit of land my father still owns out in Cumberland County is going to help him get out of a jam. Pop owes five separate contractors about twenty thousand dollars each, but he has no way of raising that kind of cash. His housing development has completely stalled, yet he does not want to stiff these men. My father has been in their shoes before and knows what it's like to do work and not get paid. These contractors, and their employees, performed all the plumbing, electrical, siding, painting and excavation work, for several of the homes my father built last year. So, Pop comes up with a plan. He offers to give these men parcels of his land, as a way to pay off the debt.

Four of the five contractors agree to the deal straight up. They would prefer to be paid—but they understand Pop's predicament, and agree to accept the land in exchange for the $20,000 he owes them.

Only, one of the contractors—a plumber, whose wife is expecting a baby in the coming weeks—is desperate for cash. He wants Pop to *sell* the land to a relative of his; this man has worked out a deal with his uncle whereas Pop would sell the land for $20k. The land would go into the uncle's name, the cash would go into the plumber's pocket, and Pop would be free and clear.

The thing is, this deal would require my father to hire a lawyer, which my father does *not* want to do, so the plumber's uncle agrees to have his lawyer handle everything. Pop reluctantly decides to go along with the deal. He would prefer that the plumber take care of the details between himself and his uncle without my father having to get involved, but the man *begs* my father. "Frank," he says, "there's no other way to do it. My uncle wants to do everything on the up and up, and I need the cash, he'll take the land. C'mon, let the lawyer work it out. It won't cost you a nickel."

Pop says, "It's not just the money, Gianni. I'm trying to help you out. I don't have the cash to pay you. Givin' you the land is all I can do. But I don't wanna get wrapped up in a big legal thing, they always turn into a nightmare."

The man promises my father that it won't be an issue.

Occasionally, Mom still rides along with Pop in his GMC Jimmy as he spends his work day checking on different projects under proposal, or following up on the status of projects ongoing. Typically, my mother just sits there smoking and reading those paperback novels she buys in the check-out line at Acme—my parents rarely engaging in conversation.

My father's primary reason for taking Mom to work, is the same as it's always been—he doesn't want to leave her home alone. Maybe she had her nightmare again, the one where my eight year old mother hangs herself in her sleep, or maybe she tossed and turned all night, paranoid about Babbo hiding in her closest.

Either way, this is not how my father envisioned himself at forty-four years old: carting around his catatonic wife, struggling to make ends meet with an underperforming construction business, and cleaning up the mess of his failed housing development.

Pop had goals, he had dreams. He wanted to be free and independent, an entrepreneur with an artistic heart, but his reality is far from that. He is struggling within the confines of a vacant marriage, his affair with Gail is ancient history; his youth is passing him by, his land is an anchor around his neck. He is hiding from his creditors, scrambling to find steady work, and now his attempt to pay-off Gianni the Plumber is turning into a headache.

Just like he thought, Pop ends up filling-out loads of paperwork, and sending them back to Gianni's lawyer via fax. Then the lawyer needs more forms and eventually summons my father to his office—which is over an hour from our house down the shore.

My father reaches out to Gianni, "Gian, do I really have to drive an hour to your uncle's attorney's office? I told you I don't wanna get involved. Can't you guys just figure it out?"

"Ah, Frank c'mon, please you've come this far. Just take a ride out there, he wants to discuss the details and get your signature on a few papers."

"Why can't you bring the papers to me?"

"Lissename, just do me this one favor and the whole thing will go away."

Pop doesn't want to do it, and he especially doesn't want to drag my mother along with him as he takes the hour drive through the Pinelands, to the attorney's office—but that's exactly what he does.

My father has long been on edge regarding finances and the monthly struggle to survive. This land deal is reminder of that, but something happened recently regarding my brother Michael, that has Pop even edgier than normal.

Michael had just finished up a baseball game that Pop was coaching. Dozens of players, parents, siblings, friends and other family members were sort of congregating behind the two-story cinderblock building that acted as the Little League snack bar and baseball headquarters. This was all typical postgame, small town routine.

Tony and a few of his friends were horsing around nearby—which was also typical. Tony was using an aluminum baseball bat, aggressively waving it back and forth, so as to keep his buddies from snatching the hat off his head.

It was a simple case of "boys being boys," but Pop saw an issue and hollered over. "Hey Toe'nooch, stop wavin' your bat around, you're gonna clock somebody," but Tony ignored him and kept fooling around, swatting his buddies away.

At the same time, my brother Michael innocently came wandering out of the snack bar, where he had just gotten a root beer. He was unaware of Tony's and his buddies' horseplay. Again, Pop hollers over, "Yo, Tone, stop bein' a meatball and put the bat down, you're gonna hit somebody! I mean it!"

But again, Tony kept using his bat like a sword; his buddies determined to swipe that hat off his head. A moment later, Michael comes walking up behind Tony and—*crack*—Michael gets whacked right above his left eyebrow. The blow split open Michael's forehead, and he falls to the ground, screaming, blood cascading down his face.

Pop was already on high alert, so he rushed right over and grabbed Michael, whisking him into the snack bar where several women were cleaning up after the game. Michael kept crying and bleeding as the women tended to him.

Meanwhile, Tony could only stand frozen in the spot where he had cracked Michael, even though his buddies scattered. Tony felt bad, and he also knew he was in hot water. Pop had told him several times about the bat—this was not going to be good.

Pop emerged from the snack bar after a few minutes and he looked possessed. He marched over to Tony, bent over and picked up the bat. He then strode a few feet over to the corner of the cinderblock building and began beating the snot out of the blockwork.

Our father fired off twenty of the hardest swings ever taken by a human being as all 6'1" and 225 pounds of *Frankie the Voice* pounded that black and gold aluminum bat with such force that all the other Little Leaguers and their families behind the ballpark remained fixated and fearful.

Pop was snarling and grimacing; he was *furious* that Tony had disobeyed him. Michael would require a trip to the Emergency Room, several stiches and be forced to carry around that black eye for weeks—but in the moment Pop was fucking pissed. With his collar popped and sunglasses in place, he beat that cinderblock with such ferocity that when he turned around and looked at Tony; everyone thought the worst was about to happen.

Instinct took over, and Pop made a mad dash for my brother. As Pop sprinted towards him, Tony took off running as well. Now, father and son were speeding away at full-speed as sixty innocent bystanders could only look-on in shock. *Was this man going to beat his son with the bat? Should someone try to intervene? Should someone call the cops?*

Michael was still being tended to, as my father chased after Tony for three blocks, flailing the bat around, cursing and shouting. Pop finally backed off, but not before throwing the bat in Tony's direction. He was disgusted and angry as he marched back to check on Michael.

Tony didn't sleep at home for two nights after that. He hid behind someone's garage for hours after Pop gave-up chase, until Aunt Teresa found him later that night. She kept him at her house until Pop calmed down.

The rage of that night, not even a week gone bye, accompanied my father as he left Mom to wait in his GMC Jimmy, and walked into the lawyer's office. Pop had called ahead to alert the attorney that he was coming, but when he arrived he is told by the young secretary that the lawyer is just finishing up a few phone calls. Pop says, "Okay, but I can't be here all day."

The secretary nods her head, but twenty minutes go by and still no lawyer. Pop speaks up. "Miss, excuse me, but what's goin' on?" Once again she apologizes, and says it shouldn't be much longer.

Twenty minutes turns into forty minutes, forty minutes turns into an hour and my father is *seething*. He thought of walking out a half hour ago, but that would almost definitely mean another day wasted when he would have to drive out here again. Giving away his land was turning into an expensive endeavor indeed.

After an hour and twenty minutes of stewing in the waiting area, the secretary finally tells my father that he can go in and see the attorney. Pop walks in, ready for a meeting. Gianni the Plumber had said the lawyer needed to discuss several details, in addition to requiring his signature on several forms; but it was not to be.

Not a moment after Pop sits down, does the lawyer casually and arrogantly toss a small stack of forms, and a pen, in front of my father. He didn't offer Pop his hand to shake, and doesn't bother looking my father in the face when he tells him where to sign the forms. This is not what Pop expected, but he does as he is told and signs the paperwork. The moment he is done with the pen, the lawyer gathers up the forms and says, "That's it. You can go."

"That's it?" My father asks.

"Yeah, you can go."

"I drove all the way out here for this? You made me sit around for an hour and twenty minutes when you could have had these forms ready and waiting for me with your secretary?"

The lawyer is dismissive. He says the real problem is the fact that Pop can't afford to pay Gianni the cash he owes him. "I'm doing his uncle a favor with this land transfer bullshit. So don't sit there and tell me how to run my office. If you were a real businessman, none of this would be happenin' anyway."

Pop is in shock. He thought he was doing the right thing by offering Gianni the land instead of not paying him at all. This is not the reception he expected. The lawyer is unmoved and coolly shows Pop the door. My father hesitantly walks out of the office, he is more in shock than anger. But the minute he gets back into his truck, the boil begins.

First, Mom doesn't acknowledge his presence when he slides into the Jimmy. She is yet again, trapped inside herself—lost in the twists and turns of her paperback novel.

Next, Pop notices the ruby ring on my mother's finger and takes a deep breath. None of this is what he wanted for his life. Internally, the boil keeps building, Pop is about to explode. For twenty years my father has practiced a Blue Collar Honor. He truly believed a man's handshake was his signature, so for this lawyer to not even offer him the common decency of a handshake scorched my father to the core. The way that attorney tossed those forms in front him gnawed at Pop's patience. After only a few moments, he gets out of the truck, slams the door behind him, *bang*, and marches back towards the lawyer's office. My mother is startled by the violent door slam, but she can only watch my father as he marches back inside the office door. Once inside, Pop storms past the innocent secretary who squeals "Sir, you can't just go in there! *Sir! Sir!*"

My father throws open the door to the lawyer's personal office, strides over to his desk, leans in across the tabletop, points his finger in the attorney's face and says, "If I had a gun, I'd put a bullet in your fuckin' head!"

The lawyer is speechless. The same arrogant attorney from only a few minutes ago is staring up at my father's Mafia mystique. Rather than barking back, the lawyer can only sit there and blink. Before he has the chance to respond, Pop turns on his heel and marches out just as quickly as he stormed in. This is the third time my father has threatened to end a man's life; this is the third time *Frankie the Voice* has flirted with fire.

If it wasn't for his three sons, Pop would surely walk away from his wife, his business and his miserable housing development. He would leave the shores of New Jersey for the sunshine of Costa Rica where he would fish his days away, with a bevy of young Latin girls vying to keep him company each night.

Instead, the boy with too many aptitudes has turned into a caged animal, trapped inside a life he never saw coming.

32

When Mom was a teenager, Babbo thought nothing of spending the evening at the kitchen table pouring himself shots of whisky between sipping on glasses of his homemade wine. Once Uncle Nick got married and moved out to start his own family, Babbo felt more freedom to get plastered drunk and fire insults at Nonna in Italian as she cleaned up after dinner.

When he tired of insulting his wife, Babbo would turn his attention to my teenage mother. He would tell Mom how much he wished he was dead, so he wouldn't have to see her ugly face anymore. He wouldn't say that he wished *she* was dead—but rather—"I hope I drop'pa dead. I no wanna see you ug'alee face no more."

Slurring his words, Babbo would then become teary-eyed as he told Mom how much he wished his two dead sons were sitting there by his side. "They dee'serve'a be 'live," he would say. "Not'a you. You no dee'serve'a nothin'...."

These sort of comments—this sort of behavior—coming from her own father, continued into Mom's adulthood, and left a lasting impression on her. When mixed with the varying forms of sexual abuse she suffered as a child, it's no wonder Mom would have felt more comfortable in a marriage with my cousin's *gavone* of a husband than with someone who "tolerated" her behavior because he suffered from a high threshold for pain.

Mom only had a brief brush with a positive male influence as an adolescent, and it was because of athletics. As a freshman in high school, my mother played volleyball and batted cleanup for her championship softball squad—splitting time between first base and catcher. Her coach was a forty-seven year old American insurance salesman, whom Mom adored.

Everybody called him Coach John. He was full of encouragement and always quick to offer a "pick-me-up." Mom began to fantasize what life would be like if Coach John were her father. She was envious of how well he treated his three daughters. On the field, she hustled and went the extra mile in order to earn his approval.

Her sophomore year she went out for Track and Field, and at Coach John's request, tried her hand at throwing the javelin. The coach had seen her strong arm on the softball diamond, and as expected, Mom became one of the best female javelin throwers in the area.

Yet, Coach John didn't know enough about proper javelin technique to take Mom to the next level. He saw real potential in her; he believed in my mother. So, he talked to her about bringing in a specialist, someone who could work with her on the nuances of throwing the javelin. Mom gushed at the idea and was bursting at the seams with enthusiasm.

But, as was her luck in this life, Coach John died before any javelin training could begin. Mom was sitting in the cafeteria with a few of her girlfriends when the tragic news made its way through the school.

Coach John was dead—heart attack, forty-nine years old, father of four. Mom couldn't believe it. She was devastated.

For two years, she looked forward to the daily practices and weekly track meets as an excuse to spend time with him. He was the only man in her young life who offered support instead of abuse. Mom cried and cried when she heard the news, which was odd for her, since concealing her emotions was part of The Cover-Up.

One thing was clear though—her sense of hope and refuge was gone. She clipped his obituary from the newspaper, and kept it for the rest of her life. Mom stopped playing sports after that—for they were a reminder of the heroic father figure she had lost.

In the summer of 1993, the Philadelphia Phillies play great baseball. They spend the entire season in first place, win the National League East, and eventually go all the way to the World Series. Even though Mom has been up and down since Easter, my brothers and I beg our parents to take us to Phillies' games every chance we get.

Mom and Pop like the Phillies just fine. They happily take us to Veteran's Stadium, in South Philadelphia, every couple of weeks. There, we purchase General Admission tickets and sit in the 700 level right behind home plate.

After the game, we always ask our parents to let us go down to the tunnel where the players leave the locker room, to head out towards their cars. Only star players like Lenny Dykstra and Darren Dalton quickly walk past the crowd of autograph seekers, without stopping to sign a single ball or glove.

I'm sixteen years old, and I know everything there is to know about the Philadelphia Phillies. Like a lot of kids, it's my dream to one day play in the Major Leagues.

Standing along the tunnel, calling out each player's name in hopes of getting their autograph, I learn something from a backup outfielder with olive skin and dark hair named Ruben Amaro, Jr.

Ruben Amaro, Jr., is not a star player. Yet, he is the only one of the Phillies who literally stops and politely signs everyone's autograph. Maybe it is because he was born and raised in Philadelphia, or maybe it is because his dad played for the Phillies back in the 1960's. But the kindness he shows my brothers and me, by standing there and signing his autograph while chatting with us for a few moments, causes Pop to say, "You see that, boys?" Amaro, Jr. is moving away from us, towards other kids along the tunnel, "That's a real class act. Look at all the guys who walked past us without even a wave of recognition. Frankie, Tony, Michael," he says, "when you guys make it big, remember this night, remember Ruben Amaro, Jr."

Pop has always been preaching Hero School, has always been preparing us for the day we would be men. On the ride home in the Cadillac, after my brothers have fallen asleep, and Mom dozes off in the front seat, Dad brings up Amaro again, and uses what happened tonight as a lesson on how to be a hero. He whispers, "Ruben may not be as good as some of them other guys, but he has greatness in him—he *gets* it. Did you see the way your brothers lit up when he stopped and chatted with them? That's what I'm talkin' about, Chichi—sometimes a hero is just an ordinary person who carries himself with class and dignity. That's what I want for you. One day you're gonna be somebody, you're gonna be a star, and when that day comes, don't be a *gavone* like the rest of them bums. Be different, be like Amaro and carry yourself with honor."

33

Weeks after Michael was born, back in November of 1981, my mother had a dream—though some may call it a glimpse into her future. In the dream, my thirty-four year old mother was still in the hospital, recovering from the delivery of a new child. She was being attended to by a young nurse. When my mother kindly asked the nurse to bring baby Michael from the nursery into her room, the nurse innocently asked, "Who is Michael?"

In the dream, Mom chuckled and said, "Oh, sorry, I thought maybe you were in the delivery room. Michael is my son. I gave birth to him yesterday."

The nurse immediately went to check the nursery, only to come back and say, "I'm sorry, but we don't have a boy here named Michael."

"Of course, you do," said my mother.

"No, I believe you're mistaken."

"How can I be mistaken? I gave birth to him yesterday, right here in this very hospital. Now, could you please call somebody else in here so we can straighten this out?"

Only, right then in the dream, my mother saw a different nurse in the open doorway of her room, holding a baby in swaddling clothes. She didn't know it was Michael until the nurse standing at the door spoke his name. That's when Mom pointed at the doorway and said, "*That's* my son. See? The nurse standing by the door has my son."

Yet, the nurse in her room said, "Now, I already told you, we don't have any babies here named Michael."

"But she just said his name!"

"I'm sorry," the nurse reiterated, "but that's not your baby."

Well, my mother had heard enough. She started to get out of her hospital bed. Only the nurse tried to restrain her, but Mom was strong and kept struggling to stand. In moments, several male orderlies arrived to assist her in pinning my mother down. As all this took place, Mom saw the nurse who was holding Michael in her arms walk away down the hall. As she struggled with the attending nurse and the male orderlies, she screamed, *"You're not going to keep me from my son! You're not going to keep me from my son!"*

In the dream, she managed to wiggle her right hand free, and cocked her arm back as if to punch one of the orderlies in the face. That's when she woke up out of the dream—with that punch—because in actuality, she was lying beside my father in bed, at our old house. Her dream punch, turned into a *real* punch, as she landed a direct shot, without warning, to my father's right eye. Sound asleep in the dark, he screamed, *"My pupil! My pupil!"*

Just as Mom landed her punch, my parents' bed erupted into a sea of chaotic sheets. Pop flailed around, covering his eye, and frantically scrambling to defend himself. Meanwhile, my mother struggled to get her bearings. *Where was she? What just happened?*

Once my father realized that Mom was the one who hit him, and not some intruder, he threw her out of the bedroom, and locked the door. He couldn't make sense of her explanation, that she had had a nightmare, and they were trying to take Michael away. All he knew was his wife had punched him in the eye, in the middle of the night, for no reason.

Immediately after being kicked out of her bedroom, Mom checked the crib where Michael normally slept and found him there safe and sound. Relieved, she picked him up, and held him to her bosom.

"Migalooch," she softly whispered to him. "It was just a dream, honey. Just a dream...."

Twelve and a half years after that dream, in the spring of 1994, Mom is hobbling around with a cast on her left leg. A few days ago she was playing videogames for so long, sitting Indian style on the floor, that she allowed her legs to fall asleep. When she tried standing up, her foot was so numb that Mom stumbled, and broke her ankle.

Since it's hard for my mother to get around, Grandmom and Aunt Ellen come over to assist her with household chores. It's a weeknight, and I have an away baseball game, while Pop has to coach Michael's team in Little League.

Tony doesn't have a game, so he is home watching ESPN, while Mom, Grandmom and Aunt Ellen sit in the kitchen. From what they tell me later, my mother is antsy, and starts hobbling around the kitchen complaining about the cast.

"I want this stupid thing off my leg," she says.

"Ann, just give it a couple weeks, that's all. It won't be long."

"Easy for you to say, Ellen, you can drive if you want to. I can't with this stupid thing on my leg. I feel like a prisoner, I want to go down to the ballfield and watch Michael play."

"Well, we can go. I'll take you. What time does the game start?"

Mom doesn't answer. Instead she starts going through the drawers searching for something.

"Ann, what are you looking for?"

At that, Mom spins back around with a knife in her hand.

"Ann, what are you going to do with that?"

"I'm going to cut this stupid thing off my leg."

"You can't do that!"

"Oh, no?"

"No, you'll hurt yourself."

Mom takes the knife, and starts to saw through her cast. Tony hears the commotion in the kitchen, and pokes his head in, "Mom, what are you doing?"

"I want the cast off, and I want it off now!"

"Mom, you're gonna hurt yourself."

Aunt Ellen and Grandmom plead with her.

"Ann, you're being ridiculous. Come on! You want to go to the game? Let's go!"

"You think I'm that dumb, Ellen?"

"What are you talking about?"

"You think I don't know about the conspiracy?"

"What?"

"I know all about it. The whole town is involved, isn't it? You too, Ellen."

"Ann!"

"And you say you're my friend?"

"Ann! What conspiracy?"

"You're just as bad as the rest of them! Everybody is against me! Frank has all of them against me—the police, the doctors, even my friends."

"Ann, calm down!"

Tony tries calling Pop on his cellular phone, but gets no answer. He hangs up and calls Uncle Bobby who lives across town and asks him to come over since Mom won't stop trying to saw her cast off, while ranting about The Conspiracy. Uncle Bobby shows up just as Mom yells at Grandmom for having suggested that she take a pill to calm down.

"You think I'm going to fall for that? It's poison! You want me dead! You've always wanted me dead! You think I'm going to take one of your pills?"

"Ann, calm down. It's not poison. C'mon, what's the matter?"

Uncle Bobby tries to talk some sense into her, but she won't listen. He decides to call Mom's doctor, and the receptionist advises him to take my mother to the Emergency Room if she continues to carry on. When my uncle hangs up, he finds Tony and Mom fighting for control of the car keys. They're standing in the foyer, each with their index fingers around the key chain, pulling in either direction.

"Tony, give me the keys!"

"Mom, you can't drive!"

"Give me the keys!"

"No!"

"Give me the fucking keys!"

"No!"

Tony finally yanks them away from her, but she goes back for the knife.

"I want this thing off my leg!"

"Let's go down to the hospital," Uncle Bobby says.

"No, I'm going down to get Michael! They won't take my kids from me! They won't do it!"

"Ann, if you want the cast off, I'll help you. But we have to go to the hospital."

"I don't want to go to the hospital."

"Well, there's no other way to get the cast off."

Just then, Pop walks through the front door. Tony finally got him on the phone and told him what was going on. So Pop left Michael's baseball game before it ended.

After twenty more minutes of arguing about the cast and The Conspiracy, Pop and Uncle Bobby convince Mom to go to the ER. The only way Mom would finally agree to go was if Pop promised that he would take her down to the ballfield afterwards to see Michael.

They walk into the Emergency Room as darkness falls. Pop signs her in, and fills out the necessary paperwork as a nurse begins to check Mom's vital signs. Only, my mother says, "Get away from me!"

"Ma'am, I need to check your vitals."

"You're trying to keep me from my kids!"

"Ma'am, I have no idea what you're talking about."

"Yes you do! You're in on it!"

"No ma'am, really I don't...."

"Oh shut up, and get away from me!"

"Ma'am, please...."

"No, you know what? Let me have a phone! Do you have a phone?"

"A phone?"

"Yeah, a phone!"

"You want to make a call? Well, there's one right there on the wall."

Mom picks up the receiver and dials our house number, but the call won't go through. She hangs up and spins towards the nurse. "I told you, you were in on this!"

"Ma'am, what are you talking about?"

"The call wouldn't go through."

"That's because you have to dial nine to get an outside line."

"Well, why didn't you tell me that before?"

She picks up the phone again, dials nine, then our house number, and—to everyone's astonishment—goes lucid. By now Michael is home and Mom's voice and demeanor become *completely normal* the moment my brother answers the phone.

"Hello Michael," she says. "How was your game, sweetheart? You hit a homerun? Wow, that's my boy. What's that? Yeah, I'm with Daddy and Uncle Bobby. We're coming home soon. I'll see you in a minute, okay, honey?"

The moment Mom hangs up, she reverts back to being belligerent and paranoid. When the nurse says, "Ma'am, I need you to come back with us to get an x-ray of your foot."

Mom says, "No, you're not taking me back there. I want the x-ray machine brought out here."

"I'm afraid that's impossible."

"Well, I'm not going back there!"

Mom turns and goes after Uncle Bobby who has the keys to the Cadillac. "Bob," she says, "I'm not going back there for any x-rays, so c'mon, let's go home—gimme the keys."

"Ann, why don't you let them take some x-rays? It isn't good for you to be walking around without your crutches."

"Bob, gimme the keys! You're not keeping me from my boys!"

"Ann, I don't want to keep you from your boys. But they need to x-ray your foot. Afterwards, we can go home and see the boys."

"You know, I never would'a suspected you, Bob. I never would'a guessed that Frank could turn you against me. Now gimme the keys!"

"Ann, I can't do that."

"Fine! You have something of mine, then I'll take something of yours!"

She tears Uncle Bobby's baseball hat off, and throws it across the room where it lands in a lady's lap. Mom starts wrestling with Uncle Bobby for the keys, only to give-up and hobble out of the ER determined to walk the several miles home. Uncle Bobby follows her outside.

"Ann, where are you going?"

"I'm going to get my sons. No one is going to keep me from my sons!"

"Ann, nobody wants to keep you from your sons!"

Just then, an empty ambulance pulls up—and Mom goes lucid again. She says to the ambulance driver, "Sir, this man has my car keys, and he will not give them to me. Would you please call security?"

Uncle Bobby is stunned. Utterly embarrassed, he tries to defend himself, "That's not true," he says to the driver. "She's here for her foot, and she isn't being honest."

The driver is confused, but a moment later, Pop comes out of the ER and says, "Ann, you wanna go home? *Fine!* Let's go home! Forget the x-ray shit, let's go!"

213

Soon, the three of them get into the Cadillac, Uncle Bobby in the backseat; Mom is in the passenger seat; and Pop is behind the wheel. Only when my father puts the key into the ignition, Mom yanks it out.

"I'm not going with *you!* There is something wrong here. You're taking me away from my kids!"

"*Jesus Christ, Ann!* We're not taking you away from your kids! Enough already!"

"Yes you are, Frank, and you even got Bob to go along with it, which I still can't believe!"

"Ann, we're sitting in the Cadillac, in the middle of the Emergency Room driveway. We're not trying to take you away from the boys. We're trying to help you. Now, will you stop being so irrational? You wanna go home? Let's go home!"

At that, she and Pop get into a tug-o-war over the keys. Only, my father realizes he'll have to either hurt her or back off. By now, several police cars arrive. They come over to the car window, and tell Mom that she has to give up the car keys immediately. The car needs to be moved from the Emergency Room driveway—this area is only for ambulances. Mom lowers the window just a little, "Officer, I don't wanna hear it. I'm not giving up the keys. I'm not moving the car, and that's that!"

The policeman remains calm, and nods his head. He can see Pop over Mom's shoulder, giving him a look that says, *my wife isn't well, please let's not escalate things. Let's find some peaceful way to end this.* The officer takes my father's cue, and gives Mom two choices. She can either give up the car keys so the Cadillac can be moved, or she can stay inside and get towed away.

"The car will be impounded," he says, "and you'll spend the night in jail."

Mom ignores the officer's offers; it is impossible to reason with her.

Uncle Bobby notices that as Mom waves her hands around, ranting and raving, she's holding most of the keys in her hand, but the ignition key is loosely flopping around.

As she turns to tell the police more of her story, Uncle Bobby grabs the loose ignition key, and yanks the rest of the keys out of her hand. Mom spins around, "Thanks Bob, thanks a lot! I can't believe you! How could you do that to me?"

Mom is *super* pissed.

She opens the door and hobbles back into the ER. The police follow her inside. Now, there are three policemen, the doctor in charge of the ER, and two security guards telling Mom she needs to calm down, or they're going to bring out the straight jacket. She turns to the cops, the guards, and the head doctor and starts yelling at them, "You're all in on it! You're all trying to keep me away from my kids!"

The doctor shakes his head and says, "Ma'am, I'm sorry, but this is it. We've given you all the chances we can."

He motions for the two security guards to grab a hold of Mom. They wrestle with her, and forcibly put her in a straightjacket, then strap her onto a gurney as she kicks and screams.

Pop and Uncle Bobby can only stand by and watch as the security guards begin to wheel her away. Mom can be heard throughout the ER shouting, *"You're not going to keep me from my kids! You're not going to keep me from my kids! You're not going to keep me from my kids!"*

After the incident in the Emergency Room, Mom spends the next several days in the Psychiatric Unit of the Atlantic City Medical Center where Pop and I go visit her. As we speak to the receptionist behind the counter, she asks, "Are you here for the Martinez family in Post-Op?"

Pop smiles and says, "No, no, we're here to see my wife. She should be in the Psych Unit."

"Oh," says the receptionist. I can tell by the way she says *oh,* that we'd be better off going up to Post-Op as Martinez men, rather than to the Psych Unit as us.

We walk through a myriad of long, quiet hallways until we find another receptionist who tells us Mom is just about to wrap up a group session in the room right behind us. We turn around and through an open doorway, can see her sitting in the middle of a half-moon configuration of desks with other patients in the unit. In the middle of the half-moon configuration, sits a man in a white lab coat, whom I know must be the doctor.

When my eyes fall on Mom, I want to look away. She doesn't know I can see her. I wish Pop and I could turn around and go back home. This feels like a movie—like a sad, freaky movie, shot in black and white, with no soundtrack or editing, where the other patients, the receptionists, even the long, quiet hallways are only here to enhance the sadness. It's like they all waited for us to show up, so they could scurry into position when the director yells, *action!* Only I know that Mom isn't acting. The other patients in the half-moon seem like extras to me who are only here for the moment until the director yells, *cut!* But Mom seems like she'll be here for life.

I'm just about to lean over and say, *Pop, let's forget this and go home.* But the receptionist is moving out from behind her desk, knocking on the open door and saying, "Excuse me, Doctor, but we have some visitors for Ann."

He looks over at her, smiles at us and says, "Great, send them right in." Pop and I smile back before slowly working our way through all the stares from all the patients so lost and distant; it scares me. We both kiss Mom on the cheek—but she looks dazed—like she doesn't know who we are. I don't feel right standing there with everybody gawking at us. I think the doctor can sense my embarrassment because he gently says that Mom can leave the group and go with us to the visiting area. Mom still has her cast on, so Pop offers her his arm, as we head towards the visiting area. There, I sit in a chair by the cold white wall and feel guilty over this movie where my mother is in the Psychiatric Unit of the Atlantic City Medical Center.

As Pop tries to make small talk, I think back almost five years to that night when we were coming home from Nonna's and Mom had that episode in the Cadillac. I think about how scared my brothers and I were, and how Nonna screeched at us in Italian to stop singing. I was only twelve when that happened. But as I listen to Mom tell Pop about the other people in her group, I can't help but remember that night as the first time I felt *afraid* for her.

For my father, though, I know the first time he knew something was wrong was when he told Mom about Gail. He expected her to slap him or get in his face hollering and screaming. Instead, the woman he watched gamble for nearly a decade, while arrogantly sleeping on the couch night after night, ran out of their master bedroom, down the stairs and hid behind one of the couches in the living room, curled up in a fetal position.

That's when Pop first thought something psychologically was wrong with Mom. He went downstairs expecting to fight, only to find himself comforting his wife and talking her out of the fetal position.

My father's friends have started encouraging him to get divorced. They say he's crazy to stay married to Mom. After all, what is he getting out of it? No housework, no sex, not even a partner who cares to shower, or change her clothes each day. They tell him that he's still young—only forty-five—and that he should find somebody nice and healthy.

In particular, Aunt Ellen and Aunt Teresa notice that Mom sometimes likes to feign being ill. Complaining of stomach pains, so that Pop would tend to her. They picked up on this routine during a weeklong group getaway to the Outer Banks. There they watched Mom transform into a bedridden wife the moment the guys mentioned a possible day of golf or fishing without the ladies.

The sisters say Pop should really consider a divorce, they feel he is being toyed with by Mom, but Pop says the image of his wife as a little girl in that greenhouse—makes him unable to get divorced. He says he can't leave her, not that he's happy, mind you, but he just can't give up and abandon her. Besides, he adds, "We're Italian, and Italians don't get divorced...."

It's more than being Italian, though, that causes my father to stay. He stays because he is different. I know I'm only sixteen, but as I sit here in my chair, by the cold white wall, feeling guilty, I tell myself that Pop stays married to Mom because he gave his word. He may not go to church anymore, or even believe that Jesus rose from the dead, but he made a promise to my mother, for better or for worse, in sickness and in health. Despite his years with Gail, he stays with Mom because he gave his word.

The night she was strapped to the gurney, Pop came home after several anxious and embarrassing hours at the ER. He poured himself a glass of wine, broke out the sopresatta, a little cheese, dipped some bread in a plate of olive oil, sat at the kitchen table, and stared out the window at Atlantic City glimmering across the meadows. He didn't say a word, but I could tell what he was doing. He was looking for the life lessons in all of this.

As I sit in my chair by the cold white wall feeling guilty, Pop can tell I'm anxious and too quiet. He tries to include me in the sluggish and sad conversation he's having with my mother, but I don't know what to say. That's when Pop gives me the look with a little twinkle in his eye. It's his Hero School look with his eyebrows rising and falling with every word. It's his way of saying *don't take this so seriously, Cheech*, like he's pleading with me to lighten up.

The look says, *I know it's tough, but we got to thank God for what we have. You know what I mean, Chichi? Some things we have control over, but other things we've got to deal with. Your mother had a rough childhood, and she's never dealt with it. So, we need to be strong, okay? We need to stay strong for your mother.*

34

Now that Mom is home after her brief stay in the Psychiatric Unit, she will sit in the Cadillac, engine off, parked in the driveway, for anywhere from forty minutes to three hours. The first time she does this, my father goes outside, and knocks on the driver's side window to see what she is doing alone in the Cadillac without a cellular phone, staring out the windshield, smoking a cigarette—talking aloud to no one at all.

It would make sense if Mom wanted to sit on the back deck at dusk with a glass of lemonade and watch the fireflies zigzag here and there above the bay. Even wanting to curl up under a blanket in her bedroom during a thunderstorm, to study the lightning bolts as they crash into the meadows would be quality alone time. But to sit in the Cadillac, like a hypnotized zombie, for hours at a time, makes no sense to any of us.

At night, we either stand in the foyer, or the living room, and look out at Mom sitting motionless in the driver's seat waiting for the bright orange of her cigarette to light up so we know she has taken a drag, and is still alive. There's nothing for her to look at out there—but our two gray garage doors. So sometimes, one of us will flash the porch lights to let her know we want her to come inside, but she never flashes the headlights of the Cadillac to let us know she saw the signal.

It's not that we really want her to come inside exactly; it's just we don't want her alone in the car, with only her thoughts to keep her company. If I had to guess, I'd say Mom is probably talking to herself about The Conspiracy—the same conspiracy that caused her to lose it in the Emergency Room, screaming about not being taken away from her kids. It was that paranoia that landed her in the Psychiatric Unit at the Atlantic City Medical Center for a week. I'm sure it's what drives her self-talk in the Cadillac, cigarette after cigarette, parked in the driveway, a million miles away.

In addition to sitting in the Cadillac, working on The Conspiracy, Mom has started to place these eerie phone calls to Aunt Ellen and Aunt Teresa at all hours of the night. She doesn't call them at three in the morning to say hello or gossip about a mutual friend; she calls to ask them a question. Mom calmly dials their phone numbers, and patiently waits for them to answer in a groggy, half-coherent voice before softly whispering the words, "What's happening to me?"

Before Aunt Ellen or Aunt Teresa have a chance to respond, Mom hangs up, only to call back a few nights later, and repeat herself in that odd, mysterious whisper, "What's happening to me?"

When the sisters tell Pop about the late-night phone calls, and the eerie feeling it gives them, it's like a part of my mother knows she is losing her mind; like she knows her life shouldn't be turning out this way. Somewhere inside of her, lives that same girl who looked out for her nieces and nephews years ago, the one who bought Aunt Colomba and her four children that triplex, so they could get away from Babbo. She is the one who shoved Babbo to the ground after he wouldn't stop teasing my cousin, Alex. Mom still has that woman inside of her, but she is lost, though. Lost in that movie I "saw" the day I went to visit her in the Psych Unit. That sad, freaky movie, shot in black and white, with no soundtrack or editing, where everything and everyone enhanced the sadness. I remember feeling like all of the other patients were extras, just waiting for the director to yell, *cut!* Yet, Mom seems destined to remain stuck in that screenplay for the rest of her life.

Uncle Bruno is Pop's brother. If people say my father is in the Mafia, they say Uncle Bruno is a priest without the collar because he's the nicest, sweetest, most soft-spoken person they've ever met.

If Pop boldly wears his ethnicity and masculinity on each sleeve, Uncle Bruno has them both neatly tucked away. Many people fail to realize the two are even brothers because they couldn't be more different.

My father makes his living working outside, so he is dark, and has that year-round tan. He is broader in the shoulders, has that broken nose, tough weathered hands, and his pencil thin mustache.

Uncle Bruno earns his money behind a piano. He was never in the army, never played sports, and never hung-out in Ducktown with those gangsters. So, he doesn't project that Italian machismo that my father proudly carries around. Uncle Bruno always wanted to be a priest, except he fell-in-love with music, married his high school sweetheart, and went to work in the casinos as a bandleader.

He fronts a very successful and well-known eight-piece band, playing weddings, parties, and casino lounges with Aunt Sofia, his female vocalist. Pop still sings when they need Italian songs, but shooting hoops in our driveway, my brothers and I can clearly hear Uncle Bruno and his band rehearsing across the street. They play everything from Motown to Big Band to C & C Music Factory.

Sometimes, I go with Uncle Bruno on his gigs to help him set-up the equipment. I watch from the wings during their performances where on breaks he tells me to, "Listen for the music, inside the music."

"Frankie," he says, "listen to the way the drummer is playing against the bass, or how the saxophone cuts through the melody."

I try to listen, but I never get it.

Tonight, Uncle Bruno isn't on stage; he is on the phone talking to my mother. She is sitting in our kitchen, smoking a cigarette, accusing my uncle of making a documentary about her; Mom's conspiracy theories are spinning out of control.

"Oh, come on, Bruno," she says into the phone. "Don't deny it. I know what you're doing. You have all the connections in showbiz. If anybody can make it happen, you can. Does Bridgid know about this little side business of yours? Does she know how you're exploiting those close to you? Because I can't believe it, Bruno, a documentary! I thought you were different than that, but I guess you're just like Frank. I guess you're just like your brother. He's been against me for years, and now I see where your loyalty lies."

She falls quiet for a moment, before saying, "Oh, please, you know I'm right."

As soon as she hangs up, Mom stabs her cigarette into the ashtray, looks up at me and says, "Frankie, do you believe Uncle Bruno is making a documentary about me?"

"Mom, he's not making a documentary about you."

"Frankie, he most certainly is."

"Mom, he's a musician, not a filmmaker. Besides, that's just crazy."

"I am not crazy."

"I didn't say *you* were crazy. I said what you *said* was crazy."

"Frankie, why doesn't anybody ever see things my way? If your father was saying something like this, you'd be the first one to agree with him."

"Mom, Pop would never say anything like that. It doesn't make any sense. You're paranoid. Uncle Bruno doesn't need to make a documentary about you. Listen to yourself!"

"Oh, Frankie..."

My mother isn't making any sense. She has it all wrong. My uncle has no desire or ability to make a documentary about anyone—let alone his lost, and helpless sister-in-law. He is a band leader. That is what he does—nothing more and nothing less. Mom's allegations are proof of just how far she has slipped.

It seems as though delusions and fantasies rule her world now. She not only fears her dead father at every turn, but her sense of reality has become totally distorted.

35

Pop says, "Chichi, didja ever notice that most of the benches along the Boardwalk in AC face the city—and not the ocean? That's because the Atlantic City Boardwalk has always been seen as a stage, a magical place where you can pretend to be more than you are."

When I hear him say that, I know that's why my father has always loved Atlantic City--for its' magic. It has always been different from the other seashore towns that dot the Jersey coast: Asbury Park, Wildwood, Seaside Heights and Cape May, to name a few. In those towns, you get what you would expect—sunbathing, pizza parlors, ice cream shops and amusement rides.

But Atlantic City has always been "Hollywood." When Pop was a kid, AC was Times Square; it was glitzy, and Victorian, grandiose and glamorous, a place where anything and everything could happen. My father always talks about the Old Atlantic City, and how great the town was forty years ago when Frank Sinatra and Dean Martin regularly played the 500 Club. Pop used to love coming down from Philadelphia for the summer to stay at his grandmother's house on *Arkansas* Avenue, for AC was his personal paradise.

He talks about the Old Atlantic City so much that I try to imagine what it must have been like because the "new" city I know is dirty and dangerous with bums snoozing on street corners, and seagulls eating trash on the Boardwalk. In a way, this idea of a "new" and "old" Atlantic City reminds me of Mom.

I have all these wonderful memories of her when she was young and full of charm. There were the countless afternoons when my brothers and I rode our bikes around the neighborhood and Mom would call us home, her voice echoing across the open lawns, *"Frankie, Tony, Michael!"* That was our cue—it was time for dinner, or a snack, or Mom just wanted to lay eyes on us and make sure we were alright.

Sometimes—after we pedaled home—Mom would greet us at the door with a big grin and usher us inside. In the kitchen she would have sliced tomatoes and mozzarella drizzled in olive oil with salt, pepper, and oregano sprinkled on top. Other days, it would be prosciutto with pieces of melon—or delicious, but simple—peanut butter and jelly sandwiches.

Mom instinctively knew how to take care of her boys, and fun was her middle name. Halloween and Easter were the perfect excuses to lavish us with the latest costumes, or fancy candies—and she always went above and beyond for our birthdays. Baking our favorite cake, serving ice cream and enjoying the big family parties she organized, as much as we did. We always had fun on our birthdays and Mom always enjoyed putting a smile on our faces, but the Christmas Season was her favorite.

We almost always received everything on our Christmas Lists. Mom would wrap the gifts herself, stashing them in the big walk-in closet she and Pop shared in their master bedroom.

Our Christmas mornings were a not so distant cousin to those magical Sunday mornings with Pavarotti and pancakes. Mom would be in her green housecoat, Pop his gray robe, and the two of them would flirt and laugh as we opened our presents, with Frank Sinatra and Andy Williams serenading us with Christmas carols.

During the school year, Mom was a whiz with our schoolwork; never shying away from helping us with book reports and poster projects. She was a woman in love with her sons, but the Mom I know now is so different, it's like she's not even the same person. I tell myself that's what Atlantic City is like for Pop—a place full of glorious memories that only slightly resembles its storied past. Just like the Atlantic City of the 1960's and 70's, my mother has become a dirty ghetto suspended in time.

The only difference is—gambling came along to "save" Atlantic City. In the nearly twenty years since that referendum passed, allowing casino gambling along the Boardwalk and in the Marina District of Atlantic City, the town has continually *strived* to resurrect itself. Despite the corruption, the filth and the crime—it regularly draws upwards of thirty million visitors yearly. It may not be the Old Atlantic City, but this new version hasn't given-up on itself—whereas my "new" mother continues to languish. She has become a mysteriously haunted creature simultaneously filled with grandiose potential, yet loaded with an incredible amount of paranoia and self-generated misery.

My father's eyes twitch because of this "new" Mom. Michael has to run to Aunt Teresa's because of this "new" Mom. And we're held hostage, on a daily basis, by The Routine of this "new" Mom. Unlike that

Monopoly board across the meadows, there will be no referendum passed to save my mother. We missed our chance last spring when Pop was going to have Mom admitted into the Institute of Mental Health at the University of Pennsylvania. That was her shot at redemption.

Now, her psyche perpetually condemns us, for her majestic potential remains padlocked and boarded up behind the dysfunctional walls of her past. Everything inside me says, my mother is Atlantic City.

I've been working weekends with my Uncle Bobby as a disc jockey's assistant. Uncle Bobby is Aunt Sofia's husband. He's in his late twenties and is a full-time craps dealer at Resorts Casino though he operates a small DJ business on the side. He used to be a disc jockey on the radio in Pennsylvania, but now he mostly works wedding receptions and anniversary parties.

For the most part, my job is pretty easy. I help him unload and organize the equipment, set-up the turntables, speakers and cases upon cases of music. I also assist with the sound-check, and go over the names of the bridal party we have to announce before slipping into my tuxedo right before cocktail hour.

Once the party begins, I stay in the background retrieving songs Uncle Bobby wants to play by rifling through the cases of albums and compact discs. When the song is over, Uncle Bobby has me file the record back in the case where I found it. Sometimes I have to monitor the volume when he takes a bathroom break or spends a few minutes talking to the bride and groom. There are other times I have to play a few songs myself, while Uncle Bobby gets cornered by a drunken guest who insists on grabbing the microphone to make a special shout-out dedication.

When the party is over, I help load-out. That's the job. It's that easy.

What isn't easy is watching all of those people get married. Even though my father wants me to carry myself with honor, I know when I get married, I don't want my mother there. The way I see it, Mom doesn't deserve to be at my wedding. When I watch the traditional 'mother-son dance,' I know that will never be she and me, at least if things stay the same. Why would I want to dance with her? Ever since she got fired from the nursing home years ago, her behavior has been on a slow and steady decline into oblivion.

By the spring of 1994, we don't even know who she is anymore.

When word gets back to Mom's family—about her not being welcome when I get married—as usual, she twists it around so all they hear is, *Frankie hates me, and says I am forbidden to attend his wedding. Why is he doing this to me?*

Edith, my godmother, calls me a few days after hearing the news, and wants to know why I would say something like that to my mother. I take the call on the phone in the kitchen where I sit at the table and say, "Edith, no one in Philly ever sees anything wrong with Mom, but she's not normal. She's up and down, and very hard to deal with."

"How can you say that about your mother?"

"Because it's true."

"That's your father talking."

"No, Edith, she's bizarre. I can't take it anymore."

"What can't you take? Is she too strict with you?"

"Strict?"

"Yeah, you know, demanding, old fashioned?"

"Edith, she's crazy!"

"Frankie, how can you say your mother is crazy? I've never heard anything more disrespectful in my life."

"Edith, she doesn't shower for days! She is always wearing this stupid pink sweatshirt covered in stains, and it's embarrassing. It's like her whole life is spent on the couch with coffee, TV, cigarettes, and her toenail clippers. If we try to say anything, she puts her back up and gets all indignant."

"Well Frankie, nobody likes to be attacked."

"Attacked! Edith, she is aggressive about it. I mean, don't you shower almost everyday? I could see once in a while not having the time to bathe, but four or five days in a row? Sometimes she doesn't shower for a week and a half. Is that normal? Is that my father's fault, too? How 'bout the floor? Isn't it weird that a married woman prefers to sleep on the floor, and not in bed with her husband?"

"Frankie, your father had an affair. If your mother doesn't want to sleep with her husband, that's his own fault."

"But that's why he *had* the affair!"

"Oh, please, you sound like your grandmother. Your mother is a good wife. Your father is just arrogant and chauvinistic. I mean he tried to put your mother away last year."

"No, he didn't."

"Yes, he did. Remember when Nonna and I came down? Had we not done that, your mother might still be locked away."

"No, had you not done that, maybe I'd want her at my wedding. Maybe she wouldn't have been taken away after that scene she caused at the ER. Maybe she'd have a grasp on reality!"

"So, you blame me?"

Taking a few seconds to calm down, I answer, "Yeah, maybe she would'a gotten some help. Maybe we would'a moved on as a family instead of bein' held hostage by her dysfunctional routine. My father's eyes twitch like mad, my brothers have to spend the weekends over friends' houses because our house is falling apart, and all we ever eat anymore is pizza. I'm tired of watching Pop go around and around with her about simple things like showering, changing her clothes, and getting up off the floor to sleep with him in bed. I love my mother, but what you and Nonna did was wrong. She needs help. Pop wasn't trying to put her away, he was trying to fix her so she could come back and stay."

My godmother doesn't like my tone or my message.

She says I'm just a puppet, repeating any and everything my father says. Edith feels sorry for my mother because she feels like Mom is living in a house with four men who are against her.

Aunt Joanne, Mom's sister-in-law, who is married to Uncle Nick, is on the phone. Everybody calls her JoJo, and she is talking to Pop, demanding to know about the movie we're making. I'm in his office, and can only hear his side of the conversation.

"Jo, what are you talking about? What movie?"

He falls silent for a moment, scrunching his eyebrows together, listening to my aunt on the other end of the line, before bursting into a fit of laughter. His face is a picture of shock and amusement.

"You can't be serious," he says into the phone. "Cause that's ridiculous! How could we be making a movie about Ann? Jo, listen to yourself. Do you think we have room down here for a bunch of actors and a film crew? I mean, how could you believe something like that?"

Pop falls silent again. He rubs his mustache with the index finger of his left hand. Listening to my aunt, my father starts shaking his head from side to side, looking at me like, *you won't believe this.*

How could Mom's family *actually* think we're making a movie about her? Aunt JoJo is a nurse, and Uncle Nick is a successful real estate agent. They have to have more common sense than to believe something like that. Pop keeps shaking his head until he starts to speak again. I can tell he's interrupting my aunt by the way he stumbles over her name.

"Jo, Jo, JoJo," he says. "I don't care what Ann told you. We're not making a movie about her. What? No, just listen! Ann accused my brother Bruno of making a documentary about her several weeks ago. What? No, he's not making a documentary about her. C'mon Jo, that's absurd. What? How do I explain it? Well, I know you don't wanna hear this, but I think Ann likes stirring up controversy. I'm not even sure she does it consciously, but it's like it takes her off the hook if she can insinuate things. Like what? How 'bout what happened at the ER? See, you guys live an hour away, and only hear what Ann tells you. She was a mess that day. She claimed there was a conspiracy in town—that I had somehow reached out to the police, the hospital staff, her best friend, my mother and my brother-in-law to keep her away from the boys. She was a belligerent bull. No! No one could talk any sense into her. Several cops got involved with the hospital staff, but she wouldn't calm down, so they finally ordered her restrained. I had to watch these security guards strap my wife to a gurney and take her away. All the while she's hollering, 'No one's gonna keep me away from my sons!' I mean, you're a nurse, JoJo. You must have seen cases like this, where people just *lose* it. I know it doesn't sound like Ann, but that's only 'cause you guys hardly ever see her anymore. When anybody from Philly comes down, she keeps things in check, or tries to, at least. But she was a disaster that day. The thing is, early on, she called home from the ER and went *lucid* over the phone.

She got Michael on the line, and went from belligerent and paranoid to calm and loving, like *that!*" Pop snaps his fingers when he says the word ***that***, only to continue, "JoJo, one minute, she's accusing my mother of trying to poison her, and the next, she's asking Michael about his baseball game. And I mean, it was something to see. The doctors, the nurses, everybody was blown away at her ability to shift gears. That's why I would hope you guys in Philly might give me the benefit of the doubt. Ann's got something super complex going on, so before you believe everything she says, ask yourself if it makes sense. I mean, do you really think I have the time, the money, the ability or even the *desire* to make a movie about my wife?"

Soon, Pop shifts the conversation from the movie to missing the girl he married. He says the girl he married was a sweetheart, who loved him, and wanted nothing more than to have a family—yet, she's nowhere to be found. It's like Pop is educating Aunt JoJo, the way he tells her how Mom acts differently, and how rude, arrogant and slovenly she has become. He says, "Ann acts more like a brutish male drunk than a mother to three boys. She does whatever she wants, whenever she wants, no matter who it hurts or embarrasses."

Pop tells Aunt JoJo that he has spent the last nineteen years of his life trying to talk some sense into my mother, but that she is the most *testa dura* woman he has ever met. He says, "Forget about trying to get through to her, our lives are passing us by. I'm trying to coach the boys in sports, avoid bankruptcy, and push Ann to get help, but she refuses to pull herself together."

My father switches the telephone from one ear to the other, and sighs as he listens to my aunt on the other end of the line. I can't help but think he's right—our lives are passing us by. I just want things to be normal. I don't want to spend Sunday afternoons visiting my mother at the Atlantic City Medical Center. I want to spend Sunday mornings playing golf with her, Pop, and Grandpop at the Atlantic City Country Club. I want to smile. I want to be happy, and I want my mother to break out of The Routine. I break out of my own thoughts when I hear my father starting to speak again.

I can tell their phone call is almost over by the way Pop tells Aunt JoJo what his friends have started saying—he should get divorced. Pop tells my aunt that his friends have seen Mom up close and personal for years now and that they're starting to think she's nothing more than a manipulating control-freak who thrives on attention.

In reality, my mother was drawn to the chaos. For 39 dark years, she had searched for any sign that Babbo loved her. When no sign was found, it broke her heart. Upon his death—emulating his often-times hidden, demented behavior—provided Mom with the elusive illusion that she and Babbo shared an intimate connection. She was a mess, just like her daddy.

We may not be making a movie about Mom, but Aunt Ellen's husband likes to say, "One day, you guys should really write a book about all this. Your lives read like a novel...."

36

My acne is unreal. We have tried everything from hanging my face over a pot of boiling water—with a touch of lemon juice—to smearing Vitamin E from my forehead to my chin. I change my pillowcase nightly, so I'm not laying my cheeks on dirty linens. I scrub my face with organic soap and pore-clearing pads; I even try to pop the blackheads before they turn into full-fledged pimples and have tried so many cleansing gels and creams that I can't remember them all.

But nothing changes.

I don't go to the Junior Prom because my zits are so big and red; I'm too embarrassed to ask anyone. What girl would want to go with me?

Even though I'm not going to the Prom, Aunt Ellen is part of the decoration committee for the "After-Prom," and registers Mom as an assistant decorator. She tells Pop that it'll be good for Mom to get out and do something rather than lay around all day in The Routine.

On the day of the Prom, Aunt Ellen picks up my mother. They both go down to the school to help the other mothers decorate the gymnasium, but Mom refuses to get out of the car.

Aunt Ellen has to battle with her about getting out and going inside. The two friends go around and around until Aunt Ellen literally pulls her out of the car and forces her into the school building. When they finally get to the gym and begin setting up, the other women notice how my mother seems like she's on another planet. They ask Aunt Ellen, "What's wrong with Ann?"

Not long after the prom, Aunt Ellen tells Pop that she feels bad about my acne, and wants to know why we don't try her son Pete's dermatologist. She says, "Pete didn't have acne anywhere near as bad as Frankie, but whenever he broke out, this guy cleared it right up. He's Middle Eastern or something, but he's very good, and I think he's worth a try."

A week later, Pop and I have an appointment with Dr. Ahmad. He takes one look at my face, and my upper back, and shakes his head.

"What have you tried up to this point?"

231

Pop clears his throat, and goes through the litany of scrubs, pads, medications, vitamins, boiling water, lemon juice and blackhead poppers until the doctor stops him and says, "Okay, okay." He slides onto the examining table next to me and says, "I think you and your son ought to consider Acutane."

"What's that?"

"I think it's exactly what you need."

The doctor looks at me and says, "Wouldn't you like to make all of this go away? Wouldn't you like to look in the mirror, and feel good about what you see?"

I want to say, *yes! Of course! I've been dying to look normal!* Instead, I just shrug as the doctor hands my father a brochure on Acutane. He tells us to make sure we go over the long list of side effects so we can make an informed decision, but Pop can't get past that word.

"Side effects? What sorta side effects?"

"Well, Frank will have to submit to a bi-weekly blood test, and may experience anything from dizziness, shortness of breath, bloody stools, chapped lips, dry mouth, blurry vision, erectile dysfunction and/or a variety of other potential and I stress *potential* problems. None of these are likely, especially in a patient as young and as healthy as Frank, but we have to make sure you are aware of the possibilities."

Pop thinks about what the doctor has to say, but remembers that he had acne well into his late twenties, and doesn't want another ten years of this for his eldest son. He looks at me on the examining table and says, "Doc, if you think Acutane is the answer, then we're ready to start."

Dr. Ahmad smiles, and in his nice Middle Eastern way says, "Great, I'll have my receptionist set-up the blood tests, and you should start to see results in a couple of months."

I smile, but I don't believe him.

The only good thing about Prom Season is that I'm finally old enough to get my driver's permit. My brothers are happy that I'll be driving soon, because like me, they're tired of putting their lives at risk every time we ride with Mom. Tony, Michael and I have held our breaths too many times, only to let out a huge sigh of relief after narrowly surviving yet another episode of Mom pulling out in front of oncoming traffic.

Just the other day we were leaving Aunt Teresa's house, waiting at the corner of a busy intersection, when Mom pulled out in front of an oncoming cement truck *for no reason*. We weren't in a rush to get home, and had only just rolled to a stop at the corner, which explains why my brothers and I were so surprised when we felt the Cadillac accelerate and lurch forward. I was in the passenger seat, and as usual, paying very close attention to every detail of Mom's driving. The three of us have grown accustomed to sitting on the edge of our seats, with our eyes fixed on the road, because we never know what's going to happen next. When Pop's driving, we relax and look out the window talking back and forth about this and that. But when we're riding with Mom, we've learned to be on high alert.

Our awareness shot through the roof when we saw that huge cement truck, with its dark red cab and faded gray barrel, barreling towards us. It was like Mom didn't see it. She has worn glasses her whole life, but there was no missing this truck. That's why I think she darted out in front of him on purpose. It's as if she could have cared less—like she was going to pull out and make the truck driver *deal* with it. The same goes for my brothers and me. We were powerless and had to *deal* with her decision, which made me think about that day Pop spoke to Aunt JoJo on the phone about The Movie.

I remember my father telling Aunt JoJo that Mom reminded him of a brutish male drunk who does whatever he wants, whenever he wants, no matter who it may hurt.

My mother could have caused a whole lot of hurt that day, which is why my brothers and I instantly panicked the moment she pulled forward. Tightening our bodies and turning away from the approaching cement truck, we screamed, "*Mom!*"

The three of us braced ourselves for impact, as the truck driver laid on his horn, and slammed on the brakes at the last possible second. We somehow avoided being flattened to death, but if *People* magazine ever did an exposé on "The Worst Driver in America," I have no doubt their story would feature my mother.

Pop says Mom has always been this way. Her first set of wheels was a small, low-riding, English sports car called an MG. He told me a story about Mom, and how she was in Center City Philadelphia one summer day in the late 1960's, and drove her tiny MG *through* Rittenhouse Square. Pop says, "You didn't grow up in Philly, so you wouldn't know. But Rittenhouse Square is a park right off Walnut Street, not far from City Hall. It's full of benches, and wide-open lawns, the sort of place people walk their dogs, or spend their lunch breaks. Anyway, your mother wasn't paying attention to the flow of traffic, and somehow left the street, and drove right into the park. She cudda killed somebody. Later, she told me she thought it odd that people were sitting so close to the road, all she could see were their knees right out the car window. It wasn't until she came up to a statue or a monument blocking her way, that she realized she had driven into a park. But that's your mother, Chichi, always been an oblivious driver."

If *People* magazine ever interviewed me, and asked me to describe Mom's driving style in one word—that's the word I'd use— oblivious. Oblivious is the only way to explain why she so frequently goes up one-way streets, in the wrong direction, or misjudges the distance on a turn so often she ends up bumping into the curb and ruining the Cadillac's tires. Mom's oblivious driving style may explain why she forgets so easily where our friends live.

A lot of our friends' parents have night jobs over in Atlantic City which makes it difficult for them to cart their sons around. As a result, my parents have spent years driving our pals home regularly after practice or a game. Mom has been dropping the same kids off at the same houses nearly every day for years now. Still, she *always* seems to forget where they live. It's like she forgets they got in the car, and are sitting in the backseat of the Cadillac. As we approach our friend's street and realize she isn't slowing down, one of us has to yell to get her attention, "Mom, Mom, *Mom!*"

Our friends are so used to us having to double-back and drop them off that they sometimes politely holler from the backseat, "*This is my street! This is my street!*" Their hope is that this will snap her out of her trance, so she'll slow down in time to make the turn into their street. If we don't catch her just then, she'll blow right by the street, and we'll be driving around the block for the umpteenth time, shaking our heads in amazement. "Mom, we just dropped Jason off last night. How could you forget where he lives?"

If she's in a good mood, she'll laugh and giggle, but if she's deep in her trance; she won't make a sound. Mom won't even look annoyed. She'll just mechanically double-back around, and stare straight ahead giving no response when our buddies slide out of the Cadillac and thank her for the ride.

This same oblivious trance can sometimes turn aggressive, and this is why there is nothing more nerve-wracking than riding shotgun when Mom is behind another car. Even though I don't have my permit yet, I know when she is tailgating, and say, "Mom, why don't cha slow down a bit? You're right on top of that guy."

"No, I'm not."

"Mom, yeah you are."

"Frankie, I am not."

"Mom, if we were any closer, we'd be in his trunk. Now, you're makin' me nervous. Can't you just drop back, and knock it off?"

The more I ask her to drop back, the closer our bumper inches to the one in front of us. I know all I can do is sit there, and brace myself for when the guy in front of us taps his brakes. Mom is so close, there's no room for error, and I know this must be why she runs so many people off the road.

Aunt Ellen has told us that several people in town have called the police from their cell phones to report Mom's reckless tailgating. They say she's a menace, a terror, only the police tell the callers they already have Mom flagged as a bad driver. They know she routinely runs motorists off the road.

Even though Mom is "The Worst Driver in America," she takes me down to the big, empty parking lot of the Acme Supermarket after it closes so I can practice driving. She sits in the passenger's seat of the Cadillac, smoking a cigarette, and talking me through the proper steps of making a K-turn, driving in reverse and parallel parking. Most nights, we put on the oldies station, 98.3 FM, and listen to the songs Mom grew-up with. We lower the windows, and sing along to the Beach Boys and Smokey Robinson as I spin around the parking lot after dark.

Mom is easier to drive with than my father. Pop likes to sit in the passenger's seat and holler at me to the point where I get jumpy and nervous. He shouts, "Cheech, slow down! You're going too fast! Take it easy! I want two hands on the wheel! Stop fooling with the mirror and pay a-ten-tion!"

Because driving with Pop is so stressful, I'm glad for those nights Mom walks into the den at dusk and says, "Frankie, you wanna practice tonight?"

Mom always drives from home to the parking lot where she and I then change spots. I get behind the steering wheel of the Cadillac, moving the seat back for my long legs, while she settles into the passenger's seat, with the window down, and puts the oldies station on. She lights a cigarette and holds it in her right hand, so the smoke escapes out of the open window. Her left leg is bent at the knee, with her left arm resting on top. Her dirty, white, Reebok sneaker, rests on the cracked and weathered, red and white leather cushion.

The Acme parking lot is only a few blocks from the ER where Mom's paranoia over The Conspiracy had her strapped to a gurney, and taken away two months ago. But on the nights we practice, it's almost like she comes alive. Mom laughs and jokes, and calls out different driving scenarios waiting for my answer. She'll say, "Okay Frankie, you're at a four-way stop, and there's a car to your left, who's also stopped. Which of you has the right of way?" Or, "Let's make believe we're behind a really slow car, but there's a solid yellow double line? Can you pass or not?"

Some nights, after I answer all of her questions, and go through all of the drills in the parking lot, Mom feels daring and says, "Frankie, don't worry about changing spots, just drive home."

I say, "Mom, I can't do that. I don't even have my permit yet."

"Frankie," she laughs, "you've done it before with your father."

"Yeah, but only on the back roads during the day—when nobody's around—I can't drive home when there's traffic at night."

"Yes, you can."

"No Mom, it's not right."

"Oh Frankie," she says, "you worry too much. Besides, if we get stopped, we'll just tell the cops we thought we saw O.J. Simpson trying to get away in his white Bronco."

I laugh when she says that, and so does Mom. We just watched O.J. last night on the big screen TV, with Tony and Michael in the den; it was unreal. Watching the news had become like watching a movie, the way O.J.'s friend drove him all over Los Angeles, while The Juice had that gun to his head. Mom says, "The Juice had everything, but now his life is over."

I wish she could see that she has everything, too, so maybe she could let go of The Routine, and The Conspiracy, and just be happy. On the nights we practice, I know that if Mom were like this more often, my brothers wouldn't have to run over to Aunt Teresa's like they do, and Pop's friends wouldn't be telling him he ought to get divorced. If Mom were like this every day, The Routine, The Conspiracy and The Movie would be things of the past. She'd go back to being that girl who wanted to be a stewardess, or go off to college—the well-groomed woman who walked downstairs like a lady, and made us breakfast on Sunday mornings with Pavarotti and pancakes. But here comes Frankie Valli on the radio and soon Mom has forgotten all about O.J. Simpson and his white Bronco, as she sings along with The Four Seasons.

I look over to see her smiling, and reaching to raise the volume, tossing her head back and saying, "C'mon Frankie, let's go!" I don't know if she's talking to me, or Frankie Valli, but I don't care because I'm driving down Shore Road without a license or a permit, on a beautiful June night, with my mother who is happy and singing.

Not long after I get my license, Pop brings home a 1986, metallic blue Chevy Camaro for me. It has oversized tires and big, shiny, metal rims. The Camaro has a tan, cloth interior, though the upholstery on the ceiling sags a bit, hitting my head and messing my hair. The speedometer doesn't work, but that's okay because the previous owner glued a glittery silhouette of a naked woman over it. The car is so loud and fast, my friends tease me and call it—The Ghetto Bomber—since you can hear me coming from a mile away.

After I spend a few hundred dollars on a paint job and to fix the sagging ceiling, my brothers and I embody the "Jersey Italian," as we run around town in my Camaro with our dark hair, deep tans and Ray-Ban sunglasses.

37

In July of 1994, weeks after my seventeenth birthday, Nonna calls my father and tells him that she's convinced we don't love Mom. She says she's had enough, and claims life would be better for her daughter if Nonna personally cared for her. My grandmother claims we physically, verbally, and emotionally abuse Mom to no end, and that Pop has become nothing more than an absentee father and husband.

With his eyes twitching a mile a minute, Pop tries to explain that she's got it all wrong, that if anybody is abusing anyone, it's Mom who's the abuser—the salt and pepper elephant in the room who holds all of us prisoner. Nonna doesn't want to hear it. She says she's been talking to Mom almost daily, and can't believe how we "walk all over her" in the morning.

"Walk all over her?" Pop thinks about it for a second—then responds, "Well, Ann falls asleep on the floor in the den. Whaddaya want them to do? It's almost like she knows the boys will have to step over her in the morning that way she can make an issue out of it later. With a clear conscience, she can call you and honestly say, 'Ma, you won't believe it, the boys walk all over me in the morning.'"

Pop goes quiet. He is listening to Nonna on the other end of the line, until he suddenly blurts out, "No, I'm not denying it. They *do* walk all over her, but they have no choice. Ann sleeps in front of the TV, and they literally have to *step* over *her* to turn it on. The real problem isn't the boys stepping over their mother—the real problem is your daughter sleeping on the floor like a drunk."

My father goes quiet again. After a few moments, he interrupts my grandmother by saying, "Look, I miss the girl I married, but this is just ridiculous. Your daughter concocts theories and accusations, and does nothing but stir up controversy. We missed our chance last year. I could have gotten Ann into the University of Pennsylvania, but you had to come down and get in the way—so, hey—if you want her for the summer, I'm not gonna stand in your way. I mean—*ti saluto*—I'll bring her up first thing in the morning."

After she has been at Nonna's for about ten days, Mom phones and wants to know why we never bother to call her. "How come I always have to call you, Frankie?"

I can't tell her that we don't call because we're glad she's out of our hair. I can't tell her that we're happier because she's not around, that we don't feel like prisoners anymore, that there isn't this cloud of negativity, and paranoia hanging over our house. I can't say any of that because she'll only get upset, and I don't want that. I want her to get better. So, I say, "Mom, you know how it is, we're busy. I have to work-out for football. Tony and Michael are on the all-star team playing baseball. Pop's busy going to their games, working, food shopping, trying to cook...."

"Well," she asks, "why don't you come up and take me to one of the boys' games?"

"Because Nonna lives so far away, I don't wanna drive up and back, up and back, all in the same day."

"So, come and get me, and take me home after the game."

"Mom, I can't do that. Nonna wants you up there for now."

"Frankie, come on, don't be like that. Just come and get me."

"Mom, I can't do that...."

"Okay, you know what? Good-bye, forget it."

She hangs up and I shake my head. Two minutes later, the phone rings again, "Hello. Mom?"

"Frankie, I can't believe you."

"Mom, you haven't even been there two weeks. Just relax and let Nonna try and nurse you back to health."

"Nurse me back to health? I love how all of a sudden, you're an expert on health. Weren't you the one that was going to kill yourself?"

She hangs up again, and I don't know what to think. Forty-five seconds later, the phone rings again, "Hello. Mom what are you doing?"

"Frankie, how can you hurt me like this?"

"Like what? Nonna wants you up there, and Pop agreed so just...."

"Pop! You know what," she says, "I don't need this." She hangs up a third time. Twenty seconds later, the phone rings again, "Yes, Mom?"

"Frankie, and another thing, why is it you take your father's side in everything?"

"Mom, he's not the one that sleeps on the floor and doesn't shower."

"Here we go with this shit again!"

"Mom, just try to make it work up at Nonna's, I mean...."

She hangs up a fourth time.

It goes on this way for the rest of the afternoon. Before I know it, she has called me ten times then twenty, thirty, forty and fifty. Every time it's the same argument, she is trying to find some way into my head, so I'll go up and bring her home. Finally, Pop calls and says that he was pouring concrete and didn't hear his cell phone, but when he checked it, there were all these strange messages from Mom. "What's going on, Chichi?"

I explain to him about the fifty calls, and how I don't know what to tell her. Then there's a click through—someone else is on the other line—when I click over to take the call, it's Mom.

"Frankie, where is your father?"

"He's on the other line."

"He is? I've been calling him all day."

"I know."

"Why? What did he say?"

"He wants to know what's going on."

"Put him on."

"I can't. He's on the other line."

"So, put him on."

"No. Mom. I mean, I can't. He's on his cell phone at work."

She hangs up, and I click back over to Pop.

"Pop," I say, "she hung up. That's like fifty-five calls."

"Really? Ah, you know what?"—we both can hear the sound of an incoming call on his line—"Your mother is calling me right now. Let me let you go, and I'll call you back."

"Alright, Pop."

He hangs up, and I start pacing back and forth in the kitchen. Mom's driving me crazy with all these stupid calls. I don't know what to do until she calls again, and again, and the number grows from seventy, to eighty, then to ninety. By the time we reach the ninety-sixth call, I'm in tears. She is pleading with me, "Frankie, please let me come home. I'll change. I'll be a good mom. I'll take my meds. I'll go to the doctor. Come on Frankie, don't do this to me. Don't you miss me? Don't your brothers want me back? Give me another shot. You know we were happy. We can do it again. Come on Frankie, please, take my side for once, *pleeeeeease!* I won't sleep on the floor anymore, and I'll do all the housework and shower every day, and we'll have breakfast and dinners like we used to and...."

This time I hang up; I throw the cordless phone against the wall; I catch my reflection in the mirror and start sobbing. I want it so bad to be 1986. I want to be with my brothers, in the front yard of our old house, playing with Mom in the snow. I wish none of this was happening, that it was all a bad dream. But the tears streaming down my face tell me this is not a dream. I retrieve the phone and call my father who can hear me crying.

"Calm down, Chichi," he says. "It'll be alright. It'll be alright."

He is soft with me, and asks what I want to do. I tell him we ought to give Mom another chance; that I can't turn her away and he says, "Okay Chichi, we'll give her another shot."

I hang up the phone with tears in my eyes; and my back against the wall, as I slowly slide down towards the bathroom floor.

The next day, I drive up to Nonna's house in Philadelphia so I can bring my mother back down the shore. It's the first time I've ever driven to Philly alone, and the whole ride up the Atlantic City Expressway, I'm torn between feelings of hope and hopelessness about Mom and everything she said yesterday on the phone. She promised she would take her meds and go to the doctor. She said she would do the housework, and shower every day, and that we would have breakfast, and dinners as a family, and that my brothers wouldn't have to run to Aunt Teresa's every weekend to claim sanctuary.

Her promises embody the reasons why I wanted Pop to give her one more shot. They are why I'm in the Camaro, with my elbow hanging out the window, speeding up the highway without a clue as to how fast I'm going. My speedometer still doesn't work, but I don't need that to feel how everything about me is in a rush. I skipped breakfast, didn't take a shower and got dressed in a blur. I've been in the fast lane all morning tailgating, and passing each and every car that dares to go below eighty miles per hour. I think I'm hurried and jittery because of all those phone calls yesterday. Mom just about drove me crazy, the way she called and hung-up, called back and hung-up again and again over ninety times. I just want to get to Philly, and bring her home as quickly as I can—though my jitters have me questioning who exactly I'm picking up today. Which Mom will I bring home later this afternoon? The mother who hides in The Routine—or the one who taught me how to drive, appearing all loving and sweet?

I hope the mother I'm picking up is the woman I remember standing at the stove making pancakes on those Sunday mornings with the sound of Pavarotti and the smell of frying butter in the air. I hope it's her, because I need it to be her. I need our lives to be different to change as they once did. Even our Sunday mornings aren't special anymore. Nowadays, my brothers and I eat cereal on the floor in Pop's office, playing Sega Genesis, while he drinks coffee in his robe in the den watching fishing shows on ESPN. On Sunday mornings, when she's home, Mom usually lays around reading the paperback novels she buys in the checkout line at Acme, or sleeps well into the afternoon. It's almost like we've stopped being a family, and have become roommates in the most random and dysfunctional of ways.

Because the heart of our Sunday mornings has changed, Pop's Pavarotti collection collects dust on the shelves above his stereo in the office. There are days I wish I could sit down and write Luciano a letter, asking him to sing to us again to brighten our lives with *'O Sole Mio*, because without him, my family is falling apart. In my letter, I would tell him how I'm 100% Italian, how I know where my grandparents are from, how I can rattle off the names of their villages, and want nothing more than to marry an Italian girl, and move to Italy. But, I tell myself that a letter is old fashioned and slow. What I need is something quick and immediate. My ferocious pace up the Expressway makes me wish I had my own cellular phone so I could call Pavarotti right here and now.

My father told me he read somewhere that Don Luciano keeps his home phone number listed in the local Modenà phonebook, even though he's known throughout the world. So, the thought occurs to me, I could just call information, and ask to be patched through to Italy, where I'd ask the Italian operator to connect me to Modenà, in the Province of Modenà, to the residence of one Luciano Pavarotti. When I got connected, I'd say, *Pronto! Pronto! Is this Don Luciano? Is this the King of the High C's?*

Only to be told by his housekeeper, *Signore Pavarotti non sta a casa.*

To which I'd say, *Look, I'm sorry. I don't speak Italian that well, but I'd like to leave a message. Could you tell Signore Pavarotti that I'm the son of Frankie the Voice. He might remember my father from years ago when they met on stage one night in Atlantic City. But if he doesn't, just tell him that there's an Italo-American kid driving up to Philadelphia in a ghetto bomber, with tears in his eyes over pancakes and bel canto, who's nervous about his mother and her promises.*

As soon as I bring Mom home, she starts complaining of that same old burning sensation eating at her from the inside. Only now, the burning is in her head. Ever since that flashback in the Cadillac years ago, where she passed out with her eyes rolling into the back of her head, my mother has complained of a burning sensation eating at her from the inside. She always said the burning was in her gut, her abdomen, and her cries for help would leave us helpless, as she rolled around on the floor in agony, clutching her stomach. Her psychologist told my parents that the burning was emotional, and that it represented guilt pains. Now that she's home, Mom will lie on the couch for hours and rub her temples, complaining of the heat and throbbing right on the other side of her skin.

She asks me to feel her head. I place my hands on both temples for a moment but tell her, "I don't feel anything, Mom."

"You don't feel that, Frankie?"

"No."

"You don't feel the heat and the throbbing?"

"No, I don't feel a thing."

Mom pushes my hands away, and shakes her head in disbelief and anger. It's as if my lack of validation makes me a part of The Conspiracy. It isn't long before I realize her pleading and promises that day on the phone were nothing more than a ploy to get me to pick her up. She wanted to be home where she could control things, and revert back to her old ways.

What with the throbbing and burning, Mom doesn't take her meds, or go to the doctor like she said she would. None of the housework or showering gets done like she promised, and Pavarotti has no chance to serenade us because those family breakfasts and dinners never happen like she said they would.

It's too much trouble for her to get up off the couch and cook something for the family she said she missed so much. So, we eat pizza, night after night, until my brothers go over Aunt Teresa's on the weekends for a home cooked meal.

With her conspiracy theory fixation, I notice a touch of disdain in Mom's attitude towards me now; like I betrayed her when I sided with Pop, and agreed she should go to Nonna's a few weeks ago. Her thoughts of conspiracy don't apply to my brothers, though. Yet, I can tell she has lumped me and Pop together—separate from Tony and Michael. That disdain I notice makes me wish I hadn't given into her that day she called me ninety-six times, and my father another sixty. If I had it to do over again, I wouldn't have picked her up because this is exactly what she wanted, to be the manipulative, yet immovable salt and pepper elephant in the room.

Mom hijacks a trip to Disney World, in the summer of 1994, with her manipulative hijinks, and reinforces the narrative amongst Pop's friends that he really ought to consider divorce. I did not go on the trip, as it would have interrupted my preparation for the upcoming football season, but Aunt Ellen and Aunt Teresa say Mom seemingly enjoyed not showering, that she took pleasure out of smelling poorly on the trip.

They also noticed, just like they had at the Outer Banks, that Mom would feign being ill. Complaining of stomach pains, out of the blue, all so that Pop would tend to her, the moment he mentioned a possible day of golf or fishing with the guys. The sisters rolled their eyes as they watched Mom transform into a bedridden wife, who seemed to be fine only a moment prior to hearing the news that their husbands were going to spend the day together having fun.

When football season begins I'm excited because this year I'm a senior, and Coach Coffey has named me the starting varsity quarterback. Throughout late August, we play three scrimmages and win them all convincingly. I play so well that the coaches pull me aside, and tell me that I'm the heart and soul of the team. Based on my impressive performance in training camp, they feel optimistic about our chances at a playoff bid.

After our season opener, in mid-September 1994, *The Press of Atlantic City* writes a little blurb on how well I played in our loss to Northern Burlington. They say, despite our 0-1 start, I seem poised for a great year.

For whatever reason though, that tiny article in the newspaper causes me to lose my confidence. Suddenly, I don't know how to handle the expectations, as doubt and superstition hijack my thinking. I feel trapped. I feel like I "need to succeed" because I have "potential," and that scares me. I start to play hesitantly, and focus more on how I "look" trotting on and off the field, rather than my performance during the game.

I become a liability, and the local sports writers notice. They write that I don't look as "sharp" as I did in the pre-season. I start to mumble the play-call in the huddle when addressing my offensive teammates. I panic when I drop back in the pocket and start throwing interceptions like I'm trying to help the other team win.

A month into the season, with our record at 1-3, we have a pep rally, and the entire student-body packs into the gymnasium. As the team captain, I am supposed to address the 1,600 students, and help get them pumped about our next game, but I chicken out. I hide in the locker room, paralyzed with fear, and ashamed of whom I had become.

Despite the fact my acne has disappeared, thanks to Acutane, I grow a full beard. My thick, brown facial hair is a sign of the depression I find myself in. Even though we lost our top wide-receiver to a broken wrist, our top running back to an arrest, and his replacement to a severely bruised elbow, I'm the reason we are having such an atrocious season. By the half-way point of the year, I'm so frustrated that I emotionally give-up.

I tell myself the coaches were wrong. I was never as good as they said I was, and I can't wait for the season to end. As I roam the hallways, I wish everybody didn't know my name. I wish they couldn't point at me and say, *there he is, there's Frankie, the guy letting us down every Saturday.* I wish I was just another senior, with clear skin, a cute girlfriend who played field hockey and a part-time job at the bowling alley. I'd rather be anything than the starting varsity quarterback, especially after they include a life-sized painting of me in the Trainer's Room.

One of the art classes is responsible for the painting of a mural of the various team sports, where the most prominent image is of me in my green helmet, white pants, and #20 jersey. I have a football in my right hand, cocked and ready to be thrown. I feel unworthy and embarrassed to be in the center of the mural. But then I get the worst news, Coach Coffey warns me that if I don't start to play better, he's going to bench me.

His threat works; it wakes me up, so to speak. Faced with the potential embarrassment of losing my "job," in front of the school, and the community, I regain control of my mind and emotions. I salvage the rest of the season. We finish with back to back victories, and I play superbly.

38

Regardless of my inconsistent season, Pop and I decide to send letters of interest, along with copies of my highlight tape, to several "big name" college programs across the country. If there was any interest, I know it would be based on my potential—not my performance. At 6'2" and 195 pounds, with a strong arm and the ability to take direction, my father and I believe that a good college coach could turn me into a star.

All during November and December of 1994, we send letters and highlight tapes to everyone from Penn State and Notre Dame to UCLA and Boston College. Aside from generically encouraging me to "walk-on," none of the major programs actively recruits me.

Since I'm committed to playing college football, Pop says we ought to widen our search and consider a Division II or III school. My parents and I have already made unofficial visits to three colleges so far— C.W. Post, Widener University, and Monmouth College. Pop and I remain unsure where I'll play out my collegiate career, which is why we're so anxious to attend a college football conference Coach Coffey turned me onto. My father and I want to find out which schools are realistic, both athletically and financially.

The conference is being held at Holy Spirit High School. Coach Coffey told me it will feature mostly Division II and III programs from the Greater Philadelphia area like East Stroudsburg, Kutztown, West Chester, Gettysburg, and Ursinus.

I'm dressed in a white button-down shirt, navy blue pants and one of my father's light blue ties. As Pop guides the Cadillac up Route 9 into Absecon with Mom quietly smoking in the passenger seat, I sit nervously in the back. I know tonight is a big night. It's almost spring 1995, and my hope is that this conference will help us decide where I'll go to college in the fall.

When we arrive, we find that representatives from the different colleges and universities are stationed at tables in classrooms throughout the school building. It's very casual; there is no agenda or itinerary to follow. We're free to stroll from room to room, and speak to whomever we choose. In the hallways, we pass other seniors from all over south Jersey looking uncomfortable in their shirts and ties. They parade around with their parents, shaking hands with prospective coaches, and chatting with the different college representatives.

When Pop and I begin talking to a representative from Montclair State, Mom starts to amuse herself. In addition to her inconsistent bathing, Mom has stopped flushing the toilet. Pop says, "Ann, I don't get it, instead of using the bathroom, and leaving your piss, shit, and toilet paper for us to find every time, can't you just flush it? I mean, what is so hard about that? It's like you like the mess you leave behind; like it gives you pleasure. But I know what it really is; it's fun, isn't it, Ann? It's fun to leave your shit there like a lazy slob. I bet you do it to amuse yourself."

The representative from Montclair is wearing a white polo shirt with the school's name, and team logo embroidered over his heart. His name is John, and he is in his early twenties.

After I introduce myself, Pop does most of the talking. He asks about the size of the student population, the style of offense the football team runs, and how they handle financial aid for an in-state student. John's polite with us, but rehearsed. He answers Pop's questions by going into a sales pitch, thus attempting to convince us that Montclair State is the best place for a student-athlete. Mom is perusing the pamphlet and informational table in front of us.

As John nears the end of his spiel, another player and his parents position themselves behind Pop and me to eavesdrop. Everything is quiet, and I can't help but think that it's very calming to be in a school building at night. It's almost like a holiday, and I feel relaxed. Mom must feel the same way because without warning, she violently and audibly farts. She makes no sudden movement, nothing to give her away as the culprit, but Pop's eyes get big—because like me—he knows that was her.

A moment later, she farts again. This time John, from Montclair, stops talking, smirks and looks over his shoulder. The expression on his face is of a humorous disbelief, like he needs to see for himself just what's going on. Mom doesn't disappoint, the moment he turns around, she farts a third time. With this one, she slightly lifts up her right leg, shifts her weight to the left, and violently pushes the gas out of her ass with another loud fart.

Pop calls to Mom in Italian—he asks what she's doing. "Ann, *chè fai?*" But she doesn't answer. He calls to her again, "Ann?" She just keeps busying herself at the table, perusing the materials like nothing ever happened. My father is too embarrassed to excuse himself, so he just walks away from John and takes Mom by the arm. He leads her out into the hallway, and I have no choice but to follow them.

My parents are standing face-to-face. We are in the corridor having a hushed conversation as the other parents and football players walk by. Pop motions to the room we just left. "Ann, what was *that?*"

"What was what?"

"You know what I mean. Why did you do that?"

"Frank, what are you talking about?"

"Ann, we know it was you."

"Yeah, Mom," I say. "What was that?"

She ignores me because Pop gets in her face. He doesn't want to cause a commotion, so he's still talking quietly, "F'Chrissakes Ann, we're here for Frankie. Now don't make a scene, *alright*? If you can't handle that, go sit in the car."

"I'm not gonna go sit in the car."

"Then please, just keep it together."

"I'm fine, Frank."

"You're fine?"

"Yeah, just leave me alone."

"Leave you alone?"

"Yeah."

"You won't fart like that again?"

"No," Mom says, as she rolls her eyes and shakes her head. She lets out a bit of a sigh before saying, "Frank, you know people do pass gas?"

"Ann, I'm serious."

"And so am I." She looks at me and says, "Frankie, people do pass gas, don't they?"

Mom waits for me to respond, but Pop says, "You know what, just stay out of the way, okay? Just stay out of the way until it's time to go."

My father takes a deep breath, wipes his left hand across his face, blinks a few times and says, "Chichi, c'mon."

He moves towards a different room where there are more recruiters. We approach a stocky, white, bald guy from Delaware Valley

State who walks us through the same routine we just experienced with Montclair. He asks what position I play, what I want to study in college, and then dives into his own rehearsed monologue about why I should go to "Del Val," as he calls it. The moment he asks whether Pop and I have any questions, Mom walks into the room. She looks normal enough, so my father decides to let her be, rather than chase her out.

As other prospects wander into the room, the big bald guy from Del Val excuses himself to say hello. It's at that point Mom farts for a fourth time. It's a thunderous, wet fart; the kind my brothers and I would have applauded if we were warming up *The Chocolate Milk Symphony* on a Sunday morning. But there will be no applause tonight, for my forty-eight year old mother has done the unthinkable and embarrassed us yet again. My father spins around and locks eyes with her. He is beside himself, but all Mom can do is open her arms like, *what do you want from me? If I have to pass gas, I **have** to pass gas!*

Pop shakes his head, and I can tell he has had it. This time, everyone knows that was Mom, and they start to chuckle, but my father turns beet red and moves towards the door with Mom not far behind. She calls to him, "Frank, I'm sorry but whaddaya want me to say? *Frank!*"

He's not talking this time.

Once I reach the hallway, I see Pop walking towards the exit. He's walking too fast for me or Mom to catch-up. She pleads her case from behind. There are other people standing in the hallway; they seem confused at the sight of my parents speed-walking down the corridor.

I trail behind, and watch them pass through the exit.

When I reach the parking lot, I see Pop to my right walking down the school's long driveway. He is heading towards Route 9, the street that runs along the front of Holy Spirit High School. Mom calls to him, "Frank, where you goin'?"

But Pop ignores her. Now, Mom and I are standing side-by-side watching him walk away from us. Without warning, my mother darts for the Cadillac. I don't know what to do. Who do I follow? I decide to get in the Cadillac with Mom.

She quickly starts the engine as I climb into the backseat. She spins through the parking lot and pulls the Cadillac alongside my father.

He is nearing the end of the driveway. Mom calls to him through the open passenger window, "Frank, c'mon get in!"

But Pop ignores her again. Looking both ways, he crosses the street. Mom reaches the end of the driveway, and looks both ways herself. Soon, I feel the Cadillac lurch forward. Mom makes a left-hand turn, and brings the Cadillac alongside my father again. From the backseat, I watch him walk south along Route 9. No, he's not walking; he's marching. Pop is marching, and indifferent to Mom's pleas.

"Frank, get in the Cadillac! C'mon, you're not being fair! You're acting like I'm the only person who has ever passed gas?"

Pop continues to ignore her. I know it isn't the fact that she farted like she did that's the issue, it's that she did it on purpose to amuse herself, to get a rise, to see how far she could take things. That's why I wish I hadn't climbed into the backseat; I wish I was marching along Route 9 with Pop.

My father has his jacket slung over his right forearm. Even though it's wintertime, he doesn't need the jacket to stay warm because he's fired up. Mom has the Cadillac crawling along the shoulder of Route 9, so I say, "Mom, put your hazards on."

She ignores me, and continues to plead with Pop.

"Frank, c'mon, get in the car," she calls out the open passenger window.

"No," he hollers back. "I'm walkin' home!"

"Frank, that's ridiculous. It'll take you forever!"

"No," he shouts, turning to his left looking into the Cadillac. "You know what's ridiculous? The way you acted in there, Ann. That's what's fuckin' ridiculous!"

"I said I was sorry. What's the big deal?"

"What's the big deal? You embarrassed your son; you embarrassed your husband!"

"Oh, c'mon, nobody was embarrassed. It happens, people pass gas."

"Yeah, people can also excuse themselves, Ann! They can walk out into the hallway, or find a restroom! They don't have to stand there, and act like that! *Jesus Ann, you fuckin' disgust me!*"

The Cadillac is still crawling along the shoulder on Route 9. Pop is marching in defiance. From the tiny droplets on the windshield, I can tell it's starting to drizzle. Cars are zooming past us as Pop slips on his jacket. I feel helpless and hopeless in the backseat. Part of me wants to reach up front, and slap my mother in the back of the head over this bullshit. While another part wants to pull Pop into the Cadillac so we can just go home.

I feel like a fool. I can't believe Mom would behave like that, though I should have known. I knew the second she got into the Cadillac back home that she was up to something.

Pop and I didn't invite her to come with us tonight because we both know she isn't very good in public; she stands out for all the wrong reasons. Even if she hadn't put on her farting exposition, Mom is out of sync with us. I look nice in my shirt and tie; Pop has on black slacks and a polo shirt, under his cream-colored sweater with both collars up. Meanwhile, Mom is in dirty black stretch pants, an oversized dirty purple sweater, with sloppy lipstick and matted hair. It's because she was uninvited that we couldn't leave home without her. She raced out to the car, the moment she knew we were heading somewhere "special."

The thing is, she's a mess and can't wander too far from her precious Routine. The safety of that couch in the den, with the big screen TV and her cigarettes, is her sanctuary. Why couldn't she have sat in the parking lot? God knows she is used to sitting in the Cadillac for hours at a time staring off into space. Maybe, she could have found a payphone, and made one of her eerie phone calls to Aunt Ellen or Aunt Teresa; anything other than come inside, and do what she did.

I hate her for doing that. I don't care if she knows she's losing her mind. I want to strap her to a gurney, and shove her into the Great Egg Harbor Bay. It's like Pop says, "Ann does things to amuse herself, to cause a scene, to stir up controversy."

The way I see it, she's addicted to upheaval and allergic to tranquility. All she knows how to do is play the role of the "innocent victim," forever the salt and pepper elephant in the room who manipulates and thrives on attention.

Sitting in the back of the Cadillac, I agree with Pop's friends; my father should get divorced. Maybe then he wouldn't have to walk home in the drizzling rain with his wife crawling beside him in the family car. Mom is still pleading, "Frank, get in! Let's go home! C'mon!" But he doesn't want to hear it. He keeps marching along the side of the road barking at her through the open window, "Ann, go the hell home!"

I don't know what's worse—standing in the classroom where I was a few minutes ago, feeling my face turn red as Mom ripped her final fart—or sitting in the backseat, helplessly watching my parents argue back and forth.

It's like our life is the same old story, again and again. I wish I hadn't given into those ninety-six phone calls last summer, and that Mom was back living with Nonna. She's not dazed; she knows exactly who we are and what she's doing.

What lessons can Pop take from tonight's "show" at the school, and "encore" on Route 9 when he sits down with his sopresatta and wine? As it starts to rain harder, he yells to Mom to stop crawling. He climbs into the Cadillac, and slams the door shut.

Now that Pop is inside the car with us, it's like I'm on the outside looking in on my parents' marriage. The image of my father sitting there in the passenger's seat, with his arms folded across his chest, indignantly looking out the window, is exactly how they live their lives anymore. Pop is Mom's hostage, just like Tony, Michael and me. She may be driving us home, but she keeps trying to plead her dysfunctional case, insisting that Pop isn't being fair, that he's overreacting, and shouldn't have walked out like that. Mom says, "Now what is Frankie gonna do about college football?"

I see her eyes searching my expression in the rearview mirror; but I'm like Pop, looking away, giving her the silent treatment all the way home.

39

Even though my senior football season didn't go as well as I had hoped, I'm still recognized around town as "the starting quarterback." Tony is in ninth grade, and is one of the freshman quarterbacks, while Michael is the starting quarterback for our town's youth team. This means my brothers and I are all "known" throughout the neighboring communities as well.

Our newfound "celebrity status" causes girls to call our house like you wouldn't believe. Sadly, they never call for me. It seems like every time I answer the phone, it's some fourteen year old girl asking, "Is Tony there?" Or some nervous twelve year old calling and saying, "Hi. Can I talk to Michael?" There's normally giggling going on in the background, and I want to say, *hey, don't you have an older sister for me?* But instead I mumble out, "Yeah, yeah, he's here, hold on a second."

When I tell the girls to hold on, I always hear more giggling going on in the background in anticipation of Tony or Michael picking up the phone and saying, *hello?* I'm so used to girls calling the house that I tend to answer with a bit of an edge to my voice, almost like I am fed-up with all the attention my brothers are receiving. Yet, when I answer the phone tonight with that same edge, I hear a man's voice ask for me specifically.

The man says he was given my home phone number from Coach Coffey. His name is Gordy Combs, the head football coach at a Division I-AA school called Towson State University, located outside of Baltimore, Maryland.

He says he is interested in recruiting me to play football. He further explains that he saw a few of my game tapes, and likes my arm strength. After I get off the phone, I go to Pop with what Coach Combs had to say. Soon we're going on an Official Visit, and I'm committing to play college football for the Towson State Tigers.

To my surprise, I'm also selected to play in a state high school football all-star game called **The Blue-Gold Rotary Bowl**. It's to be held at Rowan College in Glassboro, in June. When Pop hears the news he says, "See Chichi, people know you have talent. The team may have had a bad year, and your stats may have been weak, but you have potential written all over you. I think you're gonna surprise a lot of people at Towson."

Rowan College is a forty-minute ride from the shore which means my parents are there with a bunch of friends and family to watch me play in the Rotary Bowl. It's a clear night—Friday, June 23, 1995—and I'm the starting quarterback for the Southern squad. The thing is I become so nervous on the first play of the game that I fumble the ball, and we lose possession. I jog off the field feeling like I had just "blacked-out," but the quarterback coach gets in my face. He wants to know what I was thinking. He shouts, *"Where was your head?"* But I can't answer him because I don't *know* what I was thinking.

I calm down as the game progresses, and throw what turns out to be the game-winning touchdown pass. It isn't until the game ends that the team's water boys shyly approach me and ask for my autograph. My brothers and I have spent years filling notebooks with our signatures, practicing our autographs in cursive. I have always wanted to be in a position of recognition, and instantly feel like that olive skinned, dark haired backup outfielder for the Phillies, Ruben Amaro Jr.

When the boys hand me their Sharpies, I flash a big grin and kindly take my time signing their programs asking them if they play football, and what they thought of the game. By the time I take the Ghetto Bomber back down the shore, I feel ready for college football; I feel ready to be a star at Towson State University.

Three days after I sign those autographs, Mom disappears on my eighteenth birthday. It is June 26, 1995 and she leaves early in the morning saying she is going out to get me a cake, and spend the afternoon shopping with Aunt Ellen. Only when Aunt Ellen stops by the house around lunchtime to see if Mom wants to go to the diner Pop says, "The diner? I thought Ann was with you? I thought you guys were spendin' the day together?"

Aunt Ellen shakes her head, and says, "No, we didn't have any plans."

"Really?"

"Yeah."

At that, Pop falls silent and his eyes become distant. He looks like he is worried about something, which is why Aunt Ellen says, "What is it, Frank? Everything alright?"

"I dunno, maybe we should call Ann's mother and see if she's heard anything. I mean, we know she lied about spending the day with you."

Aunt Ellen agrees, and Pop quickly calls Nonna from the phone in his office where he learns his instincts are right. Nonna is pretty shaken up, and having a hard time speaking. It's through her emotional and heavy broken-English that she tells Pop how Mom just called to say goodbye.

"Goodbye? Whaddaya mean?"

Through her thick accent, my grandmother explains that Mom said she was headed towards the Delaware River so she could jump off the Tacony-Palmyra Bridge which is an hour from the shore in northeast Philadelphia. When Pop hears this, he just about panics. He gets off the phone as fast as he can and calls the Philadelphia police department. My father instructs them to be on the lookout for a middle-aged woman with salt and pepper hair driving towards the river in a 1987 Liberty Edition, red Cadillac Roadster.

Watching Pop flustered and frustrated on the phone is the opposite of how he always is so calm and cool—like the Dean Martin of Adversity University. He knows how unstable Mom has been since that episode last year in the ER. He knows what she's capable of, and he knows time is of the essence. The police take down Mom's description, and tell Pop they'll get back to him as soon as they can, but that isn't enough. The two of us go out searching for her. We check all the local bridges and lonely back roads just in case Mom hasn't left the area yet, but we find no trace of her and hear nothing from the cops in Philly all afternoon.

It isn't until we return home shortly after dark that we find Mom dazed and confused on the front porch. The three of us move inside and are standing in the foyer. Mom is a few feet inside the front door; her chin is down—she looks defeated and sad. Pop is soft with her, but insistent. He wants to know if she's alright; if she knows what she has put us through, and how he had to lie to Tony and Michael, shuffling them off to Aunt Ellen's in case the cops showed up to say they had found his wife dead on the banks of the Delaware. He says, "Ann what were you thinking? We were worried sick!"

"I was just looking for a birthday cake, Frank."

"All day, Ann? You went looking for a birthday cake, all day? Really?"

"Yeah."

"Okay, where is it? Where's the cake, Ann? What flavor you get?"

He's sarcastic with her, because now he's furious. All Mom can do is keep her eyes pinned to the floor, as Pop says, "There is no cake, is there Ann? You weren't looking for any birthday cake today. I spoke to your mother this afternoon, and we know all about you wanting to jump off the Tacony-Palmyra Bridge. You had your mother beside herself with worry. She sounded terrible."

Mom's eyes start to wander around the foyer. She is anxious. She is sighing. She is looking at the cathedral ceiling. Now that Pop has called her bluff about the birthday cake, it's like she doesn't know where to go with her emotions. I'm standing quietly behind my father when Mom finally looks down, and peers over Pop's shoulder. She's looking at me, but talking to Pop, "I didn't go through with it, Frank...."

"Didn't go through with *what* Ann?" he asks.

Mom doesn't answer him right away, so he repeats himself.

"Didn't go through with what, jumping off the bridge?"

She still doesn't acknowledge him, or his question, but her eyes stay locked on mine.

"I stopped myself," she says, "because I remembered today is Frankie's birthday."

By now, Mom has tears swelling up in her eyes and her speech shakes from being so emotional. She starts to stutter, and has a difficult time saying the first few words of her sentence. "I...diddddn't...waaaannnnt Fraaaankie..." she catches her breath for a moment and finishes her sentence in a rushed, high-pitched voice, "to have that memory for his birthday."

She is crying profusely. Her expression is the picture of pain. Her hands come up to her face, muffling what she says next, "I didn't want to kill myself on the day my baby was born."

Mom is sobbing, and Pop moves towards her. Whatever anger and sarcasm he had in him leaves his body as he takes her in his arms.

I remain quiet by the French doors, unsure what to feel. All I can do is continue to breathe and blink. I want to embrace her with Pop and tell her not to worry that everything will be alright, but that would be a lie. Today is my eighteenth birthday and I'm sure of one thing; my mother is not alright.

The next day Pop goes to see Mom's psychoanalyst. When he gets home, he sits at the kitchen table, where his eyes are twitching like mad. He tells me and Aunt Ellen that the doctor wants him to put his foot down; he wants Pop to stop being an enabler. As the skin around his eyes quivers and jumps, my father says he is worried about putting his foot down, worried what Mom might do, but says the doctor assured him that further enabling of her erratic behavior would only lead to more chaos and disappearances.

So, against his better judgment, Pop decides that Mom has to go back to Nonna's for the summer of 1995. He says he knows we tried it last year, when my grandmother thought Mom would be better off in Philly, only this time, he says we won't fall for her tricks.

"Even if she calls two hundred times begging to come home, we will turn her away. Ann never once called and said she missed us. She only wanted to come home using guilt and false promises to break us down." When he finally shares the news with Mom—that she'll be going back to Nonna's for the summer—she balks, and struts around the kitchen. Pointing her finger at him she says, "I won't go! I'm not going, Frank! I will **not** go back to my mother's!"

Pop leans in towards her from across the counter and peers into her eyes, "Oh, you **will** go, Ann, and that's the end of it!"

Two weeks later, on a sweltering July afternoon, my mother is alone at Nonna's house in Philadelphia.

She was invited by her nephew, Alex, to join him and our grandmother on a visit to Babbo's grave, but Mom declined. Despite the private chaos of their 56 year marriage, Nonna remains a loyal Old World widow and makes regular visits to the cemetery.

It has been nine years since Babbo slipped into that coma and slipped from this world, but his fingerprints remain all over Mom's self-esteem.

On this particular summer day, Alex and Nonna return home from the cemetery to discover my mother standing at the kitchen counter. She is barefoot and appears to be hiding something. Mom is giving them her back and seems startled by their arrival. Alex is immediately suspicious. With curiosity in his voice, he asks, "Aunt Ann, you okay?"

Mom mumbles something under her breath, abruptly turns from the counter, takes a few steps, and collapses. Within a matter of seconds, my forty-eight year old mother is lying in a pool of blood, losing consciousness. This all happens so quickly and unexpectedly, that Alex is instantly in shock. He doesn't know what just happened, his feet are frozen to the floor, but he pushes through that cloud of doubt and rushes to Mom's side, "Aunt Ann! *Aunt Ann!*"

To my cousin Alex, my mother is larger than life. She is the one that saved him from Babbo's abuse. Mom is the one who realized she needed to get her sister Colomba, and her children, out of the house. The Noose was that breaking point. The Noose was the event that pushed Mom to buy that triplex down the street, twenty some years ago. Alex always looked up to Mom, for he understood what she did for him. So, when he kneels beside his aunt, he is really kneeling beside a god.

He rolls my mother onto her back and is horrified to find that she is bleeding heavily from her abdomen. Alex glances up at the counter, where my mother seemed to be hiding something. There he spots an open container of liquid carpet cleaner, a bottle of aspirin and a bloody butcher knife.

Alex immediately knows he must call 9-1-1. With a river of emotions running through his heart and mind, he moves towards the rotary phone on the wall and picks up the receiver—but that's when Nonna desperately tries to contain him, and keep The Cover-Up alive.

With her daughter bleeding and unconscious, Nonna *LITERALLY* fights with her grandson *NOT* to call the cops. She doesn't want police cars and ambulances converging on the house. What will the neighbors say? What will they think?

Nonna has spent the past sixty plus years driven by a village girl's need to avoid bringing shame onto *la famiglia*. She doesn't want the paramedics' sirens blowing the lid off a lifetime of work.

Instead, Nonna pleads with Alex to drive Mom to the hospital himself, but he knows that's a bad idea. If they don't act quickly, Mom may die right there on the kitchen floor. The thought even crosses his mind that moving Mom himself may cause more damage than anything.

"*No!*" He shouts. "We have to call 9-1-1! She's dyin'!" But Nonna *WILL. NOT. LET. UP.* My 81 year old grandmother attempts to swipe the phone from Alex's hand, but my cousin insists they have no time to waste. As he continues to argue with Nonna, *literally* holding her back from interfering with his telephone call, he barks into the receiver and describes the scene to the 9-1-1 operator.

"My aunt is on the floor, she is unconscious, and bleeding. There is a bloody knife on the counter; it looks like she swallowed some pills, maybe some cleaning chemicals. We need help! We need an ambulance!"

Within a matter of minutes, the little girl in the greenhouse is rushed to the hospital—her life hanging in the balance....

40

When I was 10 years old, Tony 8, and Michael 6, we got the surprise of a lifetime. We were all sound asleep when Mom and Pop came bursting into our rooms at 3:30 in the morning, and turned the lights on. We covered our eyes, trying to block out the light, as we remained hazy with fatigue, but we noticed Pop holding the camcorder, videotaping us as Mom giddily shouted. "Boys," she said, "boys get up, let's go! We're goin' to see, Mickey! Were goin' to see, Mickey!"

We have a cousin named Nikki, and that's what we all thought Mom was saying, *we're goin' to see, Nikki.* We love our cousin and all, but we openly questioned why our parents were waking us up at 3:30 in the morning to go see our cousin Nikki? It made no sense—but then Mom picked up on our confusion and said, "No, you silly-billies, *Mickey.* We're goin' to Disney World! We're gonna see Mickey Mouse!"

Once we understood what was *really* happening, we literally jumped out of bed, and shook off our fatigue. We were hollering, screaming, high-fiving and losing our collective minds. We couldn't believe it! We were going to Disney World!

We made the 18 hour drive from southern New Jersey to Orlando, Florida and spent 10 days at the happiest place on earth, from Epcot Center, to the Magic Kingdom, we had the time of our lives. It was the perfect trip, the perfect time, the perfect way to celebrate Christmas 1988. But that trip was seven years ago—today our poor mother couldn't shake off her fatigue, even if she wanted to. Mom is barely hanging on; she swallowed nearly half a bottle of liquid carpet cleaner, ingested over 60 aspirin and stabbed herself in the stomach so deeply, that the doctors are worried about irreversible internal damage.

It is July of 1995, nearly 20 years removed from my parents' mythical honeymoon to Mystic Seaport, Connecticut, and Mom is in the Intensive Care Unit, at the hospital down the street from Nonna's house.

During that trip to Disney World, my brothers and I freely admitted to our parents that they had really fleeced us. We picked up not one single hint that Mom and Pop had been planning that trip for weeks. It was one big secret.

But this latest tragic turn of events would be no secret. What Mom did to herself in the kitchen at Nonna's house, sent shockwaves throughout our tiny world, and rocked me to the core.

When your mother tries to commit suicide, when she attempts to end her life, when she stabs herself in the womb—the same womb from whence you came—life, liberty and the pursuit of happiness make no sense to you. You suddenly feel claustrophobic, askew and uneasy. Your soul gets rattled. Your peace is broken. Confusion, anger, sadness and embarrassment gnaw at your own sanity, driving you into the ground.

Mother and Father are fundamental terms; built-in buzz words that represent Adam and Eve and everything we are taught from the moment we draw our first breath.

My mother is my life; and my life nearly murdered itself.

As word gets out about Mom's attempted suicide, people start bringing food to our house every night. Sometimes, it's people we've never met who knock on our front door, carrying trays of dinner covered in tin-foil. Other times, its people we know, like parents of friends we play ball with, or the friends themselves. They all come to the door with the same smile, and say, "We heard you guys were hungry."

They say it with a twinkle in their eyes, so we know, they know, they're just here to help. But, the twinkle also says, *don't worry, we're not going to stand here and ask you twenty questions. We don't need to know anything. We're not here to pry, or pray, or gossip. We're just concerned, and want to make sure you eat a decent meal.*

Aunt Ellen and Aunt Teresa call Pop and tell him that it's our local Catholic parish who is responsible for the dinners. They say they do it when families are in need, and with the news about Mom's suicide attempt circulating throughout town, it's no wonder our refrigerator starts overflowing with trays of casseroles, meatloaves, and chicken dinners. The same church group even arranges to have Mom's name read aloud as a special intention at Mass.

There was a time when I thought maybe I wanted to be a priest. I attended prayer cenacles for years, at my cousin Marco's house, where we would pray the rosary as a group and sing hymns afterwards.

Growing up across the street from a retreat center for Catholic priests and having attended Catholic grammar schools, I always admired clergymen. I even became friends with one of the Brothers who stayed at the retreat. His name was Brother Philip, and he was young; no more than thirty years old. He was a quarterback in high school, and if my brothers and I were out front with our football, he thought nothing of coming over to have a catch with us. In talking to him, he helped me discern and decipher the ancient poetry that is The Bible.

I always felt like I had a calling to help people, and thought the priesthood might be for me, though when I told Pop about it, he adamantly opposed the idea. He said, "Priests aren't what they used to be, Chichi. Anybody who goes into the priesthood nowadays is only trying to escape life, or avoid interacting with women."

No matter how hard he tried, Pop said he couldn't wrap his head around the whole "celibacy thing." He said there was no way he was going to let me go down that path. Now, if I wanted to help people, if I wanted to be a volunteer, he was all for that. It was just the idea of *Father Francesco* that scared the crap out of him. No son of his was going to be a man of the cloth—that much he could promise. In short, I guess, I wanted to be someone who did the right thing and tried to help others. But with Mom in the ICU up in Philadelphia, and our lives taking yet another tragic step closer to the abyss, we continuously find ourselves in need of help.

I'm standing next to my friend, Ron Montgomery, in a pew off to the left of the altar at our home parish. We are listening to the lector recite the litany of Special Intentions. Like everyone else, I respond, "Lord, hear our prayer," after each intention is read aloud. Only, when he gets to Mom's name, I instantly feel my face flush with emotion. It catches me by surprise. Since I was the town's starting quarterback last season, many people know who I am, and they recognize Mom's name as being that of my mother. I had no idea she was going to be a Special Intention, and now I feel like everyone is looking at me. I feel as if they know what's "behind" the Special Intention; like they know it isn't a bout with breast cancer Mom's going through, but a self-inflicted fight for her life.

Ron gives no reaction to my mother's name being read aloud, other than to say the words, "Lord, hear our prayer." Yet, the flush turns into a blush as we sit for the Offertory.

As the priest and two altar boys move forward to await the Presentation of the Gifts, I feel like I should excuse my way past Ron, slide out of my pew, genuflect in the aisle and shout, *Father, wait!*

Because the church is so quiet, I'm sure everyone from the priest to the guy standing along the wall in the back, would look at me and say, *what the heck is he doing?* But I would approach the center aisle, up near the altar, with caution. I would show the priest my hands, so he knew I wasn't up to anything sinister. I would give him a nod that said, *just give me a minute here, will ya' Father?*

At that, I would turn and face the congregation, where I would study their faces for a moment before I would go on to say, *I'm sorry for interrupting the Presentation of the Gifts like this, but for those of you who don't know, that was my mother's name the Lector just read. As some of you may know, she tried to kill herself last week. Now, I won't go into any details, but the bottom line is—she survived. The doctors don't know how—but she did. So, please allow me to thank all of you for your thoughts, prayers, and dinners you've been sending, but...you see...during my mother's recovery, the doctors found an aneurysm on the left side of her brain. They say it could burst at any time, so as soon as she's strong enough, they're going to operate...and...well...I just wanted you to know all that. I wanted you to know what the Special Intention was about.*

When I was finished, I would turn to the priest, and give him a second nod that said, *thank you Father*, before calmly returning to my seat next to Ron.

In reality though, I do no such thing. I could never interrupt Mass, especially during the presentation of the bread and the wine. It's all I can do to contain the emotions I feel inside, as the Gifts are presented, and my mother's name is left to echo amongst the rafters of the church.

With school being out and Mom in the hospital, Pop makes my brothers and me go to work with him almost every day. He's the project manager on this development back on the bay. Not only is he doing all of the masonry work, but Pop is in charge of the other tradesmen, which involves making sure they adhere to the project's deadlines.

Pop says the plan is to build several beautiful, elaborate homes along the water that should fetch close to a million dollars apiece. The profit won't belong to him, but to the investors financing the construction. My brothers and I don't do much work, since the project is still in its early stages. The only project happening is the construction of a big bulkhead along the water, but that doesn't stop Pop from finding things to keep us busy.

He makes us sweep the street along the project every day. It's several blocks long, and if we say, "Pop, we just did it yesterday." He says, "Well, I want it done again, and I want it done right."

I know he's only trying to keep us occupied, and I know that's why he has us come to work with him in the first place. He doesn't want us at home unsupervised, even though I'm eighteen and could take care of my brothers just fine.

Regardless of how much we protest, Pop makes us sweep the street, where I have to use my big push broom to brush the dirt and debris into Tony's square shovel, who then dumps it into the green Rubbermaid trashcan that Michael drags along behind us.

If there is a supply delivery of any sort, Pop has us unload it. If it is brick, lumber or block, he has us stack everything nice and neat, and out of the way. Even though it's ninety-five degrees, in the late July sun, my brothers and I laugh and horse around so much that we don't mind all the busy work.

Tony and Michael don't know the full extent to which Mom tried to end her life—those details are still kind of a secret. They were only told that she 'tried to hurt herself,' and that's why Pop doesn't mind if sometimes, after lunch, Tony passes around his carton of Nestle Quick chocolate milk, so the three of us can get the symphony warmed up like old times. Pop doesn't seem to mind if we reunite The Three Tooters, because as he wipes his brow, and drinks his bottle of Perrier, I know he must be thinking the same thing I am—at least we are together.

My father and I are inside the air-conditioned trailer on the construction site. My brothers are away picking up a load of supplies with Lester and Darryl. Pop is leaning against a desk, covered with old coffee cups and blueprints; the desk sags a bit in the middle. Behind him, is a big bay window, through which I can see the cranes and the pile drivers sitting atop those barges on the water, driving the big pilings of the bulkhead into the wet sand.

I am sitting in a brown, metal, folding chair, drinking a citrus flavored Gatorade, listening to my father handle a business call. I notice his eyes twitching like they have been for some time now. When he hangs up, I say, "Pop, I never saw your eyes twitch so bad."

Pop folds his arms across his chest, takes a deep breath, and tells me they started getting really bad the day Mom tried to kill herself. He says he called her that day, up at Nonna's house, but that she sounded woozy on the phone.

"Mom hung-up in the middle of our conversation. I tried calling back a few times, only to have her pickup on the third try and she sounded even worse than before. So, I got off the phone as quick as I could, and called Aunt Renata."

Pop says my aunt wasn't home, but that he got a hold of Uncle John, her husband. He asked Uncle John to go over and check on Mom, since he lived five minutes away. "But he never went, Chichi."

I ask Pop why Uncle John didn't go check on Mom, and he says, "Probably thought I was over-reacting. Just a few days before the same thing happened. Your mother sounded woozy on the phone, so I called the police, and asked them to stop by Nonna's house and see if Mom was okay. The police stopped by, and found Mom to be woozy, but shrugged it off as her just being tired. Nonna called me and hollered at me for calling the cops. That's probably why your uncle didn't go check on Mom."

I drink some more of my Gatorade and shuffle my feet as Pop says, "Once I found out about Mom and what she had done with the butcher knife, the aspirin and the carpet cleaner, Aunt Ellen and I drove up to Philly right away. We stopped by Nonna's house, but as soon as we pulled into the driveway, we saw the whole family sitting on the front porch. They started shouting at me as we made our way up the front steps. 'My aunt did this because of you!' 'This is all your fault!' Ellen tried to shout back, but it was useless. We got back in my truck, and went down to the hospital, where they had your mother behind this big, ceiling to floor window in the ICU."

Pop says the nurse on duty was rude to him, and said that she didn't think it was a good idea for him to be there. Mom's family told her he was the one to blame for all this. Pop says, "I got in her face and said, 'Bullshit! That's my wife lyin' in there, and I'm gonna see her!' I mean, she was on a respirator, with all sorts of tubes going in and out of her body, and Aunt Ellen started to cry. We weren't allowed to stay that long, but I just couldn't believe it. Couldn't believe the girl I married was lyin' there like that."

After he says that, Pop grows quiet and still—all except his eyes. I sit in my chair, looking up at my father, as the skin above and below his eyes, twitches and flinches uncontrollably.

Mom's aneurysm surgery has been scheduled for August 10, 1995. She has been living in the Locked Crisis Unit ever since she got discharged from the ICU. She calls Pop on his cellular phone frequently. I know because each time Mom calls, he'll stick his head out of the trailer, on that job over on the bay, and shout, *Frankie, Tony, Michael, your mother's on the phone!*

One of us will stop whatever we're doing, trot over and up the trailer steps where we talk to Mom for a few minutes in the air-conditioning.

The night before her surgery, I stay at Nonna's house, so I can be at the hospital first thing in the morning. But, as I begin to fall asleep, I start thinking about making the short walk down the street to the greenhouse—the greenhouse where all of this started. The greenhouse where Mom was abused is still there; it's only a few doors down from Nonna's house.

If I was standing in front of that thing and not lying in a sleeping bag on my grandmother's floor, I would summon all of my strength and all of my anger. I would stand in the tiny backyard where my mother used to play with her childhood friends. The backyard where that dirty old man used to lure Mom into his greenhouse, sit her on his lap, move her underwear aside, and push himself inside of her.

I would stand there, allowing my anger to grow. I would take my shirt off. I would hoist up my pants. I would focus on my breathing. I would block out the rain that came along with the night. I would shove my rationale aside. I would go crazy. I wouldn't want to know what that sick old man was thinking when his head hit the pillow each night.

How he must have known what he was doing to my eight year old mother was wrong. How, some forty years later, my mother would still be trapped in that greenhouse; forced to resort to a concoction of carpet cleaner and aspirin, with a butcher knife garnish as a way to set herself free.

As I lie in the dark, I see pictures in my head of my mother. Actually, they're photographs, mental pictures of photos she showed me from when she was young. The pictures were taken in the 1950's, black and white photos, where she looked so innocent and alive. Yet, I can also see the colored photos she showed me from the early 1960's where she looked like something was troubling her. I know from talking to Mom that she started smoking around that time.

When I revisit that scene in my mind, the one of me standing in the backyard, I know I wouldn't need to look for any stones or bring one of Pop's sledgehammers. If I was standing in that backyard, I would tear my shirt into strips, and wrap those strips around my hands. I would beat my fists into my palms, as I speak to that sick old man's spirit, dead and gone.

269

Under my breath, I would say, *you're lucky I wasn't there, old man. You're lucky I wasn't alive, because if I was, and I knew what you were doing to my mother, my eight year old mother, I wouldn't react like Nonna did. I wouldn't tell her I didn't want to hear it. I wouldn't allow you to keep raping her, to keep putting yourself inside of her. I would hunt you down, and I would slam my fist into your face* like I do in my mind's eye, when I slam my fist into the panes of glass.

I would unleash each blow and say, *this is for taking away her innocence! This is for ruining my parents' marriage! This is for robbing me and my brothers of the mother we love!*

When I am finished, there would be nothing left of that fucking greenhouse—*nothing.*

41

With the way our summer has gone, the motivation to work out for football or prepare myself for college in anyway has been nonexistent. I haven't been lifting weights with any consistency. I don't know how I'm going to be ready to play for Towson State University if I don't start working out and getting back into shape. I don't even know where to begin. I don't want to be labeled again as "the kid with so much potential," but who produced nothing but continual disappointment. I want Towson to be a new beginning, a new start, a new lease, a new life; but how can that happen when Mom's attempted suicide and aneurysm surgery have hijacked our summer and our lives?

I know I am desperate for help; I have doubts; I feel lost and alone. I don't believe in myself or my abilities; I miss my mother, yet I feel so hurt and betrayed by her. By mid-August, her health has improved and she has stabilized enough for the doctors to surgically clip off the vein in her brain that caused her aneurysm.

I drive back and forth five times between Philadelphia and the Jersey Shore the week between her surgery, and the day I'm supposed to leave for Towson State. As I sit near Mom's hospital bed staring at her bloated face, a scalp full of staples, and half a head of hair, I can't help but feel sorry for everything that's happened to her this summer—her disappearance on my 18th birthday to jump off the Tacony-Palmyra Bridge, her suicide attempt in Nonna's kitchen, her aneurysm surgery, and her weeks confined to the Locked Crisis Unit. Mom's life is a disaster; my life is a disaster; our lives are a disaster.

The night before I leave for Towson, I wait until Mom falls asleep, before I make my way back down the shore, yet I take a detour. Instead of going straight home, I drive to my high school and park in the vacant parking lot. As I walk out onto the empty football field, I feel so alone. It's nearly midnight, yet I walk the length of the field, talking to myself out loud about the challenges that lie ahead.

I know I'm not ready for college, and I know I'm not ready for football, but if I go with the right attitude, I tell myself, maybe, just *maybe*, I'll come through it alright. Despite the trauma of the summer we've had, I know I want my Towson opportunity to be a success. I know that I want to be everything I *wasn't* here in high school. I want a fresh start to prove myself. I want to be strong in the face of adversity.

I want to prove to the coaches that they made the right choice by recruiting me. I want to "walk my talk," like Anthony Robbins says, and follow through on my dreams. I want to reach my goals with enthusiasm, and stop living so hesitantly. I want to put my head down, and block out all of the distractions. I want to impress the upperclassmen, and show the rest of the Patriot League that I'm for real. I want to be methodical and purposeful as I overcome my doubts and fears.

Above all else, though, I want to embody perseverance. I continue walking the field as midnight becomes one a.m, and I realize this is it. Tomorrow marks the beginning of a new life for me. Towson will become my new home, where I'll cast my past aside, and reinvent myself. I feel ready for this challenge, and I want to do it all for Mom.

The next morning, Pop takes me down to the Point Diner. We sit at the counter, and each order a cheese omelette, with a side of home fries, rye toast, and black coffee. The diner is packed with Shoobies— those pesky summer tourists from out of town—heading to the beach on this mid-August morning. As we eat our omelettes and drink our coffee, neither one of us talks about Mom; we never mention the summer, the suicide attempt, or the aneurysm surgery. All Pop does is drink his black coffee, and flash that smile of his. The one that goes right along with that look in his eyes, the look that says, *I know this is tough kiddo, but who better to handle it all, than us?*

It's been only eight days since Mom's operation, and even though I talked to myself last night, I'm still not sure if I'm ready for Towson. Pop must sense that because he wants to know if I'll be okay to make the three-hour drive to Baltimore by myself.

"Cheech," he says. "You sure you don't need me to follow you down?"

"No Pop," I say. "I'll be all right."

"You sure?"

"Yeah, I'm sure."

"I mean, it would take some jugglin', but I could arrange to follow you down."

I turn to him, amidst the hustle and bustle of the crowded diner, and do my best to give him the Hero School look. The strong look that says, *I know this is tough, but I can handle it. Not only that, I **want** to handle it. I'm a man.*

Pop picks up on the Hero School look, and studies my eyes for a moment. He nods his head once, looks past me, raises his right arm, summons our waitress, and asks for the check. I can tell my father is impressed with my "strong look;" I sense it is the reassurance he needs.

We hurry back to our house after breakfast and I finish loading the Camaro. Pop pulls out the video camera and records my last few minutes at home. I'm standing by the Camaro, door open, engine not yet running, as my father conducts an interview of sorts for the camera.

"You ready to be a college quarterback, Chichi?"

"Ready as I'll ever be," I say into the lens.

"Got your number picked out? You know what number you want to be?"

"Twenty. You know that Pop; twenty is my number."

"So real quick, how 'bout a few words to your adoring fans...."

"Pop...."

"No c'mon, you're gonna be a star. Give us a sound bite, come on, Chichi."

Below the camera, I can see Pop's mouth is in the shape of a smile, so I smile back. Yet, I'm trying to hide the nostalgia I feel inside. The nostalgia that makes it hard for me to give him a sound bite, without thinking that Mom should be here in the frame of his shot, dabbing her eyes with a tissue over the fact that her firstborn is heading off to college. I would lay my arm across her shoulders, and say, *there, there Mom, I'm gonna be a big football star, so don't you cry. We'll see each other at all my games and on Parents Weekend.*

But as Pop lowers the camera from his face, I notice he has tears rolling down his cheeks. My father tries to smile through the tears, but as he moves towards me to kiss my cheek, I can feel what this summer has done to him. Others don't know it, the way he is always whistling, and carrying on like a frustrated Tony Danza, but I can feel it. He has stopped being just my father, and has become a fellow survivor like Tony and Michael.

The four of us now make up *The South Jersey Chapter of the Brotherhood of Sadness*, our own little fraternity, where our dysfunctional bond is built upon an oath of chaos. My father has always tried to raise my brothers and me with that Hero School touch. Always tried to model a masculine approach to handling life, but on top of all of those creditors looking for money—all of Mom's medical bills are going right to Pop.

Between the Emergency Room, the cost of her intensive care, the aneurysm surgery, Mom's recuperation, and her summer in the Locked Crisis Unit, my father has no hope of getting out of debt. My brothers and I, along with Pop, haven't had any health coverage for some time, and my father and I don't have any auto insurance either. We are barely surviving.

As I climb into the Camaro and back out into the street, my father stands at the top of the driveway with the camera down around his waist. He has stopped videotaping, and shouts through the open window, "You be careful drivin', Chichi, and gimme a call when you get there."

"Okay," I shout back.

A moment later as I reach the stop sign at the corner, I glance back at Pop through the rearview mirror. I swear I can see 'through' him—the boy with too many aptitudes, the confident Sergeant First Class, is now a lonely forty-five year old contractor with no money and little hope.

When I get to Baltimore, other incoming freshmen are walking around Towson's campus in flip-flops, with their baseball caps turned backwards, headphones on, and chewing tobacco in their mouths. They have big necks, big arms, chiseled calves with tattoos on the side and earrings that dangle from earlobes. When they shake my hand, it's like they're trying to show me how strong they are. Another thing they all have—company.

Parents, girlfriends, brothers, and sisters help the freshman ballplayers carry their boxes and bed comforters up the endless flights of stairs to our dorm rooms. When the moving is all done, mothers cry, little brothers smile, and girlfriends cling to their boyfriends' big arms, posing for pictures. I'm by myself watching all this, and I feel totally alone.

I feel alone because I wish I had taken up Pop's offer to help me move down here. I feel alone because I've never had a girlfriend to pose with, and I feel alone because my mother can't even stand up to cry if she wanted.

She's still in that hospital bed with all of those staples in her head, even though a part of me knows she's probably sneaking a cigarette every time the doctor turns his back; she's that *testa dura*.

I am unloading the Camaro by the curb outside of my dorm when Coach Combs spots me. Coach Combs is the head coach here at Towson, the one who recruited me, the one who thought he saw something worth pursuing in my game films.

All I want to do is go back home when he walks up to me with a funny look on his face and asks, "Hey son, you by yourself?"

"Yes, Coach."

"Wow, I thought you'd have half the family here. Vinny Troiano got here about an hour ago. He's a free safety from Brooklyn, big Italian family, three Lincoln Towne cars pulled up, fifteen people got out. It was like something out of *The Godfather*, all these bald guys, with little mustaches crying and helping Vinny move in. Anyway, you need anything, just let me know."

I nod and say, "Thanks Coach." But I feel more alone than ever after I run into Vinny and his entourage all hugging, crying, and saying goodbye. I wish I was standing there with my own entourage, but I'm not, and that makes me sad. I'm sad, because I'm old enough to know that going away to college is supposed to be an exciting time, filled with hope and promise, not a sorrowful sentence, marred by memories of butcher knives and blood.

From the window of my dorm room, I can see the practice fields and beyond that, I can see the stadium where I know I'll star one day. My talk with myself last night is still fresh in my mind, even if a part of me wants to pack everything up and go home.

As I begin setting up my half of the dorm, I can feel a sense of determination swell up inside of me. I just know I'm going to make Towson everything that high school wasn't. I just know I'm going to date pretty girls and break every passing record in Towson's book.

When Coach Combs was trying to sell me on the idea of becoming a Towson State Tiger, he told me all about Dave Meggett, and Sean Landetta, guys who made it to the NFL that used to play right here at Towson. He also told me about last year's quarterback, who plays professionally in the Canadian Football League. One day, I know that'll be me. Coach Combs will be telling some young recruit all about me starring for the Philadelphia Eagles, my hometown team, succeeding Randall Cunningham, and dating a whole slew of lingerie models. That'll be me, and that's what wakes me up early the next morning for our first day of practice.

There are nearly one hundred guys on the team from all over the East Coast. Black players from Florida and Maryland, white players from Virginia and New York. There are 'old' freshmen, in their early twenties, going to college on GI Bills, and then there are a lot of guys like me—eighteen, scared and fresh out of high school. One of the 'older' players, just out of the army, has the locker next to mine. His name is Donald, and he says he's happy to be here.

"Yeah, this is much better than pulling KP, back on my base in Germany."

Donald is a defensive back. When he finds out I'm a quarterback, he looks at me with a whole new level of respect. He introduces me to a couple of guys he met yesterday during check-in. I feel funny shaking their hands, and telling them where I'm from, because we're in the locker room naked. We were getting dressed for practice, but there was a mix up with the equipment; nothing fits anybody in our small little bank of lockers.

I feel funny being naked in front of Donald and the other guys because they're all black and have perfect bodies. They look like black versions of Michelangelo's *David*, with their dongs hanging down almost to their kneecaps, while their arms, necks and shoulders are bulging out all over the place. I feel like a boy standing next to them, and wonder if the equipment manager is ever going to bring us our stuff.

When we finally get suited up in our black spikes, white practice pants, yellow jerseys and brown helmets, we hit the field. At the start of practice, Coach Combs gives us a speech about his goals for the year. He calls us men, and reminds me of Pop and those speeches he used to give us years ago when I was little. Coach Combs stands before us in a pair of sunglasses, tan shorts, a white Towson polo shirt, and a whistle around his neck. He says our team mission statement is simple this year.

"It's just two words men, *show me*." He says, "Every practice, every game, every time you lace up your spikes is an opportunity to *show me* what you're made of. I don't like talk, men, I like action. The key to our success is going to be action, so on the count of three let me hear you shout it...*one two three...SHOW ME!*"

After Coach Comb's speech, we are told to break off with our position coaches. I trot over to where the other quarterbacks are loosening up, and count that there are seven of us. *Seven!* How am I ever going to beat out six other guys for one position when I couldn't even meet expectations in high school?

Six of us stand on the sidelines, as the projected first-string quarterback runs through plays on the field.

Those of us standing on the sidelines are supposed to clap after every play, even though it's only practice. So there I am, sweating my balls off, my helmet so tight it's giving me a headache, with mosquitoes singing in my ears, cheering for guys I don't even know, who when I walk by them in the shower, act like I'm not even there.

We have practice twice a day for two hours at a time. In between, we have a whole schedule of meetings with our position coach, and time set aside to watch film together from that morning's practice. The entire day is football, football, football. By the middle of the third day, I'm desperate, and on the phone with Pop.

I call him and tell him I can't take it. I'm too out of shape, too alone, and too depressed to stay here any longer. He says it'll all work out, not to panic, and to remember that Joe Montana was one of seven quarterbacks at Notre Dame, and look how he turned out. We go back and forth on the phone for hours about how out of place I feel down here with all these guys whose only focus is football, football and more football. Pop says, "Well, that's why you're there isn't it, to play football?"

I tell him he's right, "I'm here to play football, but I don't feel like I belong."

"What does that mean?"

"These guys are in great shape. I didn't work out over the summer. I'm not ready for this."

"Well, I'm sure some of the other freshmen players feel the same way. It's a big step you're making going from high school to college ball."

I fall silent after Pop says that. I was hoping to hear him say, *it's okay, Chichi, come on home*, and I fall silent because I pledged to make Towson my new beginning, yet here I am wallowing like I did in high school. I wallow, because I allow the image of my mother with all those staples in her head to haunt me. The image follows me around and reminds me of that day her name was read aloud as a Special Intention. It makes me think about my birthday, when she went to jump off the Tacony-Palmyra Bridge, or that July day with the carpet cleaner, the knife, and the aspirin.

It's because of those images and memories that I tell my father I'm not ready for this, but it's also the fact that my arm is worn out from all of the passing drills. As quarterbacks, that's all we do for the entire practice, throw, throw and throw some more. My arm feels like a wet noodle, and I'm in the trainer's room after every practice, soaking my elbow in a bin of ice, but the soreness won't go away.

By the morning of our fourth day of practice, I just can't do it anymore. I walk up to Coach Combs outside his office and say, "Coach, I think I want to quit."

"You want to quit?"

"Yeah, my arm is killing me, and I don't see how I can make this work, I'm too out of shape and..."

"Hold on, hold on a second, son. We had high hopes for you. You might even earn a Letter this year, and you know how rare that is for a freshman. As far as your arm goes, the more you throw, the more it'll improve; you know that. I really think you ought to think this over; I don't want you making a choice you're going to regret."

Standing there before him, I wish I could tell Coach about the last few weeks. How the summer has gone, how Mom is up in Philadelphia lying in a hospital bed with dozens of staples in her head. I wish I could tell him about her attempt to end it all with one of Babbo's butcher knives, or my eighteenth birthday when she disappeared to jump off the Tacony-Palmyra Bridge. I wish I could say all of that to Coach, but I know that if I did, I would cry, and who wants a quarterback who cries? Besides, if one of the guys with the big dongs saw me, they would laugh and tell everyone that the quarterback from Atlantic City is a real pussy.

Despite what Coach says about me maybe earning my Letter, I pack up the Camaro determined to go home. Yet, I start to feel guilty. *Am I just wussing out,* I ask myself. *Should I try and make this work? Do I just have cold feet?*

As the afternoon practice starts, I change my mind. I think back on all those speeches Pop used to give us when I was a kid. He didn't raise me to quit; he raised me to go all the way, and that's just what I'll do. I walk out onto the practice field in street clothes, and ask Coach if he has a minute to talk. He has his sunglasses on, and is much different than he was this morning outside of his office. He is dry, uncaring, and barely listening, as I ask him for a couple days off.

"A couple days off? Are you kidding me, son?"

"No, Coach, you see, when I said I wanted to quit this morning, I wasn't bein' honest."

"How wasn't that bein' honest?"

"You see, my mother just had surgery. She's still in the hospital, and I don't feel right being here so far away. So, I was wondering if I could go home and stay with my family for a couple days?"

"A couple days?"

"Yeah, then I'll come back down."

"Son, today is Thursday. If you want to be a part of this team, you'll need to be back here by Saturday."

"I can do that. I'll be here Saturday."

"Good. I hope your mother feels better, but I have a practice to run, so get off the field."

"Right Coach, I'll see you on Saturday."

I walk back to the Camaro and get into the driver's seat. I pull up to the exit of the parking lot, and take one last look at the busy practice field full of brown helmets and yellow shirts. I take a deep breath, apply my foot to the gas pedal, and drive back up Interstate 95 towards the Jersey Shore.

When I get back to the shore, three hours later, I head right for that construction site on the bay, where I know I'll find my father. I walk into the trailer, where he's on the phone talking business. His eyes are still twitching like they were before I left. Once he hangs up, the first thing out of his mouth is, "So, now what are you gonna to do?"

"I don't know. I figured I could work for you until I find a school where I could play baseball in the spring."

"Cheech, listen to yourself. There's a school in Baltimore that wants you to play football for them *right now*. They're going to help out with tuition. You've been accepted, you're enrolled, you have a roommate, you've signed up for classes. This is a mess! What are you talking about playing baseball? You want to hurt me? You trying to hurt me?"

"Pop, whaddaya mean, trying to hurt you? I'm not ready to play, that's all it comes down to. I asked the coach if I can have off till Saturday."

"And?"

"He said yes."

"So, you're gonna go back down?"

"I don't think so."

"You don't think so? Frank, forget about football for a second, what about school? You cannot drop out. If you don't go back right now, you're never going to finish college."

"So, what? You didn't finish college."

280

"Cheech, your mother is in a hospital bed, and nothing you do can change that. When she gets out, she's going to stay with Nonna for as long as it takes until she's ready to come back home, *if* she comes back home. Your brothers are in school; they're playing football, but you're walking out of a perfect situation. Yes, there are six other quarterbacks down there, but you know yourself, you're better than half of them right off the bat. In terms of playing baseball, Cheech, there's nowhere for you to play. There are no teams you can play for that are going to pay you anything; you're not good enough. I'm telling you right now, if you don't go back to college, you'll never finish, and it will haunt you."

"Pop...."

"Shut-up! You don't know what you're talkin' about. Now lissename, if you're not goin' back to Towson, that's your decision, but you're goin' over to Atlantic Community College tomorrow, and you're gonna sign up for courses."

"Ah, Pop, *Jesus!*"

"Cheech, *I don't want to hear it!* You're goin' to sign-up for classes at ACC. I'll pay for 'em, but you're not gonna stop college. If you don't wanna play ball, that's one thing, but you *have* to go to school. If you stop, you'll never go back, that's what happened to me."

I shake my head and start to smile. Pop notices my chuckling and asks, "What? What's so funny? Why are you laughin'?"

"Pop everything with you is, 'It happened to me. It happened to me.' *I'm not you!*"

"Frank, do you have any idea what this summer has been like?"

"Yeah, I do."

"Then why do you try to hurt me, huh? Why do you throw things back in my face?"

"Pop, what are you talkin' about?"

"That attitude, your smugness. You think you know better? *Fine!* Gimme the keys to the Camaro."

"What?"

"Gimme the fuckin' keys to the Camaro!"

"Why?"

"Because of that look on your face, because you have no clue, no idea what you're doin'. You're gonna ruin your future over this fuckin' shit. You'll get into shape with football, c'mon...."

"You ever think maybe I like hurtin' you?"

"What didja say?"

"I said, didja ever think maybe I like hurtin' you? That all this is your fault?"

"That's it, *get the fuck out! Get the fuck out!* Gimme the keys, and *get the fuck out!*"

I've never seen Pop so mad. I give him the keys, but he just throws them into the back of the trailer.

"You're a child! You're acting like a fuckin' child! Grow-up! You're eighteen years old, enough of this nonsense. You wanna hurt me? You wanna play games? Fine! Then walk home! Go ahead, get out! *Walk the fuck home!*"

When I walk out the trailer door, Lester and Darryl are working nearby, unloading bricks from the back of a flatbed truck. The odd thing is, they're working in complete silence, which is never how they do things. They're either singing, laughing, or cutting up on each other in their southern way, but today they must have heard Pop yelling through the thin walls of the trailer. They must have heard our whole conversation, and are probably in agreement with my father. They know what education means in this world. People like Lester and Darryl know that when you have the chance to go to college and play football, you can't let anything get in your way.

I know people like Lester and Darryl would stick it out. They would find a way to block out the memory of friends bringing us dinner with a look of pity on their faces. They would find a way to forget the anxiety I felt when we weren't sure what was going to happen to Mom, whether she was going to live or not, and now, the anxiety in not knowing what lies ahead. Walking out of the trailer though, I'm glad nobody calls out to me because I'm not in the mood to talk. All I want to do is walk back home in silence. Even though inside my head voices are shooting off right and left. *Fuck Mom for being so weird. Fuck Pop for the mess with Gail. Fuck Gail, stupid bimbo. Fuck football, fuck Towson, fuck Babbo for being such an asshole, and fuck anybody else I forgot who thinks they know better than me.*

The walk from the construction site on the bay to our house on the mainland is bad enough because it's so long, but it's worse when it's ninety-five degrees and you don't have any socks on. My sneakers are cutting into my heels, because of the way my feet are sweating. I start to limp, sweat, and tire, but I won't let any of it get to me. I'll show Pop I was right in coming home; I'll show him that he's wrong about me playing baseball. Doesn't he remember that I was voted the Most Valuable Player on the high school baseball team last season? Doesn't he recall that I recorded the highest batting average of any of my teammates? I'm a *fabulous* baseball player! Way better than my moronic father ever was! I don't care that no college teams recruited me to play baseball, I'll find a minor league team to play for; I'll prove *everybody* wrong. Who needs college? And what does my idiot father know about college, anyway? He failed out of Penn State, and then tried a year at The University of Dayton, that led to nothing. He knows *nothing* about college!

I'm just about to turn around, even though I'm halfway home, and let him know how stupid he is, when a white Honda Accord pulls off into the shoulder ahead of me. I instantly recognize the car as belonging to Aunt Bridgid. She rolls down the passenger side window and shouts, "Frankie, c'mon, get in!"

"No," I shout back. "I can walk. I wanna walk."

Traffic is zooming by, but Aunt Bridgid yells above it all, "*Frankie, get in the car!*" I've never heard Aunt Bridgid yell before. So, I do like she says and the moment I close the car door, she says, "Your mother just called me. She's worried to death about you. Your father told her how he was making you walk home, and she asked me to come find you."

The whole ride home, Aunt Bridgid wants to know what has gotten into my father. What does he think he's trying to prove by making me walk home? She swears sometimes he makes no sense at all, and wonders how my brothers and I can stand him without turning into a bunch of raving lunatics.

42

On Labor Day 1995, two weeks after I come home from Towson, Aunt Teresa's husband offers me a job. His name is Hank, and he's six feet six inches tall, with white hair, and a big, bushy, white mustache, even though he's only fifty-one years old. Hank is a high school dropout, and a pit-boss at the Tropicana Casino. He also runs his own landscaping business, and says he'll pay me eight dollars an hour to work twenty-five hours a week cutting lawns.

I take the job the same week Pop makes me sign up for classes at Atlantic Community College. I argue with him that ACC is a stupid college for dumb kids, but he doesn't want to hear it. He says I'll thank him when I'm older, and so I sign up for Art Appreciation, Western World, and Introduction to Philosophy.

It's late September, just days after my parents' twentieth wedding anniversary. I come home from ACC after my afternoon class, to find Aunt Ellen sitting in the kitchen with Grandmom sewing a hole in Tony's football jersey. Not even two minutes after I walk in do we hear the front door open and Mom's voice shout, *"I'm home!"*

We all look at each other like, *Mom's here? What's going on?* We file into the foyer where Aunt Colomba, Nonna, Mom and my godmother, Edith, are all standing.

I ask, "Mom, what are you doing here?"

"I live here."

"I know, but you're supposed to stay in Philadelphia until you're all better."

"I am better."

"No, you're not."

"How do you know?"

"Because it's only been a month since the surgery."

"And?"

"And, you're not supposed to be home yet."

Grandmom and Aunt Ellen wave their hands around and say, "Ann, what in God's name are you doing here?" Edith and Aunt Colomba wave their hands back and answer, "She lives here, and deserves to be with her family."

"Yeah," Aunt Colomba says, "some welcome my sister gets. First time home in two months; and this is what she gets?"

Grandmom says, "Colomba, it's only been a month since the surgery. The idea was for Ann to stay in Philly and nurse herself back to health. If it took six months, or a year, she wasn't to come home until she was better."

"That's bull! This is where she belongs! With her family! With her boys!"

"No," Aunt Ellen says, "she belongs up there where she can take care of herself. Ann, you were supposed to stay up there and start taking your medication, making the doctor's appointments and opening yourself up to therapy. It wasn't just about the aneurysm; it was about trying to put your life back together."

"I've done all that."

"*In a month?* You haven't done squat! You're only here because that's what you want! You always get what you want, don't you? Well, I'll tell you what, Ann, I can't sit here and watch you come back into this home and torture these boys again. Haven't they been through enough?"

"Ellen, I'm fine, and I'm their mother!"

"I can't listen to this anymore. You've coerced your family into *thinking* that you're fine and for that, you got your way and they brought you home."

"That's right! Her place is here," Edith says.

"Well, you only believe that because she's *convinced* you that she's okay. Don't you understand that she holds everyone hostage down here? She can convince you of anything! Nobody has bothered to ask the boys how they feel, or what they want. Why don't you try to nurse her back to health instead of dropping her off the first chance you get?"

285

Edith, Nonna and Aunt Colomba argue with Grandmom and Aunt Ellen. They go back and forth about how Mom has let our house fall apart. Specifically, they point out that all she ever does is lay on the couch, smoke and complain about the burning in her stomach, only to jump up and answer the phone like everything is fine. Grandmom says, "It's obvious; Ann needs help."

"Now wait a minute...." Edith says.

"Threatening to jump off bridges, and trying to kill yourself are not signs of healthy behavior."

"I'm not saying they are," says Edith. "But Frank and the boys don't make life easy for Ann."

"What's that supposed to mean?" Grandmom asks.

"They walk over her in the morning...."

"Yeah, because she sleeps on the floor!"

"Ladies! Ladies! " Aunt Ellen shouts, "This summer has been hard enough on everybody, but that still doesn't mean Ann coming home like this is the right answer."

"How can you say that?" Mom asks. "You're my friend, Ellen."

"Yes, Ann, I am your friend. But to come home so you can lay around all day, or gamble 'til late at night isn't what this family needs. They need a healthy mother."

"They have a healthy mother," Aunt Colomba says. "The operation went well."

"I don't mean the *operation*, Colomba! I mean emotionally healthy."

Aunt Colomba shakes her head and limps away.

"No," Aunt Ellen continues. "Ann led you guys to believe that Frank and the boys were making a movie about her. Remember that? I mean, how much more ridiculous can you get than that?"

"Why do you have to bring that up?" Mom asks her friend.

"Because," Grandmom says, "no one sees the truth here, Ann. Remember what happened that time you had the cast on your leg? More of that type of behavior is on its' way, unless you get some serious, prolonged mental help. Ann had a chance to go away years ago. She had a chance to go to the University of Pennsylvania's Institute of Mental Health, but you people didn't want to hear it. Now look where we are!"

Nonna says, "You no know nothin'! That'sa my daughter! This'a her house, these'a her boys, this'a where she'a belong!"

"Oh, God," Aunt Ellen says. "You people make me crazy! Ann needs to see a professional to get help, to worry about herself. *We'll* take care of the boys!"

"No, they're my sons!"

Trying to take control of the chaos and reveal the truth, Grandmom continues the conversation by saying, "I know they're your sons, Ann, but enough with the conspiracy theories and blaming everything on everybody else. Their lives revolve around you and your next bizarre move. My son's eyes twitch like crazy because of you."

"Oh, poor Frank...." says Mom.

"That's your husband!" Grandmom interrupts.

"Yeah, we'll tell him to start acting like it," says Edith.

This is how the rest of the afternoon goes until Edith and Aunt Colomba leave Nonna and Mom at our house. When Pop gets home, another argument ensues, and I know I made the right decision to come home from Towson. My father and my brothers are going to need me here. They're going to need all the help they can get, now that Mom is back home down the shore.

Working as a landscaper for Hank, is a lot like working for Pop in construction. We start early in the morning, work outside, and drive around in a dump truck. We go from house to house, cutting and edging lawns as fast as we can, and the funny thing is, I don't mind the work. Some mornings, when we break for coffee, I find myself thinking about the guys I met down at Towson. Sometimes, I even check the sports' section of the newspaper for Towson scores, but normally I'm just glad I'm not down there, standing on the sidelines, icing my elbow, and riding the bench.

The classes Pop made me take at ACC aren't as bad as I thought, even though I could never tell him that. I could never admit that he was right. Even though it's only been a few weeks, I know college is where I belong. I sit in my Western World class mesmerized by the professor who goes on and on about Europe and its' rich history. I scribble notes into my notebook with such fervor I shock myself. When I tell my professor that I'm going to the Meadowlands with two cousins to see Pope John Paul II celebrate Mass, I accept his invitation to earn extra credit by making a presentation to the class about the first non-Italian Pope since 1523.

In my Introduction to Philosophy class, there is a girl named Maxine who always smiles at me when she walks in to sit down. I don't know what to make of her smile because I get distracted by my heart racing like Mike Tyson working a speed bag in my chest, boom-boom, boom-boom, boom-boom. When she tosses her long dark hair over her shoulder, I feel a storm of excitement erupt inside me, yet all I can do when she smiles at me is lower my eyes and look away.

I could never smile back because then she would know I like her, and I don't want her to know I like her; I'm that afraid. Either way, I sit there in class trying to figure her out as the professor goes on and on about war. He says, in his opinion, the next Great War will be over drinking water. He's an old Hippie with long hair and a bandana who loves horses and looks like he could be Willie Nelson's twin. He waves the chalk in the air, and says, "We pay more for bottled water, than we do for gasoline. Has the war started already?"

Hands go up all over class, but my eyes never leave Maxine. I study her through a forest of raised arms wishing I had listened in on Tony's and Michael's conversations with those giggling girls, so I would know how to talk to women. When I tell Pop about Maxine, he says I'm making too much of it. My father says, I should just walk up to her, introduce myself, and ask if she'd like to get a cup of coffee at the student lounge. "She's only a girl, Cheech. You know what I'm sayin'? What's the worst she could say? 'No, thanks, I have a boyfriend?' You can't let fear dictate how you live your life. You've gotta take action in spite of it."

I try to do what Pop says, and take action in spite of my fear. But every time Maxine walks in with that smile, Tyson starts on the bag, boom-boom, boom-boom, and I keep my eyes to the floor.

43

On days when I don't have class, and I get home early from working with Hank, I normally find Mom lying on the loveseat in front of the big screen TV. She loves to watch the O.J. Simpson murder trial. On the floor beside her, will be two or three nearly empty coffee cups from 7-11 with cigarette butts floating around on top. When I kiss her on the cheek to say hello, she barely takes her eyes off of the TV to say, "Hey, Frankie."

Mom's hair still hasn't grown in all the way, so she wears a wig when we go out to one of Tony's or Michael's football games. She never wears the wig at home, which means she has one half a head of wavy salt and pepper hair, and another half of stubbly salt and pepper growth. It's strange to sit next to her and see only one side or the other, but what is really strange is that Mom has been complaining of a pain in her head again.

Not wanting to take a chance, Pop drives her back up to Philadelphia for more CAT scans and MRIs, but the doctors can't find anything. They say whatever pain exists is probably somatic and not related to her aneurysm surgery. I ask Pop what somatic is, and he says it's when your mind tricks your body into thinking there's something the matter physically, when really, there's something the matter emotionally.

I wonder if it's something somatic that makes Mom put lipstick on every hour of the day. Whether she's lying on the couch, watching the final days of the O.J. Simpson murder trial, or sitting at a stoplight waiting for it to change, Mom takes out the little mirror from her purse, and coats her lips with a heavy layer of bright, red lipstick. She does it so often that she looks like a clown, especially because lipstick is the only makeup she wears anymore. The layers of red lipstick are always crooked, and Pop has to tell her, "Ann dab your lips a little, so it doesn't look so weird. Besides, you leave lipstick marks on everything."

Mom refuses to listen to my father which drives him crazy. He especially complains at lunch, when she eats her sandwich, and leaves a heavy lipstick smudge on the bread, only to eat the smudge with the next bite. Then Mom opens her purse, takes out her lipstick, redoes her lips and eats the lipstick again, and again, and again, until the sandwich is all gone. The more Pop asks her to stop, the more she does it, until he says, "Ann, you're just like your father!"

"What are you talking about?"

"You know what I'm talking about. Anytime anybody asked him to stop drinking, what happened?"

"Whaddaya mean?"

"*What would he do?*"

"I don't know."

"Yes you do! He would do the exact opposite! If someone said, 'Hey Babbo, I don't think you should drive, you've had too much to drink.' What would he do? He would get behind the wheel of that big old Buick, and drive three sheets to the wind. Why? Because he didn't care what anybody else had to say; all he cared about was doing exactly what he wanted. This is what *you* do when I ask you to stop with the lipstick."

"No, it isn't."

"*Ay, stu gots! It is too!*"

"No Frank, it's just you've brainwashed the kids against me and...." Pop snaps at that, "*Oh! Ann, enough!* This has nothing to do with the kids or conspiracies! It has to do with you doing whatever you damn well please!"

As the cold sweeps through south Jersey, Hank tells me we have to go around and winterize his customers' sprinkler systems. When I ask him what that means, he says we have to blow the sprinklers out. When I ask him what *that* means, he nearly spits out his coffee, and says, "Jesus, Frankie, you are slow."

He explains that we have to shut each system's water off for the winter, then literally blow the sprinkler pipes out with an air-compressor so they don't freeze and burst. Hank says my job is to crawl under the houses, find the shut-off valve for the water, turn it off, and crawl back out. He says it's an easy job, even for somebody slow like me, and that I shouldn't be taking my time under there either. "Get in and get out," he quips. "We got a lot of customers to do."

What Hank doesn't tell me is that crawl spaces can be pitch dark. Sometimes, you can't see a foot in front of you. Some people are nice enough to loan us flashlights, but a lot of the time, I have to use my hands to "see," while listening to Hank's voice for direction. He'll stand outside of the house, by the sprinkler connection box, calling to me. "It's over here, Frankie," he shouts through the wall. "Over here!"

The first couple of houses we do without a flashlight, Hank laughs and tells me to look out for the mice and rats, *ha, ha, ha,* or whatever else might be waiting for me in the dark. I don't laugh when he says that, and I don't like crawling under all of these houses, especially the way some of them smell so damp and musty that I want to gag. I especially hate when I crawl into a puddle of water that I didn't see until I'm splashing around in the middle of slop. If I take too long trying to find the shut-off valve for the sprinkler system, Hank will roar at me, "What the hell are you doing down there, Frankie? We don't have all day!"

It's on those days, when he roars, that I wish I was working for Pop—pouring concrete—the most Italian thing in the world. Cutting grass isn't so bad, but crawling under stinky and wet houses is humiliating. I wish I was there with Pop, my trowel in hand, my knee pads on.

I wish I was there when the concrete truck shows up, its' big barrel swishing around with wet cement, ready, willing and able to create a masterpiece. But I'm not. My father is struggling to land any new work, with the cold winter weather fast approaching, and with that job on the bay slowing down. So, instead of honing my skills as a concrete finisher, I spend two weeks in November crawling around south Jersey in the dark, battling cobwebs out of my way with the knees of my jeans muddy and wet.

For my Western World class at Atlantic Community College, I have to write a paper on immigration. I decide to call Nonna and ask her if I can write about her coming to America. She is confused at first and laughs into the phone, "Chichi, what'a you talk about?"

"A paper, Nonna, I have to write a paper on immigration for school. Can you tell me how you and Babbo came to the United States?"

Once she understands the premise, Nonna happily agrees, and so I conduct an interview of sorts over the phone. She starts out by saying that she and Babbo married near the start of the Great Depression. That Babbo had been in the U.S. for several years with his older brother, pedaling fruits and vegetables in Philadelphia. When he finally saved enough money, Babbo made his first trip back to Italy.

My grandmother says Babbo had originally wanted to see parts of northern Italy that he had only heard about: Milan, Venice and Florence. But first he made a stop in Rome where one of his sisters was a nun living in a convent close to Vatican City. When he got there, she had some bad news though; their mother was very ill and near death. Babbo immediately canceled the remainder of his northern trip, and headed south right away. But with travel being what it was, when he got to his tiny village in Calabria days later, his mother had already died of pneumonia. She was buried the day before he arrived.

It was during the days and weeks afterwards, as he and his many siblings mourned their mother's death; that Babbo and Nonna "re-met." They hadn't seen each other in years. She was only sixteen years old, to his twenty-six, but in two short months they were married, and on their way to America. When I asked Nonna about their courtship and decision to marry so quickly, it wasn't hard to decipher that theirs wasn't a whirlwind romance—it was simple and practical—Babbo needed a wife, and Nonna was hungry to come to America.

She chuckled when she remembered how they had to offer the Catholic Church a dispensation in order for two first cousins to get married. Regardless, she was excited at the thought of going to America. After a few months in Calabria, the newlyweds caught a train north to Naples and spent nine days crossing the Atlantic Ocean. Nonna was nervous, never having been on a boat before, yet marveled at the dolphins that played alongside their ship when it passed by the Rock of Gibraltar.

Upon landing in New York, Babbo's brother was there to meet them and escort my grandparents to Philadelphia where Nonna enjoyed a bowl of chicken soup—her first meal in America.

When I turn in my paper, the professor gives it back to me days later, with a big, red **C** in the upper, right hand corner. I wait until class is over and politely ask him what was wrong with my work. Why did I only get a **C**? He tells me he was looking for a *research* paper on immigration, not a piece of memoir about my grandparents. I'm not sure how to take his explanation, since I literally don't know what the term *memoir* means. But I'm afraid if I ask for clarification, he'll look at me like I'm kidding, and lower my grade even further.

Despite the professor's contention my assignment was too personal, there were some things I couldn't put in the paper, like when I asked Nonna if Babbo ever talked about his mother. Nonna lowered her voice a bit over the phone, and softly said, "Babbo's mamma was'a no nice'a to him."

"Whaddaya mean?" I asked.

"When he was'a a boy, he al'aways wanna be with his'a mamma. He use'a to follow her whenever she left'a da house, but she would'a send'a him'a home. When he refuse'a, she would'a ben' over and pick up'a a hand'aful of'a gravel and stones and toss'a them in'a his face. She yell at'a him and made'a him go back'a home and Babbo was'a so sad."

She went on to say that Babbo never got over the fact he couldn't say goodbye to his mamma. Despite the gravel and stone showers, he loved her, and was angry he never had the chance to see her one more time. Learning that she was buried the day before he returned to Calabria broke his heart.

Hearing Nonna talk about Babbo like this made me feel sorry for him. It made me wonder if what happened between him and his mother was the reason behind his alcoholism. Was this mother-son dynamic why he spent most of his life in a self-imposed state of self-loathing? Was it why he verbally assaulted Nonna, Mom and Aunt Colomba for years? Was it why he tortured my cousin Alex and seemed to enjoy causing chaos, only to smirk as Nonna scurried to sweep everything under the rug?

Then, I think about Mom, and how she chose *not* to say goodbye to Babbo. Yet, she thought of him whenever an elderly person passed

293

away at the nursing home where she used to work. Mom claimed their deaths were a constant reminder of the guilt she felt for not paying her respects at my grandfather's viewing. Ever since he died, she has been stalked by his memory, convinced Babbo would find a way to kill her—routinely relying on her husband, or her eldest son, to calm her fears by routinely checking the bedroom closet for her dead father.

Could his disappointing daughter, Colomba, who is named for his deceased mother, have reminded my grandfather of this pain? He was, after-all, an illiterate, simple peasant who obviously struggled with the complexities of such emotions. If Mom suffers from this same broken heart and simplemindedness, is *that* why she craves so much attention, eats her lipstick, and wallows in The Routine? Are these the reasons behind her struggles, and why Pop's Pavarotti collection continues to collect dust on the shelves above his stereo?

44

Pop has always said, "In Italy, people don't get divorced as much as they do here, Chichi. It wasn't until the 1970's that you could even *get* divorced over there. Before that, it was against the law." Even now, Pop says that a lot of Italians tend to stay married to preserve the idea of *la famiglia*, above all else.

"And when the Pope lives in your backyard," he adds, "I guess you think twice about leavin' your wife."

Pope or no Pope, Pop says another practical reason Italian couples tend to stay married is because most of the men take on a mistress. He says it's never talked about, but sort of understood that a married man will behave this way. My father says Italians understand how unrealistic the 'one man to one woman relationship' can be. He says, "If the man is always gettin' laid, then couples don't have to fight about sex, and the husband is better able to deal with the day to day business of marriage."

That's the word Pop uses to describe marriage: *business*. He says, "It's a business, Chichi. That after the initial excitement dies down, you basically have two strangers living together, trying their best to survive and raise a family."

It's because of the fact that it's a business, that Pop says a man needs a woman to play with on the side. He says, "Most men, Italian or not, love their wives, and would do anything for their children. But, a man never stops being a man. When a couple first meets," he says, "they make love all the time, but once the bills and the chores and the dirty diapers start pilling up, most women get worn out and lose interest in 'playing' with their husbands. It's like sex becomes a chore, something else they *have* to do. It's not their fault; it's just the way it is. But for the man she's married to, it can be a rude awakening, especially if she seemed to enjoy sex before they got married. The guy can't help but feel like he was duped, the old bait n' switch."

Pop says most men don't want to cheat on their wives. They don't want to be unfaithful, or go through all the emotional turmoil of juggling more than one woman. "They just wanna play with their wives. That's what it comes down to, Chichi. Men fish, they hunt, they golf. Playing is in their nature, but when they get married, they're expected to somehow accept their wife's lackluster appetite to make love. This puts men in a tough spot, like his natural sex drive is bad or wrong."

He says, "Typically, you can have a guy who's committed to his wife, committed to his kids, makin' a good livin', takin' care of everythin' who has to *beg* his wife for sex, and that's just pathetic." Pop says it's a no-win situation. Either he accepts things as they are, and lives a life of quiet desperation, jerking off into a napkin before going to bed each night. Or he starts sneaking around town with another woman, risking the loss of his family, his house and all he's worked for, just so he can play with a girl.

"If he were a single man, he could go out and get laid whenever and with whomever he wanted. But, as a married man, he becomes a 'bad guy' for doing what comes naturally. The Mormons," he says, "the Muslims, they got it right, taking two or three wives. The rest of us got it backwards, Chichi, spacing our two or three wives out over forty years. We think it's weird to have two or three wives at once, but think it's civilized to marry and divorce two or three times over a lifetime. Each time, breaking up the family and forcing the man to pay huge financial penalties. Now, tell me what's better for the family, gettin' divorced, only to re-marry and divorce again, thus yanking the father away from his children, or, a man married to three women he loves, taking care of all his children, united and strong?"

If having a woman on the side is too much work, or just not their style, Pop says some men, Italian or not, turn to hookers or escorts, or frequent what they call in Italy a *bordello* as a way to satisfy their needs. Pop says in Italy, going to a bordello, or whorehouse, isn't looked down upon quite like it is here in the States. Even though it's technically illegal, some Italian fathers take their sons down to the local bordello, when they get to be old enough, pick out one of the prettier girls, pay the tab, and welcome their sons into manhood.

This bit about the bordello runs through my mind when Pop and I take a trip to Myrtle Beach, South Carolina with a few of his buddies. While we're away on vacation, we play golf everyday at a different course. Sometimes we play twenty-seven holes a day, since the February weather in South Carolina is so much warmer than back in Jersey. The thing is, when we left the shore, everyone's wife was upset that their husbands were going to spend five days having fun. None of them liked the idea of us going away all week, even though all we do is play golf, then go to a local seafood restaurant and stuff ourselves at the buffet table.

Except tonight—our last night in Myrtle Beach—there is talk of hitting a strip club after dinner. I get excited when I hear this, because I've never seen a real girl naked before. I've never even seen one in a bra and panties. So, the thought of going to a strip club, sets Tyson off working that speed bag in my chest again.

"There's only one problem," says Pop's friend, "Frankie's not twenty-one years old. How are we gonna get him into one of these joints?"

Pop shakes his head, and says not to worry. "If we get caught, just lie to 'em, Chichi. Say you've been to a few strip clubs back in Jersey and that you didn't know you had to be twenty-one. They won't know any better."

We try this routine at the first club we visit. The bouncer doesn't buy my lie and tosses us out. He checks my ID and says, "Sorry guys, but the young fella ain't even nineteen years old." Pop plays coy and apologizes. He says we didn't know how things worked down here, as he pulls the bouncer aside and asks if he knows of any other places around where I may have a better shot of getting in. The bouncer nods his big head, and tells Pop about another club, not too far down the road, where he knows no one ever works the door, and where I should have no problem gaining entry.

When we get to the second strip club, I walk right in, despite the sign out front that says—MUST BE 21 TO ENTER. No one bothers me, or asks to see my ID as we're greeted by the sound of loud music and the inviting aroma of a dozen different perfumes. The music is strong, but the perfume seems to be everywhere, and so are the girls. One of the strippers is on stage, dancing to the music in thigh high white stockings. A few girls smile, and wave at us, as they sit on men's laps topless, while others saunter around in stiletto heels and thongs. I can't believe my eyes; it's like the Victoria's Secret catalog has come to life.

We move towards a small, round table not far from the main stage. Once we're seated, Pop gives me some dollar bills to slip into the girls' garter belts and G-strings as they come by our table to say hello.

They smile, and pat my cheek. Some put their beautiful breasts right in my face, or turn around, bend over and wiggle their smooth asses for me to rub.

I take in the sights, the sounds, the smells and just want to explode. I've never seen anything like this before, though it looks like I'm not the only one. All of Pop's friends are married, but they turn into fifteen year old boys, snickering and whistling with their eyes ready to pop out of his head. They stare at each dancer like she was the first girl they've ever seen in the nude. The only one of us who keeps his cool; the only one who remains composed is my father.

It's not that he's disinterested, it's just sitting across the table from me, Pop has that same air he gets when he flirts with a pretty waitress: part entitlement, part confidence and part suave. He sits there as *Frankie the Voice*, scotch in hand, smiling at the girls who naturally seem to gravitate towards him. They sit on his lap, and kiss his cheek. The naked women flirt with my father, and soon there are girls standing on either side of him waiting their turn to sit on his lap. That's when he motions towards me and says, "That's my son, Francesco."

Pop never calls me Francesco—I'm either Frank, Frankie, Cheech or Chichi. But when he calls me Francesco, I know it is to hook the girls' attention. When he asks me in Italian which of the dancers I like best, it sends the girls in a giggle-fit. They want to know where we're from, and what we're doing here. Soon, everyone has a girl on their lap, and that's when I know our night has only just begun.

Going to a strip club with your father when you're only eighteen, and have never seen a naked girl before would make most of my friends back home uncomfortable. They wouldn't know how to act. They wouldn't be able to enjoy all the half-naked women prancing around because their father would be sitting directly across from them. They might be embarrassed or ashamed, but for me it's different; it's different because of Pop.

My father and I have never had The Talk. We never discussed the Birds and the Bees. The closest we ever came was last fall when he called me into his office and asked what I knew about the cable bill. He said there were charges for what's called the Spice Channel, the X-rated adult TV station in our area. Pop said you can sign-up for the Spice Channel as a part of your monthly cable package, or merely order it on a night-by-night basis which is exactly what someone did in this case.

He wanted to know if it was me. Did I sign-up for the Spice Channel on two separate nights like it stated on the cable bill? I played dumb. I lied and said I had no idea what he was talking about, or even what the Spice Channel was, even though I *was* the one who placed the order. I hoped he thought Tony might have done it, but I could tell by the look in his eyes that he knew it was me. He didn't get upset over the extra charges, or even push me to come clean and admit the truth. As a matter of fact, there was a touch of pride in his accusations, like he was glad to see me enjoying the sight of women fornicating.

That pride in his eyes made me think of that time years ago when he screamed at me, Tony and Michael that if we wanted to be faggots, then we should go live with faggots. It's almost as if Pop was proud that I was sneaking around behind his back, waiting for everyone to fall asleep, tip-toeing back downstairs late at night to order the Spice Channel, and go wild with myself and a jar of Vaseline.

Not long after the Spice Channel cover-up, we were celebrating Christmas Eve at Grandmom's house. Pop asked me to run out to his truck and grab a Christmas card he mistakenly left in the glove compartment. Before I ran out to the truck, he pulled me aside, lowered his voice and told me there was a picture in the glove compartment I could look at if I wanted. He said I wasn't to show my brothers, or Mom— but I could tell he wanted to share it with me. Pop said the picture was of a naked woman, a stripper, who had come to his buddy's birthday party weeks prior.

When he said that, there was that same look of pride, like he and I were now part of the Fraternity of Female Admirers. I ran out to the truck and riffled through the glove compartment. I quickly found the Christmas card, but studied the picture of the naked woman intently in the dim dome light of his GMC Jimmy.

The woman in the picture had dark hair and a perfect body. She was completely naked, except for her dark pink high heels. She was sitting on my father's lap the two of them posing for the camera. The thing is—Pop looked like *he* was the one doing her the favor. Like he was a king posing with one of his subjects, but then I remembered what Pop always says about being king. "You don't want to be king, Chichi. The king has too many responsibilities worrying about his kingdom night and day. What you want is to be the prince. The prince has no responsibilities, but reaps all of the royal benefits. He is free to spend his time playing with the lovely maidens down in the castle's basement."

That was it. The Spice Channel bill, and that picture of Ms. Smiles n' Heels, were as far as Pop and I ever got regarding the Birds and the Bees—until tonight. Watching him with all these gorgeous strippers in Myrtle Beach is a lesson in and of itself. Pop is the coolest cat in the joint, and that is why going to a strip club with my father is different than my friends going to a strip club with their fathers—with one exception: most of my friends have been laid. If they don't have an actual girlfriend, then they're just sleeping with random women, while I haven't even *kissed* a girl in almost four years.

The dancers come and go by our table. Some get called up on stage when it's their turn to dance, and some leave us after a few minutes to say hello to the other men scattered around the club. Yet, my eyes take in everything, and I must look like I'm in a trance, because one of Pop's friends chuckles and says, "Frankie, you haven't said a word in ten minutes." He shares a laugh over this with Pop and the others, but I don't care because each girl that passes by is like a walking marvel to me. I love watching the way they saunter around in their outfits and heels, and the way their skin feels when I rub their bodies, slipping a dollar into their G-strings. It's like a fantasy come true, yet Pop leans in from across the table and says, "Chichi, don't forget, they're only girls."

Now that the other men have calmed down, it must be obvious just how excited I am over the parade of scantily clad women. I don't know how Pop can say they're only girls, when I am throbbing like an animal in my pants. Yet, he motions for me to lean in across the table, as if he wants to tell me something. With the music playing, the girls dancing, and that strong perfume smell *everywhere*, Pop tells me about the two bulls. He says, "Chichi, picture these two bulls standing atop a hill, looking down on a field full of cows."

"What?"

"Picture two bulls standing atop a hill, looking down on a field full of cows."

"Okay. I got'cha Pop—two bulls."

"Now, the younger of the two bulls is excited. He turns to the older bull and says, 'Wow, look at all them cows down there in the field, whaddya say we run down there and fuck one of them real quick?' The older bull listens to him, but the older bull has been around a little bit. He's got some wisdom, got some confidence. He knows there's a field full of cows down there, he ain't blind, but he turns to the younger bull and says, 'Son, I'll tell ya what we're gonna do. We're gonna walk down this hill like we own the joint, and we're gonna fuck'em all.'"

Pop goes quiet after that, but keeps studying my eyes for a moment before continuing. "You see? That's what I'm sayin' Chichi, when I say they're only girls. Women don't like guys who worship them. They don't like men who look desperate. They want a *man*. They want the confident bull."

Not long after Pop tells me about the bulls, he summons two girls over to our table—a beautiful blonde and a gorgeous brunette. They strike a deal for a private show. Pop hands them eighty dollars, and both girls take me by the hand. They walk me across the club, leading me up a few stairs, through a dark curtain, into a dimly lit back room full of black leather couches and tiny round tables.

They sit me down on one of the couches. A moment later, I watch them undo each other's tops and kneel before me. The girls push open my legs, and run their hands across my chest and crotch. They tell me to, "Lay back and play nice, honey," as they proceed to dance and rub all over me. It isn't long before I explode inside my jeans. I couldn't contain my excitement any longer, and I know they must have felt me cum, but I don't care. I don't care, because I can't help feeling like one of those boys back in Italy, whose father took him to a bordello and welcomed him into manhood.

45

I've seen pictures of Mom when she was young and when her dark, black locks were down below her shoulders. In those pictures, her hair always looked neat and clean. As she got older, she started to keep it shorter and shorter, even letting the gray come through when most other women would have dyed it black, but it always looked classy. I even remember when we got those modeling pictures taken a few years ago, our agent loved Mom's salt and pepper hair. He said she looked so distinguished and European—and at Aunt Sofia's wedding in 1988, members of her new husband's family asked about Mom. They wanted to know about the breathtaking bridesmaid with the statuesque build, and hazel eyes—but nowadays, Mom just looks dirty.

Mom's hair has finally grown back in after her aneurysm surgery, but since she doesn't bathe that often, it always looks oily and matted. Her hairdresser even told Aunt Ellen that she has to shampoo my mother four or five times on those rare occasions Mom comes in for an appointment; her hair is that caked with filth.

Ever since her personal hygiene has become an issue, Michael has started asking her not to come to his games. He says, "Mom, Frankie's gonna drive me. You don't have to take me down to the gym." But that only makes her sit up and say, "What are you talking about? I wanna go to your game."

"I know, but you don't have to. Frankie said he would take me."

"Well, Frankie can take you, but I'm coming, too."

"No Mom, please don't come."

"Whaddaya mean? I'm your mother and if I want to go to your game, I'm going to your game."

"But, Mom..."

"Michael, enough! Now, I don't want to hear it. I have the right to watch you play, you're my son!"

"But I don't want you to come!"

I can't take anymore so I say, "Mom, just stay home this time, alright? It's not a big deal. Michael is gonna be late if we don't leave now, so just..."

"Frankie, it is a big deal. Now, why are you doing this to me? Michael is my son, and I want to watch my son play basketball."

"Mom, I know he's your son, but you smell really bad, so you're not coming."

"Who are you to tell me what I can and can't do?"

"Mom, I'm just sayin' Michael asked me to take him because he says he always begs you to drop him off at the front door, and park the car by yourself. He doesn't want to be seen with you."

"I can't believe this bullshit!"

"Mom, we don't have time for this, Michael's gonna be late."

"Well, no one's going anywhere without me."

At that, Mom *literally* dashes past me and Michael. She bolts out the front door and sits in the passenger seat of the Cadillac. With my Camaro boxed in between the garage and the Caddy, Michael and I have no choice but to take Mom with us.

During the ten minute ride down to the gym, Mom smokes a cigarette without cracking the passenger window, so the smoke can't escape. No one says a word to each other, until I slow down to drop Michael off at the front door of the gymnasium. Mom slowly opens the passenger side door, as Michael shouts, "C'mon, Mom!" He pushes her seat forward, slides out of the car, and sprints towards the front door. Mom takes off after him shouting, *"Michael! Michael!"*

I race to find a parking spot, and rush inside, only to find Michael, Mom and Aunt Teresa standing together in the hallway leading towards the gymnasium. Aunt Teresa must have seen Michael running down the hallway with disgust on his face and asked, "What's wrong, honey?" Only to have Michael tell her how tired he was of begging Mom not to come inside and watch his games because she smells so bad, and looks so weird.

As I walk up on them, Aunt Teresa is in Mom's face. "Ann, what's the matter with you? Your son is a good boy. You can't keep coming to his games smelling like this. Your B.O. is so bad that nobody wants to sit next to you. Why do you keep doing this? It's embarrassing for Michael."

"Teresa, I don't want to embarrass Michael. He's my son, and I enjoy watching him play."

"Ann, I understand that you enjoy watching him play, but he deserves better than this. It's almost like you come to his games, smelling like shit, because you get some sort of pleasure out of it."

"That's ridiculous."

"Ann, I can smell you from here. When's the last time you took a shower?"

"Teresa, the game's gonna start..."

"Ann, what you're doing to this child isn't fair. You're supposed to be his mother f'Chrissakes!"

"I am his mother."

"Then go home, and take a friggin' shower!"

My mother and Aunt Teresa go around and around about her body odor, dirty clothes and filthy hair, that by the time they make it into the gym, it's mid-way through the third quarter.

I've been sitting at the top of the bleachers, with my back against the wall, watching Michael's team lead for most of the game. But when Mom walks in, everything changes.

Michael is the star of his team. Even though he is only fourteen years old, and in eighth grade, he is skilled enough that he could be playing for the junior varsity squad at most high schools right now. His ball handling, shooting skills, and jumping ability are exceptional. But for Michael, basketball is almost an afterthought. He has already been offered and accepted a football scholarship to attend one of the most exclusive prep schools in the area.

When Mom and Aunt Teresa enter the gym, they go in separate directions, not because their sons are on different teams, but because I can tell Mom must have worn Aunt Teresa down.

She must have become frustrated and simply given up, rather than miss the entire game that her son is also playing in. The sight of my mother walking into the gym draws some attention, because she looks so odd—like someone who doesn't have regular access to soap, or a shower.

Tonight, as she moves to take a seat in the bleachers, she doesn't climb up to sit next to me. Instead, she sits about two or three rows off the court, right in the middle of a large group of parents, most of which have known her since I was in grade school. Pop isn't here, but most of the parents recognize my mother, and either say, "Hi, Ann," or offer a wave and a smile as she settles into her seat.

It doesn't take long before those sitting around her slowly begin to move away. They move away, not because Mom is blocking their view of the court, or being loud and obnoxious, but because she smells. It happens slowly, but unmistakably. Nobody can stomach her odor. Soon, Michael is paying more attention to what's happening in the stands, than he is to what's happening on the court.

Mom doesn't have to move or make a sound, but it's obvious why everyone is moving away from her. Towards the end of the game, having been completely isolated, Mom slowly turns around to look at me sitting atop the bleachers. The action on the court has stopped for a moment, but Mom is peering over her shoulder at me with a look of pitiful-innocence on her face. Her look says, *can you believe this, Frankie? Can you believe these people don't have the common decency to even watch the game with me? I'm a victim here. Tell me you've seen what they've done? Tell me you understand my pain.*

It's this look of pitiful-innocence that makes it hard for me to know what to do. There's Michael on the court going from the heroic driving force of his team's success to the distracted son of a woman who smells like a bum. He gets embarrassed, and I get ashamed for I couldn't stop Mom from coming. He asked me to take him to the game, so as to avoid this *exact* scenario. Yet, here we are, the three of us causing a scene without doing or saying a word.

In April of 1996, exactly ten years after Babbo passed away, and a little over eight months since Mom's surgery, the pharmacist who normally fills her prescriptions sends home a letter addressed to my father. In his letter, the pharmacist states that Mom appears dissociated and severely depressed when she comes to pick up her meds.

Pop and I are standing in the kitchen when he shows me the typewritten note. The pharmacist explains that Mom is taking three drugs now, an antidepressant called Nortriptytine, and two tranquilizers, Stelazine and Klonopin. The letter warns that improper use of these drugs will cause severe mood swings and continued depression. He recommends that Pop contact Mom's psychiatrist right away.

Enclosed with the letter are copies of how Mom has been signing her name recently, when she comes to pick up her prescription. ANTONIETTA, as she would normally spell it, is signed ANTONITTA on one copy, and ANTOIENT on another. As I hand the letter back to him, Pop calls into the den, where Mom is lying on the couch, watching TV.

"Ann!"

Mom doesn't answer.

"Ann!"

Mom doesn't answer again.

"Ann!" He shouts a third time. "How do you spell your name?"

Mom still doesn't answer. Pop moves to the doorway between the kitchen and the den. He looks down at Mom lying on the couch and repeats himself.

"Ann, how do you spell your name?"

We know she can hear him. So, Pop goes into the den, walks past Mom, and turns off the TV. He still has the letter in his hand, as he turns around and asks a third time.

"Ann, how do you spell your name?"

"What?"

"How do you spell your name?"

"A-N-N." Mom says dumbfounded.

"No. Your full name—how do you spell your *full name*?"

"Frank, I...."

"I have here a letter from the pharmacist, Ann, and not only does he say you can't spell your own name," Pop looks down at the letter for a second and begins to paraphrase it, "he says you seem dissociated and severely depressed when you come to pick up your meds."

"What?" Mom asks, swinging her legs around and sitting up. "That's not true."

"So, he's making it up?"

"I don't know, but I'm fine, Frank."

"Yeah, I know you're fine," Pop says. "That's why you lay around all day and shower once a month."

"That's not fair, Frank."

"Ann, we're not doing this again. We're not going through another spring and summer like we did last year."

"Frank, I'm fine."

Pop shakes his head in disgust and moves towards the wall of glass doors that look out over the meadows and the Atlantic City skyline. "Ann," he says, "you're not fine. I've known you twenty-five years, and you're not fine." He stays facing away from her, looking out the glass doors as he softens his voice. "Ann, let me ask you somethin'. When was the last time you took a shower?"

Mom says nothing.

"Ann," Pop says as he turns from the windows to face her. "People take showers; they wear clean clothes. Women get their hair done; they put on makeup. They don't go days, sometimes *weeks*, without a shower. Now, I don't wanna argue. I just wanna know—when's the last time you took a shower?"

Pop is standing over her, waiting for an answer, but I can tell he isn't angry. He glances up at me standing in the doorway between the den and the kitchen. Our eyes meet for a moment, but it's like he forgot I was there listening to their conversation—like he was surprised to see me.

Mom is looking down, so she didn't see the glance Pop gave me. It only lasted a split-second, but it said so much. It was part reassurance—that he has the situation under control—and part embarrassment. Like he couldn't believe this was his life—standing in the disheveled den of his wife's dream house, questioning her about her most recent shower.

After he looks back down at Mom, Pop moves again towards the wall of glass doors. He stands there for a moment, motionless. My father looks sad and quiet as he studies Atlantic City off in the distance.

"Ann," he finally says, his voice cutting through the silence, "what happened to the girl I married?"

My mother is still looking down and gives no response, no movement, no shrug—no nothing. "Where did she go, Ann?" He asks, turning from the windows and moving towards the loveseat. He sits to the right of my mother and continues. "Ann, do you remember that night on the Boardwalk years ago, the night with the fog?"

Again, Mom doesn't answer.

Pop glances over his shoulder at me and says, "Frankie, your mother and I used to drive down the shore sometimes, just to get a few hoagies at the White House Sub Shop. We used to drive down, and eat'em in the car on the ride home. But there was this one night, remember Ann? This thick fog rolled in off the ocean, and rather than drive right back to Philly, we walked down to the Boardwalk, where the fog was so thick, you couldn't see a foot in front of you. This was before the casinos came to town, and it was wintertime, so we were the only ones out there. Do you remember that night, Ann?"

Mom looks away from him; her eyes still down. Pop says they walked arm-in-arm that night while dreaming of their future together. He says *that* was his girl, the girl he married, and the girl he still wants to be married to. He says that night they talked about the family they wanted to raise, and the life they wanted to live together.

That's when Pop says, "Ann, this isn't *that* life, and this isn't the way it was supposed to be. You need help and I know you know that. Let me call Dr. Wydell. Let me see if he can set-up a voluntary stay at the Institute, and let's follow through this time. No more sabotage. We'll keep your family out of it. But I don't wanna see you like this. It isn't good for the boys to see you like this, and that girl who strolled along with me that foggy night years ago, wouldn't wanna see you like this either. So, whaddaya say you go upstairs and take a shower? And I'll see if I can get a hold of Dr. Wydell."

Mom is crying now. The house is quiet. My parents sit motionless on the loveseat. I don't know what to do or say. The day is overcast and gray; I feel overcast and gray inside.

The silence is broken by the sound of my mother's sniffles. Moments later, without saying a word, she rises from the couch and stands before us with her chin to her chest; she is barefoot, disheveled and dirty.

Mom takes a deep, defeated breath, turns around and leaves the room without ever looking at either of us. She goes upstairs. Soon, we hear the sound of water running. My mother must be taking a shower. I feel encouraged. Maybe my father's story about that foggy night made an impact, but Pop gives no reaction. He just stays on the loveseat, a lonesome figure, his eyes softly studying the meadows; his thoughts a mystery to me.

Days later, Pop says it is all set up. He called Dr. Wydell about getting Mom admitted to the Institute of Mental Health at the University of Pennsylvania. It was the same Dr. Wydell who could have gotten Mom in three years ago, until Edith and Nonna came down ready to feud; and the idea was scrapped.

This time around, much of the cost involved with Mom's voluntary commitment has been waived, which is a godsend—since we are uninsured. Without any health coverage, all of Mom's hospital bills have fallen back on my father. After her recovery from the suicide attempt last summer, the month in the Locked Crisis Unit, her subsequent aneurysm surgery, and ten-day recovery, Pop will never again regain his financial footing. With his development dreams a distant memory, and project manager gigs hard to land, we mostly survive on small, intermittent stucco and concrete jobs with little or no profit.

When my father tells Mom that he spoke to Dr. Wydell, and that he can get her into the Institute, to everyone's surprise, she doesn't put up a fight—and neither does Nonna. Initially, Pop didn't want to tell Mom's family about her pending hospitalization. He was concerned they would try to stand in the way again. But Aunt Ellen said, "Frank, what if they think you're trying to put her away?" So, he phoned Nonna, and was relieved to hear her agree that Mom needed to give the Institute a try. He was even further pleased to learn how Nonna requested to be involved in the process.

The first step in Mom's stay at the Institute of Mental Health at the University of Pennsylvania, is an Admissions Conference conducted by Dr. Wydell. The meeting also involves my parents and Nonna. Shortly after taking their seats, and discussing the logistics of Mom's hospitalization, Dr. Wydell wants to review Mom's personal file. In particular, he feels compelled to know why my mother tried to kill herself, some nine months prior, with the carpet cleaner, the aspirin and the butcher knife. Immediately, upon hearing his question, Mom bursts into tears. She is ashamed at what she had done, and heartbroken to admit through her crying, that it was a manifestation of what Babbo always wanted. That's the exact word she used, *manifestation.*

Nonna sat up when she heard that. "Antonietta," she snapped, in her heavy accent, "what'a you talk'a about? You father was'a my pride!"

But Dr. Wydell spoke up. "From what I understand, your daughter's attempted suicide did take place in her father's house with one of her father's knives. It sounds to me as though Ann was trying to murder herself, as she always believed her father wanted her dead. Now please, allow Ann to continue."

Still crying, Mom says, "My father used to tell me all the time if I was a boy, he would'a loved me, but I was a girl, and that meant he hated me. Oh God...he hated me...oh God...oh God...."

Mom begins crying heavily. She can barely speak, but that doesn't stop Nonna from defending her deceased husband/cousin. "Antonietta, watch'a what'a you say! Your father was'a my pride! He was'a my pride!"

"Enough!" Dr. Wydell demands. "*Enough!*"

Pop turns to comfort Mom, as Dr. Wydell says, "Ann, it is very courageous of you to make that kind of statement in front of your mother; and that's why we're here, to unearth the past. Together, we're going to do the hard work, but it'll be worth it. You're already a very brave woman, Ann. I admire you for being here today. You're in the right place. I wanna help you."

Despite Nonna's outbursts and protests, my mother is approved for treatment and accepted into the Institute of Mental Health. Hours after her Admissions Conference, when my father returns to the shore, he tells us how Mom spoke up in front of Nonna.

He says, "I think we caught her just in time. I think Mom may actually benefit from this." And then my father uses a word I never thought I'd hear in relation to my mother, and the psychological collapse she has become—hope. Pop says, "Boys, we may finally have a few reasons to hope things will turn around. Your mother really seems on board this time, and I have a good feeling about Dr. Wydell. I really think he's gonna get through to her."

46

Today is the last Saturday of April, 1996. Mom is entering her second week under Dr. Wydell's care at the Institute of Mental Health. I am landscaping for Hank and playing lots of golf, mostly on cheap public courses in south Jersey. My brothers are busy with school and baseball season, while Pop spends his time bidding work.

My father is desperate for money since both his business and personal taxes are due. He doesn't even bother to file an extension with the IRS because he has no idea where he is going to find the funds to pay what he owes. With his wife in a mental hospital and his business and finances in a constant state of flux, Pop decides to put aside his worries, and watch Tony play baseball.

My brother has a game this morning at my old high school. Pop asks me if I want to go since I'm not cutting grass today, but I turn him down. Everybody knows me there, and I don't want to spend the morning answering questions as to why I left Towson State University, and gave up football to be a landscaper and a part-time community college student.

I'm lounging in bed, trying to catch up on some sleep, when the phone rings. It is Aunt Bridgid. Her words are short and choppy; she sounds a bit frantic. She says there's been an accident. Tony is in bad shape. Pop wants me and Michael down at the hospital right away.

I'm confused, and want more information.

"What sort of accident, Aunt Bridgid?"

"I don't know all the details, honey. I think your brother collided with another player, and he's hurt bad. They took him in an ambulance. Please get down to the hospital, as quick as you can."

Michael and I jump into the Ghetto Bomber and rush down to the ER. Minutes later, we find Tony lying on a gurney in this little curtained off area of the Emergency Room, and Pop is standing next to him. Tony is still in his green and white pinstriped baseball uniform, though the front of his jersey is covered in blood. There is more blood, and long, green, strings of snot, oozing out of his disfigured nose. The

311

left side of his face from his eyebrow to his cheekbone has been shattered, and violently shoved back into his skull. His left eye is swollen, sealed and black with blood. It looks like somebody beat him with a sledgehammer.

I'm standing over my sixteen year old brother, thinking to myself, *I've never seen anybody look this bad before.* I remember how Mom looked months ago, with half a head of wavy salt and pepper hair, and another half full of staples, but that was the work of a surgeon; this is different. The left side of Tony's face has been destroyed. I am afraid for him.

He doesn't speak as we eagerly wait for a doctor, or a nurse, or somebody. We wait two minutes, five minutes, ten minutes—there is no hospital staff in sight. Pop gets so angry at the obvious lack of attention that he starts screaming. *"Hey, what the fuck is going on? Somebody get over here and help my son! Jesus Christ!"*

A young nurse finally scurries over. She takes Tony's vital signs, and tells us a CAT Scan has been ordered—which is the reason for the wait. Pop says, "Fuck that! Where the hell is the CAT Scan machine?"

"Upstairs."

"Well, let's go."

"We really should wait for the orderlies to take your son."

"We're taking him, and we're taking him now. It's been fifteen minutes, and nobody has even looked at him."

The nurse hesitantly agrees. Pop tells me and Michael to wait downstairs while he and the nurse wheel Tony into the elevator. Aunt Bridgid, and a few other parents who have come from the game, wander in and tell us that a ball was hit in the gap between Tony, the left fielder, and Chris, the center fielder. Both players charged towards the ball forgetting to look for the other when they dove head first. The centerfielder was only dazed, but Tony got the worst of it.

Twenty-five minutes later, Tony and Pop come back downstairs into the ER—only my father's chest is covered in vomit. He is *screaming.* His voice is hoarse; it sounds harsh. Pop looks pissed and panicked.

As Tony is returned to his curtained off area of the Emergency Room, Pop tells us that my brother has been fading in and out of consciousness, that the CAT Scan machine didn't work, and that Tony went into a violent seizure—thrashing around, throwing up and spewing blood. Pop and the nurse scrambled to hold him down until an orderly heard their cries and piled on top of my brother.

Pop is angry.

He complains to the radiologist, who is now standing in Tony's curtained off space. The more my father speaks, the worse he sounds. His voice is almost gone. Yet, he goes on and on about the broken CAT Scan machine, the lack of orderlies, and the lack of medical attention that Tony has been receiving.

"*What the fuck is going on?*"

Moments later, a doctor walks into Tony's curtained off area. He looks to be about Pop's age, with all his hair, and a nice gold watch on his left wrist. His white smock is clean, and crisp as he smiles and shakes the radiologist's hand.

"Hey John," he says. "How's it going? How's the golf game? I was thinking about you the other day. I played Harbor Pines, fell apart a bit on the back nine, but still wound up breaking 90. We should play next week. Maybe ask Bernie? How's Thursday work for you?"

The radiologist is made uncomfortable by the doctor's nonchalance. It is awkward to watch him motion towards my father, while acknowledging the doctor's invitation to play golf. My eyes go back and forth between my father and the doctor—this isn't going to be good. Pop cocks his head, and glares at him.

The doctor saunters over a few steps, extends his right hand to my father, and says, "Hey, I'm Doctor...." But *Frankie the Voice* cuts him off mid-sentence. My father aggressively grabs the doctor's right hand with both his hands. He looks him dead in the eye, and asks, "Do you have any children, Doctor?"

"What? No, I don't have any kids...."

"I didn't think so. Now, lissename...." Pop is squeezing the doctor's hand with all his might. He motions towards Tony, "My kid is in bad shape, and I'd appreciate if you paid a little more attention to my son and a lot less attention to your fuckin' golf game."

The doctor looks shocked. He is helpless. He can only scrunch his eyebrows together and say, "Sir, my hand. What are you doing?"

Pop continues his death grip; there is the stench of vomit in the air. "Sir," he repeats, "would you let go of my hand? This is absurd...."

"No, I'll tell you what's absurd. We've been here forty-five minutes, and I'm not impressed with this lousy excuse for a hospital. You have no orderlies, a CAT Scan machine that doesn't work, and your priorities in the wrong order. Now, just by looking at my son, it's obvious this is not a common injury. So, why don't you drop the nonchalance, and do your fuckin' job!"

No one outside of Tony's little curtained off area can see what's going on. They don't see my father standing there covered in vomit, collar up, glaring at the doctor, hands clasped together in a bone crushing handshake. They don't see Tony on the gurney, in his baseball uniform, covered in blood, with long, green, strings of jelly oozing out of his nose, the left side of his face a nightmare. They don't see Michael and me standing beside our brother, across from the radiologist, watching Pop stare at the doctor, reading his eyes.

Nobody can see any of this because of the curtain that's hanging from the ceiling, but I doubt they can hear any of it either. My father isn't screaming at the doctor, by now his voice is so hoarse, it's more like he's violently whispering to him.

It's in the moment before my father lets the doctor have his hand back, that I remember he had done something like this once before—though under much different circumstances.

Pop told me he was in a bar years ago, with a few friends having a drink over in Ducktown. He said, "My friends and I were sitting there, when a couple of people they knew came in. I had never met them before, so my friends introduced me to everybody. I turned around and shook their hands, said hello, you know. The thing is, when I got to the last person, this woman they were with, I shook her hand and said hello, but she said, 'What's this? That's not a very manly handshake. Don't you know how to shake hands like a man?' Now, that caught me off guard. I was tryin' to be a gentleman, and politely shake her hand, but she had to take my light handshake and break my balls about it. So, when I got up to leave a little while later, I went around saying my goodbyes, shaking everybody's hand—only when I got to her—I made a point to stop. I took a hold of her hand as if to shake it and say goodbye, only I wrapped my other hand on top, and started crushing her fingers together. She started screaming, '*What are you doing? My hand! My hand!*' But I wouldn't stop. I calmly stood there saying, it was nice to meet her and how I hoped we ran into each other again, and all that crap. But I wouldn't let go until

I said, 'Now, don't ever break my balls again. You wanted a manly handshake? Well, you got one, sweetheart.'"

Pop explained to me that he did that to prove a point, to save face, but here and now, as he lets the doctor have his hand back, I know he's doing it for a different reason. He's doing it because the sight of Tony there on the gurney has him terrified.

The doctor is quick to shake his hand free from my father's grip. He starts opening and closing his fist several times to restore the blood flow, and make sure nothing is broken. He is flustered, but has no choice but to examine my brother.

With his hands free, I watch Pop reach for Tony's left hand, lying there limp upon the gurney. My father is afraid for Tony, and so am I. The sight of their hands together makes me think that I want to be like Pop when I have my own family.

I want to do whatever I have to in-order to protect my children— even if it means ranting and raving, or crushing the hand of a golf-playing physician.

I want to be like *Frankie the Voice.*

Hours later, with my brother in the Intensive Care Unit, Pop paces the packed waiting room. He is worried sick. My father wants Tony moved to a different hospital. Aunt Bridgid, who has worked as a nurse in the past, recommends Children's Hospital of Philadelphia, and Pop jumps on the idea.

He calls the same doctor from the ER, who by now is at home. Pop says he wants Tony moved to Children's Hospital, but the doctor is against it. My father is on a phone in the waiting room of the ER. He is hoarsely barking into the receiver.

"Why do I want him moved? Because I feel Children's can better handle the injury, *I don't care if you think your hospital can handle it! I want my son moved!* Doctor, no! Doctor, no! Let me talk, *let me talk!* Let's be honest here. I know your hospital could use the business; the

ICU is only half full, I bet an operation like this would do wonders for your fuckin' bottom line. But what should I tell my son if you guys screw this up? Business is business? I mean when's the last time somebody flew in from Europe to have an operation at this fuckin' hospital? It's a dump, now *I want my boy outta here!*"

There is a silence after Pop says that. He is listening to the doctor—his eyebrows are pinched close together, his eyes are like razors passing the phone from ear to ear. Finally, he harshly screams into the phone, his free hand flailing around, his broken voice filling the Emergency Room. *"I don't want to hear it anymore! I want my son at Children's Hospital! If you won't set it up, I'll sign him out, and drive him up to Philly myself!"*

The doctor finally relents, and agrees to the transfer. It isn't until we get to Children's Hospital of Philadelphia, that we find out the severity of his injuries. He has a broken collar bone, a broken nose, a damaged sinus passage, his left eye has been knocked out of place, the eye orbit that surrounds his eye has been shattered into ten pieces, and the membrane between his skull and brain tissue is torn in two spots.

The surgeons make an ear-to-ear incision at the top of Tony's scalp. They peel and roll the skin of his face down below his eyes. Then, they reset the ten broken pieces around his eye orbit—using forty-eight titanium screws, and ten titanium plates. The doctors also suture the membrane between his brain and skull and successfully move his eye back in place.

During the eleven hours of surgery, Michael and I get something to eat in the cafeteria with Pop, Hank and Aunt Ellen's husband, Mr. Welsh. As we sit eating our food, Pop notices a foursome of nurses crying quietly across the way. He stops by their table, when he gets up to discard his trash, and I know he's going to ask them what they're crying about. I think he's worried that they may be part of the team working on Tony. But when he comes back to our table, he has a soft smile on his face, and tells us why the nurses are teary-eyed.

He says, "You won't believe this. Those nurses said they just finished a procedure where the doctors opened up a pregnant woman, only to open up her baby inside the womb, and remove a tumor the baby developed. Then, they were able to close everybody up after that."

Pop's soft smile explodes into a full ear-to-ear grin as he says, "If they can do *that*, Tony's gonna make it through this. These people are miracle workers. And besides," he adds, "my grandmother is gonna make sure of it."

Pop stopped going to Mass long ago, and was never one to truly accept the teachings of the Catholic Church, but he believes in the soul of his dead grandmother—Giulia. She died when I was a baby, but it is she who Pop turns to in times of need. He always says, "My grandmother is gonna look out for us."

I know he believes it. He feels that way because she was 'special,' and used to be able to 'see' things, and communicate with our relatives who passed away. The one piece of advice she gave him—that he *always* repeats—was actually a critique.

When she used to watch her grandsons sing and play, during the years they had that band in Philadelphia, Great-Grandmom Giulia would tell my father, "Do me a favor, sweetheart. When you're up there on stage, stay away from the sad songs; the world is tough enough as it is. People don't need any reminders. What they need is inspiration. Sing the happy songs, and put a smile on people's faces"

With his wife in the Institute of Mental Health, at the University of Pennsylvania, and his middle son in the midst of eleven hours of life altering, reconstructive facial surgery, my father needs his grandmother and her advice more than ever.

Not long after Pop talks to the nurses, we get word that Tony has made it through the surgery. He is in recovery in the ICU. His lead surgeon finds us in the cafeteria. The doctor sits down next to Pop and pulls an index card from the pocket of his knee-length white coat. On the index card is a drawing of a person's face. The surgeon begins talking to Pop about Tony's operation; he motions to the drawing and explains how my brother was put back together. He says, "By bringing Tony up here, you very well may have saved his life. You see, the CAT Scan machine down the shore, can only do cross sections of one's head, where ours allows for a three-hundred-and-sixty-degree view. Had Tony stayed there, complications would have surely arisen as a result of the inaccurate read. And to be honest, that hospital just isn't as well equipped as we are. Some of the tools and accessories needed would not have been on hand. Tony could not have been put back together properly had he stayed down the shore."

The doctor hands Pop the index card. He stands up as if he's ready to leave. When Pop rises to thank him, I can tell my father is emotional, but he doesn't want to cry with Mr. Welsh and Hank sitting right there. Both men are standing in the crowded cafeteria of Children's Hospital, as Pop extends his arm and shakes the doctor's hand. He cups the surgeon's elbow with his left hand, and looks him straight in the eye, "Thank you, Doctor. Thank you for saving my boy."

Once word gets out about Tony and Mom *both* being in the hospital, dinners start showing up at our door just like last summer. The thing is, only me and Michael are home to eat them. Pop has been staying with Tony up at Children's Hospital, sleeping on a reclining chair right next to Tony's bed.

Michael and I go to see them every day. It's hard to look at Tony lying there with his head twice the size it has always been. Pop says the swelling will go away, and that we're to be positive around Tony especially since he hasn't seen himself yet. My father says Tony can't get out of bed, and hasn't been in front of a mirror to see the huge zig-zag of a scar at the top of his head, or the way his left cheek bone bulges out past everything else.

As Tony slowly recuperates, we know his recovery is progressing when he begins to share a room with another patient. Streams of visitors come to visit him—baseball teammates, football teammates, coaches, parents, cousins, aunts, uncles. They all come with balloons and cards, or girly magazines, to cheer him up. The thing is, whenever someone comes to visit, they have to block out the constant moaning coming from the other side of the curtain.

Tony's roommate is a nineteen year old boy. He just had cancer surgery and moans so much that the nurse comes in and whispers to everybody that he has been sick since he was a kid, and his situation doesn't look good. I don't like it when the nurse says things don't look good. I don't think it's fair that this nineteen year old has to suffer and moan like he does. What did he ever do to deserve this? Sometimes in our comings and goings we'll bump into his mother, and she doesn't look good either. But how can she, the way he moans there in the bed?

Through the curtain we hear her say, "Come on, Brian, sit up, honey. You gotta eat your lunch." But we can tell he pushes the lunch away, and I feel bad because I'm eighteen going on nineteen, and the worst I ever suffered was with acne. Sometimes I wonder what Brian would do differently if he and I swapped places. I bet if Brian were healthy, he'd carry on like Jimmy Valvano did years ago on the *ESPY's;* he would live and laugh and enjoy his life.

If I was the one confined to that hospital bed, I'm afraid to say I don't think much would change. When I stop and listen to myself, all I ever do is whine and complain. It's like I want the whole world to pity me, or pray for me—like I want to be the eternal Special Intention. Instead of carrying on like a kid who had his own mural in high school, I see myself as the ugliest, wimpiest, saddest creature on the planet.

When I hear Brian moan through the curtain, I feel guilty for ever having told my parents I wanted to commit suicide. I feel guilty for having come home from Towson, after only four days—and now I feel guilty because Mom has no idea Tony is in the hospital.

There has been one question on everybody's mind since Tony dove for that ball, *do we tell Ann about all this?* By the time Tony is half-way through his recovery, Mom has been in the Institute of Mental Health just under three weeks. Pop says the last thing he wants is for my mother or her social worker to sign her out and come down here to Children's Hospital. He says, 'come down here,' because the Institute of Mental Health is *literally* fifteen minutes down the road. Pop says, "What good would it do to have Ann roaming the hallways, causing a scene?"

Aunt Ellen agrees; she says Mom calls her every night going on and on about getting her out of that place, about how she doesn't belong there, saying, "I'm not like these people, El. I'm not sick. Come get me out! C'mon Ellen, come get me!"

After initially feeling hopeful about her chances at 'turning things around' while under Dr. Wydell's care, Pop says Mom's social worker called and complained that she was showing very little interest in her therapy. The woman told Pop that Mom kept insisting she was fine, and that she didn't need help. The social worker told Pop, "I'm sorry, but this is starting to look like a simple case of a husband trying to get rid of his wife."

Pop says he got off the phone as quickly as he could and called Dr. Wydell. He asked him to lobby for the Institute to keep Mom just a little longer.

"She'll start to unravel," he told the doctor. "She can only keep up the 'everything's fine face,' for so long. Please, we've worked so hard to get her in there. Don't let them discharge her before anything's happened."

My father says Dr. Wydell agreed. In a few short days, Mom's social worker calls back and says she saw what Pop was talking about; Mom has started to disassociate from everyone and everything.

With Tony and Mom both in the hospital, Aunt Renata calls my father and says she is tired of all the talk about her sister being sick. She says this latest stay in the Institute of Mental Health is nothing more than a ploy—a chance for my father to carry on an affair with Aunt Teresa. My aunt says she won't rest until she can prove it.

Aunt Teresa is livid. She doesn't know where Aunt Renata gets off making up something like that. She is worried because Mom is so impressionable that she is liable to believe the lie. Aunt Teresa says she has to talk to Mom as soon as possible. After stopping to see Tony at Children's Hospital, she makes the short drive down to the Institute and tells Mom that there's no truth in what Aunt Renata is saying.

"It's all a lie, Ann. Your sister is making this shit up. I would never do anything like that to you. Rena is just angry. She has never forgiven Frank for the whole affair with Gail."

When I see her next, Aunt Teresa tells me that Mom believed her. She said she knew Teresa would never do that—for weren't she and Ellen her best friends in the world?

"It's just the drama of it all," says Aunt Teresa. "Rather than coming together as one big, united family, Renata has to stir the pot and continue The Cover-Up. It couldn't be that Ann needs help, and that's why Frank pushed to get her into the Institute? No, no, no, it was so he and I could have an affair; that's just ridiculous! She should be ashamed of herself. What kind of sister is she?"

Seeing Aunt Teresa all worked up like this reminds me of how Aunt Renata reacted to the news that Mom had been abused. When it first came out, a few years ago, she didn't want to hear it, didn't want to discuss it, thought Mom was making it up.

If twenty years from now, Tony or Michael came to me with something similar, I would give them the benefit of the doubt. I would listen and discuss, looking to see what made sense, and what didn't. But I wouldn't say, *no way, didn't happen. You're out of your mind!*

Yet, that's exactly what Aunt Renata did to Mom, and all my cousins in Philadelphia followed suit. "The reason your mother is where she is," they would say, "is because of your father. That man is no good."

I think about where my father is—sleeping night after night on that reclining chair next to Tony in his hospital room. I wonder if he stays up late at night to softly serenade Tony with his repertoire of Neapolitan songs, for that's what Pop does when the chips are down.

Then I wonder if he ever thinks about the guy Mom was engaged to before him—the one who had her crying the day my parents met back in April of 1969. I wonder if that guy ever thinks about Mom, or knows about the favor Pop did in taking her off his hands.

47

Weeks after Tony's accident, Pop arranges for a meeting to be held at the Institute of Mental Health at the University of Pennsylvania. The meeting is to be conducted by Dr. Wydell, and is open to anybody from both sides of the family who wishes to attend. Pop's hope is to clear up some of the bad blood.

Ten of us attend the meeting: Uncle Bruno—Pop's brother, Grandmom, Michael and me, Uncle Nick, Aunt JoJo, Aunt Teresa, Aunt Ellen, Nonna and my father. We're all sitting in an oval, some on couches, others in chairs, looking at each other—not sure what to do.

Finally, a scholarly looking older man with gray hair comes into the room—this is Dr. Wydell. He sits at the 'front' of the oval, and proceeds to welcome us, and warns us that fighting will have no place in our meeting. "It will serve no one, and nothing. If there is an argument, the instigator will be asked to leave. This meeting was called to facilitate clarity, and understanding. We're not here to argue, but to explain things. Our objective is to get everyone on the same page as we put together a strategy for Ann."

After his welcome address, Mom is brought into the room by her social worker—a large woman in her forties, wearing a flowered dress with librarian like glasses.

I feel a pain that slices through my chest the moment I see my mother. Mom looks defeated and lost. It's not that she has put on weight, but something about Mom looks "heavy" as she sadly sits next to my father. Mom shyly waves to me and Michael; we are sitting across the room. She then turns to Pop and casually asks, "Where's Tony?"

Even though he was discharged from Children's Hospital a few days ago, Tony still gets dizzy, and complains that his vision is blurry and poor. He can't walk very far under his own power, and his head and face still look bloated from the operation, so Pop plays down the accident.

He tells Mom that Tony got hurt playing baseball but makes it seem like his injuries are much more routine than they actually are. This causes Mom only mild concern since she thinks Tony just 'knocked his head,' therefore allowing us to start the meeting without delay.

Dr. Wydell takes a deep breath, and explains that he would like to go around the room so each of us can express our opinions on what has been happening with Mom. "Would it be okay," he asks, "if Ann's mother begins?"

Everyone sort of shrugs their shoulders as if to say, *that's fine,* and so Nonna begins to talk. Her accent is heavy; her speech is slow, but it isn't long before she's up, out of her seat going on and on about how my father is no good, and how my brothers and I are worthless.

Pop sits there, calmly rubbing his mustache as Nonna calls us selfish. She says we walk all over her daughter, and have never cared about her welfare. Soon she is in a tirade. She gets right in Pop's face, pointing her finger at him like the wife of a Mafia Don who got double crossed. Nonna screams at him, "This all you'a fault! This what'a you get for be with'a you *puttana!* This what'ta you get when'na you a'buse'a people!"

Aunt Ellen interrupts, "That's not true! I've been there, I'm sorry, but I've seen the way Ann lays on the couch all self-indulgent. These boys don't nag her, they never complain; I mean this is a good group of guys."

Nonna spins around and snaps at her, "Shut'ta you mouth! This no you'a biz-a-ness. You no even'a part of'a the family! Who you think talk'a 'bout my daughter?"

"But how can you hurt these kids any more than they've already been hurt? They're your grandchildren. Can't you see you're putting another knife in their back?"

Uncle Nick gets out of his seat and moves towards Nonna.

"Mu," he says, "c'mon, calm down, enough, let somebody else talk."

As he walks her back to her seat, Nonna mumbles under her breath in Italian that Aunt Ellen is out of line, and better keep her mouth shut.

Dr. Wydell shakes his head, and says that's exactly what he was talking about. "We're not here to point fingers. We're here to come together, to work together."

The doctor doesn't hesitate to tell Nonna that one more outburst like that, and she will be asked to leave. He takes another deep breath and says, "Let's try something else. Why don't we discuss Ann's suicide attempt last summer? She was brought to me soon after that happened. I believe from talking to her that it was a manifestation of what her father always wanted for her. For those of you that don't know, Ann stabbed herself in the stomach with as I've come to understand, one of her father's old butcher knives, drank from a bottle of carpet cleaner and ingested nearly 60 aspirin. Now as you might imagine this was of great concern because I believe it speaks to the root of her problem..."

Before the doctor can continue, there's the explosion of someone sobbing off to my left; it's Michael.

He's the only person in the room who didn't know what really happened that hot July day. All Michael was told was that Mom tried to 'hurt herself.' I can only imagine what he's feeling crying there in Aunt Teresa's arms. She cradles him into her bosom as Mom leaves her seat and scurries across the room.

She kneels beside him, "Michael," she says. "I'm here honey, I'm sorry."

Michael pulls away from her. He buries his face in Aunt Teresa's bosom and sobs like a son should sob when he realizes the truth behind 'Mom tried to hurt herself.'

I watch Michael sobbing there in Teresa's arms—the arms of his second mother—and think about all those weekends he has spent at her house over the past few years. I know in many ways he has a stronger bond with Aunt Teresa than he does with Mom—especially the Mom kneeling by his side.

Michael just got Confirmed, and will graduate this month from grade school, but sobbing there in Aunt Teresa's arms, I know he wishes he could make all this go away, and I wish I could, too. I wish I could take the forty-eight screws and ten titanium plates out of Tony's face, and chuck them into the ocean. I wish I could stop him from ever diving for that ball. I wish I could go back in time and stop Mom from going into that greenhouse decades ago. I wish I could take the stones out of my great-grandmother's hands, the ones she threw at Babbo when he was a kid back in Calabria. I wish I could cover our family history over in snow, and make it all go away so we'd be happy again with a buffet of Pavarotti and pancakes.

It isn't fair that all that is gone replaced by hospitals and meetings. I want to build a snowman, I want to make snow angels, I want to be nine years old again. I don't like being eighteen. I don't like cutting grass and dealing with a mother that smells and embarrasses us right and left. I don't like taking dinners from strangers, or quitting football, or watching Nonna scream at Pop about how we're no good. I want it to be 1986, but it's not and it never will be again.

Once Michael calms down, Dr. Wydell asks Aunt JoJo and Uncle Nick if they have anything constructive—not argumentative—but *constructive*, to add to the conversation. Aunt JoJo sits forward in her chair and says, "Frank, Nick and I are here to hear your side of the story, to see if it makes sense. The rest of the family wants your head on a platter. It's very easy to hate you based on what Ann tells us, but we're here to at least find out from you what's going on."

That's the first time anyone has ever said they're willing to hear Pop's side of the story and I know why that is; my father seems to handle things too well. Aside from his eyes twitching, my father has appeared seemingly unaffected by my mother's collapse. He seems to carry on without a care in the world, going around the house singing *'Finiculi, Finicula,'* as Mom has slowly lost touch with reality.

Even members of his own family have a hard time feeling sympathetic for him because Pop always seems to take things so lightly. I know from talking to them, that some of my father's relatives would have preferred he fall on the floor and whine like a crybaby, confessing it would be easier to 'believe' just how impossible life is with Mom, but that isn't my father.

His black leather jacket with the popped collar, his sinister mustache, and *Frankie the Voice* persona hasn't allowed anyone to see behind the curtain. It's not their fault; they weren't listening in on the other end of the line when Pop used to call the police worried for Mom's whereabouts on those nights she spent gambling. Nobody but my father lied in that empty bed, while his wife slept on the couch, then the floor— ignoring him night after night when he came home from work.

My father never mentioned these things to anyone; never felt it was his place to complain, but now all that has blown up in his face. No one can see through his affair with Gail, and his indifference to the drama of our lives. They've labeled him a 'bad guy,' just like the FBI did years ago in Ducktown. He's Italian, wears a leather jacket and works in concrete; he must be a gangster.

Both sides of the family—except his parents—look at Pop and say, *he's an arrogant, male chauvinistic pig, with no feelings of empathy who is indifferent to his poor wife's troubles, and only cares about getting laid.* He is why poor Annie is struggling so much; it's Frank's fault, and he is the problem.

My father follows a different code. I remember reading when members of the Mafia in Atlantic City were paraded in front of news crews—going in or out of jail—they were instructed by their higher ups to smile, and wave to the cameras. Even if their hands and ankles were shackled, they were to act as if everything was okay, like they could care less whether the judge gave them fifty years behind bars.

An icy, cool, macho indifference was what they wished to project; *I ain't scared. I can take it. I'm a real man*—that's Pop—he comes off like he can handle anything.

But at least Aunt JoJo seems open minded. At least she wants to hear his side of the story. "Okay Frank," she says, "even if I take your word for it, and believe how impossible Ann has been to live with, I still gotta know one thing: how can you let your boys ignore their mother, and not call her for weeks at a time? I mean, how are her problems any different than if she had cancer? If she was laid up in some hospital somewhere, you'd be at her bedside every night, rallying around her, and offering her support. Why is this any different than that?"

"Because Ann doesn't want to get better. If she had cancer, it's the *cancer* we're trying to beat, but in this case, I don't know what we're trying to beat. I mean, whether it's because she feels sorry for herself, or because she doesn't feel worthy of it, bottom line, Ann doesn't want to get better. We're always on guard. We don't know what to expect of her anymore; we've grown past sympathy, and just want peace."

"Frank, that sounds cold if you ask me."

"Jo, call it what you want, but Ann craves chaos."

"That's ridiculous."

"No, let me finish. This isn't a conspiracy like everybody in Philly thinks it is. This is a sick girl; she needs help, but everybody has always fought the idea."

"Frank, c'mon, you've never given her a chance."

Pop looks right at her and says, "We most certainly have given her a chance."

"Yeah, some chance—dump her off at her mother's—or get her into some hospital. What does that prove? She's still the same woman you married twenty years ago."

"No, she's not. She has changed. The girl I married twenty years ago isn't this girl."

Nonna interrupts.

"At'sa right! You no wanna be marry to my'a daughter no more. You wanna go back'a to you *puttana!* Say it Frank, say 'da tru! You wanna the *puttana!*"

Nonna is out of her seat again, finger back in Pop's face. That's when Dr. Wydell shouts, *"That's it! She's out!"* He turns to the social worker, who gets up along with Uncle Nick, and takes Nonna out into the hallway. Mom follows behind them as Dr. Wydell shakes his head and makes a heavy sigh.

"It's obvious," he says to us still sitting in the oval, "that there are a lot of issues that need to be worked out amongst the extended family. But I'd like to explain what I feel is the next step in Ann's treatment."

Even though Mom, Nonna and Uncle Nick are out in the hallway with the social worker, Dr. Wydell explains to us that he wants my mother to live in an apartment on campus here at the Institute. He says that way she'll be able to get the proper therapy from a doctor trained in Dissociative Identity Personality Disorders.

Aunt Teresa raises her right hand when he says that. With Michael still by her side, she asks, "Doctor, what exactly is this dissociative identity thing? I've heard Frank mention it a couple of times before, but I don't think any of us know what it is."

"A Dissociative Identity Personality Disorder," he says, "describes a condition in which a single person displays multiple or distinct personalities."

Aunt Teresa asks, "I thought that was multiple personality disorder?"

"Individuals eventually diagnosed with Dissociative Identity Personality Disorder frequently receive other diagnoses first. Ann's case history includes diagnoses of schizophrenia, multiple personality disorder and bipolar disorder...."

"So, why is she being diagnosed with this Dissociative Identity Disorder?" Aunt JoJo wants to know, "What makes you so sure?"

327

"Ann has at least two personalities that routinely take control of her behavior. In addition, she presents an associated memory loss that goes beyond normal forgetfulness. I mean, have you ever seen Ann exhibit an inability to recall important personal information, like the spelling of her own name or home address?"

"No, I haven't. That's not Ann," Aunt JoJo says.

"Wait a second," Aunt Ellen interrupts. "That's *exactly* Ann."

"Yeah," Pop says. "She's been that way her whole life. I mean I just got a letter last month from the pharmacist who fills Ann's prescriptions. He sent along a copy of the way she's been signing her name as of late, and it was spelled three different ways. *Three different ways, Jo!*"

"Well, how would I know that?"

"You wouldn't," says Aunt Teresa, "unless you were there. I've heard how Ann drives right by my street, and right by my house, when she's been there a thousand times. My sons will tell me, 'She drove right by the house, and we had to circle the block before she could drop me off.' It's like she forgets or something."

"Right," says the doctor, "she does forget. Since I've begun working with her, Ann consistently presents an amnesia type quality, which again falls in line with my Dissociative Identity Personality diagnosis."

Aunt JoJo says, "Well, where does this disorder begin? How does it originate? I don't get it...."

"It starts in childhood, normally in response to trauma, coupled with insufficient childhood nurturing. What happens is people develop an innate ability to dissociate memories, or experiences from consciousness. A high percentage of patients report having suffered sexual abuse as children, which as you know, Ann claims to have experienced."

I listen to the doctor, and watch Aunt JoJo's face, wondering what Aunt Renata or Aunt Colomba would say to Dr. Wydell if they were here. If Nonna and Uncle Nick were sitting here in the oval, and not standing with Mom out in the hallway, I'm sure they'd object. Nonna would just go on and on about how Babbo was her pride, and how the sexual abuse Mom says she experienced is only her imagination. How the men she claims abused her, were Babbo's friends, respected men from the neighborhood, who would never hurt an innocent little girl. Yet, as the doctor continues, I feel like we may finally have someone who has a real handle on Mom's struggles—like Dr. Wydell may actually be able to save her.

He goes on to say, that individuals diagnosed with Dissociative Identity Personality Disorder often demonstrate a variety of symptoms such as headaches, and other body pains, that can't be explained even through a thorough medical examination. When he says that, I can't help but think of all those nights Mom was lying there on the couch, holding her head, or rolling around on the floor, complaining of the burning inside.

The doctor goes on to say that, "Severe sexual or psychological trauma in childhood predisposes an individual to the development of Dissociative Identity Personality Disorder."

He says most abused children are abused by someone they trust, and that this causes them to split off the awareness and memory of the abuse so they can continue to survive in the relationship. The doctor says that these memories and feelings enter into the child's subconscious, only to be experienced later in the form of a separate personality. He says the dissociation acts as a coping mechanism, but that this individual may experience memory loss, and literally develop the habit of waking up in unexplained locations. In short, he says they will suffer a chaotic personal life until they are able to receive treatment for their Dissociative Identity Personality Disorder.

"Which," he says, "is exactly why I feel Ann needs to stay here on campus. She needs to work at this full-time. No distractions—no changing doctors mid-stream. If not, I fear she may only continue to deteriorate."

When Mom and the social worker return to the oval, Dr. Wydell explains to them what he just explained to us—he wants Mom to live in an apartment, here on campus, so she'll get the proper therapy from a doctor trained in Dissociative Identity Personality Disorders. He says, "Ann, now I want you to understand something, by agreeing to stay here on campus, you may be away from home for six or eight months, but in the end, it'll be in your best interest. You know you can't be committed against your will, so whaddaya say? Whaddaya think? Are you willing to give it a try?"

Before Mom has a chance to answer, Pop turns to Dr. Wydell and raises his hand as if to say, *give me a second.* He turns to Mom and says, "Ann, do you agree with Dr. Wydell? Do you think you need therapy? Do you need to stay in the hospital?"

"No, I don't think so, you know that, Frank."

"Then, why are you in the hospital?"

"Because you put me here, I'm not like these people. I don't need help."

Pop turns back to Dr. Wydell with his arms open like, *see what I mean?* The doctor lowers his eyes, takes another deep breath and says, "Ann, I can't be more emphatic. If you pass on this opportunity, you may never get it again. Now, are you sure you don't want to give it a try?"

"I'm sure. I'm not going to stay here. I need to be back home with my boys taking care of my family."

"Well Ann, you're not coming home," Pop interrupts.

"Whaddaya mean, I'm not coming home?"

"If you don't stay here, then you're going back to your mother's."

"What?"

"Ann," Dr. Wydell says, "that's on my recommendation. You need a doctor who specializes in Dissociative Identity Personality Disorders, and you'll need to stay with that person for an extended period. No more switching doctors all the time, changing people in mid-stream would be disastrous."

If she refuses to stay on campus, then Dr. Wydell recommends that Mom see a female doctor not far from Nonna's house in Philadelphia. He knows this woman who specializes in dealing with Dissociative Identity Personality Disorders.

"The challenge," Dr. Wydell says, "is this particular doctor recently found out that she's pregnant. She will be suspending her practice for about eighteen months. So, if Ann opts not to stay here on campus, then I believe going back to her mother's house for the summer is the next best option."

"But," Aunt JoJo says, "you just said this dissociative doctor won't be around? Why would you want to keep Ann away from her kids for the summer?"

"Jo, I'm not tryin' to keep Ann away from her children for any length of time. I'm tryin' to restore her health so she can *return* to her family permanently. As I said before, and as I'm sure you would agree, if

Ann continues to regularly change doctors mid-stream, the results could be disastrous. Now, I can arrange for her to attend out-patient therapy sessions at the hospital down the street from her mother's house until the specialist returns from her pregnancy leave. I don't know anybody down the shore; I could ask around and try to find someone, but I truly believe Ann's best option is to remain here on campus."

"Well, that's just not gonna happen," Mom interrupts.

"Then," Pop is quick to add, "you're goin' back to your mother's."

48

In late June 1996, just days before my nineteenth birthday, me, Pop and my brothers drive up to Uncle Nick's house in Philadelphia for our cousin Samantha's college graduation party. Sammie has just finished four years in college and all our cousins from Mom's side of the family are at Uncle Nick's for a barbecue, and so is our mother who has been living at Nonna's all summer.

She was discharged on her own accord from the Institute of Mental Health over a week ago, and has been staying at Nonna's ever since. Mom doesn't have the Cadillac to drive—that was part of the plan Dr. Wydell laid out; he didn't want her to have that much freedom. So, my mother's only responsibility is to attend her outpatient therapy sessions at the hospital down the street from Nonna's house.

When the four of us slide out of Pop's GMC Jimmy, Mom is waiting for us in the street. She looks anxious. Instead of saying hello, she immediately tells Pop she wants to take a walk. My brothers and I nod our heads at her, but none of us move to kiss her cheek or give her a hug.

Mom doesn't seem to notice us; she's only interested in one thing—taking a walk with Pop.

"But Ann," he says, "we just got here. Let me say hello to everybody first. Let me at least say hi to Samantha."

"Why can't we take a walk?"

"Ann, we're here for the party. Let's go around back, c'mon."

"I wanna take a walk."

"Ann, we're not gonna take a walk."

"I wanna take a walk."

"Ann, how 'bout you say hello to your sons?"

Mom looks at us and blinks. Her face is expressionless, "Hi, boys."

"Hi, Mom," we say in unison.

I can tell she's not angry, or ignoring us for any other reason than she wants to take a walk with Pop. Michael moves to kiss her on the cheek, though Tony and I stay back.

Mom keeps badgering Pop about wanting to take a walk—*needing* to take a walk—until Aunt Colomba limps out onto the porch and calls to us.

"Hey, boys! Hey, Frank! Come on in. Everybody's 'round back, hope you guys are hungry...."

We wave and call out, "Hi, Aunt Colomba!"

Soon, we are walking up onto the porch, and making our way through the house to the backyard. Everybody seems happy to see us; everybody except Aunt Renata.

Aunt Renata won't talk to us. Anytime any of us walk near her, she moves away. When we move to kiss her hello, she sticks her nose up in the air, and walks right past us. Pop shakes his head and motions for us to ignore her. He tells us to say hello to everyone else, which includes one of our aunts who has come over from Italy for the party and to spend a few weeks with Nonna.

Her name is Concetta, though we all call her Zia Concetta because *zia* is the Italian word for aunt. Zia Concetta is younger than Nonna by fifteen years, which means she's in her late sixties. She has a round face, with big, brown eyes, and a nose that slopes up at the end. Her dark hair is short, but her shoulders are broad, and her body is thick. She was married to one of Nonna's younger brothers, but he died last year from lung cancer, making Zia Concetta a widow.

It's uncomfortable and strange, to have Aunt Renata ignore us at every turn, but it's unexpected and odd to have Zia Concetta lecture us through Nonna, who sits beside her and translates. My brothers and I are sitting next to one another on the same side of a light brown picnic table, eating our hamburgers and drinking lemonade, when Zia starts talking to us in Italian.

Now, the only Italian I really understand are the words and phrases Pop or Nonna have taught me over the years. Whenever Zia Concetta would call our house to say "hello" or speak to Nonna, who may have been down visiting, it was all I could do to tell her to hold on, as I ran and got my grandmother in the next room. I couldn't carry on a conversation to save my life.

Regardless of whether or not we understand her, Zia Concetta speaks directly to us, in a fast staccato, with her hands waving around like she's leading some imaginary orchestra. As she speaks and waves her hands, Nonna is beside her studying our faces, and nodding her head. Sometimes, they turn towards each other and say a few things back and forth in Italian. But mostly, when Zia stops talking—Nonna starts talking—repeating everything in her broken-English.

From the sounds of it, it seems Nonna has told Zia her side of the story, regarding Mom's suicide attempt last summer, her various hospitalizations, and the constant shuffling between our house down the shore and Nonna's place in Philadelphia. Through Nonna's translation, it seems like Zia thinks it's all our fault, because all we do is walk all over Mom, talk all over Mom, and do everything we can to keep her down. Nonna tells us that Zia hasn't seen Mom in almost fifteen years, and that she is very troubled to find her niece in such poor condition.

Zia goes on to tell us—through Nonna—that we have to love our mother, and not to allow Pop to brainwash us into abusing her. She says it's our job as her children, her sons, to stand up for her, and make things right. The three of us sit there as Nonna continues to translate, until Pop comes over and stands behind us. He listens for a minute before trying to defend himself in his broken-Italian.

If I could translate what he's saying, I would imagine Pop's telling Zia all about the meeting we had at the Institute of Mental Health, where Mom opted not to stay on campus, but to check herself out, thus ruining her best chance at working through this Dissociative Identity Personality Disorder. From listening to him, I would imagine he's trying to say Mom is the one who needs to stand up and make things right, that she has to stop being so stubborn and take Dr. Wydell's counsel, and attend her sessions in anticipation of the return of that pregnant specialist.

I would imagine he's trying to say all that, but I can tell Pop's Italian is different than Zia's, or Nonna's. He can't possibly be saying all that. There are more pauses when he speaks, more of a searching for words on his part and soon he breaks out of Italian completely.

"You're bending the truth," he tells Nonna. "These boys don't abuse their mother. Their mother abuses *them!* Now, Rena won't even say hello to us, won't acknowledge her own *nephews*, but you sit there and translate this load a bull about how I'm brainwashing my boys against your daughter. Well, I'll tell you what if we're so terrible, then you and the rest of your family can stay the hell away from us. From here on, none of you are welcome at my house!"

My cousin, Alex, hears the commotion and comes over, "Hey, Uncle Frank, Nonna, what's goin' on? Why don't we calm down?"

But Zia keeps saying things to Pop in Italian; soon Nonna joins in. The two women are angry and peppering my father in a fast staccato, and that's when Pop says, "Alright boys, c'mon, we're outta here!" He marches towards the side gate; we follow him out into the front yard. Mom and Aunt Colomba are trailing behind us.

"Frank," Mom calls to him. "Take me home. Take me with you!"

Pop is ahead of us, he is striding towards his truck. Aunt Colomba is limping behind Mom, "Frank, you don't have to leave like this. Zia Concetta was just surprised to see Ann in this condition. Frank, boys, come back in!"

We climb into the truck. Pop starts the engine. Mom is standing by the driver's side window, Aunt Colomba is behind her. I'm in the passenger seat. I look over at Pop who is staring straight ahead, his sunglasses on, collar up.

Mom tries again, "Frank, take me with you." But Pop stays staring straight ahead—he puts the truck into gear. Then, without a glance in her direction, he says, "Goodbye, Ann," as we slowly pull away from the curb and make our way back down the shore.

Days after Samantha's graduation party, my forty-nine year old mother steals money from Nonna's pocketbook, hails a cab, and plans to commit suicide.

She has the taxi driver take her to the Ben Franklin Bridge, a massive suspension bridge connecting Philadelphia with the city of Camden, on the Jersey side of the Delaware River.

At the last minute, Mom calls Uncle Nick from a payphone to say goodbye. She tells him of her plan to end it all, but Uncle Nick is able to keep Mom on the line long enough for the police to trace the call. Soon, the cops arrive and find my mother outside a bar in downtown Camden. They take her to the Locked Crisis Unit at Our Lady of Lourdes Hospital.

When Pop gets the call that Mom is locked up, he is relieved that she was found, but tells everybody, "I'm not gonna pick her up right away. I'm gonna make her wait until tomorrow. I want her to stay the night. I want her to learn she's not the center of attention. We're not going to jump whenever she does something bizarre. She expects everybody to drop everything, and make a fuss over her? Well, not this time."

The next morning, Pop drives the forty minutes up to Camden, and signs Mom out of the Locked Crisis Unit at Our Lady of Lourdes Hospital. His plan is to bring her back to Nonna's house in Philadelphia, then return home in the afternoon. Only, after he signs the papers to secure Mom's release—she turns to him and says, "Frank, I want you to know that the Ann you used to know isn't here anymore."

Now, Pop has always claimed to miss the girl he married, and would probably concur that the Ann he used to know, *isn't* here anymore, but he is not in the mood for discussion. He just wants to get Mom into the truck, and back to my grandmother's. My mother seems calm—so my father leaves her and her statement alone.

Minutes later, as they're leaving Camden, crossing the Ben Franklin Bridge, my mother realizes they're going back into Philadelphia, and that's when she suddenly opens the passenger side door, and makes a move to jump out. My parents are on the incline of the massive bridge. My father is driving full speed. They are in heavy traffic. But as soon as he hears that door open, Pop throws his body on top of my mother. He has her pinned against the corner of the seat, using his right hand to keep the door closed, even as Mom starts punching him, and slapping his face. She is screaming, "*Let me out! Let me jump! I wanna jump! Let me out! I wanna die!*"

"*Jesus, Ann! Calm the fuck down! Knock it off!*"

"*No, I wanna jump! I wanna die!*"

Mom continues to slap him, and plead with him long after they have crossed the bridge. On the entire thirty-minute ride from the Ben

Franklin Bridge to Nonna's neighborhood, Mom is screaming, slapping and begging my father to let her jump out into traffic.

She wants to be run over by a car, a truck, a bus—anything—just, "Please, let me jump Frank. I wanna die."

Somehow, my father is able to keep his truck on the road as he continues pinning Mom against the passenger side door, enduring her pleas and slaps—until finally—he snaps.

Instead of going straight to Nonna's house, my father decides to stop at the cemetery where Babbo is buried. He drags Mom out of the truck. He carries her over to my grandfather's headstone.

Pop shouts, "Ann, I've had it! You're gonna get this out right now! You got a problem with your father? Well, here he is! This whole mess, our entire lives, revolves around this little prick. *Now, make your peace!*"

Standing atop Babbo's grave, Mom is in tears. All of a sudden, the same woman who was screaming and slapping and begging to die, becomes sheepish and shy.

She softly says, "I don't want to be here, Frank."

"Ann, you *need* to be here!"

"No, I wanna go."

"You need to get this out of your system, Ann. He's dead. He's been dead ten years. Now make your peace. Have it out! Yell at him! Tell him you hate him! Do whatever you gotta do! *But we can't go on like this!*"

Sadly, Mom never makes her peace; she never says a word.

As my mother continues to study the marble headstone inscribed with her father's name—Pop is so fed-up, standing in the middle of a thousand gravesites, on a hot July day, that he contemplates pissing all over my grandfather's grave. It's only his fear of getting caught in the act that stops him from going through with it.

49

We have two cats—Oreo and Midnight—and just like everything else in our house, they are a mess. Though we have had them for years, they have never been to a veterinarian. We don't stay up on their 'shots,' or make sure they are properly spayed or neutered. Midnight is so ill that she begins to sneeze all over the place—leaving long, slimy cat snot on everything: our walls, cabinets, kitchen counter, pillows, couches and carpet.

Since we don't make regular trips to the supermarket, we never have enough cat food. Sometimes Oreo and Midnight go days without being fed, so they hunt whatever they can. They are really "inside cats," but since they're normally starving, they sneak out and like to kill the mice that live in the meadows behind our house. Then they leave their dead corpses to rot on our front porch, where they stay for days.

On the rare occasion we have a fully stocked cupboard, Pop will open a can of tuna fish and place it in the hallway behind the den. Oreo and Midnight will notice him with the can, and meow in anticipation, only to *devour* the tuna like lion cubs in the wild.

We have learned to be careful where we step when walking down that hallway, since those empty tuna fish cans and lids will stay there for weeks, lining the wall. The stench of kitty litter is also strong in that hallway—because we never bother to change it. The kitty litter is left to pile up with mountains of cat shit, and valleys of soggy feline piss everywhere.

We're not proud of the way we treat Oreo and Midnight, but we don't even think about it; our neglect is universal. We don't do the dishes. We don't change the sheets on our beds. We never sweep, dust, vacuum or organize anything. Our bathrooms reek of urine and the mirrors and sinks are spotted with toothpaste scum and shaving cream residue.

Even though I have access to all of Hank's professional landscaping equipment, our huge lawn goes weeks and weeks without being cut. Our two-car garage is so over-run with concrete tools, fishing gear and sporting equipment, you can barely walk; and, we *never* wash our clothes.

For the past few months, we have been using two separate thirty-two gallon trashcans as hampers. Pop sent me and Tony down to the local hardware store, where we bought the huge, green trashcans. When we got home, we lug them upstairs to the landing, where we use one for colored clothes, and the other one for white clothes.

In addition to the trashcans, there is always a waist-high pile of clean clothes sitting on the landing, waiting for Aunt Teresa, or Aunt Ellen to come over and fold them for us.

When Pop's friend, Charlie, comes over, he takes a look at our kitchen, the filthy carpets, the disheveled landing with the trashcans and huge pile of clothes, the lawn with its' knee-high grass, and a half-dozen cat food cans scattered throughout that wretched smelly hallway; he says he's never seen a more helpless bunch in his life.

"Italians," he says. "This would only happen to Italians. You all think you're too high and mighty to wash a dish, or fold a towel! What's the matter with you guys?"

Uncle Charlie, as we call him, is an Irish-American bachelor. If Uncle Charlie was Italian, he wouldn't feel the need to wash our dishes when he comes over—but there he is—our 5'10" 325-pound silver haired dishwasher, smoking a cigarette, with a dishtowel slung over his shoulder. The cigarette dances on his lip as he mumbles, "Helpless bunch of princes. Frankie, get over here and help me dry these dishes."

I look at him like, *dry the dishes? What is he talking about?*

When Nonna used to turn our kitchen into Calabria, we used to help her with the fun stuff—rolling the meatballs, or closing the edges of the ravioli with a fork. She never asked us to do anything that was a *chore*. Chores were something our friends had.

But Uncle Charlie is impatient. "Frankie, I don't have all day. Get your ass over here. I'm going to teach you how this is done."

I feel like I should talk to him—tell him what Pop told me years ago that doing the wash is for women. Loading the dishwasher is for women. Ironing clothes is for women. We, as men, don't do any of that because we are Italian.

Yet, Uncle Charlie won't stop. He starts stomping his foot, "Frankie!"

I go over, and swipe the dishtowel off his shoulder.

"Now, dry these pots and pans," he commands.

I pick up the frying pan. I take the towel and start to dry it. Uncle Charlie orders Tony to get the broom, and sweep the kitchen floor. He calls Michael in from the den, and shows him how to properly load the dishwasher.

Just then, Pop walks into the kitchen. My brothers and I look at each other with knowing smiles, Pop will put an end to this. He'll take one look at Uncle Charlie, making us do this silly housework, and say, *whoa! Whoa! Whoa! What are you doing to my Italian boys?*

But to our amazement—and great disappointment—Pop doesn't do any of that. Instead, he throws his head back and laughs, ha, ha, ha, before slapping his hand against the counter in excitement. With a grin on his face, he sarcastically asks, "So, what are you guys up to?" My brothers and I look at him in disbelief. Not only doesn't Pop stand up for the "code," he says, "I like what I see. When you're done in the kitchen, I want the hallway cleaned up, the grass cut, and your rooms put in order."

Even though Pop has said no one from my mother's side of the family is welcome down the shore, he drives up to Nonna's house to take Mom to dinner every once in a while. Sometimes we go with him, and sometimes we don't; but, it's hard for me to believe he would even want to speak to his wife after that time she tried to jump out of his truck, and die on the Ben Franklin Bridge.

Mom was a mess that day, punching and slapping my father, until she completely shut-down when brought to Babbo's grave. If my father thought that was a stressful afternoon filled with chaos and drama, it's safe to say that incident merely served to prepare him for what was to come. Several weeks after the events of that blistering July day, Pop drove up to Nonna's house and took Mom to a diner where they had a simple dinner and discussed her progress, or lack thereof, with those outpatient therapy sessions she had been attending. Afterwards,

340

my parents stopped for ice cream. It was as they sat in Pop's GMC Jimmy, finishing their sundaes that Mom said, "Frank, I wanna sleep with you tonight."

Pop chuckled to himself and rolled his eyes, "Ann, I really don't think that's a good idea."

Intimacy had long been a complicated subject for my parents. Having both come from traditional Roman Catholic families, they did not engage in premarital sex. And of course, their honeymoon was marred by Mom's emotional discomfort after their first time making love.

Throughout the 1980's, after Nonna called Mom a *puttana*, she escaped my father's advances by sleeping on the couch, and gambling late into the night.

Eventually, my father became so fed up he started locking their bedroom door to discourage Mom from coming to bed, even if she wanted to. He was just that disgusted. By this point, engaging in sex with Mom was weird and too much work. It was only during Pop's affair with Gail that Mom seemed remotely interested in being playful or sexy.

In the five years post-Gail, Mom has shed all signs of femininity. Without a mistress to compete with, Mom goes days without a shower, and rarely brushes her teeth. It's easy to imagine that her feminine hygiene leaves much to desire. So when my mother says, "Frank, I wanna have sex."

My father tries to let her down easy. "Ann, I think we should just say goodnight."

"I don't wanna hear that, Frank. Stop at the next hotel, and get us a room."

"Ann, that's crazy...."

"Frank, stop at the next hotel and get us a room!"

Pop stopped at the next hotel. He went into the office, and asked about a room. Even though there were plenty of vacancies, he lied to Mom, "They're all booked, Ann. No rooms available."

"Well," she said, "let's go back to my mother's and have sex there."

"Ann, it's late. I wanna get back down the shore."

But Mom was insistent, and my father wasn't in the mood to fight. He pulled his truck into the driveway at Nonna's house. He turned the engine off, and calmly said, "Ann, I really don't think having sex is the best idea." But Mom didn't want to hear it. She reached for the truck keys, and yanked them out of the ignition. "Frank, you're not leaving until you have sex with me!"

"Ann, give me the keys."

"No, come up stairs and have sex with me."

"Ann, just give me the keys."

Fighting an uphill battle—Pop decided to go inside. Aunt Colomba, who sometimes slept at Nonna's was home alone. My grandmother was staying with Zia Concetta, over Uncle Nick's house. Aunt Colomba was upstairs in bed when Mom started pulling at Pop to have sex in the living room.

"Ann," he said, "this is ridiculous. Give me the keys and let me go home."

"Not until you have sex with me!"

"Ann, *Jesus Christ!*"

After a few minutes, Aunt Colomba heard the commotion and came limping downstairs in her robe. "Frank, Ann," she said, turning the hallway lights on. "What are you doing?"

"He won't have sex with me," Mom said.

"Excuse me?"

"She has the keys," Pop said. "I need to get going, but she won't give them back."

"Ann, come on, give him the keys, it's late."

"No, Colomba, this is between husband and wife. Now, he's gonna have sex with me, or he's not goin' home." Mom proceeded to get undressed in front of the both of them. She took off everything, but her white undershirt. Aunt Colomba got in her face, "Ann! Jesus Christ! Give Frank the goddamn keys, and let's go to bed! I'm tired of this shit, enough already! Now, c'mon!"

For twenty minutes, the three of them went around and around, until Aunt Colomba got back in Mom's face and Pop was able to grab her wrist, wrestle the keys from her hand and make a break for the front door. He ran down the front steps, and quickly hopped in his truck. As he turned the ignition over, and started backing out of the driveway, Mom came charging down the front steps, and launched herself onto the hood of his GMC Jimmy. Now, Pop was lowering his window, "Ann, get off the hood! *Let me go!*"

"*I want you here!*"

"Ann, let me go!"

"I want you here!"

As he inched his way out of the driveway, Mom rolled off the hood, over the sidewalk, and into the gutter. She got up and chased Pop down the sidewalk—half naked—angry, and screaming. She was running down the street where she grew-up, in only an undershirt, begging my father to have sex and carrying on like a woman gone mad.

"Get back here! Frank, get back here and have sex with me!"

Pop slowly drove up the block to the hospital; he didn't want to leave Mom alone in the street—and of course Mom followed him.

When he got to the Emergency Room entrance Mom was still insistent on having sex, so Pop had the hospital staff and security guards help him corral my mother. She was ranting and raving in the middle of the road; the security guards tried to reason with her, but Mom was not in the mood to negotiate.

After exhausting all their options, they had no choice but to physically restrain my mother. For the second time in twelve months Mom was readmitted into the Locked Crisis Unit, at that hospital down the street from Nonna's house.

50

On Pop's side of the family, I have a cousin named Romeo, who is five years older than me. Romeo lives in Southwest Philadelphia, and comes down the shore a lot in the summer. Once in a while, he brings down his friend Carmine, who is so 'Italian,' even Pop rolls his eyes.

Carmine dresses in designer suits, wears pinkie rings, and talks like he is in *Goodfellas*. He hangs out with the wiseguys from South Philly, the Italian neighborhood, where *Rocky* came from. It's where the biggest mobster in the area lives, a young, handsome gangster whom Carmine idolizes.

I quickly learn that Carmine has no fear. He likes to hang out on Passyunk Avenue, in the heart of South Philadelphia, where he makes the acquaintance of several *Mafiosi*. All summer, he tells me and Romeo stories about the wiseguys. He drops their names as we walk the Boardwalk in Atlantic City, or enjoy a pizza at Tony's Baltimore Grill. Carmine loves talking with his hands, and boasting about hanging-out with Made men.

Pop grows suspicious of Carmine. My father says, "If he really knows those people, he shouldn't brag like he does." My father is worried, and says, "Chichi, you know that I did a lot of work for those guys over in Atlantic City years ago. Through Uncle Sal, I even shared an occasional drink with them. But I want to make sure you understand, I **never** got involved with them. Anybody who talks like Carmine, who brags like Carmine, is a *gavone*, and only gonna get himself and those around him in trouble. You gotta promise me, you're gonna use your head with this kid."

"Alright, Pop. I will."

"'Cause I'm tellin' ya, you're too soft, Chichi. These guys will push you around, and you won't know when you're walkin' into a bad situation. Because you're Italian, people will assume things, and we don't need that." I smirk, when my father says I'm too soft. "Pop, I get it. I won't get involved."

"Chichi—you don't understand—they'll *make* you get involved." —and that's when Pop tells me The Seventy Punches Story.

The Seventy Punches Story—is exactly that—the night my father got punched seventy times by a Mob associate from Georgia Avenue in Atlantic City.

In the early 1980's, Pop was hired to do all the concrete work at a bar in Ducktown—a Mob joint. It took him about eight months to complete the project, knowing full-well who hired him; who really ran the place.

Through Uncle Sal, and the fact some of the local Mob figures worked in concrete, my father got to know them well enough to shake their hands and say hello. Though he was never afraid of them, he always felt strange shaking the hands of known killers. He rationalized it by saying, *they're Italian, and I'm Italian. As long as I don't bother them, they won't bother me,* but he was wrong.

When gambling first came to Atlantic City, a dispute immediately arose between the New York and Philadelphia crime families over control of the resort. Everyone wanted a piece of the action. Anyone associated with organized crime was constantly on the look-out, fearing a hostile take-over by an out-of-state rival.

Frankie the Voice was just coming into his own back then. My father was pouring concrete every day. He was learning how the city worked, and developing that Mafia mystique. By the time he was in his early thirties, Pop was 6'1" and weighed 225 pounds, and with a sledgehammer in his hand, he was an animal.

One of the local Mob associates noticed my father's confident strength, and made him a "job offer." Even though this particular fellow always carried a loaded forty-five caliber revolver in the waistline of his pants—and was known to be a hothead—he wanted my father to start carrying a gun, and get involved with him as "muscle."

My father knew he couldn't turn the man down without insulting him. So, Pop didn't give him a direct yes or no. Instead, he just hoped the guy would drop it and leave him alone. But the Mob associate kept pestering my father, badgering him for weeks about getting involved. Pop finally told him—in no uncertain terms—he had a family, and didn't feel right getting mixed up in anything. But, that only served to piss the hothead off.

Not long after he turned him down, Pop was at another bar in Ducktown. He was eating dinner with Uncle Sal. They were sitting at the bar, enjoying a plate of spaghetti and a glass of wine, when the hothead came up behind my father—and without warning—began to pound him in the back.

The thing is—when the hothead landed his first punch, Pop didn't even flinch. He kept eating his dinner, and drinking his wine. But then the guy *really* started to lay into him. He was pounding my father so hard, that Uncle Sal, who was sitting on the stool next to him, slowly got up, and backed away.

Uncle Sal may have hidden that tiny twenty-two caliber pistol under his hat, but he was Sicilian enough to know how this worked. If someone associated with *La Famiglia* wants you to do something—even if you're an innocent bystander—you're going to do it, or be punished. This was my father's punishment.

The thing is—Pop was making the hothead look weak by not reacting to the beating. This was even more of an insult. The whole bar stopped and watched; it was hard to believe someone could take that much punishment.

Even though he would have a bruise the size of a football for weeks afterwards, it wasn't until the hothead hit Pop on the spine that my father even acknowledged what was going on. After a few dozen punches, this deranged Mob associate hit my father directly on the spine, and it hurt so badly it brought tears to Pop's eyes.

That's when Pop half turned around, "You wanna keep hittin' me? Go ahead. But don't punch me on the spine again."

But that's exactly what he did, and that's when *Frankie the Voice* snapped. My father spun around from the bar and clocked the fellow in the face knocking him off balance. He then aggressively lifted the hothead up, threw him over his shoulder and called for one of the waitresses to open the door. Pop then carried him out into the street where he dropped him in a dumpster across the way.

Then, my father calmly walked back inside to finish his dinner, but not before it crossed his mind that he might get killed. He knew these guys from Georgia Avenue didn't fool around. You can't do what he just did in front of a bar full of people without some sort of retribution.

Mobsters, and their associates, don't like to be out manned. They can't allow anyone to embarrass them. They need to be the toughest guys in the room. Members of this Atlantic City gang killed a concrete contractor just a few years earlier for merely insulting the quality of their masonry work. The authorities found the man's body stuffed in the trunk of his car.

So, my father knew what could happen. Yet, he went back inside, sat down and continued eating like nothing had happened. Five minutes later, the door swung open, and in walked the hothead. My father was certain he was going get a pistol whipping, or a bullet to the back of the head. He had just stood up to an armed associate of the Philadelphia / Atlantic City crime family—even worse—Pop embarrassed him.

No one knew what to expect. He walked over to my father— people were thinking they were about to witness the end of someone's life. After all, this was Georgia Avenue.

Yet, to everyone's surprise, the hothead started boasting about my father. He wasn't angry; he was impressed.

He started shouting to everyone how he couldn't believe how Pop just sat there while he beat on him. *Then* had the strength *and* the balls to carry him outside and drop him in that dumpster. The hothead was even more convinced that Pop had to come work for him as muscle; but in the end, he paid for my father's spaghetti dinner, and decided to give him a pass

—and that's The Seventy Punches Story.

51

It is autumn 1996, and my brother, Michael, is a freshman at a prestigious prep school in southern New Jersey; while Tony is a newly registered junior at the local Catholic high school. My brothers may go to different schools, but they do so for the same reason—football.

Even though Michael is only fourteen years old, he is the starting varsity quarterback for his squad, and the recipient of a full athletic scholarship. Tony, on the other hand, transferred out of my alma mater over the summer. He wanted to give himself a better shot at winning the starting varsity quarterback position at his new school—a perennial south Jersey powerhouse.

The fact Tony is back to playing football, just four months after breaking his collar bone, damaging his sinus passage, knocking his left eye out of place, shattering the orbit around that eye into ten pieces, and tearing the membrane between his skull and brain tissue in two spots—has everyone in our circle of friends and family questioning the decision.

To most parents, the thought of their son playing football again after all that—would be impossible. They would say, *you're lucky to be alive. Football is way too dangerous, and completely out of the question. Why don't you take up something like golf?*

But, that's not Pop.

I can still remember the way he crushed that doctor's hand in the Emergency Room, how he fought to get Tony transferred to Children's Hospital, and how he slept by his side during the eight days it took my brother to recover. If the doctor says Tony's face and head can handle the physical pounding football entails, then Pop is on board; and, that's just what we were told.

Over the summer, Tony was medically cleared to play football by his surgeon. He said my brother's face is actually stronger now than it ever was, thanks to those ten metal plates and forty-eight screws around his left eye and forehead. Yet, everyone from Aunt Ellen to Grandmom say it doesn't seem worth the risk. They try to talk him out of it, but after he got the doctor's okay to play, Tony immediately started getting back into shape and talked with Pop about transferring schools.

Personally, I knew Tony was on the mend when he started poking fun at himself after the injury. He would regularly snatch a few magnates off of our refrigerator and stick them to his face where they would remain stuck to his skin. It was nice to see him making us all laugh. It put me at ease. It was a long and difficult recovery for my middle brother, but after watching him crack us up with those magnates, I knew Tony was back.

Yet, the idea that he would be jockeying to position himself for a better shot at "playing time" by changing schools just months after nearly dying in leftfield, spoke of something else—Tony is basically fearless now.

He starts using a certain phrase over and over—*say I won't*. Whenever something challenging arises, climbing a tree to the very top, paddling out past the waves—well beyond where anyone should be swimming—Tony will challenge those around him to dare him to attempt the risky move. *Say I won't* becomes his mantra, his way of showing the world he ain't afraid of nuttin'.

With both of my brothers playing high school football, I can't help but think if Mom hadn't tried to kill herself two summers ago, I'd be going into my sophomore year as a Towson State Tiger. Instead, I attend community college and cut grass all week—spending my Friday nights and Saturday afternoons watching my brothers from the bleachers.

On game days, Pop and I ride in his GMC Jimmy, and stand high atop the bleachers where he videotapes each and every offensive play. Pop is not only creating a highlight tape to send to colleges at season's end, but a film for my brothers to review and study from weekly. In the stands, Pop beams with pride every time someone singles him out as the quarterback's father—or when one of my brothers' names are announced over the loudspeaker. I know he did the same thing when I played, but I can't help but think if there's nothing like playing quarterback, there must be nothing like being the quarterback's father.

Watching my brothers play every weekend throughout the fall is one of the ways Pop puts aside his worries over Mom's future and the approaching New Jersey winter. The winters down the shore are always the toughest for those in construction, and I know he has very little work lined-up; he must be concerned about money.

When it comes to Mom, he has no idea what to do next. Nothing substantial came out of her seven-week stay at the Institute of Mental Health at the University of Pennsylvania. Ever since she has been released, her behavior has only gotten more bizarre and erratic: threatening to jump off the Ben Franklin Bridge, trying to jump out into high-speed traffic, and chasing my father down the street, begging him to have sex.

The thing is—Mom was *always* the biggest football fan in the family. When I was seven years old, she took me to my first game, a preseason contest at Veteran's Stadium for the Philadelphia Eagles. Our parents even surprised us one Christmas with Eagles' tickets right on the 50 yard line—my brothers and I couldn't believe it...!!! And it was Mom who told me about one of the biggest games in Eagles' history, the day in January 1981, when they beat the Dallas Cowboys for the NFC Championship, and the right to play in Super Bowl XV. That game took place on her thirty-fourth birthday and she was there to witness it in person, attending the game with her brother, Nick.

Some fifteen years later, Mom is staying with Uncle Nick and his wife, Aunt JoJo. She has been out of our daily lives for nearly five months which means the four of us have been free of the day-to-day dysfunctional mess Mom has become.

We have been free to be as 'normal' a family as we can. Football has become our way of communicating. It has replaced those Sunday mornings when we used to feast on Pavarotti and pancakes.

Aunt Sofia, Pop's much younger, only sister, is concerned about Mom, and she has an idea. Where my father has long been pragmatic in his view of the world, Aunt Sofia is dogmatic. She lives her life according to the rules of the One Holy Catholic and Apostolic Church. Aunt Sofia and her husband want to take Mom to a woman named Margaret who has visions of the Virgin Mary. The walls of her church in Maryland, where she has these visions, are covered with the crutches of people who were healed when the Virgin appeared.

My aunt believes the same healing could happen for Mom in an emotional sense. The thing is—Margaret only has her visions on Thursday afternoons. When he hears this, Pop smirks, and says, "What's so special about Thursday? Is Mary booked the rest of the week?" Pop in his sarcasm adds, "I'm comfortable being Roman Catholic—because we're Italian. But you can't tell me the Virgin Mary comes and talks to this lady in Maryland. That's just ridiculous."

Even though he was skeptical and sarcastic, Pop allows Aunt Sofia and Uncle Bobby to drive up to Philadelphia, and take Mom to see Margaret the Visionary, as long as they promise not to bring her back down the shore afterwards.

Another relative of ours makes arrangements so my mother could sit in a designated section up by the altar, where Margaret would be able to pray over her.

Before Mass, Mom goes to confession. When she comes out of the confessional, my aunt says it looks like a weight had been lifted from Mom's shoulders—like she was relieved. My aunt and uncle are pleased.

Following Confession, Mom, along with the rest of the congregation, prays the rosary. She doesn't even flinch when her name is read aloud during the litany of Special Intentions.

After Margaret is visited by the Virgin Mary, all the people for whom the Mass was offered are taken into the back of the church, where the visionary anoints them with Holy Oil, and offers a prayer.

When Mom comes back out into the congregation, she sobs in Uncle Bobby's arms. She stays in his embrace for the longest time— almost as if a damn had broken—and all the grief is rushing out.

My Aunt Sofia and Uncle Bobby again feel pleased. In their hearts, they feel like they have done the right thing. It seems as if this visit with Margaret has done wonders for my mother; like maybe she is on the road to recovery.

But when Aunt Sofia tells my father how the visit had gone, all Pop can do is roll his eyes and say, "Oh, please, nothing that 'visionary' did, or didn't do, is going to have any effect on Ann. Trust me. You got her away from her brother's house for a day, and for that, she put on a good performance. What you think 'helped' her, actually did nothing but help her convince you that she is a sweet girl who needs to be handled with kid gloves. You played right into it; Ann got you good."

"Not true," Aunt Sofia shoots back. "Ann had a wonderful experience with Margaret. It really helped her."

After that day with Margaret, and the Virgin Mary, Mom starts to read a series of religious booklets about the Sacred Heart of Jesus.

She gets these books from Uncle Bruno, Pop's brother.

This series of religious literature soon takes the place of those supermarket paperback novels she used to read. If Mom isn't lounging on the loveseat in the den staring at the big screen TV like a zombie, she is quietly sitting in the living room, reading about Jesus Christ.

52

Weeks after Mom sees Margaret the Visionary, she comes home unannounced. It is Saturday night; Michael is over Aunt Teresa's house, and Tony is home alone. I'm over at Grandmom and Grandpop's house watching TV when Tony calls with panic in his voice. "Frankie," he says, "I don't know what to do. Mom is home."

"Whaddaya mean?"

"Uncle Nick and Aunt JoJo brought her down. Aunt Colomba is here too."

"Where's Pop?"

"I think he's down at the field."

"Alright, I'll be right there."

As soon as I hang up, Grandmom wants to know what's wrong. I tell her Tony needs a ride to the movies, and not to worry.

I race out the front door, and hop in the Camaro. I rush across town with one thought in my head; *Mom wasn't supposed to come home like this.* The idea was for her to get herself together, get a job, take her meds, make her appointments, and *prove* to us that she is ready, willing and able to come back down the shore.

When I walk inside our house, I find Uncle Nick sitting calmly in the den watching TV. His hands are clasped behind his head. He rises to greet me, just as my aunts come spilling out of the kitchen with Mom. We make our way into the living room. I sit at one end of the couch; Mom sits at the other. Aunt Colomba and Aunt JoJo on the love seat, and Uncle Nick is across from us in a chair from the kitchen, but there's no sign of Tony. I ask Aunt Colomba, "Where's my brother?"

"He left."

"He left?"

"Yeah, on his bike."

"Where did he go?"

"Who knows?"

"What does that mean?"

Before I can get an answer, Aunt JoJo chimes in, "Frankie, our house is over-run. I don't know if you know, but Sammie's house flooded. She and her husband are staying with us, along with all their stuff, so there just isn't room for your mother right now."

"Besides," Uncle Nick says, leaning forward in his chair, "she should be *here* with her family."

"Yeah, Frankie," says Aunt Colomba, "you gotta start taking care of your mother. It's because of you guys that she is acting the way she has been acting. All she talks about are her boys. 'Take me to see my precious boys.' Would it kill you to be nice to her? To think about her needs for a change?"

"Yeah, maybe come and visit her," adds Aunt JoJo. "I can't believe you three. My mother had some emotional problems when I was young. She was away from us for a whole year, nursing herself back to health, but my father made sure we saw her, and made sure we wrote her. Goddammit! I don't understand you three—especially you, Frankie."

"Yeah, *especially* you, Frankie," Aunt Colomba says. "You can drive. There's no good excuse for why you don't come up and take your mother out to eat, to the movies, someplace. I mean would it kill ya'?"

In my defense, I just blurt it out: "Don't you think Babbo has anything to do with how Mom has been acting? I mean...."

That's all I get out before Uncle Nick is all over me, "I don't want to hear that shit! That is nothing but pure bullshit! Who do you think you are dragging my father into this? He was a good man. It's *your* father that needs to be looked at, shuffling his wife off to Philadelphia whenever he feels like it. How 'bout takin' responsibility for the mother of your children? Huh? Where's that? So don't you dare pin this on my father, but it's easy to see who you take after."

"Right," says Colomba. "Where is your father anyway? *Fishing*?"

"I think he's with Michael at a football game for Teresa's son."

"Oh, there's another one," Aunt Colomba says. "She and her sister—a royal pain in the ass, the both of them."

I look to Mom to say something—*anything*. Aunt Ellen and Aunt Teresa are her friends, her *only* friends. They have gone out of their way to help us for years, but my mother says nothing, and I know I'm wasting my time waiting for her to pipe up.

She just sits there going right along with everything, playing the innocent victim—when the phone rings.

I walk into the kitchen, pick up the receiver, and I hear Aunt Teresa scream into my ear, "Frankie, are they still there?"

"Who?"

"You know who! Your mother's fuckin' family—that's who! Tony is a mess. He rode his bike all the way to my house in his bare feet. He is crying. What the fuck did that stupid ass Colomba say to him, huh? A liar? She called him a liar?"

"I don't know."

"Tell me what she said!"

"I don't know."

"Fine, put her on the phone then!"

"Aunt Teresa, calm down, please."

"I am calm. Now, put her on the fuckin' phone!"

"I can't do that; you know I can't do that."

"Why?"

"Because it'll only make matters worse; I got things under control."

I pace the dark kitchen, talking as quietly as I can, so they won't hear me in the next room. But Aunt Teresa is livid; she wants answers, and she wants them now. "I'm comin' over, Frankie."

"No, Aunt Teresa."

"I'm comin' over because I've *had* it with them. I'll come over and tear them a new one! If they want to bad mouth your father—that's one thing—he's a grown man. But you kids? Jesus Christ, you're kids! What do they think you do to her?"

"Aunt Teresa...."

"Your mother brings it on herself."

"Please don't come over. I'm fine; we're okay."

"I have a better idea. Put that fuckin' Nick on the phone. What does he know? Showin' his face once a year! Goddammit, Frankie!"

"Aunt Teresa, I can handle it. If you come over, things are only gonna get worse, but they're askin' for my father. Do you know where he is?"

"He should be pullin' up any minute. He just dropped Michael off; they went to dinner after the game."

"Okay."

"But Frankie, you call me if they get out of hand. I'd already be there, except my nephew is gettin' married tonight, and I gotta go. But Goddammit, they piss me off. They got to learn to leave you fuckin' kids alone!"

I hang up the phone, and take a deep breath before heading back into the living room. When I do, I find Pop's brother, my Uncle Bruno, sitting in the pink chair in the corner. He gets a different treatment than I get from Mom's family. They are more cordial with him, and less indicting. They like Uncle Bruno, and catch him up to speed with what has been going on. But all I hear is Aunt Teresa's voice in my head, *you tell them to leave you kids alone!*

Pop walks in minutes later, and Uncle Nick starts complaining. He says he doesn't like how his sister has been getting treated down here. Aunt JoJo can't wait to add how cruel she thinks it is that Pop can stand by and watch as we abandon our mother.

At first, my father does nothing but stand there in his black leather jacket, collar up, looking like a mobster from Central Casting. When he finally speaks, he cocks his head and says, "Ann needs to show us that she's ready to try and get better. That she is willing to take her meds, see her doctor, and make a serious effort, otherwise...."

"Otherwise what?" Uncle Nick asks.

"Otherwise, we're only gonna go through the same thing again. She doesn't shower; she doesn't cook anymore. When she does cook, it's barely edible. She neglects the housework, eats her lipstick, does nothin' but sit on the couch and drinks coffee, smokes cigarettes and watches TV. Over the past few years she has concocted God knows how many conspiracy theories, suicide attempts and threats. I mean, it's been a lot to deal with. We need Ann to show us that she is ready to change. We need her to admit that there is a problem, and that she needs help because we can't keep livin' like we've been livin'. And Jo, to be honest, it's a relief when Ann goes to Philadelphia. We're provided with a much needed break from the daily torture of living with her."

"That's cold, Frank."

"Call it what you will, Jo. But that's the truth."

Now that Mom is home again, she falls head over heels back into The Routine. She doesn't cook, she doesn't clean, she doesn't shower, and she doesn't change her clothes. She never flushes the toilet, she never washes her hair, and she is obsessed with applying and reapplying her heavy red lipstick. Her body odor smells of a homeless person, and any discussion of what it would take for her to get better has all but vanished from our daily lives.

With Mom so caught up in The Routine, my brothers, me and Pop try to avoid her at all costs. If we used to plead with her about not coming to my brothers' games, now we just sneak out of the house when it's time to go. If we used to try and cover-up or explain away her behavior, now we let things lie—knowing that our friends have certainly heard about her suicide attempts and disappearances, or witnessed firsthand The Routine in action.

Sometimes if I'm parked behind the Cadillac, Mom will ask me to borrow the Camaro so she can drive down to 7-11, and purchase a cup of coffee and some cigarettes. But other than that, she will go hours without speaking to us—sitting in a trance in front of the big screen TV.

Because she is often in the trance, the four of us carry on as if she isn't around, and rarely include her in anything we do, or any place we go. The fact that she talked her family into bringing her home before we were ready or even able to set anything up with a mental health provider puts Pop in a bad spot. He stays in his office most days working on blueprints and proposals, while Mom wallows in The Routine.

My mother's trance is so deep that most days she won't answer or turn to us until we shout—*Mom*—four or five times. Even then, she looks at us like she has been somewhere else for the past half-hour; some place other than lying on the couch, watching *The Maury Povich Show*.

When I see her like this, I think about Dr. Wydell, and the explanation he gave us for Mom's Dissociative Identity Personality Disorder. He said it is the sort of condition in which a single person displays multiple or distinct personalities, and that this person may have the sort of memory loss that goes beyond normal forgetfulness almost like amnesia.

That's the best word to describe how Mom looks at us when she comes out of her trance—amnesia. If you asked her what Maury Povich is talking about, she would have no idea, even though she is in the middle of watching his program. If I asked her where the Camaro keys are she borrowed, she would look at me dumbfounded, clueless as to who I am, or even what a Camaro is. It's almost like she has been hypnotized, and I know from what Dr. Wydell said it's because she was traumatized as a child.

I remember him saying that severe sexual or psychological trauma in childhood may cause a person to develop a Dissociative Identity Personality Disorder. He said that most abused children are abused by someone they trust, and that this causes them to split off the awareness, and memory of the abuse. Those memories and feelings go into the child's subconscious only to be experienced later in the form of a separate personality.

It must be a separate personality that causes Mom to race to answer the door or the telephone the moment someone calls or comes around. She has done this for years. When she does it, she always magically changes her voice, posture and demeanor so much that no one would believe just how comatose she was a second before. She still isn't completely normal in those moments, but she is the closest I have seen to the mother I knew years ago. It is like she has become a different person, and it is because of this ability to transform herself that I get an idea of how to nurse her back to life.

I know from talking to Nonna that in Italy it's common for adult sons to live at home with their mothers well into manhood. She has told me I have several male cousins in Calabria who do just that. They have great jobs, with good salaries, and lots of perks—but choose to stay with their *mamma*. I know that if we lived in Italy, I would be the same way. Tony and Michael would probably get married young, and move out to start their own families, but I would stay home with Mom.

I'm nineteen years old, and even though she has been falling apart since I was twelve, I have memories of her when she played with us in the snow and always had smiles. Yes, she may have slept on the couch and gambled a lot—but as a kid—all I knew was Mom was the nicest, prettiest and sweetest girl I had ever met. Sadly, Mom is now a living, breathing, disaster of a person with a resume of trauma and drama to back it up. Still, part of me figures that if she can 'turn it on' when someone calls or comes around, then maybe what she needs is someone to help her 'do it' more often. If Dr. Wydell is right, and Mom does have these separate personalities as a result of having been abused by men she trusted as a child, then maybe someone she trusts as an adult can help her find which personality answers the phone or comes to the door.

I have literally listened to Anthony Robbins' *Personal Power* so many times, that I have most of the twenty audio cassettes committed to memory. I feel if given the chance, I can do what all the doctors haven't been able to and save Mom. They may have lots of certificates hanging on their walls, and experience in dealing with human behavior, but what they don't have is an Italian son's devotion to his mother.

I started feeling older than Mom years ago, when my brothers and I came home from school to find her crying on the couch because of those pictures of Pop and Gail. Since then, I've become the adult in our relationship and she has become the child. I feel that way because I change when I talk to her; I slow down, and I listen to what she says. I think my patience, combined with listening to Anthony Robbins' tape program on a daily basis will be better than her seeing some no name once-a-week therapist until that pregnant specialist re-opens her practice.

Dr. Wydell said any further interruptions in Mom's care would be devastating, and since I plan on being her son all my life, I figure I can be her doctor, too. I won't leave her, or suspend my practice, and that's because I have something to gain if she gets better; I'll get my mother back. A doctor is only going to get paid. What do they care if she beats this Dissociative Identity Personality Disorder?

The thing is I don't want Mom torturing my brothers or chasing Pop into his office where he spends each day now that she is home. I want her free of distractions. That's why I walk into my father's office, and tell him I want to move out and live with Mom.

"*What?*"

"I wanna move out and live with Mom."

"I heard you the first time," he says. "Why would you wanna do that?"

"To get her away from you and the boys—to give her a chance to...."

"Get her away from me and the boys?"

"Not 'cause you do anything to her, but so you can go back to enjoying your days."

"And what about you?"

"I'll take care of Mom. I figured you could pay for the apartment, since we'll probably only need two bedrooms, and a small kitchen. It can be local. But not too close where she can just walk home—someplace where she and I can work on her problems."

"Chichi, what are you talking about? Some of the best doctors in the area haven't been able to reach your mother, let alone help her."

"I know, but that's 'cause they're just doctors. I'm her son. I'll try longer, and harder than they will."

"Chichi, you're a good son, but we need to worry about you. Cutting grass? Community college? This wasn't what you had in mind when you graduated high school."

"I know...."

"Then lissename," he says. "I know you wanna help your mother, but she needs prolonged, professional help."

"But hasn't she already gotten that? Haven't the last seven years been all about trying to find her prolonged, professional help?"

My father looks at me with confusion on his face. That's when I remind him of that big, tall, bearded marriage counselor who Aunt Bridgid and Uncle Bruno set-up years ago. I'll never forget how he came to the house for six months, concluded he couldn't help them, and emphasized that Mom may need to be medicated and hospitalized.

From there, I ask my father if he remembers the three days of analysis he took her for in New York City. Or what about all those trips to Methodist Hospital, Jefferson Hospital and the Princeton Biological Brain Center to see if her problems were of a neurological or chemical sort?

He tells me I don't have to remind him; he was there. But, still I say, "Finding Mom prolonged professional help has never worked. Even those times she went to the Children of Alcoholics meetings were a waste. The week in the Psych Unit after she tried to cut-off her cast and the seven weeks at the Institute of Mental Health at the University of Pennsylvania both added up to nothing. I can help Mom," I say. "I wanna move out, and give it a shot before she tries to kill herself again."

My father falls quiet after I say that only to ask whether I ran all this by my mother. He says that before I get all worked up about moving out, I should see what she has to say.

Pop can tell I'm serious about wanting to help, but says, "I'm tellin' ya Chichi, she'll **never** agree to it. She'll never agree to movin' out just you and her. Not in a million years."

When I talk to Mom about moving out together, she chuckles and thinks it's funny. She is lounging on the red leather loveseat in the den—smoking a cigarette—staring at the big screen TV.

"Move out? Frankie, are you kiddin' me? Why would I ever move out with you?"

"It might be easier for you to focus on getting better if the two of us lived together."

She chuckles some more.

"Mom, I'm serious. I think you and I could work on some things until that pregnant lady re-opens her practice."

"Frankie, I'm not goin' anywhere—and neither are you. So, just go back to cuttin' grass, or whatever you do, 'cause we're not movin' in together. Okay?"

"But Mom, I'm afraid if we don't do something, you're only gonna get worse. I don't want you to try and kill yourself again."

"Jesus, Frankie!"

Mentioning suicide sets her off. She is angry now—swinging her legs around—sitting straight up. "Who put you up to this?"

"No, Mom, I...."

"No! Who put you up to this—*your father?* Frankie, this is where I live. This is where I belong, with my family. You and I are *never* gonna live in some stupid apartment some place talking about God knows what. Now, I'm fine. I don't need your help. I don't want your help, and I don't wanna hear this again."

Ever since Mom's family dropped her off at our doorstep, she has reluctantly and sporadically been seeing a therapist. He's not a specialist in Dissociative Identity Personality Disorder, but someone my father found through a colleague of Dr. Wydell's.

Pop says, "Chichi, if you really wanna help, maybe you should be the one to take Mom to her Tuesday appointments. It's important that we get her there every week—going whenever she feels like it is not the idea. We gotta get her there on time, and we gotta get her there regularly."

My father explains that Aunt Ellen has been taking Mom to her therapy sessions recently. Pop is finally getting busy—bidding work on this big concrete job down in Wildwood.

"The thing is—Ellen is gettin' worn-out. You know how Mom is. She drags her feet, and Ellen has to fight with her about leavin' on time. Sometimes, Mom protests so much, El can't coax her into the car, and they end up missing that week's session. Since you don't cut grass on Tuesdays, why don't you think about takin' Mom to her ten o'clock appointment?"

I don't have to think about it. I want to help. I tell my father he can count on me. I don't care that Mom blew off my idea about moving out; I'm her son, and I'm going to make this work.

Pop says I'm a good kid. But he doesn't want me to get upset if Mom gives me the same hard time she has been giving Aunt Ellen. "She's the most stubborn person I've ever met, Chichi. You know that—a real *testa dura*."

"Oh, I know, Pop. I know."

The following Tuesday I wake up *determined* to take my mother to her ten a.m. therapist appointment on-time. Pop told me the session should last about fifty minutes, and for me to sit in the waiting room and read a magazine until Mom is done. He gave me a blank check to fill-in with the amount of the cost of the visit, and reminded me a second time, "You know your mother Chichi, so just be ready."

I know what Pop is talking about. I know how *testa dura* my mother can be when she is forced to do something against her will, even if that something is what's best for her. Still, I feel like I can handle it—like I'm the one who will save her.

When I get out of bed at nine o'clock Tuesday morning, Mom is still asleep. She has been rotating a few nights on the floor in the den, and a few nights with Pop in their room. I see her lying in bed when I walk past my parents' door, on my way downstairs for a glass of water. When I come back up five minutes later, I poke my head into her room and say, "Mom, c'mon, it's after nine. We gotta get up and dressed."

It's only a fifteen-minute car ride, but I'm not sure exactly where the office is, and I don't want to be late. When I call to her, Mom is awake, and lying on her back. Her eyes are open. She looks at me, and nods her head as if to say, *okay, I'll get up.*

I go down the hall to my bedroom and throw on a sweatshirt with a pair of jeans and sneakers. My father is away, looking at that big concrete job he mentioned while my brothers are in school. After I brush my teeth and walk back to my parents' bedroom, I find that my mother hasn't moved an inch.

"Mom," I say, "its quarter after nine. I thought you were gettin' up?"

She doesn't say a word. She only stays there lying in bed blinking her eyes. I walk into her bedroom and pull the curtains open. I turn from the window with the morning sunlight now filling her room.

"Mom, let's go."

She sighs, and rolls over away from me. With her back towards me, she says, "Ellen normally takes me."

"Well, I'm taking you now."

"Why?"

"Because Aunt Ellen is busy this morning."

"Busy doing what?"

"I don't know, but you gotta get up—it's almost nine twenty."

After a few more minutes of going back and forth, she finally sits up, and swings her legs out of bed. My mother sits on the edge of her side of the bed in a white dress-shirt. Her back is to me as she reaches to her right and picks up a pack of cigarettes lying on the nightstand. She lights a cigarette, and starts smoking. Mom is staring at the floor in silence, until I come around to stand before her with a pair of jeans, and a sweatshirt for her to wear.

"Mom," I say, offering her the clothes, "put these on and meet me downstairs in five minutes. We gotta go."

She never looks up at me, but nods her head *yes*, as she pensively runs her left index finger across her upper lip. Fifteen minutes *after* I tell her to meet me downstairs, we finally climb into the Cadillac where the green digital numbers of the clock radio read **9:47**.

I back out of the driveway, and speed down Shore Road towards the doctor's office. We still have a chance to arrive on-time. But when I ask Mom for help with exactly where the office is located, she just stares out the window, smoking and running her left index finger across her top lip.

With no help from Mom, I find the office complex. I locate the doctor's name on the big directory board out front, and park the Cadillac as quick as I can. I rush to get out of the car, but Mom is slow to do the same.

I'm standing on her side of the Cadillac, with the door open, looking down at my mother in the passenger seat. She insists she won't go anywhere until she finishes her cigarette. I check my watch and shake my head; it's a little after ten and we're late.

Only because I start badgering her, Mom gives up on her cigarette. She tosses the still burning butt into the parking lot and looks ready to go, until she reaches into her purse and starts poking around.

"Mom, what are you doing?" She pulls out her lipstick. "Mom," I say exasperated, "we don't have time for this. We gotta go."

She ignores me. My mother is focused on her reflection in the small flip mirror of the passenger side visor. She coats her lips—like she always does—until they are bright red, like a clown. I look at my watch again—10:06.

Mom flips the visor up, screws the lipstick closed, presses the cap back on, and sighs.

"Mom, c'mon…" I extend my right hand so as to help her out of the Cadillac, but she ignores it, and moves to place the lipstick back in her purse. When she starts poking around again, I grab her purse with my right hand. "Mom, you don't need to put on more makeup. You need to get out of the car."

She sighs again, and stays focused on her purse.

"Mom, we gotta get goin'."

She says nothing—but she does swing her legs out of the Cadillac without me forcing her. As soon as she stands up, I quickly close and lock the door behind her. Not a second after I close and lock the door—does Mom start pulling at the door handle, trying to get back inside.

"Mom, what are you doin?"

She doesn't respond, so I say, "Mom," as I gently, but firmly, pry her hands off the car door, "we gotta go."

"Gimme the keys, Frankie."

"Mom, I'm not giving you the keys."

"Please, Frankie, gimme the keys."

"Mom, we're gonna go inside, and you're gonna talk to the doctor, and *then* we'll go home."

"I don't wanna talk to anybody!"

"Mom, c'mon...."

"*I don't wanna go, Frankie!*"

"Mom, enough already, calm down."

Frustrated, she storms away from me and the Cadillac. She stops after a few paces, digs into her purse, pulls out her pack of cigarettes, and lights one up. Mom takes a long, deep puff of the fresh cigarette in her right hand, while shaking out the match in her left hand.

"Mom, c'mon, we're already ten minutes late."

She looks at me a moment—exhales after that long, deep puff—then very matter-of-factly states, "I don't wanna go in there, Frankie. I wanna go home."

"But Mom, we just got here."

"I don't care; I wanna go home."

"Mom, we're not going home."

"Frankie, I don't wanna be here."

I take a deep breath and realize that I'm not going to win this battle. I'm not going to be able to force her inside. I tell myself to be patient, and pick my spots. Maybe, *just maybe*, I'll be able to coerce her inside—but it's already ten after ten.

I think for a second and say, "Mom, I'm gonna go inside and tell the doctor we're here. I'll tell him you're finishin' your cigarette, and that it was my fault we're late. Maybe he can push your appointment back to ten thirty and you can get a full session in."

"Why would you do that?"

"Because he's expecting you."

"So?"

"So, I want him to know we're here and that you didn't skip out."

When I say that, Mom gives me a look of smirk and arrogance; *you're not the boss of me.* She squats and sits on the yellow concrete parking chock in the space next to the Cadillac. I look down at her and say, "So, I'll be back in a sec. Okay, Mom? Just let me tell him we're here."

"You go inside, and I won't be here when you come back."

"Mom, don't make a scene. Just let me go inside, or you can come with me, but Pop said it's only a fifty-minute session, so I want the doctor to know we're here."

"Pop!" she says sarcastically.

"What?"

She doesn't say anything.

"What?" I repeat.

"You wouldn't be doing this to him."

"Doing what?"

"This."

"What's *this?*"

"Torturing him."

"Mom, I'm not torturing you."

"Yes, you are."

"No, I'm only tryin' to bring you to your doctor's appointment."

"Well, you ever think I don't need a doctor's appointment? That I'm fine? That what I need is to go home?"

"Mom, Dr. Wydell said any further interruptions in your care would be devastating, so why don't we just go inside?"

"*My care?* That guy's an idiot, Frankie!"

"I think what he said at the big family meeting made sense."

"Oh, Frankie, you're supposed to be on my side. Why aren't you ever on my side?"

She looks up at me a moment, the two of us in silence, mother and son, the smoke from her cigarette slowly rising past me towards the sky. I soften my voice and say, "Mom, I'm on your side, that's why I'm here. Now, will you please get up?"

She acts like nothing was said—looking away indignantly—flicking away the ashes from her cigarette. "Mom," I try again, "it's already ten fifteen. You're only gonna have thirty-five minutes with the doctor. So, can we please go inside? I won't go in by myself. But, can we go in together? Can we go in as a family? Before you know it, we'll be on our way home."

Again, Mom says nothing. She just stays seated, looking away, rubbing her thumb across the butt of her cigarette. Still with softness in my voice, I go over to her on the concrete parking chock, and half try to pull her to her feet.

"Mom, c'mon," I say. But she yanks her arm away from me, and for the first time my patience starts to weaken. I think of Aunt Ellen and what this must have been like for her the last few times Mom had an appointment. I'm afraid to tug on Mom's arm again; I'm afraid she'll cause a scene. I know how she can be. I know Mom can turn everything around in a flash, and make it look like I'm trying to hurt her—like she did with Uncle Bobby that time in the Emergency Room. That was two and a half years ago, but I don't want someone in the parking lot to mistake me for a mugger, or think I'm trying to harass her. So, I repeat what I said about going inside, and letting the doctor know we're here. I say, "Mom, let me just run inside real quick, and tell the doctor we're here. If you wanna come with me that's great; if you wanna wait here that's fine, too."

After I say that, and turn towards the doctor's office, Mom jumps to her feet and rushes around to block my path. She scrunches her eyebrows together in disbelief, looks up into my face and angrily shouts, "*No, Frankie!*"

"Mom...."

"*No!* Can't you just stay outta this?"

"Stay outta what? I'm only tryin' to help."

"I don't need help! *Don't you understand that? I'm fine!*"

"Mom, can we just go inside?"

"No!"

"Mom...."

"*No! I'm fine!*" A second awkward silence falls between us as we stand face to face. I wish I could dive into her hard head—her *testa dura*—and steamroll it over with reason. Why can't she understand I'm only trying to help? Why does she have to fight me every step of the way? We stand there a moment, as I try to think of what to do next. If I take her home, without ever making it in to see the therapist, Mom will know she can do this every week. If I physically force her inside, she could turn things around to the doctor and make it look like I'm abusing her. He doesn't know her that well; he's only seen her a few times, and he doesn't know me at all. I get tired of not knowing what to do. I decide to stick with my original plan. I'll walk into the office, and tell the doctor we're here only to add that my mother is giving me a hard time about coming inside. As I continue towards the doctor's office, Mom stops bullying me and starts crying.

"Why are you doing this to me, Frankie? Why can't you just leave me alone?"

I keep walking towards the door—giving her my back and ignoring her pleas. Only, out of the corner of my eye, I catch sight of my mother and watch as she suddenly sprints past me towards the doctor's door and ducks inside.

By the time I walk in more than a half-hour late, I can only watch as Mom transforms herself into a complete mess. But not the sort of mess I'm used to. She just started crying out on the walkway, but now that we're inside, she takes it up a notch. It must be that separate personality she has, I tell myself, the one that causes her to race to answer the door, or the telephone, the moment someone calls or comes around.

The same personality that pathetically tries to change her voice, posture and demeanor for the 'better'—now changes everything about her for the 'worse.' Instead of Mom magically transforming into the shell of a healthy person, with the sound of a telephone ring, or doorbell chime—the moment we walk inside—she becomes a battered and abused mother.

Standing behind the counter, in the empty waiting room of the doctor's office, are two people. One is a man in his late fifties, with silver hair and matching goatee—the other, is a frumpy brunette woman, a decade his junior.

I imagine the woman is the receptionist, and from the way Mom whimpers out the word 'doctor,' the silver haired man standing there in a white shirt and crimson necktie must be her latest therapist. Even though this is where people come for counseling and therapy—the sight of my mother crying upon arrival, thrusts a look of concern and bewilderment upon the doctor's face.

"Ann," he says, with empathy in his voice. "Is everything all right?"

"No," she says, motioning towards me. "My son, Doctor, it's my son...."

I look at the doctor, and nod my head, as if to say, *she's talking about me*. The doctor offers a soft, "Good morning."

"My son, Doctor, he's so unfair. He's so unfair to me."

I hope the look of exasperation on my face tells the doctor not to believe everything Mom is saying. I can already tell her tears are for his benefit. Mom wasn't sad about anything out in the parking lot, she was just angry that I had brought her down here. Yet, now that we're face to face with her therapist, Mom is going to make sure nothing of any consequence gets accomplished today—save trying to turn the doctor against me.

Mom is sitting in the first chair by the door. She has her face covered with both hands. I am standing behind her in the doorway. The doctor comes out from behind the counter, "Ann," he says, "why don't we go back into my office? We can talk there."

She gives no reaction to his words, other than to remain seated with her hands to her face. From where I'm standing, I can see that her hands aren't *touching* her face at all. They are about a half-inch in front of her cheeks and nose—acting more like a curtain—than a sincere reaction brought on by grief. Her hands are together, as if she were holding an imaginary book up to her eyes.

"Mom," I say, looking down at her. "Let's go back into the doctor's office."

When I say that, the doctor approaches me, extends his right hand and politely asks my name. I reach out to shake his hand and say, "I'm Frank." He nods at me reassuringly, before looking down at Mom.

"Ann, why don't you and Frank come back into my office so we can discuss what's troubling you this morning?"

Mom still has her hands in front of her face, but it's easy for the both of us to watch her shake her head *no*—she doesn't want to go back into his office. Maybe because he wants to put her at ease, or maybe because he's not sure what else to do, the doctor sits down across from Mom.

"Ann, if you don't wanna go back, we'll just sit here till you're ready then. Okay? We'll just sit here, the three of us and wait."

The doctor motions for me to sit down. I take his cue. We sit in silence for several moments. Mom with her hands in front of her face, the doctor, with his legs crossed—studying her from the edge of his chair. While I shuffle my feet, seated two chairs to Mom's left feeling guilty and confused over how this morning has gone so far.

My plan—my hope—was to get Mom to her appointment promptly at ten a.m. I wanted her to want the same thing. I even envisioned us having a pre-session discussion during the fifteen-minute ride to the doctor's office. Maybe we could have discussed The Routine, breaking it down into categories: poor personal hygiene, lack of engagement in everyday life, and low self-esteem.

In other words—as her oldest son—armed with Anthony Robbins' *Personal Power* program, I would coach her on what to bring up during her fifty-minute session with this latest therapist. I would arm her with an agenda and the inspiration to change. I even saw us going for an early lunch or cup of coffee after her session. We could discuss the points her doctor made. The answers behind her addiction to The Routine, or that amnesia she has displayed for years. I hoped we could talk as two adults. This was my hope; this is what I thought my role would be. I would give up eighteen to thirty-six months in exchange for total immersion into Mom's past, present and future.

I feel like if the roles were reversed, she would do the same for me. That notion makes me feel a little bit like Pop, and his reason for not getting divorced. My father always says he can see his eight year old wife alone in that greenhouse, and it breaks his heart. It breaks his heart so much he stays married to her, when most other men would have skipped town years ago. It is that same image of my eight year old mother alone in that greenhouse that makes me want to help. It breaks my heart even more to know that greenhouse wasn't all the torture she had to endure. There was also Uncle Larry crawling out of her closet to feel her up under the covers, and Nonna's friend's husband waiting in the basement to put himself in her mouth. That innocent image of my eight year old mother makes me want to try, but it makes Mom unable to.

My mother sits next to me, a lost and broken person. With her hands in front of her face, hiding behind that curtain, she is a prisoner to her past. Sitting here in silence, across from this latest doctor, I can already tell Dr. Wydell was right. He told us at that big meeting at the Institute of Mental Health at the University of Pennsylvania that Mom was beyond casual, once a week therapy. He told us that because she has something so complex going on, that one doctor specializing in her Dissociative Identity Personality Disorder working with her three times a week for several years, was the only option. Otherwise, he said, Mom would just lead the 'doctor of the moment' down a different path each time, knowing where and when to take turns that would throw them off her scent—thus sabotaging any attempt at a true recovery.

This latest 'doctor of the moment' quickly glances at his wrist watch, and I think I know why. He must have an eleven o'clock appointment with another patient, yet Mom sits there before him, hiding behind her hands, showing no sign of going anywhere soon.

He tries again to coax her into going back into his office, but she does nothing but ignore him. I feel so frustrated and guilty over us having arrived late. I wish Mom would just put her hands down, and walk with us back into the office, but I know she never will. She just keeps sitting there, hiding behind her hands.

Anticipating the arrival of his eleven o'clock appointment, I clear my throat and start talking to the doctor. I tell him that we're here because my mother suffers from a Dissociative Identity Personality Disorder. I tell him she lies on the couch day after day smoking, drinking coffee, staring at the TV, picking her nose, farting and vanishing into a trance so deep she doesn't answer us until we shout, *Mom* four or five times. I begin telling him about her suicide attempt with the aspirin, the butcher knife and the carpet cleaner. Then, I enlighten him about her seven week stay at the Institute of Mental Health at the University of Pennsylvania—but right in the middle of my explanation—Mom starts to moan.

Her moan is a steady monotone. It gets louder as I continue talking to the doctor. It's like she's trying to drown me out, so he won't hear what I'm saying. Confused, I look over at her and notice Mom peering at me ever so slightly from behind her hands—almost as if she wants to know what I'm going to do. Her peer is to determine whether I'm buying her charade. She stops moaning only to break into a completely normal speaking voice like a bad actress failing a screen test.

"Doctor, my son is not being honest."

I shake my head, and calmly say, "*She's* not being honest."

Only, Mom starts moaning again and cuts me off. I try to speak over her, but she matches my volume, and I don't know if the doctor can make out my words when I say, "She had been stalling and smoking out in the parking lot for the last half-hour—wanting nothing to do with coming in here."

Mom breaks back into her normal speaking voice after that, saying, "Doctor, that is false. I wanted nothing more than to arrive on time, but...."

"But *what* Mom?"

I look directly at the doctor. "She's just trying to confuse you, or waste your time, because nothing she's sayin' is honest." That brings on more moaning, though now Mom adds a long, drawn out, "Oohhh, Frankie! Oohhh, Frankie!"

Mom does all this from behind her hands—every few seconds glancing to her left—to catch a glimpse of my expression.

When the eleven o'clock appointment finally arrives, Mom instantly drops her hands into her lap and kindly smiles at the lady who seems surprised to find the doctor sitting in the waiting room. Watching her transform like that makes me feel foolish for ever thinking she and I could have moved-in together, and nursed her back to health. My mother is so far removed from being healthy that it's like what she told Pop over the summer that day she tried to jump out of his truck, "The Ann you used to know isn't here anymore."

We make another appointment to see the doctor, but I can't imagine she'll ever agree to come down here again. As we drive home, we pass my old high school. We pass the football field where I was supposed to star, the same football field I visited the night before I left for Towson some fifteen months ago. Mom was in the hospital then, recovering from her aneurysm surgery, and I was on the verge of going off to college. But sitting beside me in the Cadillac, all Mom does is smoke and stare out the window as we approach the football field on our left.

The empty bleachers and lonesome goalposts make me think back on that August night in 1995. I walked the field as midnight became one a.m. and told myself that I wanted to be confident and powerful during my move to Towson, and that I wanted to be sure of myself and real. I wanted to be the best I could be, and that I wanted to do it all for Mom. None of that came true, of course. My Towson experience amounted to just four days, one very sore elbow, and an offer to cut grass. Yet, as we continue home in silence, the turbulence of the last fifteen months comes back to me in snippets of sound and color like a montage of movie clips I can't forget: First, I see my father and me at the Point Diner, giving each other the Hero School look at breakfast. Then, I see him crying, as I back out of the driveway. I see the other incoming freshmen and their entourages. I see the way Coach Combs treated me when I asked for a few days off. I see myself walking home from that jobsite on the bay, my sneakers digging into my heels. I see Edith, Nonna and Colomba dropping Mom off unannounced. I see Pope John Paul II in his Pope Mobile waving to me at the Meadowlands, while Mom and O.J. Simpson sit on the couch eating lipstick for lunch.

I see myself crawling around in crawl spaces, the knees of my jeans wet and soggy. I see golf balls, boobies, Spice Channel bills, G-strings, bulls and bordellos. Then, I see Mom sitting courtside, isolated for the way she smells, reading the letter from the pharmacist, and the way she signs her name. I see Dr. Wydell and medical bills, Nonna shouting, "He was'a my pride!" I see Tony in the hospital, his face and head a mess. I see my father crushing the doctor's hand. I can hear Brian and his mother moaning. I see Nonna pointing her finger at my father, while he calmly rubs his mustache. I see Michael burying his face in Aunt Teresa's chest. I see the words **Dissociative Identity Personality Disorder** in big, bold, black print. I see Zia Concetta at the picnic table gesturing with her hand. I picture my parents wrestling across the Ben Franklin Bridge. I see Oreo and Midnight emaciated and sick. I see Uncle

Charlie with the dishtowel and that cigarette dancing on his lip. I see my mother chasing Pop down the sidewalk, half naked, angry and screaming. I see Romeo and his long, slick, brown hair listening to Carmine talk about them wiseguys, as my father takes seventy punches in the back. I see the Virgin Mary riding shotgun in my Camaro as Margaret the Visionary says a prayer. I see Tony crying on his bike running from The Routine. I see Maury Povich and Anthony Robbins arguing with my mother as she stares off into space with one half a head of wavy salt and pepper hair, and another half of stubbly salt and pepper growth.

53

My mother refuses to go back to see that doctor again. Mom says she's going to prove to everyone that she's fine. My father's wife of twenty-one years insists that she's going to get an entry-level job and begins applying for work at several local businesses. Mom tells us, "You'll see I don't need help."

But without a college degree, or recent work experience, she gets widely rejected. My mother knows enough not to mention how she worked at that nursing home years ago. For if one of those businesses calls for a reference, they would surely find out she was fired for talking suicide in the bathroom.

So, Mom tells them she's a long-time housewife looking for work for the first time in two decades. To qualify for some of these jobs though, Mom has to take a written exam. Inevitably, the prospective employer comes back to her with the news that she *almost* made the minimum score required to begin the hiring process. They have to apologize though, and say they can't bring her aboard. They wish her luck, and never follow-up beyond that.

Pop tells Aunt Ellen he thinks these written exams are just a ploy. He says, "These people take one look at Ann and think, *something's wrong with this lady. We can't hire her.*"

My father says they let her down easy, by making her take some "made up exam," because Mom can't hide it anymore; everything about her says *I'm a desperate catatonic mess.*

Pop likes to say, "Our family is special, Cheech. We're full of talent." When he says that, I know he means his mother's side of the family—the talented Neapolitans—who write and compose, paint and invent. It's also her side of the family that fails to live up to its' potential.

The rest of my "make up" is Calabrese—Nonna, Babbo and Dad's father all come from humble, Calabrian backgrounds. They would never label themselves 'special.' They simply focus on making a living, and trying to get ahead. They are not actors, or writers, or "thinkers." No one can sing or play an instrument. No one would dare write a musical like they do in Grandmom's family.

My Calabrese cousins seem content to work, spend time with one another, and come down the shore for two weeks in August. But my grandmother's family has always thought 'highly' of itself—always had *Big Ideas*. This explains why my father financially backed his brother for a year so he could try his hand at writing an album. It also explains our foray into acting, and Pop's half-finished manuscript—*Thoughts of a Common Man*.

How many other concrete contractors in the world would attempt to write a book about their thoughts on life? It's only because he comes from a family that believes it's different, and that it's special.

Within Grandmom's family, there exists a sense that we're all destined to be great one day, and that we're *un*common. The family-wide belief is that one of these days something somebody writes, or paints, or sings is going to fetch us all millions—but that someday never seems to happen.

Everywhere you turn on Grandmom's side of the family, there's another relative loaded with talent and large ideas who can barely pay his bills. Now that I'm a teenager, I take issue when older, cynical cousins say our family motto should be, "Buy high, and sell low."

These same cousins say our family crest should be the silhouette of a man floating through the air, reaching for a dollar bill that lies perpetually just beyond his reach. Pop laughs and says, "They're only kiddin', Cheech."

But I know what they are saying is true. We *are* full of talent, but have yet to realize any of it. I guess that's why I sit in my room and listen to Anthony Robbins so much. Ever since I stumbled upon *Personal Power*, I have been listening to Anthony Robbins say: *you need to know your outcome because without knowing your outcome, how will you know if you have hit your target?* My outcome is simple—I want to take the Calabrese work ethic of the other three sides of my family, and combine it with the Neapolitan potential of Grandmom's people. If I ever sit down to write a book, I don't want it to end up like my father's *Thoughts of a Common Man*—stuffed behind some bills in the bottom drawer of a filing cabinet. I want it to be read; I want it to be real.

It's because I want to "do" something with my life that I decide to take Pop's advice, and break off my friendship with Carmine from South Philly. One of Carmine's black girlfriends is pregnant. He told me he tried to talk the girl into having an abortion, but that she wanted to keep the baby. Carmine said, "Frankie, then I tried bribin' her. I told her I would give her a couple grand, *and* pay for the abortion, if she would just go along with it and get rid of the baby." Carmine starts getting louder. "Except that cunt *kept* the money I gave her, and still wants to have the baby! When she told me that, I just about lost my mind. I reached across that table, and grabbed that girl. I shook her and said, *'You don't know who you're messin' with, you dumb bitch!'*"

Carmine's scare tactic worked; she agreed to have the abortion. But shortly thereafter, he came down the shore and picked me up. Though neither of us is twenty-one, he decides he wants to go to the Sands Casino and gamble. Even though I could easily pass for thirty years old, with my new mustache and receding hairline, I feel funny when we walk past security out onto the casino floor.

I feel funny because we're breaking the law. But I couldn't turn to Carmine and say, *dude, let's go bowling or something*. He would only look at me and laugh and probably say I was some sort of chicken shit, and that I had to grow a set of balls.

It isn't until I finish watching him play blackjack that he walks me out onto the Boardwalk, and says, "Frankie, I've been thinkin'—I wanna get a gun."

When Carmine tells me he wants to get a gun, I know what Pop told me months ago is right; I'm too soft. Here I am walking into a situation I should not be anywhere near. Carmine doesn't want a gun so he can go hunting. He doesn't want a gun because that right is guaranteed to him by the Second Amendment. He wants a gun because he wants to be a gangster—like the other *malandrini* from South Philly.

I want to be different. I want to do something special with my life. Yet, here I am with Carmine—a *gavone* to the bone. A little voice in my head says, *Frankie, don't miss the obvious.* The obvious is that my friendship with Carmine has to end, and it has to end now. I give no reaction when he tells me about the gun, which he takes to mean I'm on his side, and that I not only support him, but I might want one myself.

When I get home and tell Pop about Carmine wanting to get a gun, he explodes. "That's it! What did I tell you? I knew this kid was not for you!"

Pop makes me promise I will stop being his friend. Over the course of the next few weeks, I begin ignoring his phone calls, and eventually sever ties with him after an uncomfortable discussion over the phone. Carmine is hurt, and accuses me of being a pussy. But Pop says, "Yeah, yeah, yeah, whatever, that kid's a wannabe. Just be glad he's outta your life. Trust me, Chichi."

Even though he could grow it long, Tony keeps the hair on his head "army short," so everyone can see the huge scar from his operation. It's in the shape of a zigzag, and it runs from ear to ear at the top of his scalp. To me, he wears the scar like a badge of honor; the physical embodiment of his *say I won't* mentality.

In our hometown and the neighboring towns, Tony is the best known of us brothers. He has a network of buddies who worship him. To be Tony's friend, is akin to rolling with a celebrity because he has what Pop calls '*it.*'

Tony isn't afraid of anyone or anything; he is cocky. He does what he wants, dresses how he wants, talks how he wants, and fearlessly flirts with older girls.

In plain English—Tony is the Confident Bull.

54

I am on a date with a girl named Sara. She has blonde hair and blue eyes, and was first runner-up for Miss Atlantic City last summer. I met her a week ago when I went to dinner with a bunch of cousins from Pop's side of the family; Sara was our waitress.

For our first date, we go bowling, and for whatever reason—throughout the entire evening—I keep telling her she has a pretty smile. I pick her up at her house in my Camaro, she smiles when she answers the door and I say, "Geez, you have a pretty smile." We get to the bowling alley, I rent the shoes, carry two balls over to our lane—she smiles—and I say, "Geez, you have a pretty smile."

After each time she bowls and walks back to her seat, I say, "Geez, you have a pretty smile," even if she's only slightly grinning. I know I should stop, but I can't since I'm so nervous. I haven't been on a date in five years. I literally tell her she has a pretty smile *two dozen times* during the course of our night together. After the first few times, Sara politely responds with a *thank you*, but as I continue, she just starts looking at me blankly.

I wish I was the Confident Bull, but I'm not.

To my astonishment, she accepts an invitation to go on a second date, and even suggests we go for a walk on the Boardwalk. This time I know I have to redeem myself, so I stop and buy a rose at the Acme Supermarket and hide it in the backseat of Pop's truck. When I pick her up, she notices I have a different car, so I play it off as if I own two vehicles and she is impressed.

When I open the passenger's side door, and hold it for her to get in, I reach into the backseat, pull out the rose, give it to her and say, "Pretty girl, pretty rose."

She says *thank you*, but her expression is that of concern—like—*here we go again.*

It's a nice night, so we drive into Atlantic City, but as we make our way down the promenade, I start to ask myself, *how do guys get girls to kiss them? What do they do?*

The answer I come up with is brilliant—*take her out on the beach!* When I suggest a stroll along the waterline, Sara enthusiastically agrees. Soon, we are walking side-by-side along the water's edge when I begin to struggle with the next dilemma—*how do I make the first move?*

The thought that comes to me is—*A Bronx Tale.* After a summer of listening to Carmine talk about his life with them wiseguys in South Philly and all his black girlfriends, I have *A Bronx Tale* on my mind. I decide to use a scene from that movie to woo Sara. We are sitting in a lifeguard stand when I turn to her—and as suave as I can—I say, "Have you ever seen *A Bronx Tale*?"

"What?"

"You know the movie, *A Bronx Tale*?"

"No."

"Well, you know the part where Calogero asks the black girl if she can make sauce?"

"No, I just said I never saw it."

"Oh, right, well, there's this part in the film where the main character falls for this beautiful black girl, and right after their first kiss, he asks her if she can make spaghetti sauce."

"Okay...." Sara is confused.

"Well, it goes like this...."

I look deep into her eyes and ask, "Can you make sauce?"

She looks at me like, *what are you talking about?*

But I am already in the moment. I lean into kiss her, but when I do, I stick my tongue out as our lips meet, which makes for an awkward first peck, that only gets worse. As soon as our mouths separate, when they aren't even a *millimeter* apart, *out loud* I say three words that I wish I could take back immediately.

I say, "That was gay."

When Sara hears that, she asks, "What?"

"Huh?"

"What didja say, Frank?"

"Nothin."

"Yes, you did."

"No, I didn't."

"You said that was gay."

"No, I didn't."

"Yes, you did!"

"No, I didn't."

"Yes, you did!"

Oh my God, she heard me. Here I am with the runner up to Miss Atlantic City, on a quiet, romantic beach with no one around, and all I can say is, *can you make sauce*, poke her with my tongue and close with *that was gay*.

The ride back to her house is filled with an awkward silence. I try to explain my gaffe when we pull into her parents' driveway, but Sara quickly gets out of Pop's truck, slams the door, and never returns any of my calls.

I drive home thinking, *there is no hope for me when it comes to girls, no hope at all.*

55

Nonna is going back to Italy. She is going to stay with Zia Concetta in Calabria for the next several months. Mom wants to go to the *bon voyage* party her family has planned. But my father is uncomfortable with her driving herself to Philadelphia. We know he can't take her because he isn't welcome in Philly anymore. Ever since that argument with Nonna and Zia when he defended himself with his broken-Italian, Pop has become *persona non grata*. Mom's family is disgusted by him—especially after my mother was locked up that night she chased him down the street, screaming about wanting to have sex.

Mom *begs* my father to see Nonna off at the party, so I volunteer to take her up to Philadelphia.

The night of the party, I can tell Mom is up to something. Although she is quiet on the ride to Philly, smoking and staring out the window, the moment we pull into Nonna's neighborhood, she becomes anxious. Mom is not thrilled that I have to circle the block several times looking for a parking spot. When we finally find one several doors down from Nonna's house, Mom scrambles out of the passenger seat, just as I put The Ghetto Bomber in park.

She rushes up the sidewalk, practically speed-walking away from me. I call to her, "Mom, wait up!" But she is a blur hustling up the driveway. I sprint to catch up and when I step into the skinny hallway off the backdoor, Mom is several steps in front of me. The hallway leads into the kitchen where I can hear everyone inside. I'm close enough to Mom now that I can see her squat down like a linebacker in the entranceway to the kitchen and holler, *"I'm here! I'm here!"*

Even though she looks goofy, and is obviously not the same *Aunt Ann* from years past—the room erupts with a collective, "Annie! You made it! I told you she was coming." When I appear in the doorway behind her a moment later, the kitchen falls quiet. My relatives are surprised to see me, especially my cousin Luke, who is Aunt Renata's youngest son.

Luke is a former soldier, with a bad attitude, especially when he's drinking and tonight he points his beer bottle at me, "What are you doin' here?" My pulse quickens. I don't know what to say. I wasn't expecting a fight; Luke is slouched in his chair like a renegade. He stares right through me. "I said, what are you doin' here? You know you're not welcome. You and your fuckin' father make me sick...."

Luke adjusts himself in the chair, "Maybe we oughtta go outside...."

As he continues to stare me down—I know Pop was right; I'm too soft, too nice. I don't know how to handle confrontation. I keep staring at Luke, but I can hear my father's voice in my head, *Cheech, Luke has nothing to lose. He lives to fight. Don't back down, but be smart, or he'll hurt you.* I tell myself that I have enough adrenaline running though my veins that I could rush him, but after that, Luke would tear me up. Either way, I summon all my courage and mumble out, "I'm ready whenever you are."

Luke gladly accepts my challenge, and moves to his feet, but that's when Nonna steps in. She knows Luke; she has seen this happen before. "*No,*" she snaps, "he's 'a my grandson. He's 'a my grandson."

Our grandmother literally comes between us, and takes me into her arms. Luke's eyes are still locked on mine as Nonna gives me a kiss on the cheek; her way of signaling—*enough!* Nonna stepping between us doesn't stop Aunt Renata from expressing her disgust at my presence. She hurriedly gathers Luke's cigarettes and car keys from the kitchen table as he continues to glare at me. "C'mon Luke," she shouts. "Let's go! I don't wanna be here with *him!*"

My aunt and my cousin storm out of the kitchen with a vow and a point in my direction. If I'm still here tomorrow, they say they won't see Nonna off at the airport. "Do you hear me?" Aunt Renata shouts to all of us in the packed kitchen. "If *he* is here tomorrow, I will *not go!*"

The next day Nonna's flight isn't until eight in the evening, out of Newark International Airport. That means everybody comes over again in the afternoon for one last goodbye—everyone but Luke and Aunt Renata. She called ahead, and when Aunt Colomba told her I was still here, she hung up—but not before saying, "Colomba, tell Frankie he can go to hell!"

56

In December of 1996, I begin working for my father full-time throughout the winter. We get up at a quarter to six each morning, so we can have a quick breakfast, before making the forty-five-minute drive down the Garden State Parkway to Wildwood. We ride in Pop's GMC Jimmy, with his long-time employees, Lester and Darryl.

Tony and Michael leave after we do. They catch rides to school with upperclassmen friends; which means Mom is home alone and left to wallow in The Routine all day.

Wildwood is a touristy beach town, further south along the Jersey coast. It's where we've started doing all the stucco and concrete work on this huge, three story condominium complex.

In the summer, Wildwood is crawling with Shoobies. They come down the shore to enjoy the beach, Boardwalk, amusement parks, and cheap 1950's themed motels. In the off-season, Wildwood sits by the sea like a deserted ghost town. The dozens of ice cream parlors and miniature golf courses that dot the strip, sit boarded up in anticipation of Memorial Day Weekend.

The condominium complex where we're working is right on the beach, which means there is nothing to block the wind from whipping off the ocean and pelting us with misery. "The work itself is hard enough," Pop says. "But between the wind and the cold, we're lucky to still be in one piece."

We wear big, rubber, yellow concrete boots, light brown, full-body Carhart overalls, black cotton hats, and dark brown gloves—but still the wind cuts right through us—and we freeze.

It's during the forty-five-minute ride down to Wildwood that Pop softly tells me, what I already know; he loves concrete. He speaks softly because Lester and Darryl tend to fall asleep in the backseat. But it's during those morning rides that Pop tells me how he thinks concrete is romantic, that it reminds him of the Old Country, of our ancestors and of how life should be.

It's on this job that I can finally use the term—'concrete finisher'—in reference to myself. There is something different about the way Pop treats me, and I think it's because he has realized I dropped out of college. He is so distracted with Mom coming home, and this job getting started, that he wasn't able to force me to sign-up for classes for the spring semester. Pop doesn't seem angry about me dropping out; he just seems worried.

In addition to working for my father, I've started delivering pizzas on the weekends—but this does nothing to quiet Pop's concerns. He says being a landscaper and a part-time pizza delivery boy are not career paths where I belong. If I don't go back to college, he feels like he needs to do right by me—and teach me how to properly finish concrete—once and for all.

"At the very least," he says, "it'll give you something to fall back on, Chichi."

I have worked for my father ever since I was a kid. I'm already a bit of a natural with the trowel in my hand. But this job is the *first* job where I am expected to not just apprentice, but to produce and perform like someone who has years of experience.

Now, when the concrete trucks arrive, Pop ushers me in, and expects me to know what to do, as I take my float, my edger and my trowel—and get to work. The more concrete we pour, the more I begin to feel like Pop; concrete is in our blood. I love everything about it, from the moment we first hear that big concrete truck approaching to the singing lessons my father has started giving me in *bel canto*.

We will be finishing concrete together, or putting stucco on the wall, when Pop will start with these singing exercises. We will be on the side of the building where the wind isn't blowing that hard—with our finishing trowels in hand—when Pop starts teaching me how to breathe from my diaphragm—so the notes can 'sit on top of the air.'

We practice vocal scales for several weeks. As my breathing begins to improve, my father says we're ready to start working on my first song. He selects an Italian piece, written in 1935, called, *Non ti Scordar di Me.*

Since we have no sheet music, Pop sings a line and tells me to sing it after him. I don't understand the words, so Pop translates. He says

385

the title means—*don't forget me*—and that despite the warm melody, the song is about two lovers whose romance has ended. Pop says the narrator of the piece is particularly sad—since his lover left without saying goodbye.

We spend days working on the opening verse, and the repetitive, enchanting chorus. I like when Pop and I finish concrete together, as the sun sets, and we sing—*Non ti Scordar di Me*. The winter sky turns the color of wine as our voices echo through the corridors of the empty Wildwood streets, and I finally understand what my father means when he says concrete is romantic.

57

Nonna is on the phone calling from Italy. It's Saturday morning—January 11, 1997 and today is my mother's fiftieth birthday. Tony is watching ESPN in the den, with both Oreo and Midnight lying at his feet. Michael would be in there too, but he spent the night over at Aunt Teresa's house. I'm sitting at the kitchen table watching my father at the stove. He is making Italian bread French toast. Mom is asleep on the couch in the living room, or she would have raced into the kitchen to answer the phone, before I had the chance.

Nonna has been in Italy for nearly four months; her English is rusty. She struggles with certain words, and ends up saying a few words in Italian that I don't understand. The one thing that's clear is Nonna has called to wish my mother a happy birthday. But first, she wants to know how my brothers are doing. I know to keep my answers short and sweet. I tell Nonna that my brothers are both doing well in school, and are crazy as ever over sports and girls. She likes hearing that, and asks what I'm doing—since it's too cold to cut grass. I tell her that I'm working for Pop down in Wildwood on that big concrete job.

I ask if she ever heard of *Non ti Scordar di Me*—but when I mention working for my father, she clears her throat, and changes the subject. She wants to talk to Mom. I was going to sing her a few bars over the phone, but I can tell Nonna isn't interested.

Just as I'm about to put the receiver down, to go and wake my mother in the living room—Mom walks into the kitchen. She sits in the chair opposite mine, with her hair matted a bit from the couch. She motions to me—wanting to know who is on the phone. But before I can answer, Pop turns from the stove. "Cheech," he says, "ask your grandmother what she thinks about you comin' over for a visit. She has always wanted to take you to Italy. See what she says."

I look up, and nod to him. The thought of going to Italy excites me. I have long fantasized what life would be like for me "over there." Now seems like the perfect time for me to go. It's getting so cold we may have to pull off the job down in Wildwood. We can't pour concrete only to have it freeze overnight. Since I'm not in college anymore, going to Calabria for a few weeks really is possible.

Only when I mention it to her, Nonna says it doesn't sound like a good idea. She says Zia Concetta's house in Calabria doesn't have any heat, and that neither she, nor Zia know how to drive. I tell her the lack of heat doesn't bother me. And, if she and Zia can't drive, I can. But Nonna insists now isn't a good time for her, and I know to drop it.

As I'm about to say goodbye, and hand the phone over to my mother, Nonna says she has one more thing she would like to ask me. She wants to know what my brothers and I did for Mom's birthday. "What we did?" I ask. "Whaddaya mean?"

"What'a you get'a you mother?"

What did we get our mother? Is she serious?

The thought of doing anything for Mom's birthday, never even crossed our minds.

Who wants to celebrate another year of disappearances, suicide attempts, and lipstick lunches? I say, "Nonna, we didn't do anything for Mom's birthday."

"*Niente?*"

"No. We didn't get her anything."

"How you no get'a nothing? No even'a card? It's her'a fiftieth birthday! *Disgraziato!*"

Nonna starts to mumble to herself in Italian. She can't believe her grandsons could be so inconsiderate.

She breaks back into English only long enough to tell me, "Put'a you mother, on'a da' phone."

I hand the phone to Mom, knowing I'll never get to Italy now. But I am half-tempted to say, *Mom, make sure Nonna puts Zia Concetta on the phone, so we can thank her for berating us at Samantha's graduation party. Or better yet, make sure to thank Nonna for the tirade she went into at that big family meeting at the University of Pennsylvania last spring. That was very helpful; it really resolved a lot.*

Sitting here helpless in the kitchen, I feel like diving into the phone only to come out in Reggio di Calabria and say, *Nonna, I know you're my grandmother, but you have a lot of nerve getting upset over what we did or didn't get for my mother's fiftieth birthday when you cursed Mom years ago as a child. If I had a daughter who came to me and told me that old men were doing dirty things to her in a greenhouse, I never would have abandoned her. I would have defended her, protected her, not kept things a secret. So really, it's your fault we didn't do anything for my mother's fiftieth birthday. Va fan culo!*

A week after Mom turns fifty years old, Pop goes to Costa Rica. Thanks to the big concrete job we have down in Wildwood, my father has been able to catch up on some bills. Because of the extra money in the bank, and the weather being too cold to work, he decides to go away.

He and Uncle Charlie are going to meet up with a few other guys who are already in Costa Rica for a fifteen-day fishing trip. The thing is—Pop doesn't tell anyone he is going on vacation until Mom finds him packing his suitcase. I'm in my bedroom when I hear Mom say, "Frank, where do you think you're going?" She says it with such an indignant tone that I wait for his response—but he says nothing.

"Frank," she says again. "I mean it. Where do you think you're going?"

I wander down the hallway to see what's going on. When I reach the doorway to their bedroom, I see Pop folding clothes, and placing them in a black suitcase lying open on the bed. Mom senses me behind her and half turns around. Our eyes meet only briefly—she quickly turns back to Pop.

"Frank, answer me goddammit!"

He looks up only long enough from his folding to say, "Ann, leave me alone. Alright? Charlie will be here soon to pick me up."

"Leave you alone? What are you talking about? I'm your wife, and I have a right to know where you're going."

"Ann, I'm going to Costa Rica with a few of the guys. We'll be back in two weeks."

"Two weeks?"

She glares at him as Pop continues to calmly place clothes in the suitcase. I stand in the doorway shaking my head. *Is he really going to leave us alone with Mom for two weeks?*

There is tension in the air.

While Pop moves to the bureau, Mom approaches the black suitcase lying open on the bed. She reaches in and starts yanking clothes out. Mom is shouting, "You're not going anywhere!"

"Ann!" Pop says, turning from the bureau. "Will you knock it off, fChrissake?"

He rushes to the bed—ignoring the clothes Mom just threw on the floor. He butts in front of her, and quickly zips the suitcase closed. Mom is still hovering behind him. My father uses his left hand to take the suitcase by the handle; he picks it up off the bed. Pop moves towards me in the doorway. He throws a satchel over his right shoulder. Mom moves in front of him to block the way.

"You're not leaving!"

Pop stops only briefly, and lowers his eyes. "Ann, get out of the way."

"No, this isn't fair! I'm not moving!"

"Ann, get the fuck out of the way!"

"No, you're not going to Costa Rica!"

"I am too! Now, move!"

Mom tries to pin him against the doorjamb. I back out of their way, onto the landing. I am more confused than ever. *What do I do? Should I help Mom make him stay? Or help Pop get out of here?* I don't know. I don't like this. I don't like him leaving like this. It's too bizarre. He had to have known this was going to set her off. *What was he thinking?*

As I struggle to find an answer, Pop starts slowly edging his way past her. When they reach the staircase, Mom wraps her hand around the handle of his suitcase; she won't let go. She is trying to yank it from his hand—or at the very least—stop my father from descending the stairs. But she's no match for him. Pop is determined, and methodical, in the way he starts dragging the suitcase and my mother down the steps with him. They move slowly. Mom is grunting, and pulling—while Pop is stone-faced, and silent. I feel stupid just watching them. I'm still not sure what to do until I blurt out the words in my head. "Hey Pop," I say. "Maybe you don't go this time? I mean, it's not the end of the world, right? There'll be other trips."

When I say that, Pop looks up at me. I'm his oldest son, but standing there atop the landing, looking down on my parents, fighting on the stairs, I'm a delay he won't have. He speaks nothing—but his eyes say, *Cheech, stay out of this.* Despite his glare, I can't help but feel like he is doing the wrong thing. He's leaving without any notice—without even telling me and my brothers ahead of time. *What does he expect us to do with Mom for two weeks?*

Outside I can see the headlights of Uncle Charlie's car in the driveway, as Pop lowers his gaze and says, "Ann, Charlie is waiting. Now, let me go before we miss our flight. This is ridiculous!" Mom acts like he didn't say a thing. She still has her hand wrapped around the handle of Pop's suitcase—trying to yank it from him. But step-by-step, Pop drags her all the way down the stairs. When they reach the foyer, he pulls her over to the front door and with his satchel hand, he is able to get it open. He starts backing out the storm door, with Mom screaming, "*You're not going! You're not going!*"

Pop is hunched over, and stone-faced. Using his rear-end to prop the door open—he continues to struggle with my mother for control of the suitcase. Then Mom wraps *both* her hands around the handle and tries to pull Pop, and his suitcase, back inside one last time.

When she realizes she can't, Mom lets go of the handle and starts kicking Pop in the shins. She screams and kicks, "*You bastard! You bastard!*" Pop doesn't try to stop her. He doesn't even cover up. He has control of the suitcase, and that's all he cares about now. Just as he's about to straighten up and back out the door once and for all Mom reaches up and slaps him across his left cheek.

She screams, "*I hate you!*" Then she spits in his face.

Mom may have spat on him, but Pop doesn't reach up to wipe it away. He just stands there calmly glaring at her. Then, without a word from either of them Pop calmly backs out the door. My father has that satchel slung across his right shoulder, the suitcase in his left hand, and Mom's saliva splattered across his nose and mouth.

391

With Pop in Costa Rica, and Tony staying over a friend's house, Michael goes over Aunt Teresa's like he always does. Mom and I are the only ones home. She is on the phone in the kitchen talking to Michael. It's seven o'clock, and she's saying that she doesn't want him to spend the night at Aunt Teresa's.

Mom wants him home.

She says she'll be over soon to pick him up. I can tell from her tone that my brother is giving her a hard time. He probably doesn't understand why he has to come home. But Mom barks into the phone, "I am your mother, and I want you home. I'm coming over to pick you up, so be ready!"

No sooner does she slam down the phone—then she's marching out the front door to retrieve Michael.

A half an hour later the phone rings. When I pick up the receiver, and place it next to my ear, I hear a shaken Aunt Teresa.

"Frankie, hey sweetie, it's Aunt Teri. Listen, I'm sorry to bother you, but your mother is really acting strange. I can't get her to calm down. She's downstairs trying to get Michael to leave with her, but I'm worried about him getting in the car with her. I'm gonna try and stall them. But I was wondering how quick could you make it here? Maybe you could take him home?"

"I could be there in a few minutes."

"Alright, don't get into an accident, but hurry over. I don't know how much longer I can stall her before she just flips-out. She doesn't look right tonight."

I hang up the phone—and race across town in the Camaro. I get halfway to Aunt Teresa's house when I see what looks like Mom and Michael in the Cadillac.

They're slowing down at a stop sign—coming in the opposite direction. All of a sudden, Michael jumps out of the Cadillac as it rolls to a stop. He must have recognized the Ghetto Bomber. Michael scrambles through the intersection without looking to see if any other cars are coming. He reaches my passenger door, opens it, and gets in. He is crying.

"Michael, what's the matter?"

Sobbing, he slams the door.

"Michael, what's wrong?"

392

"I hate her Frankie. *I hate her!*"

"What happened?"

Before he has the chance to answer, I'm startled by the sound of Mom shouting at us while laying on her horn. She has pulled beside us. Her window is down. She is shouting to me that she wants to talk to Michael. Mom looks possessed; her eyes are big and angry. I don't know what to do except lower my own window and holler back, "Mom, let's go home and talk."

"No! I want to talk to Michael right now!"

"Mom, we're in the middle of the intersection."

"No, Frankie!"

"Mom, just follow us."

She lays on the horn again as I start to pull away. Through my rearview mirror, I watch her make an illegal U-turn, and follow behind us. The whole ride home Michael is quiet, and Mom is tailgating me. When we get to our street, something tells me not to pull into the driveway. I don't want Mom to box us in, so I park at the curb.

Mom pulls into the driveway and gets out of the Cadillac right away. She is marching towards us. I get out of the Camaro and tell Michel to stay put. Standing on the sidewalk near the top of the driveway, I say: "Mom, what's goin' on?"

"Where's Michael?"

"He's in the car."

"Tell him to get out!"

"Why, what's the matter?"

"I want my son out of the car!"

As she marches towards me, the anger in her eyes makes it clear to me that Michael can't go inside. Mom can't be allowed near him like this. I turn around and get back into the Camaro, locking the door behind me. A split second later, Mom is pulling on the handle of my door. She is screaming, "Let me in goddammit! Let me in!"

Michael is in the passenger seat saying, "Frankie, she's crazy!"

Mom begins pounding on my window. "Let me in! Frankie! Let me in! Michael, open the door!"

I shout through the glass, "Mom, take it easy! He'll get out, but you gotta calm down."

"Don't tell me what to do!"

"Okay, but you gotta tell me what's goin' on."

"I'll tell you what's goin' on. You and your fuckin' father always against me, that's what's goin' on! If I want my son home, I want my son home, *period!* He's not Teresa's son He's mine, and he'll do what I say!"

"But Mom, he always goes over there. What's the big deal?"

"He is my son, and I say where he can stay. I say what he can do! Now, open the door because no one is taking my family away!"

"Mom, we are your family. We're sitting right here. Jesus, calm the fuck down!"

"Open the doors! I want my family!"

We go on like this for five minutes, then ten minutes, then fifteen minutes before I decide Michael and I have to leave. Nothing I say to her makes any difference, and nothing she says to me makes any sense. She lets Michael go over Aunt Teresa's as much as he wants—whenever he wants. But suddenly he has to come home? No matter how much I try to explain to her that she needs to calm down, the more frantic she becomes.

When I start the engine—prepared to leave—Mom shoots me a look that says, *where do you think you're going?* She leaps onto the hood of the Camaro. Her face is glaring at us through the windshield. Her hands are wrapped around the top of the hood; her legs are dangling off of the front grill. I shout at her through the windshield. "Mom, get off the hood!"

"No!"

"Mom, get off the hood! We're only gonna take a ride!"

"No, get out of the car! I want my son home!"

"Goddammit! Get off the fuckin' hood!"

When I say that, Mom looks up at me through the windshield and raises the middle finger of her right hand as if to say, *fuck you!* That's when something inside me snaps. "You wanna act like this?" I shout. "You wanna throw a tantrum over nothing?"

"I want my son!"

"Well, get off the fuckin' hood!"

"No!"

"Get off the fuckin' hood!"

"No!"

I don't know what to do. My fifty year old mother is clinging to the hood of my 1986 metallic blue Chevy Camaro. She refuses to get off.

I'm screaming myself hoarse; Michael's crying himself crazy. I can't believe this is happening.

"Mom, get off the fuckin' hood!"

"No!"

"Get off!"

"No!"

I've had it. I don't know what else to do except put the car in gear and shout, "You don't wanna get off? Fine! Don't get off!"

I start rocking the car back and forth. I put the Camaro in reverse—step on the gas—then slam on the brakes. Then I put it in drive—step on the gas—then slam on the brakes.

"How do you like it now, Mom? You sure you wanna stay on the hood?"

My mother has panic on her face. She is fighting not to lose her grip, but after a few sets of back and forth, Mom slips off the hood, and rolls into the gutter. I edge up slowly, so as not to run her over—then quickly speed away. The problem is—Michael and I are facing the wrong direction. We're heading towards the cul-de-sac, which is a dead end. In order for us to leave, we first have to drive down and turn around.

We race down the avenue. As we start speeding back in the other direction, I see a figure standing in the middle of the street—it's Mom.

We're one hundred and fifty yards from her, but I can tell what she's thinking. *If you wanna leave, you're gonna have to run me over*. I take my foot off the gas and hesitate for a split second. *Am I really willing to do this? Am I really going to run her over?*

As quickly as that question comes to mind—so does the answer—the weight of my foot against the accelerator. I step on the gas, and Michael and I start racing towards our mother. With my foot to the floor, her image becomes larger with each passing nanosecond. As we bear down on her, I scream, "Michael, hold on!"

It looks like she's not going to move. I try to trick her by yanking the wheel to the right, then to the left, but Mom just mirrors me. Whatever direction I swerve in, she goes the same way. That's when a voice inside my head screams, *this is it!*

I don't hear the engine anymore. I don't feel Michael to my right. I am staring at my mother through the windshield as we race towards her with my foot to the floor. She's fifty yards in front of us squatting down with her arms open like a football player ready to make a tackle. She is stubborn. She is crazy. She is ready to die.

Move! I think to myself.

She's at thirty yards....

Don't make me kill you!

She's at fifteen yards....

I'm not stopping!

Ten yards....

She's in my headlights....

Five yards....

This is it! This is the end! She's not moving. You're gonna kill your mother! You're gonna kill your mother! At the last possible second—Mom dives out of the way. Michael and I crane our necks to the right; we watch her tumble past us into the gutter. I don't stop. We race to the corner. I look to my left—no traffic coming. I make a right. We are gone. We are free.

Something happens to you when you come within feet of murdering your mother, in a 1986 metallic blue Chevy Camaro. You start to feel a rush of adrenaline fill every cavity of your soul. It's the sort of rush you feel when you realize—you didn't let up on the gas—you made your peace. I was willing to run her over right there on the street where I grew-up. It's that adrenaline that makes it hard for me to think about where Michael and I should go.

Do we go to the police?—No.

Do we go back to Aunt Teresa's?—No.

Do we go to Grandmom's?—No.

Do we go to Uncle Bruno's?—No.

If I know Mom, she has already gotten herself out of the gutter and into the Cadillac. I bet she is casing the streets right now, looking for a fight. I have to clear my head. I can't think straight. Where do we hide? What do we do? Why is this happening? As I search for an answer, Michael and I approach a small church complex off to our left when the thought comes to me that Mom will never think to look for us there. I don't know the name of the church. It's not Catholic, so we've never paid any attention to it before. But tonight, I race into the parking lot, and pull behind the church to hide. There are other buildings around. They look like part of a school. All of the lights are off. I feel safe here—far out of view from the road.

I turn the engine off, take a deep breath, and stare out the windshield. I try to swallow my adrenaline and gather myself, but I can't. I can't because I can still see her in my headlights. I can still see her mirroring my every move like she wanted to get hit. The thing is—I was going to do it. I didn't let up on the gas. I was beyond the point of being able to stop. Had she not dove out of the way—I would have killed her.

Sitting here in the dark, hiding behind the church, with the image of Mom in my headlights ready to die, I look over at Michael who is in tears. He is facing away from me, staring out the passenger side window. He is crying and sniffling so heavily that his chest rises and falls with each breath. My brother is a mess. I need to say something. I need to calm him down. I need to make this right.

"Michael." He doesn't answer. "Hey, Migalooch...."

He turns towards me just slightly. There are tears on his cheeks, and his eyes are red. His chest is still rising and falling, but the look on his face is of a sad anger.

"Migalooch, you alright?"

"Why," he stutters out, "doesssss ssssshe doooo these thingsssss, Frankie?"

"I don't know."

"Why," he keeps stuttering, "can'tttt she jjjjjjust be nnnnórmiiiiiiiimmol?"

His face cringes when he says the word 'normal.' He starts to cry again. I place my hand on his back to console him, but Michael turns away from me. He turns away because he doesn't need consoling; he needs answers. He wants a normal mother, not one who dives onto the hood of her son's Camaro, or stubbornly stands in the middle of the street ready to die. Tonight, I need to give him answers. Tonight, I need to be a father.

I clear my throat, and take my hand off of Michael's back. I turn towards the windshield, and start talking to him without talking *at* him. My voice is soft; my speech is slow.

"Migalooch," I say, "ever since we were kids, Mom's had problems. You know that. I mean for years she slept on the couch at our old house. When we moved, she started sleeping on the floor, going days without showering. Now, I know she has embarrassed you at some of your basketball games, and she embarrassed you tonight over Aunt Teresa's, but I think she's acting this way because she's sick, Michael. She's doing all this because she wants to be like Babbo. You're too young to really remember him, but he didn't like Mom very much. You could even say he hated her. So, when I hear you say that you hate her, it worries me, because I know you love her and I know she loves you. It's just she wants us to hate her right now. She wants us to treat her poorly. She wanted me to run her over just now, because that's what she thinks she deserves. You follow me?"

I pause, and look over at Michael to see if he's listening—to see if my words make any sense to him. He is still looking out the window. But his chest isn't rising and falling anymore, so I decide to keep talking.

"Michael, do you remember when Dad used to go away, and Mom would ask one of us to check the closet for her to see if Babbo was hiding inside?"

"No."

"No? You don't remember that?"

"No."

"Well, you were probably too young. But she used to ask me, or Dad to make sure Babbo wasn't hiding in her closet—that's how scared she was of him. Even after he died, she had to make sure he wasn't hiding in her closet ready to jump out and kill her after she fell asleep. Now, that's what I mean Michael; Mom's stuck in the past. It's like she's a prisoner. We can't be mad at her for that. We can't hate her for that. Things happened to her when she was little, bad things, you kn..."

"I don't care, Frankie."

"But Migalooch...."

"I don't care what happened to her when she was a little girl. She's fifty years old now."

"Yeah, but Michael, she's still the same girl who got abused years ago. You have to understand; Mom wouldn't have turned out this way if that stuff didn't happen to her."

He doesn't say or do anything more after that, except fold his arms across his chest. I feel like an idiot for talking to him like this. But he is too upset to see the truth of my words, and I'm too upset to convince him of it. I stop talking, and we both end up sitting in silence for a few minutes—me staring out the windshield, and Michael staring out the passenger's window.

I start to get a chill from the winter air, and decide to turn the car back on, and crank up the heater. Michael is still staring out the window in silence with his arms folded across his chest. I wish I knew what to say, because what I *did* say has only served to shut him down. My adrenaline may have subsided, but I still feel like I did something wrong, like I said something wrong, and made this night that much worse for him.

I'm supposed to be his big brother—his Hero of the House when Pop goes away. All I can think is how much I wish I could take back what I said to him about Mom. *He doesn't care about any of that,* I tell myself. *He's almost five years younger than you, Chichi. He wants Mom to be like Aunt Teresa, normal and healthy. It's not that he could care less about what happened to her all those years ago in that greenhouse; it's that all he knows is he wants a mom who is happy to see him. A mom who makes him snacks when he comes home from school. A mom who doesn't embarrass him by the way she smells. A mom he is proud to call his own—yet all I can do is make excuses for her.*

It's with a mixture of guilt and shame that I look over and say, "Hey, you wanna go home, Migalooch?"

He still doesn't say anything. I know his silence means that he's tired of talking, and that—*yes*—he wants to go home. Still, I wish he would say something—so I could explain myself—so I could explain our mother.

58

A week and a half later, Pop comes home from Costa Rica with three things I can't help but notice right away. I'm standing in the small terminal of the Atlantic City International Airport, watching my father and Uncle Charlie walk towards me through the crowd. I am here to take them home. They have their luggage in hand, and smiles on their faces.

The first thing I notice is my father's tan. Pop is wearing a black, Philadelphia Flyers' baseball cap, but that doesn't camouflage just how dark he got while in Central America. Amongst the other white people in the terminal, he stands out as being brown like a man from Syria or Egypt.

The second thing I notice is Pop's stubble. His upper neck and face are covered with a scruffy black and gray beard. It's obvious he hasn't shaved in days—yet my father looks handsome and rugged.

But the third thing I notice is somewhat different. It's different, because you would have to know him to 'see' it. The tan stands out. It tells everybody else at the airport; *I was on vacation down south.* The stubble says almost the same thing; *I was away and didn't feel like bothering.* But the third element of his new look isn't as easy to recognize. I say that because I've been looking at him for nineteen years, and even I have to study him an extra second to notice the slightest hint of a swagger to his walk.

At first, I thought it was a limp, due to the weight of his satchel and suitcase. But the closer I look, the more I'm convinced I see The Confident Bull. Immediately, my instincts say: *he was with a woman.*

A few days ago, when I was trying to remember what time I had to pick him up at the airport, I went looking in Pop's office for the flight information. I started shuffling through the drawers of his desk looking for some sort of clue, but found nothing. Next, I rifled through the papers in his briefcase, and that's when I came across a picture of Gail, along with some love letters. The picture and letters were way in the back, hidden behind some business documents. When I pulled the picture and letters out, I wasn't sure what to make of them. I studied the photo of

Gail; she looked just like I remembered her, dark circles around her eyes, blonde hair, with dark roots.

She was even wearing a gray business suit—like she was the day I met her. The picture was a headshot, something she had gotten done professionally. As I stared at the photograph, I couldn't help but wonder why it was there. I thought Gail was history.

The picture wasn't enough. I had to read the letters and the cards. I was shocked when one of them mentioned Costa Rica. *Costa Rica? Did she go with Pop to Costa Rica? Is that possible? Are they back together?* I was more confused than ever, and still didn't know what time I had to be at the airport. Unsure what to do, I put the letters, cards and picture back the way I found them, and called the airline.

Yet, watching my father saunter through the parking lot without a care in the world—is in stark contrast to the way he left—arguing with Mom, her spit splattered across his face.

But then I start to think, *What if it's not Gail? What if there's someone else? Did Pop meet some young Latin girl on vacation? Did he bring someone with him? Did that someone just blend into the crowded terminal undetected? And if it wasn't Gail—how would she know to mention Costa Rica in her letter?*

My friend, Ron, invited me to a weekend Catholic youth retreat. On a Saturday night in February, I find myself sitting in one of the most elaborate churches in all of the Camden Diocese, with the lights dimmed and surrounded by hundreds of candles that line the aisles and envelop the altar. I feel like the shadows of the statues are dancing upon the walls. It appears as if the entire church—and everyone in it—is sitting around a holy campfire with the aroma of incense in the air. Dozens of teenagers quietly sit and kneel in pews throughout the church as they await their turn to make a face to face confession with the waiting priests, some of whom are sitting in between the aisles, up next to the altar, or back near the doors. From where I'm sitting, I watch as many of the teens return to their pews after having given confession, with tears in their eyes as they examine their consciences and fulfill their penances.

It is my turn to make confession. As I sit in front of a young priest up by the altar, I shuffle my feet feeling anxious and nervous. The priest looks at me somewhat confused when I don't automatically go into the Act of Contrition. I have something else in mind. "Father," I say. "If it's alright with you, I'd like to ask your advice on a family problem, instead of giving confession." The priest nods his head, and gives me a reassuring look. "Well, Father, you see, my mom is not well."

"Oh, I'm sorry to hear that."

"No, no, that's not what I mean. I mean she's not well, but I mean she's not well mentally or emotionally, or whatever. I mean she has had some health problems, but she has had many more, ah...emotional problems, you could say."

The priest is quiet, and nods his head. He is trying to understand me. "I mean...she has tried to kill herself before, threatened to jump off bridges, and stuff like that. You know, mentally ill? But the question I have for you is about both my parents. You see, they're still married, though it really isn't much of a marriage anymore. I mean, my father had an affair a few years ago that I didn't understand back then. But now that I'm older, I know it was because my mother was driving him away. She was forcing his hand, and because he wouldn't leave my brothers and me, he had no choice. The thing is Father; I thought his affair was behind us. Yet, I found a picture and some letters from my father's old girlfriend in his briefcase recently. And I'm not sure what to do about it."

"Whaddaya mean, my son?"

"Well, I mean...the thing is...my father took a trip to Costa Rica a few weeks ago. One of the letters mentioned Costa Rica, and how she hoped he would have a great time when he was down there. The thing I'm not sure about—is whether she and my father are back together again. As far as I know, the affair ended with them years ago. I'm just a little worried about it all. I'm not sure if I should ask my dad about it, or just pretend I don't know."

The priest looks at me, and nods his head some more as I explain to him that I just want my father to know I am on his side. I'm not going to judge him or get upset, if he and Gail are back together. I just want to know how to act around him and Mom if their marriage is a farce. I want to know how I can be the best son I can be to meet *both* their needs.

The priest's eyes wander down and to the right for a moment before they come back up and meet mine. "It all sounds very complicated, my son. But as you know, marriage is one of the seven sacraments. And it is a very sacred institution at that. It is when a man and a woman promise themselves to each other for life before God. The sacrament of marriage then enables that man and that woman to start a family, and raise their children with the values and morals set forth by the Ten Commandments. So, my very first piece of advice would be prayer. Ask God for guidance. Ask Him to speak to your heart about whether approaching your dad is what He intends for you. I've never known Our Lord to lead anyone astray, but you must listen my son. You must be open to what the Lord offers. You are obviously a very courageous young man for sharing this with me; it must be a very difficult thing for you and your family to be going through. But you must never forget that God turns his back on no one, and I know that if you pray about this, things will work out as they are intended."

"Okay, Father," I say. "It just feels good to get it off my chest."

"And if I could offer you one more piece of advice?"

"Sure, Father."

"If indeed you do speak to your dad, try not to approach him with anger. Do your best to allow him to explain what you found without any hint of accusation in your voice. He is your dad, and must be honored as is taught to us through the Fourth Commandment. I'm sure he is very proud to call you his son. So, approach him softly and with love. Tell him just what you told me; that you found these items, and simply wish for an explanation. Anger and accusation never lead to healing. Do you understand, my son?"

I nod my head in agreement, and listen as he suggests that we might say an Our Father together before I go back to my pew. I bow my head, as he closes his eyes, and follow his lead when he begins....

Our Father, who art in heaven, hallowed be Thy name.
Thy kingdom come, Thy will be done, on earth as it is in heaven.
Give us this day our daily bread, and forgive us our trespasses
As we forgive those who trespass against us, and lead us not into temptation,
But deliver us from evil. Amen.

When I get back to my pew, I reflect upon the priest's advice. As I sit in the dark church with the candles burning, music playing softly in the background and the shadows dancing along the walls, I think about that day I told Pop I wanted to be a priest. My father got so adamant about that. He said there was *no way* he was going to allow me to become a man of the cloth. Looking back, I know what I really meant to say was that I wanted to be a hero. Not a comic book character with a cape, and a hideout, and a sidekick, but a soft-spoken sage who studies the past and doles out advice to those in need.

Even though I'm expected to produce and perform like a veteran on that big concrete job down in Wildwood, come break time, I'm still the one who gets sent out in Pop's truck for doughnuts and coffee, but I don't mind. It gives me a chance to get out of the miserable, Wildwood wind. But today, as I approach his truck, I notice something white taped to the driver's side window. As I get closer, I can tell that that "something," is an envelope.

I'm alone around the side of the building while Pop and the guys are on the beachfront. They don't see me peel the envelope off the glass and look around. *There's no one else here;* I think to myself. *Where did the envelope come from?* I take it, and turn it over. *It must be from the investors, probably something business related.* As I study it more closely, I can see what looks like a drawing or a picture inside. The envelope isn't sealed. I look around to see if anybody is watching; I decide to peek inside.

I flip the envelope open, only to find a full page computerized drawing of a red and gray airplane with the words, **YOU** and **ME**, in big, bold, blue capital letters. The picture and the words are easy to decipher. Whoever placed this here is looking to go away with my father. I have no idea who could have left this. Literally, we are the only human beings around. Wildwood is like a deserted movie set. I stand there utterly shocked beyond belief. I don't understand. I need more information. I look back inside the envelope, and find a little hand written note. It is addressed to my father; the note is from Gail. Immediately, I think of that swagger I saw at the airport, and that picture I found in Pop's briefcase. *I knew it, they must be back together!* Yet, as I read the note, I realize I am mistaken.

Gail states that every night when her head hits the pillow, she thinks of one man—her special Frank—and she wants him to know that. She says that this is her last try; it has been nearly six years since they were last together. If he doesn't respond—if my father doesn't reply—she will finally know it's over.

I'm more confused now than I was before. I can't make sense of what I found that day in his briefcase and what I am now holding in my hand. Yet, the moment I finish reading the note, I quickly fold everything up, and put both the papers back into the envelope. I look around once more to see if anyone is watching me, before I climb into the truck. As I make my way through the empty streets, I keep my eyes peeled for any sign of life—any sign that Gail is still here—but I don't spot a single car.

When I get back to the condominium complex, twenty minutes later, I meet Pop and the guys in our makeshift break room—an unfinished condominium unit—where Lester and Darryl are sitting on upside down buckets. Pop is on his cell phone, and Gail's envelope is in my back pocket. I pass out the cups of coffee. When my father hangs up, Darryl takes a bite of his chocolate doughnut, and with his mouth still full, mumbles, "Frank, we got an ocean, down in North Carolina." He takes a moment, and swallows the bit of doughnut. "Is this here the same ocean?"

"What?"

"I said we got an ocean, down in North Carolina, and…"

"I heard what you said, Darryl."

"So, is this the same ocean?"

"Please, tell me you're not serious."

"I'm serious as a heart attack."

My father shakes his head, and smirks. "Yes, Darryl, it's the same ocean."

"Jesus, Lord, Almighty. That sure is one big ocean. Lester, you know that was the same ocean?"

My father and Lester share a laugh at Darryl's expense because they know he isn't kidding. But the moment Darryl stops his babbling, I approach my father and show him what I found.

"Pop," I say. "There was an envelope taped to your window when I went out for break." I take it out of my back pocket, but before I hand it over I direct him a few feet away so we can have some privacy. In the moment before I begin to speak, I recall the priest's advice, and approach my father softly without the slightest hint of accusation.

"When you were away," I say, "I found something in your briefcase, and I've been meaning to ask you about it. But now with *this*," I motion towards the envelope in my hand, "I don't know what to think."

When I say that, Pop's eyebrows do what they always do when things don't seem right, they scrunch together above his nose, and he cocks his head to the left as if to say, *oh, really?* With that look of curiosity locked on his face, Pop puts his coffee down, and folds his arms across his chest as he waits for me to ask my question.

"What's goin' on with you and Gail?"

"What?"

"I found a picture of her and a few letters in your briefcase. One of them mentioned Costa Rica, so I figured you must have started seeing her again. But, after reading this...I...."

"Cheech, Gail and I haven't been together since 1991—that's six years ago. The cards and the picture are all I have left of her."

"I know."

"Whaddaya mean, you know?"

That's when I hand him the envelope. Pop flips it open. He studies the plane and the note. My father nods his head and says, "Chichi, Gail has tried a number of times to reconnect with me over the years. She even called over Christmas saying how much she missed us being together. I must have told her we were working down here. Though I purposely refrained from telling her *exactly* where we were 'cause I wanted to avoid something like this, but she must have gone from street to street looking for me. When she called, I told her there were too many complications going on, that Mom is really struggling, and that the two of us getting back together would only add to the whole mess."

"So, she wants to get back with you?"

"Chichi, you haven't had a girlfriend yet, so you may not understand what I'm talking about, but when a man and woman are considerate to one another, when they think about one another, and truly feel appreciated by one another, it's very hard to walk away from that. It's very hard to walk away from love, but that's what she and I decided to do. I was never going to leave my family. But Gail *did* leave her family. She moved out, took the kids, and wanted me to do the same. I told her that was never going to happen, and that she should go back to her husband. And though she tried to go back, it wasn't the same."

"What wasn't the same?"

"Her feelings weren't the same. She had fallen out of love with him."

"And had fallen in love with you?"

"Well, she had fallen in love with *us*. She said she had never been as happy before in her life and wanted us to be together. Gail was very sweet to me, Chichi. That's what it comes down to. The two of us being apart has been very hard on her. I feel bad about that, but what are ya gonna do? That's life sometimes. I mean we burned just about everything we had ever given each other one summer day back in 1991. We tried to make a clean break—but as you can see, it wasn't that easy for Gail."

"Well, how did she know about your trip to Costa Rica?" He pauses before he responds. "I don't know if you remember, but I went to Costa Rica back in '91 with Uncle Charlie. Whatever you read probably had to do with that."

I want to ask him about that swagger I saw at the airport; and the possibility that he may have someone else in his life, but my father goes on to tell me how badly he feels in terms of the hurt that Gail is experiencing.

He explains that it isn't her fault, and that people don't stop loving each other just because things don't work out.

Pop says she was always good to him, but that he just doesn't know what else to do. I tell him I understand, and not to worry, I'm not going to say anything to anybody. I'm on his side, and he is right; none of this is Gail's fault.

Even though the twelve year old in me whispers to the nineteen year old that Gail is a whore—a real *puttana*. The twelve year old says *she had a husband, and two kids, yet chose to fuck up my parents' marriage. Let her suffer, let her miss my father.*

But I tell the twelve year old to shut up; things are different now. We can't go back and change the past. So, I blow on my coffee as Pop borrows a lighter from Lester. We walk outside, and my father sets the envelope on fire right at the foot of the beach.

As we watch the envelope burn, Darryl comes out and stands next to me. I can feel his voice in my ear. "Frankie," he says. I turn my face to him only slightly because I want to watch the envelope burn, "You think your daddy pullin' my leg?"

"Whaddaya mean?" I ask, my eyes studying the flames.

"About the ocean?"

"What about it?"

"Is that really the same ocean we got in North Carolina?"

I know he isn't joking. I feel bad for him. "Yes, Darryl, it's the same ocean."

He pauses a moment, blows on his coffee and studies the horizon. "Well, I'll be," he says in his southern accent, "that sure is one big ocean, Frankie."

59

Weeks after my father burns that letter on the beach in Wildwood, Aunt Ellen stops by our house curious about my mother. She wants to know how Mom has been acting lately.

Aunt Ellen is standing in the foyer, by the front door. She looks haggard and disheveled. She is dressed in a white cotton sweat suit, with matching Keds sneakers. The dark bags under eyes match the fatigue she projects. Her short, dirty blonde hair is wild; it is obvious she got dressed in a hurry. Her body language is rushed as she tells Pop that she can't stay long, left the car running, and wants to be gone before Mom gets back from Aunt Teresa's with my brothers. She says, "Frank, I had to stop by. I had to tell you what happened yesterday."

My father scrunches his eyebrows together. "What are you talkin' about, Ellen? What happened?"

"Ann stopped by my house—unannounced. She looked weird, even for her. I had a dentist's appointment first thing in the morning, but I wasn't dressed yet, just having a cup of coffee. As soon as she walked in the door, I could tell something was wrong. I couldn't put my finger on it, but as we sat down at the kitchen table, I got this eerie feeling inside. I only had a few minutes before I had to get dressed, and go to the dentist's—but I didn't feel right getting up from the table, and leaving Ann alone."

"Whaddaya mean, you didn't feel right?"

"I was scared."

"Scared of what?"

"Of Ann—I think had I gotten up, and left her alone, she would'a done something."

"Like what?"

"I don't know. I didn't even go into the bathroom and brush my teeth. I didn't get dressed properly. As much as I didn't want to go to the dentist's office in my pajamas, I wasn't comfortable leaving Ann alone. It was like she had something sinister in mind—some sort of plot."

Pop studies Aunt Ellen for a moment; he looks concerned. He takes his left index finger and runs it across his mustache a few times with his eyes sharp and focused. "It's funny you say that," he says. "Just this morning I was up in the master bathroom when I noticed a lump in one of the fishing magazines I keep next to the toilet. I wasn't sure what it was, but it looked like there was something stuck in between the pages. I picked it up, opened to that page, and inside was a knife. I thought to myself, *now, what in the world is this doing here?* I finished in the bathroom, and brought the knife into the bedroom where I asked Ann about it."

"What did she say?"

"She said she was using it to clean the tile in the shower, but I didn't believe her. I asked her why it was hidden in the magazine, and she couldn't give me a straight answer. I kept at her until she started crying. Finally, she said she brought the knife upstairs to use on herself."

"God, Frank," Aunt Ellen says. "Didja ever think she could use something like that to hurt you, or the boys?"

"No," Pop says. "I don't think so. She's not like that. She would never hurt one of us. Ann has never been violent."

"But she did try to kill herself with that butcher knife."

"That's what I mean. She has tried to hurt *herself* in the past, but she would never hurt one of us. It's not in her nature. She begged me not to tell the boys about the knife; she was really ashamed."

Though Aunt Ellen left as quickly and as hurriedly as she arrived, her story leaves an impression on my father. He spends the remainder of the morning mulling over the knife he found—and Aunt Ellen's fears of a 'plot.'

By early afternoon, he decides to call Aunt Colomba. He tells her he wants to get my mother readmitted into the Institute of Mental Health at the University of Pennsylvania. He tells my aunt about the knife in the magazine, and Aunt Ellen's experience.

Pop says it might take a week or two to get a hold of Dr. Wydell, and make all the proper arrangements; he wants to know if Mom can stay with Aunt Colomba in the meantime. She immediately agrees. Pop thanks her, and says he will bring Mom to Philadelphia first thing in the morning.

When Mom is told about the plan later that night, she says, "Frank, I'm not going back into that stupid hospital, and I'm not staying with Colomba."

"Ann, I don't care what you *want* to do. You're going to Colomba's tomorrow. Then we'll see just how soon Dr. Wydell can get you readmitted."

"I'm not going Frank. The hospital is for sick people, and I'm not sick."

"Ann, lissename—you have to go."

"I'm not going."

"Yes, you are. Now, I don't want to hear it. Help me pack your things, because I'm taking you up to your sister's in the morning."

"Frank, I'm not going!"

I'm standing in the doorway to their bedroom. Mom is sitting on the bed in an old dress shirt she uses as nightgown. She's running her right hand through her short, salt and pepper hair. Pop is looking out the window; he is staring at the Atlantic City skyline.

Neither one of them turns to me as I say, "Mom, I think Pop is right. Why don't you stay with Aunt Colomba for a little while? Give us a chance to regroup down here and...."

"Regroup? What the hell does that mean, Frankie?"

"Well, it's just things aren't right with all of us living together."

"What are you talking about? We're a family, right? Families live together...."

"Yeah, but Mom you know things aren't normal. I mean Pop has to talk you into taking a shower half the time because you smell so bad. Now, is that normal?"

"I do not smell."

"Yes, you do."

"I do not."

"Mom, yes you do! You always do!"

"*Ann! Frankie!*" Pop shouts. "*Enough!*"

We both stop and look at my father. He has turned from the window. Pop takes a deep breath, and lets out a long sigh. "Ann," he says, "the boys and I need a break."

"*A break!* What kind of a thing is that to say to your wife?"

Mom searches my expression looking for help—but I agree with Pop. She has been home with us since October, but nothing has changed.

She clings to The Routine day and night, won't listen, doesn't try and *never* admits that she needs help—but my mother won't give-up that easily. "Not over my dead body," she says. "I'm not going back to Philadelphia! I hate it there! I'm staying here with my family!"

From there, the conversation escalates to the point of exasperation. Mom starts going on and on about how she's fine, and how she can't understand why we have to pick on her so much. I tell her we're not picking on her, but that we can't keep living this way. I tell her that the last few months have been very difficult for us—that we need a break, and that if she's not careful—there won't be any future for her to come home to. When I say that, she raises one eyebrow higher than the other, and slowly walks towards me. "Okay, Frankie," she says. "You know what? I get it now; you win and I lose. Is that how it is? Sound better? Isn't that what you want to hear? I'm going to Philadelphia because that's what you, and your father, want me to do."

"Mom, come on...."

"No, it's simple. You win and I lose. I get it now." She walks past me, out onto the landing. Pop calls after her, "Ann, this isn't working for us. Can't you see that? Now, you're going to Colomba's tomorrow, and that's the end of it!"

With the three of us still going around and around, Tony pokes his head out of his bedroom down the hall. He calls to us, "Night, guys."

Pop and I call back, "Night, Tone." But Mom doesn't respond. She stays standing in silence, staring at a black and gold crucifix hanging on the wall at the top of the stairs. Tony waits for Mom to answer, before repeating himself, "Night, Mom." She continues to stare at the crucifix in silence. This makes Pop crazy. "Ann," he says sarcastically, "your son is trying to say good night to you."

But Mom keeps staring at the crucifix—ignoring him. "Ann, you think this is a game with a winner and a loser? You think it's that easy? Well, you're wrong, 'cause I'm not doin' this anymore. I've bent over backwards to try and help you. But you're so *testa dura* nothing ever changes. So, fine, if that's the way it's gonna be—then go live with Colomba!"

"Frank," my mother says, slowly turning from the crucifix. "I'm not gonna go."

"Yes, you are."

"No, I'm not."

I interrupt. "Mom, just go to Philly for a few weeks, and *prove* to us that you're fine. Take your meds, take a shower every day, look for some part-time work. But *show* us you're fine. It's not enough to *tell* us. You can't keep coming home and doing the same thing over and over."

"Oh, *Frankie,*" Mom snaps. "What the hell do you know?" She has a scowl on her face. "The two of you have been against me for years, and I don't get it. I don't know why you keep doing this to me. But I'll go to Philadelphia if you want. I'll go, because you win and I lose."

My mother is indignant. I get choked up when she repeats that bit about winning and losing. She waves me off at the sight of my tears— lighting a cigarette, and sitting back down on the bed. Pop can only muster a sigh of exasperation, and a shake of his head.

This is too much, I think to myself. Mom is destroying us by being so stubborn. She won't admit she needs help. She won't admit that leaping onto your son's Camaro, or eating lipstick at lunch are things that healthy people don't do. She can't see that The Routine has become her life—or that it has taken over our lives.

All she wants is chaos and dysfunction, while cultivating sympathy from everyone. Well, I'm tired of the dysfunction.

I turn on my heel, and storm back to my bedroom. Pop is right behind me. He walks into my room, and sits on the edge of my bed. "Chichi," he says, "I need you to be a man about this."

That's the word he uses—*man*.

"You're not a little kid anymore. I know it's hard. But you can't react like that. When the chips are down, you need to be your strongest. Now, your mother needs help. I'm gonna see if I can get her back into the Institute, and arrange for the doctor to *make* her stay for a few months this time. But enough of the tears; you need to be a man. You're almost twenty years; it's time to start acting like it."

I hear my father—but there are images in my head that make it hard to be a 'man'—images of confusion. Images of my mother jamming that butcher knife deep into her abdomen—doing shots of carpet cleaner—while chasing my father down the street—begging him to have sex. Mom is giving us no choice but to send her back to Philadelphia. I want a choice. I want to be happy. I want the chaos to end—and Pop says it will, if we can just get through one more night....

60

By five o'clock the next morning, I'm lying peacefully in bed. Our house is so quiet; I'm hesitant to even roll over. I like the darkness of my room. In the silence of the morning, I start to think Pop was right—all we had to do was make it through one more night—and everything would be fine. Except right at that moment, at the height of my relaxation, with my body and mind at peace under the covers, my father lets out a blood curdling scream from his room down the hall. I am instantly filled with panic. Pop only shouts three words, *"Oh God, no!"* But each word is laced with a growing fear—a realization that he is about to die.

Any other time—if my brothers or I screamed like that—Pop would come charging into our rooms. He would have a towel wrapped around his waist, and his hair would be a crazy mess. He would shout, *"What happened? What happened?"*

But today, I throw my covers off, and leap from bed in the instant I hear his cry. I feel the adrenaline grow with each step, as I race down the hallway for my parents' bedroom with everything I got.

When I get to their doorway, I see them both wrestling on the bed. I smell what I think is gasoline in the air. Mom and Pop are facing me on their knees. My father has my mother wrapped in his arms; he is struggling to control her, and Mom is fighting to get free. I'm not sure what is going on. *Why do I smell gasoline?* My parents' faces are frantic as they flail around in a sea of sheets and covers. Mom looks possessed; Pop looks panicked. He shouts, *"Cheech, come grab her! I gotta flush my face! I can't breathe!"*

His voice is strained, and I don't know why. It's like he can barely talk, but I do as he says and jump onto their bed. I struggle to take Mom from his arms. Still, I don't know why I smell gas—or why I'm suddenly struggling to wrestle with my mother.

From the bathroom, I hear Pop's voice straining to say how much his mouth and eyes burn. He sounds afraid. Pop screeches for me to hold her. He knows she has matches, and doesn't want her near his face. His voice is cracking in ways I've never heard a human voice crack before—squeaky and soft, weak, yet panicked.

414

Mom is in my arms, but she won't calm down. We violently flail around on the bed, taking out the lamp on the nightstand, and falling to the floor. I'm on top of her shouting, "Mom, knock it off, calm down!" But she screams, "Get off me, Frankie! Get off me!"

Soon, Tony appears at the bedroom doorway. He sees me struggling with Mom. He instinctively moves to help me, and jumps on top of her. Tony wraps his left hand around Mom's throat and screams, *What the fuck is wrong with you?* Pop strains to shout from the bathroom. "Don't hurt her! Whatever you do, keep her away from me, but don't hurt her!"

I don't know how Pop expects us to keep her away from him, while not hurting her; it is like Mom has the strength of ten men the way she won't stay on the ground. Tony takes his hand off of Mom's neck. He and I end up sliding off her. She gets up and starts going after Pop. My father is stronger than she is—that much is true—but she has matches. If she gets a chance to strike one, his face will go up in a flash.

Pop helplessly hollers, "Keep her away from me! She has matches! Keep her away from me!" He scurries from the bathroom where he was flushing his face. He rushes past Michael who is now standing in the bedroom doorway. Mom is giving chase and Tony shouts, "Michael, keep her away from Pop! Keep her away from him!" But Michael has no idea what's going on. He can only watch Mom and Pop blow past him.

As the three of us run after them, I'd like to know how the peacefulness I felt minutes ago has turned into this—I'm chasing my mother down the stairs, who's chasing my father down the stairs, whose face is covered in gasoline, with my mother and her matches ready to strike.

When we got downstairs, Tony and I catch up to Mom and *pummel* her. Pop may have said he doesn't want us to hurt her—but we hit her so hard, she flies over the back of the loveseat, and lands in front of the big screen TV. This time, Tony and I don't let her up. We jump over the loveseat, and pin her down like a pair of tag-team wrestlers. Pop is on the phone, screaming at the police in his hoarse voice that they need to get here as quickly as they can. When he hangs up, he sees me and Tony on top of Mom in only her underwear and that dress shirt she uses as a nightgown. Pop moves towards us. "Let me have her," he says. "Let me have her!"

He takes control of Mom by coming behind her and wrapping his arms around her and squeezing. The two of them are kneeling next to the loveseat, with Mom's chest and face smushed into the red leather cushion. With his arms wrapped around her, squeezing with all his might, Pop hoarsely grunts, "You have no idea what you've just done, Ann! You're in some deep shit now!"

The roles have been reversed—now, my father looks possessed, and my mother looks panicked. Pop has her wrapped so tightly, Mom can hardly move. Michael is crying near the steps that lead into the living room, while Tony shouts at Mom, his face red, his breathing hard. He wants to know what the fuck she was thinking, and what the fuck is wrong with her. I shout, "Jesus, Mom, what the fuck is the matter with you? You're fucking nuts!"

But Pop half-shouts—in his strained way—that he wants us to stop fucking screaming. We do as he says, but I can't stop the thoughts that fire off in my head—I hate the sight of my parents kneeling beside the loveseat, Mom squirming, and Pop squeezing. I hate the smell of gasoline. I hate screaming. I hate feeling my heart racing like it is. I hate the darkness in my head. I hate the way my chest is rising and falling. I hate the word pummel. I hate my mother. I hate confusion. I hate fuck. I hate this morning. I hate the sun rising over the meadows, and I know I will always hate the memory of this day.

Pop wakes me from my hate fest when he hoarsely hollers, "Cheech! Cheech, get some ice cubes and rub my eyes—they burn!" I sprint into the kitchen, where I reach into the freezer and grab a tray of ice cubes. I dump a few into my left hand, and bolt for the den. I kneel beside my father, who already has his eyes closed because they burn so much. I rub only his left eye, until he whisper-shouts, "Do the other one too! The other one, Cheech!"

I'm rubbing and shaking and breathing and watching my mother struggle there in Pop's arms—*is this really happening?*

My father wants me to give the ice to Tony. He struggles to support the words, in his airy voice, as he says, "Frank, call Uncle Bruno and Aunt Ellen. Have them get over here right away!" As I rush back into the kitchen to make the calls, Pop sends Michael out to the curb to flag down the police. Tony stays in the den with my parents, rubbing my father's eyes with ice.

When the cops show up, Tony is still kneeling beside Pop, rubbing his eyes, as tears of melted ice stream down my father's face. Tony's voice is hoarse from all the shouting he's done. He yells to the police, "This woman is trying to kill my father! You need to get her the hell outta here!"

As I watch Tony and Pop get up, and give control of Mom over to the police, my first thought is—Tony is right. This woman is trying to kill my father. So, can somebody please tell me where my mother is?

The police take me, Tony and Pop into the kitchen. Michael is still outside. At first, the cops are laid back—figuring this is a typical domestic violence call. They casually ask Pop if he wants to press charges, half expecting him to say, *no, don't worry about it.* He's bent over, with his head in the kitchen sink, rinsing his eyes under the faucet. When he hears the question, and the nonchalant tone—he suddenly straightens up and screams at the police, "Fuck yeah, I wanna press charges! What the fuck do you think?"

Pop starts ranting and raving. I've never seen him this angry, this hostile—this human. He has always shrugged things off, always whistled his way through Mom's problems. But this morning, he is the opposite of the Pop I know—the opposite of the calm figure who sat on the corner of my bed last night, and told me I had to be a man.

Next to arrive after the police, are the EMT's. From the kitchen, I watch them file in the front door and recognize one as a guy I went to high school with. We weren't close friends, but we played ball together for a season. When I see him walk in, I'm not sure whether I should be embarrassed, thankful, or say, *hey man, what's goin' on?* I decide just to nod, but he can tell by the look in my eyes that I'm lost and embarrassed. He's being debriefed, along with the rest of his crew, about a victim doused in gasoline, and a suspect that won't cooperate with the police.

The cops have moved my mother out into the foyer, but it takes them a little while to get her under control. After getting word from Pop that he wants to press charges, a young policeman with a light mustache tells Mom, "I need you to come with me, ma'am." But Mom insists that she has to go to the bathroom—and that she has to take her purse with her. "Ma'am, I can't allow that."

"Well, some gentleman you are. I only want my purse so I can freshen up."

"Ma'am, if you have to use the facilities—that's one thing—but I'll have to escort you into the bathroom and observe you. As far as your purse goes, that's completely out of the question."

Mom defies him. She makes a move for her purse that is lying on the floor next to the couch in the living room. Only, when she begins to leave the foyer, she gets covered in blue. A few of the police officers standing nearby converge on her. They keep her from making any move towards her purse, or from walking freely throughout the foyer. The cops insist that she stay put, but she feels boxed in, and takes steps towards the kitchen where me, Tony and Pop are standing. The police have no choice but to corral her. Because she appears ill, they treat her a little differently than they would some young burglar—but still it is clear—they won't hesitate to use force if they need to restrain her.

That same young officer, with the light mustache, is able to coerce Mom into the bathroom. Pop is moved upstairs because the police say they don't want to take any chances. Tony and I stay downstairs. We watch through the front door as Aunt Ellen walks in amidst the labyrinth of ambulances and police cars parked on our front yard—their lights flashing and swirling—cutting through the early morning mist.

Just as Aunt Ellen walks in, Mom is led back out into the foyer. There is a certain defiance in Mom's step after she notices Aunt Ellen. For a second, the two women lock eyes. Aunt Ellen screams, "What did you do, Ann? What did you do? The house reeks of gasoline?" Mom doesn't answer. She just struts around the foyer—surrounded by cops—with her head held high. Pop notices that same defiance in Mom's step. His voice is coming back to him. He starts shouting from the landing, high above us all, "She's history! She'll never be back! She's outta here! That's it! *Outta here!*"

A few members of the rescue squad, and two police officers, stop Mom from strutting around. They struggle to strap her down onto a gurney. Mom tries to fight them, but she's no match for five grown men. As they start to take her away, they ask Aunt Ellen to call the Crisis Center at Atlantic City Medical Center, and let them know all the medication Mom has been taking. Aunt Ellen asks for my help. We go into the kitchen, and sort through the bottles of pills in the cabinet next to the stove. Just then, Hank shows up, and takes my brothers with him back to his house. In the melee of the morning, I have lost track of my brothers. It is hard to gauge their temperature, I can barely read the labels on mom's prescription bottles, let alone read my brothers' thoughts. But I know they must be glad Hank has shown up, glad that they are being carted away, removed from the madness of this morning.

After Mom is carried out the front door, and Pop is escorted to his own ambulance, I am left standing in the foyer where the police ask me about the rifle. I look at them confused, "Rifle? What rifle?" A police officer is walking down the steps from my parents' bedroom. His arms are extended in front of his chest; he is carefully carrying my father's hunting rifle. Aunt Bridgid has arrived. She and Aunt Ellen are standing next to me when I tell the police Pop used to hunt with that gun. I say he hasn't used it in years, and that I don't think it works anymore. I tell them he always used to keep it in his closet, hidden behind a bunch of clothes. The police say that's just where they found it, and even though I claim it doesn't work, they remove it from our house as a precaution.

Aunt Bridgid is going to drive me down to the Emergency Room, so we can check on my father. But before we leave, I remember that Lester and Darryl will be showing up for work soon; it's almost seven in the morning.

I tell Aunt Ellen to go ahead of us—that we'll meet her at the hospital. I scribble a quick note to Lester and Darryl, and tape it to the front door. In the note, I tell them not to worry, but that we have had an emergency. I ask if there's any work they can do without Pop's instruction—if not—I tell them they have the day off, and that I'll call them later. I ask Aunt Bridgid if she has any cash. I take the ten dollars she gives me, and tape it to the door as well. Darryl is always broke, and may need a few dollars to catch the bus back to Atlantic City.

After we climb into her white, Honda Accord, Aunt Bridgid shakes her head at me. "Frankie," she says, "I know you're only nineteen honey, but to be that aware, to think about Lester and Darryl, and their welfare...to have that much presence of mind...on a morning like this...I don't know...I...I think you're more of an adult than most adults. I'm proud of you sweetie. You should know that."

My father is discharged from the Emergency Room with an assortment of drops and solutions for his ears, nose, throat and eyes. To look at him, you wouldn't think anything is wrong. His voice still is scratchy, but he doesn't look like a victim—in fact—he has the "strut of a survivor." Watching him walk out of the ER is impressive. Every step says—I am *Frankie the Voice*. It is a relief to see him looking so strong and formidable.

From the Emergency Room, Aunt Bridgid drives us to the tiny police station—where Pop and I receive subpoenas—and are questioned about the events of the morning. Pop does most of the talking, and answers most of the questions.

He starts off by telling the cops about last night—about the argument we had with Mom, how he wanted her to go to Philly, to stay with Aunt Colomba, and how the argument didn't end well. Pop says he went to bed with an eerie feeling—like something was about to go down.

Not wanting to cause a scene, he waited until we all fell asleep, then quietly slipped out of bed. He went out into the garage, where he found an old ice chest. He brought the ice chest into the house and grabbed a towel from the powder room. Next, Pop went into the kitchen and rounded up all the knives. He wrapped the knives in the towel, and placed the towel in the ice chest. He then hid the ice chest in the extra shower we never use downstairs—making sure to pull the curtain closed.

The officer wants to know why Pop would do all that. So, my father tells him about the knife he found the other day in the magazine, and the conversation with Aunt Ellen, when she felt like Mom was up to something sinister. The officer makes a lot of sounds to show he is paying attention, as he scribbles into a small notebook. He looks up from his scribbling and asks, "And then what happened?"

"Well, after I hid the knives, I tried to stay awake as long as I could. But by three thirty in the morning I just couldn't do it anymore. I was exhausted. I went upstairs, got into bed, looked over once to make sure my wife was asleep, and closed my eyes. I figured nothin' was gonna happen after all."

"So, you went to bed at three thirty. But the attack took place at about...?"

"I guess it was what—five o'clock, Chichi?"

"Yeah, Pop. About five o'clock," I say.

"Well," the officer asks, "what led up to that?"

"Let's see. I think I woke up around a quarter to five. When I rolled over, my wife wasn't in bed. The only reason I woke up was because I kept hearing the sound of drawers opening and closing down in the kitchen. Any other time I would have gotten out of bed to see what was going on, but I could barely open my eyes, and kinda just fell back to sleep."

"You fell back to sleep?"

"Yeah, I had hidden all the knives, so I knew she wouldn't find anything. I guess I slept another twenty minutes. Then I remember hearing the creaking of our staircase. Whenever somebody is on the way up our stairs, they sort of make a creak that lets you know someone's coming. So, I rolled over onto my back and saw my wife at the top of the stairs. She was just standing there, staring at this crucifix we have hanging on the wall; she seemed mesmerized by it. I called to her, but she didn't say anything. I called to her again, but she still didn't say anything. Only, this time she turned, and slowly walked into our bedroom."

"Did she attack you right then? Was there any conversation? How did it proceed?"

"She—now let me think. Ann made her way across the foot of the bed, and stopped at the window. She was facing away from me. I think she said something about not wanting to go to Philly."

"Philly?"

"Yeah, remember how I said we were gonna take Ann back to stay with her sister today?"

"Right, okay...and?"

"Well, she turned from the window, and walked across the room. Then she did the strangest thing. She stopped at the bureau where we have a bunch of pictures of my sons when they were little. She took all the pictures, and turned them face down. It seemed so strange to me. I didn't know what to make of it. But looking back, it's obvious she didn't want the boys to see what she was about to do. I rolled to my right, and propped myself up onto my elbow to talk with her. That's when I noticed her holding a sweater. At first, I thought it was a towel because she had it bunched up. But then, I realized it was a sweater. She was holding it at about the middle of her waist; it looked like she was trying to hide something, but I didn't know what. Ann started to lean towards me from across the bed. I thought she was comin' closer in order to talk me better—but in a flash, she dropped the sweater and hit me with the gasoline."

"Where would she get gasoline?"

"I'm a contractor. I always keep gas, acid, oil—things like that—in the garage...."

"Alright, so, she had the gas under this sweater—this white sweater. Then she threw it in your face when she leaned in from across the bed?"

"Yeah, as soon as it hit me, I couldn't catch my breath. I mean, the gas went in my mouth, my nose, my eyes; it just took my air away. Plus, I knew Ann always had matches on her, so I panicked. I screamed, and tried to hold her until one of the boys could come and grab her. If it wasn't for Frankie, I don't know what would'a happened. I was just about outta air...."

Pop glances over at me when he says that, and I have to fight to conceal the confusion I feel in my heart. For the first time in my life, I was the hero. For years, my father has put my brothers and me through Hero School—teaching us how to turn adversity into a lesson. But this morning's attack feels more like a total loss, than a Hero School lesson. It fills me with a confusion I've never known. It would be different had I saved my father from some intruder who had broken into our house, or some washed up old Ducktown wiseguy, looking to exact revenge for being thrown in the trash.

But it was my mother who wanted to light him on fire this morning, my own mother....

After the officer finishes his paperwork and hands us our subpoenas, he allows Pop to call Uncle Nick—Mom's brother—and tell him about the attack. As I sit quietly cornered by my confusion, I eavesdrop on my father's brief conversation with Uncle Nick. I can tell that my uncle isn't at all surprised by what has happened.

I haven't seen him in months—since that day we took Nonna to the Newark airport. Though I can tell he's not shocked, my uncle can't possibly guess what I'm feeling as I hold the subpoena in my hand. There's no way he can imagine the weight I feel on my shoulders—the way my throat hurts from all the screaming this morning, the panic I felt when I heard Pop scream, the way my pulse quickened, and heart pounded. He can't possibly know how heavy the subpoena feels in my hands, how it represents the end of an era, the end of my innocence, and the end of life as we know it.

My uncle simply can't feel what I feel as I look at my father, knowing I may have saved his life today, but still confused about what it means to be a "hero" on a day like this. My confusion won't go away. It snaps at me that if this is what it feels like to be a hero, then I don't want any part of it. Sitting here, silent and motionless, as my father hangs up with my uncle, being a hero feels like a burden, not a prize. It feels like I did something wrong, or sinned against humanity, or lied to a priest, or tripped an old lady.

Heroism feels sticky and thick. I tell myself this is why people like Bruce Wayne need an alter ego to change themselves into. A hero is something you can only be when you step outside yourself. You can't be a hero and be afraid; you can't be a hero and weigh the odds. You have to charge into that burning building with all you got, even if it means you may not come out alive—and charge I did. But it wasn't courage that pushed me down that hallway this morning; it was fear. Fear that my father was about to die.

I have watched him for years, living behind those dark sunglasses, with that collar popped, and bravado in place. He was impenetrable, undefeatable. He was my father, but he was also the Italian Stallion, *Frankie the Voice*, the heavyweight champion of the world, the underdog who never gave up, and took no shit; the eternal optimist who threw armed Mob associates in the trash, and rubbed elbows with Made Men.

Yet, when I rushed into that bedroom a few hours ago, I found a man fighting for his life.

A man who was rendered helpless, forced to his knees by a fifty year old woman in panties and a dress shirt, armed with matches and gasoline.

61

For the next few days, our house is filled with an incredible sadness that makes everything feel empty. Meals somehow get eaten, and TV somehow gets watched—but that's about all we do. Things are so bad Pop doesn't even have the energy to make his Blue Collar Carbonara. All he can do is boil a pot of water, throw in some spaghetti, and dump a jar of tomato sauce into a smaller pot on the stove.

We've never eaten sauce out of a jar before, but Pop is too depressed to care. When he sends me to the supermarket, he orders me to buy Barilla tomato sauce—the number one brand in Italy. He says, "Don't buy any of that other shit. You hear me, Chichi?"

Pop doesn't even care if Tony and Michael stay home from school, because he and I stay home from work, which means the four of us stumble around the house like Italian zombies in a shocked, silent and confused daze. We don't laugh. We don't play. We don't talk, and we don't hear Pop whistling his Sergio Mendes songs. Everything is out of sync, and we barely function.

There seems to be only shadows and sadness in our house now. Like everything we ever loved, everything we ever dreamt of, perished in a vicious head-on collision late last night. Only, last night happens every night, over and over and over.

It's hard to escape, or hide from the shadows, and the emptiness seems to follow us everywhere. That hollow emptiness is there when we go to bed each night, and lingers still to wake us up each morning; it cannot be ignored, and it cannot be willed away. It drains us of our energy, and robs us of our hope. Sometimes—without warning—the emptiness will drag me back to that morning and I'll be rubbing ice on my father's eyes, screaming at my mother, or watching the policeman with the light mustache keep Mom away from her purse.

It is the emptiness that accompanies me as I sit alone at the kitchen table—staring out the window—three mornings after The Gasoline. My brothers are over Aunt Teresa's, and our house is quiet and still. Sitting there, my chin cradled in the palm of my left hand, my elbow resting on the table, I watch clouds drift above the endless sea of cattails. I can see Atlantic City rising in the distance across the meadows, ignorant and cold to the reality we now face—Mom in jail, and the four of us in a total freefall.

As I watch the wind tickle the meadows, bending the stiff cattails nearly in half, I can feel Oreo rubbing against my shin under the table. He and Midnight haven't been fed in days, so they lick the half-dozen empty cat food cans that line the hallway leading to the garage. I know I should get up to feed him. I know he must be starving. And I know that if I looked hard enough, I might find an old can of tuna fish hiding in the back if the pantry.

As I get up from my chair to find the cats some food, I begin to hear what sounds like crying coming from another room. First there's a yelp, soft but high, followed by the sounds of sobbing. My father is home in his office trying to work on some paperwork. I move from the pantry and call to him. "Pop! Hey, Pop! Is that you?" I get no response. I walk out of the kitchen and head for his office—where the sound seems to be coming from. When I get to the office doorway I find my father crying on the small brown couch by the window. He is wearing jeans, and a white, tattered, polo shirt with the collar popped.

Pop is looking down at a dark blue photo album; he is crying like a child. I have never seen him cry like this before, and when I walk in, he doesn't try to stop. He doesn't try to pull himself together, or wipe away the sadness. He just looks up at me with tears streaming down his face and asks, "Does she look like she hates me, Cheech?"

I don't know what he is talking about, until I sit beside him, and realize he's looking at pictures from my parents' wedding album. The photograph that has him in tears is of my parents and four grandparents—posing for the ages—smiling and happy—a brand new family.

My grandfathers look handsome in their brown colored tuxedos. And my grandmothers look pretty in their fancy dresses. My mother and father are both wearing white—they are standing in the middle of their parents. They look as perfect as two young people could hope to look, on the day they begin their lives together. Yet, as Pop and I study the picture, he chokes out, "Everybody looks happy, right? Even her father...."

"Right, Pop," I say. "Everybody looks happy."

425

"So, what happened?"

"I don't know, Pop."

"How did we end up here? How is it possible that this is really happening?"

When he says that, he looks up from the album and searches my expression for an answer, but I have none to offer. He looks lost and sad. I wish I knew what to say to make the sadness leave his face, but I don't know how we got here, and I don't know how this can be happening. All I can do is soften my expression, and take my father into my arms because his eyes film over with fresh tears. His lips begin to quiver, which leads to an emotional eruption that brings on more crying as he buries his face in my chest. When Pop sobs, his entire body sobs with him. I can only rub his back and stare out the window—my chin on his shoulder—saying, "It's alright, Cheech. I'm here. I'm here."

Through the window I gaze upon the meadows with that Monopoly board just staring at us, as we sit there a moment not speaking. It's during the silence that I realize I just called my father Cheech. I didn't call him Dad, or Pop, like I have my whole life—but Cheech.

I don't think he even noticed with the way he is crying as he knocks the photo album to the floor. But as he starts to calm down, it makes me wonder who we are, and what we are becoming. Aunt Bridgid may have said I'm more of an adult than most adults, but if Pop is Cheech, and I'm Cheech—then who is going to fix all this? Who is going to make things right? Our roles are reversed, and there is no turning back.

The only people that ever call my father by that name are his friends or relatives off the boat from Italy. Other than that, he has always been Frank—because **I'm** Cheech. So why did I call him, Cheech? *Why?* I want my father back. I know I've lost my mother, but I want my father back. I can't lose them both—not at the same time—not like this. Not, now. I need him. I don't want to be an orphan. I don't want my brothers to be orphans. I want my father. Where is my father? Where is *Frankie the Voice*?

62

My mother calls collect from jail every day, but my brothers and I never accept the charges. We don't want to talk to her. But the more we decline the charges, the more she calls back again and again and again. Mom will call two, three, four times in a row, until her time at the jailhouse payphone must run out.

We spend most days pretending she doesn't exist anymore, but Mom is everywhere. She is in our parents' bedroom where the smell of gasoline is so strong that we keep the door closed all day long. She is in the den, flying over the back of the loveseat, after Tony and I pummeled her. She is the foyer, strutting around in defiance. My mother is in the Cadillac. She is in the garage. She is in the sky. She is in the meadows. She is at the top of the steps, staring at Jesus. She is on the cross. She is in the kitchen—looking for a knife. She is at the bureau—turning over our pictures. She is in Calabria. She is strapped to a gurney. She is in my heart. She is in my soul.

My mother is missing; but she won't go away.

The only person who accepts the charges when she calls from jail is my father. He even goes to visit her. Pop says the other female inmates call my mother 'mom,' because she's so much older than they are. When he took Aunt Ellen to see my mother, both she and Mom wept over the telephone, talking through the glass—like one might see in a movie.

When the visit was over, Aunt Ellen interrupted the conversation next to her. She was sobbing, but she got on the phone and pleaded with the young, black, female prisoner, to watch out for my mother. Aunt Ellen said Mom didn't belong there—that she was sick. The young woman was in agreement. She said Mom wouldn't shower, or sleep in her cot. Instead, my mother sleeps on the hard-concrete floor of her jail cell.

My father may accept her calls—and he may go see her in jail—but, my father can't bring himself to sleep in the same bed where Mom nearly killed him. My brothers sleep across the hall, but Pop and I have become roommates since the attack. He sleeps on a cot next to my bed. Pop only goes back into his bedroom for the few fresh clothes that lie in his drawers or to quickly shower.

Other than that, we try to wall off that part of the house from everything else. I like knowing my father is safe lying beside me, because in my head, I can still hear the way he screamed that morning, and in my heart, I know this could have turned out much differently. Had Pop not hidden those knives the night before, Mom may have driven one into his chest. Had he not been as aware that morning, she may have burned him to a crisp.

I think these same thoughts and feelings are running through Pop's head and heart as well. I think he knows how lucky he was—how lucky we all were. Had I gotten to their room, and if Pop's face was in flames—I think my brothers and I would have beaten Mom to death. Now, not only would Mom be dead, and Pop in a burn unit, but Tony and Michael would be in a juvenile holding cell and I'd be in jail awaiting arraignment.

We were lucky—but that doesn't stop Pop from sliding out of his cot in the middle of the night, crawling over to my bed, kneeling beside me and burying his face in my sheets to sob. He sobs in my sheets twice the first week after The Gasoline. I console him like I would a child. I rub his shoulders, and stroke my fingers through his hair, trying my best to tell him everything will be alright. We never talk about it the following morning—never bring it up even when it's just the two of us alone sitting in the den watching TV. I know it's to remain between us as part of the tight brotherhood we have become.

Seeing my father sobbing in my sheets reminds me of that August day out in the driveway when I was getting ready to leave for Towson State. Pop had the video camera out beaming with pride as he recorded my last few moments at home. It was the summer of 1995, and I remember how when he lowered that camera from his face, I saw tears rolling down his cheeks. I remember thinking what that summer meant to him, the summer of Mom's suicide attempt with the aspirin and the carpet cleaner and the knife.

It was the summer that nearly destroyed him. Others didn't know it, they didn't see it, the way he was always whistling and carrying on like a frustrated Tony Danza, but I knew it; I saw it. I knew it because he stopped being just my father, and became a fellow survivor like Tony and

Michael. It was the survivor in him that came out that morning of The Gasoline, but it came out in a way I didn't really understand until now.

Pop went to court the other day to hear the charges filed against Mom. But when he arrived in the courtroom, he wasn't sure where to sit, so he asked the sheriff's deputy who seemed to be directing people. The deputy was a heavyset black woman, about ten years younger than Pop. When he politely asked her where he should sit—she naturally sat him on the defendant's side of the courtroom. After all, Pop was wearing his black leather jacket, with his collar popped, and those dark sunglasses. He told the deputy he was there for a domestic violence hearing, so it made sense to her—he must be here to defend himself. The thing is, after Pop took his seat, he realized he was sitting on the wrong side. He got up to move to the victim's side, across the aisle—but the same female deputy approached him. "Sir, where are you going? Please stay seated. Court's about to be in session."

"But, I think I'm on the wrong side."

"Whaddaya mean?"

"I think you sat me on the defendant's side."

"Right, I did."

"Well, I'm not the defendant."

"But you told me you were here for a domestic violence hearing?"

"Yeah, but I'm the victim."

"Oh c'mon, big man like you, what could your wife have done?"

When Pop tells her how Mom had doused him in gasoline at five in the morning, and wanted to light him on fire, her eyes got big; she realized she had made a mistake. She quickly softened her tone, and moved my father to the victim's side.

It's this idea of perception that must have been running through my father's mind the morning of The Gasoline. Even as he frantically flushed his face, Pop strained to shout from the bathroom, "Don't hurt her! Whatever you do, keep her away from me, but *don't hurt her!*"

I didn't know how he expected us to keep Mom away from him—yet not hurt her—because it was like she had the strength of ten men. I didn't understand how he could be so concerned for her welfare, when she had just doused him with gasoline; but now I know he was making sure we looked innocent.

Mom has always had that unique ability to turn things around and make *you* look like the fool. It's like she's the master of perception. No matter the circumstance, she always vied to play the victim. Pop knew that if she had come out of that morning bruised and battered—manhandled by her teenage sons—it wouldn't have taken much for the police to arrest us. In the confusion and adrenaline of that morning, he was thinking about survival in the immediate sense; *I need to get away from this woman and her matches.* But he was also thinking ahead. He knew that when the smoke cleared, Mom needed to look completely guilty, and we needed to look completely *not* guilty.

Days after the attack, Pop learned that Mom had planned to take us all to "be with Jesus." That's the phrase she used when talking to the paramedics. She was going to light Pop on fire, then set the house on fire, then do everything she could to stop my brothers and I from escaping the inferno. We would all die together; so we could all "be with Jesus."

That was the plan my mother and her madness had decided upon that dark and gray winter morning.

Eight days after The Gasoline, I find a piece of paper lying on the pillow of my father's cot. I pick it up, and sit on the edge of my bed to read it over; it is a hand-written letter from my brother, Michael.

Dear Dad,

I know this is hard for you, it is hard for me as well. You've known her for thirty years and now you can't do things that people are telling you because you don't want to be a jerk, but maybe it is time for you to be a jerk to her because where has nice gotten you? Also, don't listen to anything that woman says. I HATE HER get her away from me. I don't want to ever see her again, and if you talk to her on the phone hang up for me because I don't want you talking to her either because you are making it harder on you. Next time she calls, call the police, because she is breaking the law and YOU'RE LETTING HER talk to you. DON'T, as far as I'm concerned she is not part of my family anymore. You did your best and now that is it, OK, no more let her go. She didn't do anything when you helped her so let her sit in a hospital somewhere far away. Get a divorce and more restraining orders because I'm scared, I'm scared I might lose my dad, my brothers or me. Also, tell Aunt Teri and Aunt El and everyone that is close to us to get a restraining order too, because I don't want them hurt, as well as are close relatives. I don't know if you know how much I love you, Dad, but that morning when I thought I lost you it only made me realize how precious life is and know I love you more than ever. These are my thoughts on 3/19/97 at 10:15 pm. Thank you for all the great things you have done for me; you are my hero.

I love you,
Michael

There is a line halfway through Michael's letter that stands out—*as far as I'm concerned, she is not a part of my family anymore.* It stands out because of what Michael did the morning of The Gasoline. In the immediate aftermath of the attack, while the police were corralling my mother, and questioning my father, my brother slipped back through the front door. He was out by the curb, waving down the police, but when he came back inside, he grabbed a pair of scissors, marched into the den, went over to the mantel above the fireplace, and literally *cut* Mom out of our lives.

Sitting on the mantel—for the last decade—has been an eight by ten color photo of the five of us lounging as a family on the couch. We looked so tan and Italian; relaxed and united. There was Pop in his crisp white tee-shirt with Tony scowling on his lap; my brother's hand resting upon my father's huge paw. Then there was little Michael smiling in the middle of the photo, his left arm behind Mom's body—but now that Mom's head is missing, the next face you see is mine. My right arm is behind my mother's decapitated body and I am smiling brightly.

Behind us are two framed photographs of Atlantic City, but the morning of The Gasoline, Michael swiped that photo down from the mantel. He undid the fasteners on the backside of the frame, slipped the photo out, took the scissors in his right hand, and carefully cut Mom's head out of the picture. Just like that, her image was headless. The odd thing is—Michael put the picture back in the frame. He redid the fasteners, and returned the photograph to its' place on the mantel, as if nothing happened. Mom was no longer on display above the fireplace, or in our lives.

When Pop reads the letter, he sighs, shakes his head and says, "You know, Chichi, I have the best three boys I cudda asked for." He folds the letter in half, clears his throat, and puts it on the nightstand next to his cot. Then Pop looks over at me. "Chichi, I went down to Wildwood today. I told the investors about The Gasoline. I wanted to be honest with them, and let them know what happened. Otherwise, they would'a started wonderin' where we've been, and why no work is gettin' done. The thing is—they didn't take the news so well."

My father says he told them about the attack, and how Mom is in the Atlantic County Jail—and though they seemed to "understand," they want him off the job. They were cordial, but they made it clear that they have deadlines to meet. They would not allow my father and his family problems to hold them back. Pop assured them that he would live up to the contract he signed, if they could just give him a few days to regroup. But they said Memorial Day is right around the corner, and they need to be fully operational by then.

Again, my father gave them his word. He would work to get everything done in the next two months—if they just gave him a few days to get back on his feet. They tried to talk him into leaving on his own terms, rather than being forced out. But my father stood his ground; and in the end, they hesitantly and nervously, agreed to let him stay.

It's after he got home from Wildwood that my father says he felt Babbo's spirit in the house.

My grandfather has been dead for more than ten years. But ever since he passed away, my mother has been terrified of him hiding in her bedroom closet. My father or I always had to check the closet and reassure her that Babbo wasn't hiding inside waiting for her to fall asleep, so he could kill her.

Yet, here it is—late March of 1997—and my father is telling me that he felt Babbo's spirit today.

He says he walked in the front door after his meeting with the investors and felt "something" in the house—a presence in the air. Pop says he called out, but nobody answered. My brothers and I weren't home. So, he called out again, and that's when he realized it was Babbo. My father says the presence felt evil. He immediately started shouting.

"I went from room to room barking at him. *'Get out you son of a bitch! Get the fuck out! There is no place for you here!'* I'm bein' dead honest, Chichi. I'm gettin' goose bumps just thinkin' 'bout it. I went around hollerin' and screamin.' Tellin' him he wasn't welcome, that he had done enough damage, and that he wasn't gonna drag us down with him. I asked my grandmother and all our family that is passed on to help keep us safe, because we are not giving up. We're gonna beat this, Chichi, you hear me? We're not gonna allow this to ruin the rest of our lives. We gotta be strong."

Days later, Tony has a similar experience. He is home alone, he feels an eerie presence in the air. The presence is so real to him that my seventeen year old brother picks up our Louisville Slugger for protection.

Spooked and afraid, Tony cautiously goes from room to room just like Pop had done days prior. After several tense minutes, Tony's fear boils over into anger. He erupts into a rage, aggressively swinging the bat at the presence in the air, and violently shouting at the spirit.

This is our life now.

This is our home now.

This is our truth now.

63

As winter turns to spring, my father decides that we have to sell the house. He uses the words 'have to,' because he knows that if the investors in Wildwood get nervous again, they'll throw him off the job. "So, before we lose the house," he says, "we should try and sell it." At the same time, Pop decides to sell the house, he stops making the monthly mortgage payments. He would rather spend that money on something that will help clear his mind—like maybe a boat.

In May of 1997, with his credit ruined, and his taxes having gone unpaid for a second year in a row, my mother in jail, and the concrete job in Wildwood barely keeping us going, my father buys a beat up old fishing boat for seventeen hundred dollars cash. It comes with a trailer that he attaches to his truck. He tows his boat down the gravel roads that lead to the bay behind Atlantic City. There he launches his humble vessel and starts spending his afternoons and evenings out on the water. Sometimes he takes my brothers or me, and sometimes he takes Uncle Charlie, but most of the time Pop goes alone. He guides his boat through the marshes and focuses on placing his fly casts into just the right pocket of water along the banks of marsh where the striped bass are known to hover. We always used to go surf fishing when I was a kid, or use spinning rods whenever we went out on our old boat. But now, fly fishing is what captures my father's imagination. He thinks of fly fishing as a method, or an art, that lies at the intersection of thought and skill. He says, "Anybody can drop their line in the water, and wait for some poor fish to take the bait. But only a fly fisherman, only an *angler*, can place his line softly upon the water, and lure a powerful bass out of the shadows."

When Pop isn't out on his boat, he is practicing his fly casting on the front lawn. It's nothing for one of us to come home, and find him standing at the top of our long driveway, fly rod in hand, casting back towards the house. He and the fly rod work in perfect harmony, as he majestically guides it back and forth through the air—building the momentum needed to cast the fly as far and accurately as he can.

While my father falls back in love with fishing, I throw myself completely and totally into the game of golf. Whatever Pop finds out on the bay, I find on the golf course. Whatever peace he gleans from studying and rehearsing the proper moves of a fly cast, I glean by studying the golf swing. The two moves require much of the same: focus, discipline, desire and passion. I love spending hours out on the driving range, working on my swing, video-taping my sessions, and doing everything I can to perfect my golf game. Because golf costs money, I sneak onto different golf courses, or make friends with some of the guys who work there, so they'll let me hit balls, or play a few holes for free. My hustle and dedication pays off. A month shy of my twentieth birthday, I shoot par for the first time in my life, and I'm convinced golf is my future. I want nothing more than to play golf daily, for it has become my sole passion, distraction, and escape.

Some nights, when the house is quiet, and it's too dark to stand out front and practice his fly casts, my father sits alone at his office desk and writes about his experiences on the bay. He stopped working on *Thoughts of a Common Man* many years ago. But since The Gasoline, he has turned his focus to writing a short fishing article for publication in a salt water fly fishing magazine.

Pop writes the article on the computer in his office. He says it is about the romance he finds fishing in the back bays, with the lights of the casinos of Atlantic City radiating in the background. Pop prints out a rough draft of the article, and shows it to me. I can't help but think that he sounds just like Grandmom; only to remember that he was told years ago that he should have been a writer, that he had all the insight and perspective necessary to bring a story to life on paper. The problem was he could never get himself to sit still long enough to flush something out. Now, with Mom in jail, our house for sale, and fly fishing his escape, writing has found him.

It's interesting because the same thing that has happened to Pop has happened to me; I am keeping a diary.

Every day or every couple of days, I find myself typing my thoughts into a Microsoft Word Document on that computer in his office, and saving it in a file called MY LIFE. Though keeping a diary is something I've never done before, it quickly becomes a habit, a way of recording all that has been happening, and all that I've been feeling since The Gasoline.

In addition to writing his fishing article, my father has been writing an essay of sorts, a recount of his life with Mom entitled: *History of Events*. The recount is simply a nine-page, single spaced essay about Mom's childhood, and Pop's experiences as her husband.

His hope is to share it with my mother's family so they may better understand our life, for they have done nothing but curse us—what with Mom in jail, and charges pending. Nonna will be coming back from Italy this month, and from what I've heard, she knows nothing of The Gasoline or Mom's incarceration. Uncle Nick didn't want to tell her over the phone. He wanted to wait until she came back to America.

Pop wants to have the *History of Events* finished by the time Nonna comes home, but I don't see the point. "They'll never understand," I tell him, "they'll never see things our way."

64

On Father's Day, 1997—three months after The Gasoline—Pop and I decide to visit Mom. She has been transferred from the Atlantic County Jail to the Trenton State Forensic Hospital. We don't bring Tony and Michael because Pop doesn't believe they are emotionally "ready" to see her yet.

We take my father's GMC Jimmy up the Atlantic City Expressway to Route 206, and head north for Trenton. I'm silent for those ninety minutes on the road, as I stare out the passenger window, and watch Mexicans in big hats work the fields along the road. A caravan of tractor trailers blows past us on this two-lane highway, as on the radio, Bobby Darin sings, *Beyond the Sea*. The Trenton State Forensic Hospital is surrounded by a parking lot of the darkest, blackest asphalt I have ever seen. It has two large maroon colored doors that stand out amidst the gray, cinder block building.

Once inside, Pop approaches a receptionist behind the kind of glass window you would find in a police station. Peeking at her, from over my father's shoulder, I watch the lady with short blonde hair force her lips into the shape of a professional smile. "Can I help you, sir?"

"Yes. We're here to see Antonietta?"

"Who is that?"

The woman half turns her head—as if to say—*could you say it again?* Pop moves a little closer, and speaks directly into the slotted circle in the middle of the window. He is embarrassed—like when he used to apologize from stage—but tries to conceal it.

"Yes, I'm sorry," he says "I'm mumbling. We'd like to see my wife, Ann."

"Oh, yes. You called ahead, didn't you sir?"

"Yeah, that's right."

"Okay. Here's what I need you to do. Sign this book—date it, and put the time down. Then just have a seat and we'll bring you back to the inmate."

Inmate? Is that what she said? *Inmate? Jesus fucking Christ,* I think to myself, *my mother is an inmate.* I thought this was supposed to

437

be a hospital? She was an inmate at the Atlantic County Jail, but this is the Trenton State Forensic *Hospital*. No mention of inmates. My mother is a patient. *Isn't she?*

After we both sign-in, Pop and I slide into the slightly cushioned maroon seats bolted to the concrete floor of the Trenton State Forensic Hospital. My father crosses his legs and as always, tries to keep things light. He can tell I'm anxious, so he rubs my shoulder, and gives me the look with that twinkle in his eye—the Hero School look. His eyebrows rise and fall with each word, like he's pleading with me to lighten up.

"I know it's tough," he says. "But we gotta thank God we're all alive—Mom too." He continues with his eyebrows alive and pleads, "Cheech, some things we have control over, but other things we've got to deal with, you just can't...."

"Gentlemen," a voice interrupts from behind. "I'll take you back now."

We both turn halfway around to find this gargantuan, mountain of a black man dressed in a guard's uniform. He has the deepest voice I've ever heard in my life. "Follow me."

Pop and I rise from our slightly cushioned maroon seats, and follow him through hallways of concrete, metal detectors and sliding jail doors. Pop's right arm rests over my right shoulder as we trail the mountain man into a smaller hallway where he stops and turns around.

"Gentlemen," he says, in his low rumble, "this visit will last thirty minutes. Is that understood?" Pop shakes his head yes. But I can only stare at him blankly. "There is to be no contact with the inmate. Is *that* understood?" We both shake our heads yes. "And there will be two of my men waiting inside to keep an eye on things."

The guard turns around, and I take a deep breath as he rat-tat-tattles his keys into the hole, and opens the door. I walk in first, and see two big black men dressed as guards standing behind my mother, who is sitting alone at a small square table, dressed in a tan inmate's jumpsuit.

There's a sharp pain in my chest. It feels like someone has punctured my lungs with an ice pick, and tied a cinder block to my soul, heaving it over the side of a deep sea trawler leaving it to rot at the bottom of eternity like all the other souls of everybody else who have ever had their guts rearranged by the sight of their mother looking a desperate mess.

Her hair is matted. Her hips are heavy. Mom reeks of sadness as she stiffly rises from her chair and sobs. We move into the room, but all I want to do is to run back down Route 206, past all the Mexicans in the fields, and the tractor trailers blowing by. I want to run until I reach our old house; the home we lived in when I was a little boy. I would knock on the door—knock knock knock—and when someone answered, I would say, *Hi, I'm Frankie. I'm sorry to just barge in like this, but I used to live here a long time ago. I've come to see if my mother is here.*

If they looked at me like, *what the hell are you talking about?* I'd burst past them scouring the house. *Mom!* I would say, *Mom! It's Frankie. Where are you hiding?* I would go from room to room, frantically searching for her, because it can't be that she is gone. It can't be. But I can't run back down Route 206, and I can't change the fact I'm standing between my parents—the two people who made me—in the Trenton State Forensic Hospital with my mother coming into my arms crying and moaning so awkwardly, that when she lets go of me, my right shoulder has small little wet spots from her tears and snot.

Mom stays in my arms for the longest time. Pop rubs my shoulder with that soft Hero School look on his face. *Cheech*, it says, *I'm sorry about this. But we can make it, we can get through this.*

I don't cry as she pulls away, because Pop always makes me feel like this is some sort of lesson—like I should be thankful for the adversity because one day I'll look back and realize how much I've grown. But today I don't realize anything, and today I don't grow anywhere, because today I have come to visit my mother in the Trenton State Forensic Hospital. It's all I can do to make it across the room to that little square table in the corner.

The room is whiter than white—all cinder block—with nothing on any of the walls, no signs of life. There are three doors—one across the room to my left, where the inmates are housed. The second door is straight ahead—it has a small window—I can see outside. The third door is being locked behind us by the gargantuan, mountain of a black man who just walked us back here.

When we sit down, Mom is across from Pop—I am next to her. There are tears rolling down her face. Pop tries to comfort her. "Ann," he says, "it's okay. We're here. It's okay Ann...." But as he says that, one of the black guards hollers out, "Remove your hand, sir." Mom looks to her left, then her right. She is trying to find the owner of the voice. "I said—remove your hand, sir." Mom is confused. She says, "But, he was just...I mean, he's only my hus...." *"Remove your hand from the inmate!"*

Mom reached for Pop's hand when we all sat down. She hasn't yet let it go. Her crying suddenly stops with the third demand. Pop has to give her a look that says, *do what he says, Ann,* to make Mom let go of his hand, and allow him to pull it back into his lap.

My mother's eyes are only half open. She looks like she is stoned. Her left leg keeps jumping up and down so fast that only the ball of her foot touches the ground. She looks nervous. Not nervous to see us, but nervous to be alive. It's like something has wrapped its legs around her sanity, and is fucking the shit out of it.

My father looks tired, even though he hasn't sobbed in my sheets in weeks. I know he is relieved to have finished the Wildwood job on-time, and is passionately distracted by his fishing and writing, but today is a Father's Day he'll never forget. It is awkward sitting here between my parents. I feel sick. I don't know what to say. This place feels like a jail. I am intimidated by the silent, expressionless guards. They just stand there with their backs against the wall watching our every move.

A few minutes into the visit, my mother asks the guards if she can smoke a cigarette. My father brought her two packs of *Virginia Slims*—Mom's favorite. The guard closer to Pop says she can smoke—but that we have to go out into the tiny courtyard and stay by the doorway to be watched. Even though we have to be watched, I'm happy to get away from that table where my mother's leg was starting to drive me mad. It was jumping so much—so fast—that it almost didn't seem human. No one I've ever seen can move their leg that fast.

I'm glad when my parents and I leave the table and walk to the door that leads outside, but I should have known better. The door leads to a small concrete courtyard surrounded by twenty-foot-high walls of cinder block. There is a chain link fence bellied across the top of the cinder block walls. I feel uncomfortable. I feel sad.

My father stands with his right leg up against the door-jamb bent at the knee. I'm standing the furthest out the door, with Mom next to me. She is swaying, trying to light her cigarette, as it twitches in her left hand. Mom can't get the lighter Pop gave her, to ignite. So, he calmly takes the cigarette, and the lighter, and lights it for her—but I have a hard time watching that. I have a hard time watching the two people who "made me" light a cigarette. Every time I look at Mom, I get that sharp pain in my chest. I have to bite down real hard to keep the tears away.

Pop tries to start a conversation as he hands the cigarette back to Mom. He folds his arms across his chest, with his leg still bent at the knee, lowers his face down to Mom's and softly asks. "Ann, how are they treating you?" Pop studies her eyes and waits for an answer, but Mom just stares at the floor and puffs on her cigarette. She looks up when he asks about her sleeping on the floor, but still doesn't answer. I know Pop wants to know whether she's sleeping in her cot or not, but Mom can only nervously puff on her cigarette and blink. She blinks at him once, then twice, but the third time her eyes rest on me.

Mom tries to smile when our eyes meet, but I don't know what that means. She is my mother; she is my soul—but standing there watching her smoke that cigarette in her tan inmate jumpsuit, I don't know who she is anymore. I have memories of when she was slim and young and healthier—of when she would never have dreamt of dousing my father in gasoline. But now those memories have been stained by the word *inmate*. She may be a mother and a daughter, a sister and a wife, but it's that word that describes her now. She has always been a prisoner of her past, but now her only chance at parole may lie in my eyes. I know she's looking for forgiveness. Will I forgive her? She doesn't have to say a word; it's written all over on her face. This is the first time we've seen each other since that morning, and though she must be glad I'm here, she needs to know what sentence I will hand down.

Mom always told me that she first realized she was pregnant with me on a trip to Italy back in 1976. When she got back to Philadelphia, my parents spent the rest of her pregnancy dreaming about me. But as I stand here, watching her blink and smoke that *Virginia Slim*, I have to say this life feels more like a nightmare. Forgiveness is the last thing on my mind—an explanation is what I want. How did we go from Pavarotti and pancakes, to gasoline and incarceration?

Since I don't give her the forgiveness she seeks, Mom asks of my brothers. "Why didn't they come?" She hopes they don't hate her, and asks us to please tell them to call her. Pop is very sweet with her, very calm. But I know Tony and Michael won't call. Neither will I; this visit has been enough. I feel so awkward struggling to find something to talk about, biting down so I don't cry, that I'm glad when the mountain who led us back here opens the door behind us with a, rat, tat, tattle of keys and tells us, "Times up, gentlemen, please follow me."

Pop and I give Mom a hug goodbye, which brings on more tears and snot. She is sobbing. The little girl who was lured into that greenhouse some forty years ago, now stands before us a broken person. It is a sin. Her life has been a sin, but what lies ahead? What will become of her? What will become of us? As we leave her, and walk towards the door, I turn around one last time and see those two big black men—one on either side—lead my mother, who is still sobbing, back to her cell. It is the saddest scene I have ever seen.

When my father and I make it back out to the lobby, he speaks to the same lady who was behind the glass when we arrived. She tells us to sign-out. Then Pop speaks directly into the slotted circle in the middle of the window and asks, "Is there any need for money here?"

"Excuse me?"

"I mean—my wife. Is there any reason she would need money?"

"Yes, she can purchase some extra items in the cafeteria. We have vending machines."

"Okay, then I'd like to leave her some cash, and these two packs of cigarettes."

The woman nods her head, and says, "Okay." A moment later she slides a manila envelope, and a white paper under the glass. "Just put the cigarettes and the cash in this envelope. Print your wife's name on the form, and sign it at the bottom. I'll make sure she gets it."

"Thank you."

"Yes sir. You're welcome." Pop nods and grins. He is trying to be polite, but I can tell he is uncomfortable and embarrassed. When we climb into his truck, and my father starts the engine, he looks over at me. "Cheech," he says, "you alright kiddo?" I lie and say, "Yeah, I'm cool, Pop."

"I know she doesn't look good, Champ, but keep your chin up. We gotta thank God we're alive." I turn towards him ready to say, *you're right. We are lucky to be alive.* But when I look over, he's staring out the windshield with a dark, serious expression on his face. The darkness tells me, this isn't like all the other visits, to all the other hospitals—there's no going back now—nothing will ever be the same.

65

Today is my birthday. It is June 26, 1997, and I am twenty years old. I'm supposed to go golfing, then to dinner, with Mr. Welsh, Hank and Pop—but we're running late. My father is seated behind his desk talking to Mom on the phone. She calls all the time, and he's the only one who accepts the charges, and agrees to speak to her. But today he is angry.

There is a light breeze coming through the windows behind him as he barks into the receiver, "Ann, you gotta stop this. You gotta stop controllin' everybody. This isn't fair! You got us all wrapped up in you!"

Pop is leaning forward in his chair, moving his free hand—trying to make a point. "Ann, we have tried. We've been trying for years, but you don't want to change. *What?* No, you're the one who doesn't want to change. No! I don't want to hear what Rena thinks...because I don't...."

As they continue to argue, I think back on all the conversations like this I've overhead. What have they ever amounted to? My mother is in a forensic hospital, and my father is an emotional and financial mess.

Lying there on the floor, between the desk and the filing cabinet, I can see my father's eyebrows alive with anger. I watch the index finger of his free hand rub across his mustache. I continue to listen as his voice suddenly softens with the sound of my name. "Yes, Frankie's here. He's right next to me. What? Okay, let me ask him." Pop takes the phone and presses it against his chest. He looks down at me. "Cheech, you wanna talk to Mom? She wants to wish you a Happy Birthday."

I shrug my shoulders as he reaches the phone out to me. I sit up, and put the receiver to my ear. "Mom," I say.

"Hey, birthday boy."

I can tell she is trying to camouflage her sadness. "Hey..." I say—trying to camouflage my own confusion.

"S'what you doin' for your birthday?"

"Oh, I don't know. I think we're gonna play golf...."

"That sounds like fun...."

When I take too long to answer, Mom asks, "What's the matter sweetie? You, okay?"

What's the matter? Am I okay? How can she even ask me that? I'd like to tell her the matter is I'm horribly upset, and that I'm *not* okay. I can't get her out of my mind. I'm still hung up over that visit ten days ago—but I know I can't say any of that. Instead, I mumble out, "I miss you, Mom."

"What? What's that honey?"

"I said I miss you."

The line goes quiet after I say that. My hope is, Mom will get back on and say—*I know you miss me, Frankie. That's why I've decided the time has come to get better. This time I promise nothing is ever gonna happen again that involves gasoline, or knives, or hospitals. Things will be like they used to be. We'll play in the snow, and go to Nonna's for pasta fazule.*

Because this is what I want to hear, I burst into tears when Mom ignores what I said about missing her. I drop the phone, and sprint out of Pop's office without giving him an explanation. I am hysterically crying as I run through the foyer and out the front door. I can hear Pop in his office hollering, "Jesus, Ann! What did you say?"

I don't want Mom to get into trouble. I want to turn back around and tell Pop that she didn't say anything at all—that was the problem. I told her I missed her, and she didn't say it back. Maybe she couldn't say it back—but it's too late for me to know that. I'm at the top of the driveway, nearly in the street, with tears streaming down my face. I stand there and think about the fact I miss Mom more than I ever thought I could. *How is that possible?*

I don't miss the smell of her dirty feet, or watching her eat her lipstick at lunch. I don't miss dragging her to the doctor or charging towards her in the Camaro, but I do miss those Sunday mornings, when everything seemed perfect. I miss those days when she flirted with Pop, and made us breakfast with Pavarotti and pancakes. But what I miss most—is the pride I used to feel in being their oldest son. I was always proud of that fact—proud to be first—but recently, I've grown jealous of Tony and Michael, and find myself longing for a big brother to protect me.

The morning of The Gasoline—Michael heard Pop scream—just like me. He leapt from bed—just like me. But when he threw open his bedroom door, and poked his head into the hallway—he did something very different. Michael saw me racing towards our parents' bedroom; he knew something was terribly wrong. Yet, he immediately darted back into his own room, hurriedly closed and locked the door behind him, jumped back into bed, and quickly pulled the covers over his head.

When Tony demanded to know what was going on, Michael didn't answer. He couldn't answer. His father had just screamed like a man under siege, and his big brother was rushing to salvage what was left of him.

Michael was terrified; he felt safe under the covers.

Sometimes, I wish I could have stayed hidden under the covers that day—but as the oldest child of *Frankie the Voice* and *Swing-Set Annie*, my reaction was instinctual. My training began years ago when I used to check the closet for my dead grandfather, and comfort my mother when news of Pop's affair came out. I don't know what good I did trying to help her, but I know I did right by my brothers. I sent them out to play. I stayed inside and consoled her.

Now that *Frankie the Voice* sobs in my sheets, and has turned to me for that same brand of counseling, I have become his confidant—his *consigliere*—which means I'm the first to learn the big news; Pop has sold the house. He sold it to an Egyptian doctor, for five thousand dollars more than he paid for it ten years ago. We have to be out by Labor Day. That news mixes with the sadness in my heart over Mom's silence on the phone; it feels like a bomb went off in my chest. I am angry. I am crying. I am hopeless. It is my birthday.

I need someone to tell me—*it's gonna be alright*—that's all I want. And just as that rage is about to burst within me, just when I'm ready to scream to the heavens over the jealousy I feel towards my brothers—Tony comes dashing out the front door. He is shouting, *"Frankie! Hey, Frankie! Wait up!"*

He quickly catches up to me, and we hug. Tony pats my back, "What she say, Frankie? What she say?" But I don't answer him. I can't answer him. Mom didn't say anything; that's the problem. We stand there in silence, hugging in the middle of the street—the same street where Michael and I nearly killed Mom in the Camaro—the same street where I used to ride my bike as a child.

As we separate from our embrace, Tony turns me around, and starts walking me back towards the house. We don't say another word, but with Tony by my side, I raise my head and see Michael standing on the front walk. He has a soft smile on his face. When we get close enough he says, "You gotta cheer up, Frankie, today is your birthday."

My brothers smile. They have never seen me like this; they want to cheer me up. The sight of their smiling faces causes me to smile through my tears. Soon the somberness turns to silliness. My brothers start to giggle, and I start to giggle and sniffle.

It is unspoken, but we know we are laughing at the same thing—the absurdity of who we are—of what we have become. The unpredictability of Mom's mental illness has ravaged the tranquility of our lives; it has taken us on an emotional and complex journey.

On the front walk, Tony offers me to Michael—who takes me into his arms. We stand there hugging on the walkway. I am the luckiest kid in the world. Mom may be in that Forensic Hospital, and Pop may have sold the house to Egyptians, but I will always have Tony and Michael. Decades from now, I wonder who we will become. What sort of lasting affect will Mom's turbulent life have on the three of us? Sometimes I feel doomed—like a prisoner shackled to her insanity. But as we move onto the porch, my brothers help me pick the lock of those chains. They smile, and tell me they love me, and I relax.

I relax because at least we are together—*Frankie the Voice* and The Three Tooters. As we sit on the porch, and enjoy the summer sun, I know I'll never forget this day—the day I turned twenty years old, and felt like a little brother for the first time in my life.

66

A week after I turn twenty years old, my father surprises me with a belated birthday present—a fire engine red, Jeep Wrangler, with a tan interior, and matching soft top.

Pop was able to buy the Jeep, thanks to the additional work he landed on that job down in Wildwood. The investors were so impressed that he kept his word—and finished by Memorial Day Weekend—that they awarded him all the block, stucco and concrete work, for the addition they're building to their beachfront complex.

My Jeep may be three years old, but to me it represents a brand-new lease on life. I love to fold the soft top down, and cruise all over the Jersey Shore. Some days after work, instead of going straight to the golf course, I drive for miles and miles, so I can clear my head, and remind myself to breathe.

There are many nights when I put the Jeep into four-wheel drive, and follow these narrow dirt paths that lead out into the marshes behind Atlantic City.

The marshes border the back bay, where sometimes the air is so salty, I can taste the sea upon my lips. The night sky is dark in all directions, but Atlantic City acts as a beacon of sorts. Her twelve casinos, and mini-metropolis, create a dome of light—a glow that illuminates my world. From across the bay, I like to sit in the Jeep, and stare at her majesty.

I think about a lot of things when I'm back there, but mostly I think about the future. I know that one day I want to shine like Atlantic City does, that I want to be a hero, a beacon that burns for all the world to see.

I get these ideas from Pop, because he says I'm special....

The one thing my father liked about my former friend Carmine was the nickname he gave me—*Frankie Special*. Carmine gave everybody a nickname, whether you liked it or not, it was part of his wiseguy approach to life—and Pop loved the one I received.

447

Frankie Special had nothing to do with *being* special, and everything to do with *eating* a Special. Carmine was impressed that I could eat an entire *Special* from Tony's Baltimore Grill in Atlantic City all by myself. A *Special* being a cheese pizza topped with sausage and pepperoni—I routinely ate the entire pie with no help needed. This so amused and impressed Carmine that I forever became *Frankie Special*.

Pop loves that nickname for me because he says it sums up the fact that I have talent, and that all this adversity we're going through is only going to make me stronger and *more* special. My father says what I'm learning is how to be perseverant, and that one day, I won't believe how far I've come. I think his Hero School curriculum has finally worn off on me.

Pop has preached perseverance all my life, and by the summer of 1997, I begin to long for a future where I can be an inspiration to others.

On nights when it rains, or when it's too foggy to sit in the Jeep and gaze at Atlantic City, I go to our Catholic church for what's called—Perpetual Adoration. I don't go to Mass as often as I would like, but for the past few years I have attended a weekly Bible discussion at Aunt Bridgid and Uncle Bruno's house, and it's there that I learned to appreciate the wisdom of the carpenter's son.

During Perpetual Adoration, the Eucharist is displayed on the altar, and not kept hidden in the tabernacle. The church is dark, except for a few lights and candles. There are never more than a few people kneeling and praying by the altar, or silently reading from The Bible, in pews near the center aisle.

I'm too intimidated by the Eucharist to go anywhere near the altar, so I stay off to the side, slouched in one of the back pews. There, I allow my eyes to drift up to that huge cross hanging on the front wall.

Surrounded by stained glass, and images of The Stations of the Cross, I talk to Jesus like a friend—since that's what Sister Ruth used to say.

Even though she taught us that God was a girl, Sister always said, "Whenever you have a problem, just talk to Jesus like you would talk to a friend," and that's just what I do. I tell myself he was a carpenter's son, who picked up the hammer like his old man—if anybody is going to help me, it is going to be Him. From my pew in the back, and off to the side, I start telling Jesus about my visit to Mom with the metal detectors, and

448

the armed guards. I tell Him how we couldn't hold hands, and how she looked bad with her leg jumping up and down.

I tell Him about that phone call, when I told her I missed her, and she answered with silence. But mostly, I tell the carpenter's son how lonely I feel. Though I am committed to perseverance, I have never felt more alone. I have my brothers, and I have my father, but I need more; I need love. Sometimes, when the loneliness overwhelms me, I get down on my knees and plead. *Please, Lord, help me. Let me know you're there. I'm tired of being sad. I'm tired of being alone, please send me an angel. I know it's wrong to be selfish, but just this once, please do me this favor. I know others need more help than me. I know there are starving babies in Africa, but I'm having a tough time down here in Jersey. So, could You please send me someone to love?*

There is a small, spiral bound, Mead notebook, kept in the back of the church. It acts as an informal sign-in book for those who have come to Perpetual Adoration—a casual way for the monsignor to know how many attendees pass through each week.

I notice that the notebook also seems to act as a "Special Intentions Log," for some people have anonymously scribbled a few lines about their husband's drinking, or the lump in their mother's breast. I imagine their hope is that other parishioners will pray for them. I never write anything that could be construed that way, though I do take the pen lying beside the notebook, and sign my name. Without even thinking, I don't sign my real name; I sign in as *Ciccio Antonietta*. The first time I do that, I look down at my "new" signature and realize I did it to honor my parents; *Antonietta*, being my mother's full-name, and *Ciccio*, being the proper spelling for the Italian nickname "Cheecho," my father and I share. As a kid, I called him Dad. In high school, I switched to calling him Pop, but ever since that day I found him sobbing over those pictures in my parents' wedding album, I have started to call him Cheech because he is no longer simply my father—but an extension and reflection of myself—a connection to the past and the future, as well as a manifestation of all that I want to become, but yearn to avoid.

So, amidst the other signatures, Special Intentions and scribbled prayers in that ordinary notebook, the parishioners will read the words *Ciccio Antonietta*. They may not know who 'he' is, or even who we are, but my hope is that one day my life will come to represent the most basic of Catholic themes—that of redemption.

Those two Italian kids from Philadelphia, who brought me into this world, have been through more than most couples should ever have to endure. Something inside me knows that if I ever do anything worthwhile with my life, it will be to honor them: Ciccio and Antonietta.

67

In August of 1997, with my mother an inmate at the Trenton State Forensic Hospital, and our house in complete disarray—weeks prior to our moving out—I stumble upon a voicemail intended for my father. I am upstairs in my brothers' bedroom, where there is an extension of our house phone line. I want to call my friend, Ron, and see if he can play golf. I pick-up the receiver, ready to dial his number, when I hear the "tone" that alerts me to the fact that we have a new voicemail message waiting to be checked.

I wonder if Ron has already called, telling me where and when, we are going to tee-off. I enter the password to retrieve the voicemail, but when the message starts to play, I go cold. The message is from a woman. It is obvious she has been drinking. It also seems like she placed the call at night, since she sounds tired. The woman leaves a soft-spoken, romantic message for my father, sharing with him the news of her daughter's recent engagement, and how much she misses Pop, and hopes to see him soon.

I listen to the message a second time—trying to place the voice—but I can't. The caller doesn't identify herself, so my first thought is Gail. It has only been a few months since she came to that big concrete job down in Wildwood, and left that note for Pop; it *has* to be her. Yet, something in my gut says no. Something in my gut says—*this voice belongs to a new woman.*

At first, I am angry—I feel betrayed. *What does my father need with a girlfriend when he has me to rely on?* After all, he came to *me* with his emotions. He didn't go to his brother, his sister, Aunt Ellen, or Aunt Teresa—not even his own *mother. Frankie the Voice* shared his fears and his tears with *Ciccio Antonietta.*

I am his rock. He doesn't need some woman who leaves mushy messages for him on the same phone line he knows his sons use to call their friends. *What is he doing? Couldn't he have given her a different number? What is wrong with him?*

But then I stop myself. I stop myself because I love my father. He has been through enough since The Gasoline, and if he has met someone who makes him happy, who am I to say anything?

In the nearly six months since the attack, Pop has started to rely more and more on the cash he has withdrawn from his IRA. Despite the early withdrawal penalties he has to pay, we desperately need the money since the work in Wildwood has slowed down for the summer. The investors want Pop to wait until after Labor Day Weekend, before he can continue with that expansion project he was awarded, meaning we have no cash flow.

With no work, Pop spends most of his time fishing, and fiddling with his writing, as we begin the enormous and emotional task of moving-out. Meanwhile, his friends have started urging him to get divorced. They don't know what he is waiting for. They say it's time for him to face the facts; his marriage is over. I don't think they know about his voicemail mistress, but Pop says he doesn't feel right getting divorced. He says it feels too much like abandoning Mom—he does, however, agree to a structured Catholic Separation.

Even though Pop hasn't been to church in years, his lawyer—a personal friend, who is working pro bono—sells Pop on the idea of a Catholic Separation. He said it will allow a mediated separation agreement that addresses all the issues of living apart. Basically, it means my parents will be "divorced" in the eyes of the State, but still viewed as "married" in the eyes of the Catholic Church.

Pop likes the idea because it will allow for a sensitive and dignified approach to ending his marriage. Only, when it comes time to appear in court, and file the proceedings, my father becomes overwhelmed with guilt, and calls it off right there in front of the judge.

Later, he told us that he just kept thinking about the little girl in the greenhouse. He said, "That little girl grew-up to be my wife, and for better or worse, I still think of her that way."

It's just, after The Gasoline—he can never trust her again. He can never close his eyes at night without wondering if Mom will be standing there with another white sweater, and something much more lethal than a glass of gas to throw in his face.

My parents' marriage may still be legal in the eyes of Church and State—but it's over in the eyes of reality. That's why I simply decide to erase the voicemail, and mention nothing of it to anyone.

In late summer, I quit cutting grass for Hank, and stop filling in on my father's construction crew—I even give-up delivering pizzas on the weekends—because I want to find a job on a golf course. My plan is to get my game in shape before moving to Florida in the winter, and tryout for a college golf team next spring. The thing is—the only course hiring this late into the summer season—is Cape May National Golf Course—an hour's drive from home.

Cape May is at the very southern tip of the New Jersey peninsula—where the Delaware Bay meets the Atlantic Ocean. It is the nation's first—and oldest—seaside resort. The whole town is considered a national historic landmark, with award-winning beaches, and hundreds of Victorian-era buildings. It is the opposite of Atlantic City's "glitzy-ghetto," with a tiny year-round population, that *explodes* in the summer.

Cape May National Golf Course offers me a position on their ground's crew for six dollars an hour—and I'm just happy to find work where I can play golf for free every afternoon. I have to get-up at four thirty in the morning in order to clock in by six, but I don't care. It is with excitement that I speed down the Garden State Parkway for my first day of work, on August 18, 1997.

When I arrive at the golf course, the morning sky is still dark. I walk into the huge, airplane hangar type garage loaded with lawn care equipment, and members of the ground's crew. A couple of them are high school aged kids who nod *hello*. The rest are drifters, or men like me—looking to enjoy the free golf.

The superintendent's name is Stan. He is in his mid-thirties, with gray hair and piercing blue eyes. After introducing me to the rest of the crew, he tells me to go out onto the course in one of the old golf carts parked nearby. With a weedwacker, my job is to trim anything I see that the mowers can't get.

I take one of the old golf carts out to the first hole, knowing this course is going be my home away from home until I leave for Florida. I'll know every nook and cranny—every break of the greens. When I make the PGA Tour, they'll write articles about this place saying: *This Jersey native honed his skills on a wonderful little course, set back into the marshes, off historic Cape May.*

When I get to Hole #1, I'm filled with so much enthusiasm that I don't mind all the weedwacking I have to do. I don't mind that my shins are covered in green clippings like they used to be when I worked for Hank, and I don't mind because the thought of getting off at two thirty, to go hit balls until dusk, pushes me forward.

By seven thirty in the morning, I'm working on the fourth fairway, when I hear the hum of a gas-powered golf cart approaching from behind. *It's probably Stan,* I tell myself, *coming to check on the new guy.*

Only, it isn't Stan at all. Instead, it's a girl who obviously works here thanks to her gray shirt that says CAPE MAY GROUNDS. She is wearing a baseball cap. It's pulled way down over her dark eyes. Before she even opens her mouth, something about her tells me she's not from around here, yet I get this feeling like I know her. I try to act nonchalant as she gets out of her cart and approaches me. She says her name is Marina. I extend my hand and introduce myself, but I'm confused by her accent, "Are you French, or something?"

"No, I'm Spaneesh, from 'dee Spain."

"Oh...."

She says she came out here because I took her golf cart by mistake, which means I must have all the tools she needs for pruning flowers. Marina rummages through my golf cart, grabs what she needs, and as quickly as she pulls up—she's driving away with an, "Adios, amigo." Even though she disappears behind the fifth tee, I keep thinking about her accent, and those dark eyes, until break time—some two hours later. When I walk inside the airplane hangar type garage, in search of a cup of coffee, I'm caught off guard. I'm instantly overwhelmed by the strong presence of gasoline in the air, from all the lawnmowers and tractors nearby. Immediately, I think of Mom. The fumes trigger a sense of loneliness, and a feeling of desperation. The despair of these last five months suddenly rushes through my veins, and I feel the grief rising. In an instant, I am sad and hopeless—but then I turn the corner, and walk into the break room where Marina is standing there smiling at me, sipping a cup of coffee....

It's been exactly one hundred and sixty days since that March morning, as I stand there staring at her staring at me, with a white styrofoam cup just leaving her lips, to unveil a smile. Marina asks if I'd like some coffee, and out of habit I can't help but say, "Sure." But it's her pleasant manner that enchants me, as the coffee splashes into my cup, and the rest of my life begins.

Marina puts the pot back in its place, and starts telling me how she has been here all summer, that she comes in late—around seven thirty—and works only on flowers and flowerbeds, but gets off like everybody else at two thirty. She keeps explaining, as I blow and sip on my coffee, that she lives here on the golf course, in that house out by the road. That it's her first time here in the States, and yeah, she likes it, but for two months all she has seen is the beach and the golf course. She would like to travel a bit beyond what she's seen in New Jersey and Philadelphia and can't imagine going back home and telling her family all she saw was sand and flowers. When I ask her about home and where she's from, the answer I get is Madrid. She says, "You know where is'a Madrid, Franco?"

Franco? Did she just call me Franco? It takes me a second to gather my thoughts. I tell her I *think* I know where Madrid is, and Marina says she came for the summer to improve her English. As she says that, I want to tell her it's cute the way she wraps her Spanish lips around American words, but I decide I better not, for she might get offended and turn on her heel and never speak to me again. Then, where would I be without her pretty smile and dark eyes? As we finish our coffee, we begin to walk back outside, when she tells me I'll have to excuse her, because she has to load all these trays of pansies and tulips onto the back of her golf cart. "Let me give you a hand," I say.

"No, Franco, is okay. You drink'a coffee, I do." I ignore her, and start loading trays two at a time. She softens her eyes and says, "Franco, you are'a different."

"What's that?" I ask, wiping my brow with the back of my hand.

"I say you are'a different than other mans here. The American mans never help'a me."

She smiles and says, "Is easy see you are'a EE-talian boy from'a EE-talian family. You hold door'a for me, you ask where I from'a, you help'a me work...you'a different, Franco."

I stand there looking at her with a blank expression on my face, but inside I'm smiling from ear to ear. *Did you hear that?* I want to ask the other men walking past us. *Did you hear her say I'm different? That it's easy to see I'm Italian?* After I finish with the trays of pansies, Marina smirks and says, "Muchas gracias."

I smile back, but she drives off for the second time in two hours.

Come lunchtime, I make sure to sit next to her on this bench in the shade, as the rest of the guys spread out on golf carts, pick-up trucks and tractors. I'm longing for a big, Italian sandwich full of peppers and prosciutto, but all I have is a ginger ale, and some fried chicken. In between sips of ginger ale, I peek at Marina every chance I get, but Tyson's easy on the bag. I don't want to get all worked up over nothing. Yeah, she told me I was different, but a girl as pretty as Marina has to have a boyfriend. Her hair is dark with highlights of blonde; her legs are smooth and toned; and her breasts are small but ample. Tyson is easy on the bag because she probably has some bullfighter back home with this great big cape, and an even bigger tamale who calls her everyday just to say—*olé*—and remind her how much he loves her.

Or, maybe I'm wrong about the bullfighter—maybe it's some American guy she met this summer. A bit older, tall and slender with sprinkles of gray in his hair, who is into real estate and showing her a good time in his convertible as they discover hidden make-out spots along the by-ways of Route 9. Marina is probably defenseless against his American real estate charm, which means they may have even danced the *Cha-Cha* in the back of his convertible, and that image ruins it for me entirely. Come quitting time—a few hours later—I don't even look for her. I could never compete against a bullfighter with a big tamale, or a guy with real estate on Route 9.

After I punch-out, and grab my change of clothes from the Jeep, I make my way onto the driving range to hit some golf balls. I start with my pitching wedge to get loosened up, half swings, nothing fancy, stretching my back out, working on crisp cuts—when from behind I hear, "*Franco!*" I turn around, and there's Marina climbing the incline of the driving range. "Franco," she says, "I'm sorry for make interrupt."

"That's okay," I say. "What's up?"

"Well, I was go to dee' beach. You want go to dee' beach with me?"

Without even thinking about it, I hear myself say, "Sure, I'll go. I love the beach." I slip my pitching wedge back into my golf bag, and walk away from the pile of balls lying there on the range. With my golf bag slung across my shoulders, I hear a voice inside my head, *hey, Franco, yoo-hoo, Franco, you came here to be a golfer, not to go to the beach. What are you doing?*

Marina takes me to Cape May Point where we follow this narrow path through the dunes that leads out to a tiny beach, loaded with Shoobies. We pick a spot not far from the waterline. I melt at the sight of Marina slipping off her shorts and pulling her tee-shirt up over her head. She is wearing a dark pink bathing suit that cups her small breasts, and hugs her bottom like she was born in it. All I can do is take my shirt off, and puff out my chest. I hope Marina notices me noticing her as we swim and laugh and talk until sunset.

After our time on the beach, we go to dinner in the heart of historic Cape May—where it's quaint and quiet and romantic. I am embarrassed to wear my work boots that are covered in grass clippings, so I put on my golf shoes. The problem is—my golf shoes have metal spikes, and I am aware of the sounds the loud metal spikes make as I walk.

So, I crunch, crunch, crunch along the sidewalks and cobblestone streets as people turn their heads in our direction—wondering who on earth is making all of that noise. We decide to sit and eat at an outside deli where it's nice to be able to talk without my shoes causing a scene.

We order hoagies and fries, and Marina walks me through Spanish history from Queen Isabel to Francisco Franco.

All her talk of Europe reminds me of a class I had at Atlantic Community College on European History, and that's what I tell her. But what I hold inside, is that sometimes a study group would meet at my house—and that meant I had to cover for Mom. These weren't people I grew up with. These were new people entering our world. They didn't know my mother, hadn't seen her slowly deteriorate, so I always had to make something up. I would see them pull into the driveway, meet them on the front porch and say, "Hey, you know, just wanna tell ya', my mother isn't feelin' too hot. I think she's got the flu or something. So, if she seems a little out of it, you know, don't think nothin' of it."

"Oh, no problem," they would say. "I know how my mom gets when she's sick."

"Yeah, no problem, Frank." That was normally enough to explain why she was laying around in a trance—*poor lady isn't feeling well*. I never liked covering for her like that, but they were outsiders—what else could I do? And that's what Marina is; an outsider. I need to cover-up— but she notices the distance in my eyes. "Franco, is you okay?" I was daydreaming, but I can't tell her the truth. "Yeah, yeah. I'm fine."

"You sure?"

"Yeah, I'm fine."

She studies my eyes an extra moment. "Franco, what is?"

"Nothing."

"Franco, tell me what is...."

Do I tell her the truth? What if she doesn't understand my English? What if she gets up and walks away? I take a sip of water. I look down. I lean in towards her. I look into her eyes. I lay my arms across the table. I smile and say, "I was thinking about my mother."

"Oh, what about you'a mother?"

"Well, she's kinda sick."

"That's a shame'a. What is'a problem?"

"She lives in a hospital."

"How sad. Does she have da' cancer?" *Here comes the moment of truth*, I tell myself. *Stop beating around the bush. You can't fear the consequences. Just say it.* "No, Marina. She doesn't have cancer. My mother is mentally ill."

"Oh," Marina looks right back at me. She doesn't bat an eye. She says she wants me to continue, but to please speak slowly. I can tell she is sincere. Maybe it's because I don't know her, or maybe it's because her English makes her sound innocent, but I don't feel any shame when I share Mom's history with Marina. In fact, it flows out of me like a story.

I choose my words carefully, and tell her about that greenhouse back in 1955, and what that meant to my mother, and parents on their honeymoon. Then I go to Babbo, and my great-grandmother, and how he held a grudge against Aunt Colomba and Mom for being girls. I tell Marina how my mother changed after Babbo died. How she gambled and slept on the floor—fearing he was hiding in her closet. I talk about my father's affair; and how Mom kept getting worse and worse. Then, I mention Mom's attempted suicide with the butcher knife and the carpet cleaner and the aspirin, and how that led to her aneurysm surgery, and my Towson disaster.

By the time I get to The Gasoline, and how Mom has been shuffling between the Atlantic County Jail, and the Trenton State Forensic Hospital—Marina is silent, with her arms folded across her chest. I speak factually, not emotionally, mainly because I was making sure to speak slowly so Marina would understand my English. When I finish, she nods her head a few times and says, "Interesting, very interesting. I hope I no offend'a you, Franco, but I study psychology in'a Madrid, and for me, what you say, is'a very interesting."

I slouch back in my chair a bit. *Interesting?* I never thought of it as interesting. *Is she fucking out of her mind?* I don't know whether to take my glass of water and throw it in her face—or get out of my chair and propose marriage right here on the cobblestone streets of Cape May.

We move from the deli, to the beach—where we spend the next few hours sitting by the water's edge, discussing my mother in more detail. Marina and I are side by side, as the ocean reaches for the sand, then backs away, reaches for the sand again, and backs away. The moon is bright white, and as we talk, I realize I feel calm inside.

I don't feel betrayed, or scared, or any of the thousands of sad tinglings I've felt since the madness of that March morning—one hundred and sixty days ago. With Marina by my side, I feel at peace. She sits there half lying back, both hands extended behind her, legs straight out, right crossed over the left.

During a break in our conversation, I gaze out over the dark ocean—and think of Mom. She must be so scared in that forensic hospital—scared to be locked away in her cell. I wish I was there to protect her—but I'm not. I'm sitting next to Marina, who is dusting the sand from her legs, saying it's late and that we ought to get going. We both stand and make our way off the beach. We stop near the building by the edge of the beach so she can slip her sandals back on. That's where I notice how the yellow light coming from the building shines upon the spiked footprints my golf shoes have left behind in the sand.

Since Marina and I didn't return to her house until one in the morning, I didn't bother driving home. I slept in my Jeep—in the deserted parking lot of the golf course—which means I have some explaining to do when I call Pop from the phone in Stan's office the next day. I tell him I'm sorry for not calling, but it didn't make any sense for me to drive all the way home, if I was just going to have to come back down in three hours. At first, Pop is stern with me—hollering through the phone that he was worried to death. He doesn't care what time it was—I should have called. "That's no excuse, Cheech. You should have known better! Where did you sleep anyway?" I explain to him how I slept in the Jeep—in the parking lot—but he says, "I don't get it. This is so unlike you. What the hell happened?"

"Well," I say, "I met this girl, and time sorta got away from us." When I say that—the line goes quiet for a moment, until he asks, "What's her name?"

"Marina."

"She a nice girl?"

"She seems like it."

"What'd you guys do?"

"Went to the beach after work—then hung out all night."

460

"Sounds good. You have a nice time?"

"Yeah, she's an exchange student from Spain"

"Yeah? How old is she?"

"Twenty-one."

"Twenty-one?"

"Yeah. Why?" The line goes quiet again, until Pop says, "Cheech, lissename."

"Yeah, Pop...."

"You don't have that much experience with girls."

"Pop...."

"No, no, it's not your fault. But the truth is, you haven't dated much and...."

"Pop, c'mon it wasn't even really a d...."

"Now, Chichi, sometimes older girls—especially older foreign girls—are a little more aggressive than boys. You follow me?"

"Pop, she's only a year older...."

"That doesn't matter. Just hear me out. I want you to use your head."

"Pop, I just met her. She doesn't even think of me that way."

"Today she doesn't—but tomorrow she might. You gotta promise me that if anything happens you're gonna use your head. I'm serious, right now you're thinking you're just friends, but that's not how these things work. Pretty soon, Mother Nature takes over and...."

"What's that mean?"

"That means you gotta be ready...."

"For what?"

"For sex."

"Oh my God! Pop, you're crazy. I think she's got a boyfriend."

"That doesn't matter, Chichi. I know how these things work." He makes me promise I'll use a condom not *if*—but *when* Marina and I sleep together. I tell him he's nuts, but Pop says he doesn't want a little Francisco running with the bulls in Spain. I can't get off the phone until I promise him that I'll use a condom. Even though I know that would *never* happen in a million years. Marina doesn't even think of me that way. "Besides," I tell him, "I made a promise to Mom that I wouldn't do anything until I got married."

"You can make all the promises you want—but when the moment has arrived, and it *feels* right—ain't nothin' gonna stop ya'."

For the next six days, Marina and I go to the beach every day after work—and my golf clubs never leave the backseat of the Jeep. Day and night, we laugh and talk so much—that by the third night—I start to feel what Pop was talking about. Mother Nature is taking over. I find myself wanting to lean in and kiss Marina. I find myself wanting to say, *Marina, you're amazing. Would you like to go out on a real date?*

The problem is—I'm afraid of saying something like that. I'm fearful of that boyfriend back in Spain—with his tamale poised and ready—so I keep my feelings to myself. But it gets harder and harder to keep my emotions bottled-up, especially when I see Marina in her pink bathing suit each day. When we get to the beach, she dribbles off her shorts and peels off her shirt, and Tyson starts to beat the bag like a man possessed. My heart pounds so much that I'm afraid Marina might hear. My palms get sweaty, the back of neck gets hot, and by Friday afternoon, I can't stand it anymore.

As the beach empties out, and the sun begins to set, I walk to the water's edge. In the light splish splash of the waves, I hear Pop's voice in my head. I spoke to him on the phone at lunch, told him I really like Marina, but that I'm hesitant to say anything. He said, "You just gotta tell her, Chichi. You can't wait. If you feel it—then just be honest. You're a sweet guy, you're handsome. If you like her, then tell her, not apologetically, don't apologize for liking her, just tell her how you feel, and what you would like. If she doesn't want the same things, well then you'll have to accept that, Chichi. Life's just too short to fear the consequences."

The sky is bright orange, when Marina walks up behind me with the hood of her sweatshirt covering her dirty blonde hair. She comes close to me. "Franco, what you think'a about? Is long'a time you stand here think." I turn to look at her. I study her eyes. "Marina," I say, "I really like spending time with you...."

"Me too Franco, is'a fun."

"....and I don't know your situation, if you have a boyfriend, or not. But I was wondering if we could be more than friends." She looks at me a second, then looks down and kicks at the sand with her bare feet. When she looks back up, she says, "Franco, you are'a sweet boy, and I like'a be with'a you. But I no wanna boyfriend right'a now. I no wanna hurt'a you. I go back'a to Spain in'a few weeks. So, I thank'a you, but I no think'a is good idea for be more than friends."

—I am devastated.

68

After being rejected by Marina, I spend the next two days wondering what's wrong with me. I call Pop and tell him how she turned me down, but he says, "Chichi, you have to feel good about what you did. Don't beat yourself up. She isn't leaving tomorrow, and you never know what could happen."

Pop is always telling me not to beat myself up. He says I always get wet before it rains, that I live in my head too much. So, just this once I decide to take it easy on myself, and step outside my head—which might be why Marina accepted my invitation to go to the Dodgers-Phillies game as friends. This new attitude, on my part, also might be the reason why right there during the seventh inning stretch, during the singing of, *Take Me Out to the Ballgame*, Marina leaned in and touched her lips to mine.

I had no idea it was about to happen. But as we kissed, our tongues brushed against each other's so passionately, I felt a warmth rush through me from head to toe. From that moment on, my whole world changed—as Marina and I become inseparable.

While my romance with Marina quickly develops in Cape May, I learn that Mom has been moved to a Psychiatric Hospital—located halfway between Philadelphia and Atlantic City. Pop says there will be no more shuffling between the Atlantic County Jail and the Trenton State Forensic Hospital; this is Mom's new home.

Situated in the middle of the Pinelands—on eighty acres of land—Mom's new home is New Jersey's largest psychiatric hospital. Built in the 1950's, it can house up to six hundred patients, Mom stays in the involuntary commitment unit.

Through his involvement with her doctors, my father comes to understand that this hospital will offer a multidisciplinary team approach to the development, and implementation of Mom's care. Though there against her will; I'm glad my mother is no longer viewed as an inmate; she is a patient.

With Mom in the Psychiatric Hospital, my brothers move into Grandmom and Grandpop's house. My grandparents live with Aunt Sofia and Uncle Bobby, at the other end of town. Their house is already overrun—with four adults living in a cluttered, awkward rancher. But that's where Tony enters his senior year of high school, and Michael begins his sophomore campaign.

Both of my brothers share a tiny bedroom—and the gridiron spotlight. In August of 1997, they enter training camp as the starting varsity quarterbacks for their respective high school football teams. Since there isn't room for Pop to comfortably stay at Grandmom's house, my father divides his nights between Uncle Bruno's guest bedroom, and his friend Charlie's living room couch.

The thing is—my father starts to 'come and go' a little bit. Sometimes my brothers don't see him for several days, or he won't answer his cell phone consistently. This new pattern on Pop's part irks members of the extended family, and his close circle of friends. They want to know where he is.

They say, "These boys just lost their mother to the loony bin. Where the hell is their father?"

But I know what's going on—my father must be in love. Though I have never mentioned a word about it to anyone—I imagine Pop must be spending time with that woman from the voicemail. That's the only way to explain his, 'now you see him, now you don't,' behavior.

On the eve of his forty eighth birthday, my father has either abandoned—or lost—everything. His business is a sham, his finances are in shambles, his wife is in a psychiatric hospital, her family hates him, his own family questions how much "blame" he deserves. His friends criticize his whereabouts, and his sons are confused by his absence. Pop is seen as the 'bad guy' by *everyone.*

He is even ridiculed for supporting my involvement with Marina.

As my parents and my brothers settle into their new routines and living arrangements, Marina and I spend every day together. We spend the balance of August and all of September, traveling as much as we can. Both of us quit the golf course and take my Jeep all over the Delaware Valley—and beyond. We go to Washington, D.C., and Baltimore, Maryland. We sightsee in Philadelphia, New York, and the Poconos. The two of us even spend a day in Asbury Park, looking for Bruce Springsteen—though we find no trace of The Boss.

Marina and I squeeze an entire summer of travel into four weeks, and I'm so happy I can't think straight. She is the angel I prayed for, and nothing or no one has ever made me feel so alive. But back home, everyone wants to know—*where is Frankie?*

Despite the fact we had to be out of our house by September first, my father told me not to worry about coming home to help move. He wanted me to enjoy whatever time I may have had with Marina, considering her return to Spain was fast approaching.

Pop said he and my brothers could handle the move, along with help from my aunts, uncles, cousins—and a bunch of Tony's friends. But this only caused my relatives to ask—*why is big Frank allowing Frankie to get away without helping us move? When did Frankie become so irresponsible?*

They didn't care that I had met 'some girl.' They felt taken advantage of. In addition to assisting with the move, I was supposed to help prepare my grandparents' house for our arrival. While Tony and Michael were going to share that tiny bedroom, I was destined to sleep on the back porch. I was supposed to help Grandpop enclose the porch—turning it into a bedroom of sorts—but with Marina and I unwilling to separate for even a day, nothing gets done. When I finally showed up on the last day of the move, I got the cold shoulder from Aunt Sofia—my father's much younger, only sister. My aunt wouldn't speak to me. This caught me off guard. But I quickly realized there was more behind her coldness than hurt feelings—she was worried about me—and thought my father was guilty of leading me astray.

When Marina and I aren't traveling—that tiny beach in Cape May Point is our home—and her bed is my lifeboat. We sleep together every night, in a little twin bed, in the house she shares with a few other employees from the golf course. Even though we sleep together; we're not 'sleeping together.' I told Marina about the promise I made to Mom when I was fifteen—but she has been saying she can't imagine us being together like we are without 'being together.' When I ask Pop about it, he tells me that I'm a man now, that I'm twenty years old, and shouldn't worry about some promise I made when I was fifteen. He says I should follow my heart. If I feel being with Marina is the right thing, then I shouldn't think twice about it. His only concern is pregnancy. He says, "Just remember, Cheech, I'm on your side whatever you decide. But I don't want any grandchildren running around just yet. *Capisce?*"

With my mother out of the picture, Aunt Sofia feels the need to say something—and she doesn't hold back. My aunt corners me, and wants to know what happened to the sweet church-going boy that knew better than to put himself in a situation where he might find himself sleeping with a girl. She says I could cause irreparable damage to my eternal soul. I tell her I understand, but, "It's just Marina. We've grown so close in the past few weeks."

"*A few weeks!* You've known her a few weeks, and already you're thinking about sleeping with her?"

"Aunt Sofia, I like feeling close to her and...."

"Frankie, you have to understand something; you're the oldest cousin. Don't you know how everybody looks up to you? Don't you know that if they see you doing something wrong, they're going to think it's alright? You have that power over the rest of the kids. You're not thinking, Frank! You're not seeing what repercussions this decision could have on the family."

I have nothing to say to my aunt; she is right. I'm not only the oldest of The Three Tooters—I'm also the oldest cousin in our faction of the family down the shore. I've always known that what I say, and do, 'mean' something. I am "the example," and I don't want to disappoint anybody—but Marina says the waiting is over. It's time. She wants us to be together—and wants us to be together *tonight*.

We are in Baltimore, and had a glorious day together at the city's well-known aquarium. Before we get ready for dinner, Marina sends me out to buy some condoms. She drops her towel as she enters the bathroom of our hotel room—just to prove a point—and I think I'll need a thousand condoms the way my body hardens at the sight of her nudity.

But then I think of Aunt Sofia, and the consequences, and my thoughts quickly turn religious.

Though I agree with Marina that it's time for us to start 'sleeping together,' I decide to ask the Blessed Virgin for guidance. I ask the carpenter's wife for a sign. I climb into the Jeep and say, *Mary, if this is supposed to happen then please make it obvious. If not, then please do the same.*

On a busy Saturday in late summer, as tourists crawl through Baltimore, I stop at two pharmacies in search of condoms. The thing is, both pharmacies turn me away at the door. "Sorry," they say, "we're closing." When I get back into my Jeep after the second pharmacy turns me away, I take it as Mary making her point—*now is not the time.*

I go back to the hotel without any condoms, and Marina is disappointed. She says she was looking forward to making love tonight, but can see that I'm not ready yet.

I don't tell her about Mary, and the message I gleaned from the closing of the pharmacies. Marina doesn't believe in prayer like I do. She says Spain may be a Catholic country, but nobody goes to church anymore, especially people our age. I know she would ridicule my talking to Mary, or the carpenter's son. But Marina pushes her disappointment aside as we spend a romantic evening wandering around Baltimore's Inner Harbor, happy and smiling, and holding each other's hand.

69

During the process of moving out, my brother Tony found a small, handwritten note my mother composed almost five years ago. It was hidden under the box spring in my parents' bedroom. The note was addressed to my father, though Mom had never given it to him. In her own words, she provided a self-diagnosis of sorts:

November 1992

Dearest one, I love you. My whole being, soul, heart and mind has always been devoted to one person, my special Frank. Please excuse me for the hurtful, insensitive, ugly side that I've displayed with shame to you. I didn't expose my soft side out of fear, and in reaction to the endless years of turmoil, and abuse, I saw at home. My mind set was so mixed up. I truly thought I didn't deserve to be happy, because I thought my mom wasn't happy. I'm so grateful that I have you. My husband, my hero, my love, my life.

Yours always, Antonietta

Mom's note reminds me of something I gleaned from Marina, and her psychology studies: *the level of happiness we experience on the outside—is simply a reflection of how we feel about ourselves on the inside.* Marina helps me to understand that Mom's self-esteem was like a thermostat, set to maintain a certain temperature.

No matter what happened to her on the outside, Mom's emotional thermostat kicked on the "heat," or the "air conditioner," and kept her stuck in the same place. She was a prisoner of her past, and her self-worth. Mom even writes that she thought she didn't deserve to be happy—because Nonna wasn't happy.

No matter how many reasons she had to feel good about herself—and the life she *could* have led—my mother continued to sabotage herself.

She never wanted to change—never wanted to grow. After the years of sexual abuse—and the way she suffered under Babbo—it's easy to see how Mom felt worthless.

But after reading her note, I think a part of her was afraid that if she "got better," she would somehow betray Nonna, and that was something Mom would not allow. It went against her code. It was something no psychologist, or "emotional electrician," could ever re-wire.

I believe my mother lost her mind—*in part*—out of loyalty.

Buried beneath that loyalty and hidden beyond the decades of dysfunction stood four words that foretold my mother's future—*oh no, not her*.

In the tiny Italian enclaves from which my parents hailed in Philadelphia, there remained a certain connection, a certain affection amongst the immigrants from the different regions of Italy. The Sicilians tended to favor other Sicilians, those from Calabria tended to favor other *Calabresi* and so on and so forth—it was only natural. They were all Italian in the eyes of the Americans, but these regional loyalties were a very real thing.

Grandpop—Dad's dad—is Calabrian. He and his *Calabrese* relatives knew Nonna and Babbo before my parents ever met. As a matter of fact, Babbo used to park his fruit stand on wheels at Grandpop's auto mechanic garage. This meant my two grandfathers saw each other daily throughout the 1950's and 60's, and although they were not "friends," Grandpop didn't share his wife's concerns over my parents' plans to marry. He was happy his oldest son was not only marrying an Italian girl—but a Calabrian girl. He liked Nonna and Babbo just fine and from what he could tell they treated his boy wonderfully—which they did throughout my parents' long courtship.

Grandpop saw his wife's concerns over my parents' wedding as nothing more than a Neapolitan mother claiming *no Calabrian girl is good enough for my son*—that is until one day in the spring of 1975.

My grandfather was visiting one of his longtime pals, a fellow *Calabrese* named Luca. Now, Luca lived several doors down from Mom's family in their almost entirely Calabrian neighborhood. The two men were on the front porch enjoying an ice cold beer when Grandpop casually happened to mention in his *Vito Corleone* like voice, "Luca, I dunno if you heard, but my oldest son is gettin' married soon."

"Oh, that's great."

"Yeah," Grandpop continued, "and I think you know the girl."

"Oh? Who's that?" Grandpop nodded towards a house across the street. The house belonged to Mom's family. Their rowhome stood near the corner of the avenue and Grandpop said. "Ann. You know Ann from down the street, right?"

At that Luca stopped drinking his beer and his expression went blank. Grandpop couldn't make sense of his friend's reaction, but before he could ask him what the matter was, Luca shook his head and uttered those four words, "Oh no, not her...."

My grandfather was confused. He thought highly of my mother. He figured Luca would be happy to hear that his son was marrying a nice *Calabrese* girl, but those four words cut through their afternoon visit. These were blue collar men and Old World friends, yet my grandfather didn't know what to say to Luca's *oh no, not her*. He was actually a little offended. After all that was his future daughter-in-law Luca was talking about. Yet, Grandpop decided to leave Luca's comment alone as the two buddies continued on with their beers, and quickly changed the subject.

The thing is—Luca had lived down the street from Mom and her family his entire life, he watched her grow-up, he probably saw through The Cover-Up. He may have known things weren't "right" behind closed doors. He may have even heard rumors about the greenhouse, and all that took place in that wretched place.

Regardless of what Luca did or did not know, Grandpop never mentioned anything about his visit that day or those four words his friend uttered until long after my parents' marriage—and Mom's life—had completely fallen apart.

Luca's *oh no, not her* intuition seems to connect the dots between the little girl in the greenhouse, and the lady now living in New Jersey's largest psychiatric hospital.

The clues were there—you just needed a front row seat, and a few decades to realize what you were looking at.

Mom was 28 when she married my father. Luca knew that whomever she married was in store for a confusing and mysterious walk down the aisle.

Yet, Mom's family continues to see her demise as being completely and entirely my father's fault. They roll their eyes, shake their heads and utter, *"Va fanabala"* if any other theory is given breath.

As far as they're concerned, Mom was a healthy woman when she left Philadelphia and was forced to move down the shore in 1978. It was her two decades married to an overbearing and abusive partner that did her in.

Marina and I are on the Cape May-Lewes Ferry, crossing the Delaware Bay. Our plan is to spend the entire day in Rehoboth Beach, Delaware, looking for knick-knacks Marina can bring back to her friends and family in Spain. The bay is calm, though the huge ferry is crowded with lots of people and cars.

I'm sitting next to her on the back deck of the ferry. The sun is high and bright in the sky, as a couple stands at the rail feeding a bunch of seagulls hovering behind us. I sit with my arms folded across my chest, with Marina by my side, as she asks me if I remember the first time I mentioned my mother.

"You remember, Franco, 'dat dinner you wear'a golf shoes, an'a we talk'a of the Spanish history?"

"Yeah," I say. "I remember that. It was our first date."

"Well, remember how I say, you mother was'a interesting?"

"Yeah, you said you're studying psychology and hearing me talk about my mom was like listening to a real life case study."

"*Sí, sí, sí*," she says, "*pero* there is 'nother reason I thought'a was interesting."

Marina points at the couple standing by the railing, feeding the seagulls. "Franco, what you think'a 'bout them?"

"About what—the seagulls?"

"No, the man an'a the woman."

"I think they're probably a few years older than we are."

"*Sí, sí, sí*, but'a you think that'a is'a the only way?"

"Marina, I don't understand."

"I mean, you think man an'a woman is'a the only way?"

"Man and woman is the only way? What?"

"Do you think only man an'a woman can'a fall in love?"

"Are you trying to ask me if I think only men and women can fall in love?"

"*Sí.*"

"You mean fall in love with each other?"

"*Sí.* Do you think'a only mens can fall'a in love with'a womens, or can fall'a in love with'a mens?"

"You mean like gay guys? Like homosexuals?"

"*Sí, sí, sí, como homosexuales.*"

"I don't get it. What are you talkin' about? Why would you want to know that?"

"Because...ah...because'a mi madre, ah...my mother is in love with'a woman. She is—how you say—*lesbiana?*"

"You mother's a lesbian? I thought you said your parents were divorced?"

"*Sí, están divorciados.*"

"So, how can she be a lesbian?"

"My parents dee'vorce two years a'go. Now, my mother say to me an'a my family she fall'a in'a love with'a a woman from'a her work. She name is'a Beatriz."

Marina goes on to tell me that her mother sat her, and her two younger sisters down, and told them that she had fallen in love with a colleague of hers named Beatriz. She says it was very difficult for them to accept, since her parents were married for twenty-one years. Marina says her mother coming out as a lesbian, was very insulting to her father, and difficult for her sisters and her to deal with.

She wants me to know that she used that word *interesting* on our first date because she immediately felt a connection with me, and my own struggles with Mom. She says her mother and Beatriz live together in Madrid, and that her father now has a girlfriend who is much, *much* younger than he is.

Her sisters and she are still struggling to get used to their new lives. It has been very challenging. Marina says she didn't want to wait any longer to tell me. She thought it was important for me to know.

Marina telling me the truth about her mother, only serves to bring us closer together, to cement the fact that we are perfect for each other. We understand one another, and get along so well, that even though it has only been a month—Marina says she has been thinking about marriage and a family.

She says she has never met anyone like me before. That I'm so kind and generous and handsome, that she would love to be my wife. But a funny thing happens when she mentions marriage; I become cold and grumpy towards her.

I have always wanted to get married. So, I don't know why I get so glum when Marina uses that word, but it's like someone hits a switch in my brain when she starts talking about us like that. Marina says she can feel the change in me, and wants to know why I'm so against getting married—but then she answers her own question. "Of course," she says. "Is'a what'a you saw grow up. You no wanna get'a marry after watch you parents."

She says she could say the same thing about her parents' marriage, but then she wouldn't be allowing herself to be open to the possibilities of where life could lead. Marina says she understands my fears, but says she can still see us together forever.

Our feelings for each other only get stronger come September, when Marina has to go back home.

The thought of being away from her, makes me so sad, I have a hard time hiding it from her. I tell her I don't want her to go. I say I don't care about my parents' marriage, I want her to stay, that I can't imagine going back to the life I had before we met.

I can't imagine going back to Perpetual Adoration and asking the carpenter's son for more angels, because He would never send me one as perfect as Marina. I get a chill down my spine, when I think of her in Spain and me here in Jersey. The great thing is—she feels the same way.

She tells me she loves me, and I tell her I love her. It isn't long afterwards—that I break that promise I made to my mother. Pop was right—Mother Nature took over one hot September night—and our young bodies came together as one.

When Marina and I first make love, it's over so quickly I am embarrassed, but she is sweet with me. We are on the floor of her room, in that house she lives in, here on the golf course. When my body is ready to perform again, I discover the sincerity of my desires towards her, and realize Marina is the perfect girl for me. Being inside of her is both erotic and pure—I only hope the carpenter's son understands.

474

Once our relationship becomes sexual, Marina is convinced her life is meant to unfold here with me in New Jersey. She wants to stay in the United States. Only when she calls her father and tells him that she wants to drop-out of college in-order to remain with her Italian-American boyfriend, he says that's completely out of the question. He says college is more important than anything, but if she really cares for me that much, then I'm more than welcome to stay with them in Spain.

When I tell Pop that Marina's father invited me to Spain, he says, "See, Chichi, I told you. You never know where things are going to go, how they're going to turn out. A month ago you were depressed because she shot you down. Now look at you, halfway to Europe."

Even though Pop and I are excited about the idea of me going to Spain, every other adult in our family, including Aunt Ellen and Aunt Teresa, think it's the wrong move. They want to know why he would spend the money it will take to get me to Spain, when we don't have a real place to live.

They say, "Think about it, Frank, you're not doing right by Frankie. He just met this girl. You're setting him up for disappointment. What if they break-up over there? Then what will he do with the five words of Spanish he knows?"

Pop argues with them. He tells them that he thinks it's very important for me to go. If not only to stay with Marina, but so that I'll have a chance to see a little bit more of the world. He wants me to get out of south Jersey, and discover who I really am. My father says, "The trip will do wonders for Frankie. He has been floundering here anyway. So why don't you get off his back, and wish him *bon voyage?*"

70

Today is Wednesday, October 8, 1997, and I am leaving for Spain. Marina had to go home ten days ago, so she wouldn't miss the beginning of the semester at her university. Even though we've been in constant contact ever since she left, I simply can't wait to see her again. Memories from our month and a half together mix with the excitement I feel inside, as Pop takes me up the Atlantic City Expressway, to Philadelphia International Airport.

After we park my Jeep, and I check-in with the airline, my father says we ought to get me a pack of gum for the flight. I'm not sure what he's talking about, or why I would need a pack of gum to get on an airplane, but I can only trail behind him as he approaches a small kiosk inside the terminal.

I have to trail behind my father because he's taking big strides, like he's the one going to Spain. Like he's the one with the European angel waiting to show him what life is like on the "Continent." But I know his strides are big because he's happy. Happy to see me with Marina—happy I belong to a woman. As I watch him stride towards the kiosk, I think about that lady from the voicemail, and wonder if he belongs to her, too.

It has been two months since I heard that message, but something in me knows they are together. Pop has been singing and whistling a lot recently—a far cry from the father who just six months ago used to sob in my sheets late at night. He has that cool air about him again—that *Frankie the Voice* feel—with his collar up and bravado back in place.

A little stucco work he has gotten recently is the only project keeping us afloat. But that doesn't stop Pop from giving me twelve hundred dollars for my trip to Spain. He knows what confidence I've found in Marina, because he has probably found the same thing in Ms. Voicemail.

Being with Marina has allowed me to see things differently. When I think about Mom in the Psychiatric Hospital, or the Egyptians living in our house, I feel a peace inside. A silent strength that says, *appreciate what you have. Your father could have died that morning. Your house could have burned to the ground with you and your brothers trapped inside.*

I think these thoughts standing beside my father, who is standing in front of the cashier station of the kiosk, studying a rainbow of chewing gum colors and flavors, on a small shelf at waist level. Pop reaches out and plucks up a lime green pack of Wrigley's Spearmint gum. He turns to me and says, "Chichi, take this, and make sure you chew it when you take off, and when you start to land. It'll keep your ears from popping."

I look at him funny when he says that—I've never flown before. But Pop gives me a nod that says, *trust me, I know what I'm talking about.* Before we pay for the gum, Pop weaves through the other travelers. He walks towards the magazine racks where he picks up a small, red book full of Spanish/English phrases. As he begins flipping through the phrase book, I say, "Pop, I don't need a dictionary. Marina can translate for me. We already talked about it."

"That may be true, Cheech, but you might wanna pick up some of the language when you're over there."

Pop pays for the gum, and the phrase book. He walks me to my gate where we sit and wait for my flight to start boarding. Outside— through these huge floor to ceiling windows—I can see dozens of planes. Some are parked next to long metal corridors, while others are being driven from here to there.

Every minute or so, I catch sight of a plane barreling down the runway, only to be lifted into the air so smoothly that it looks effortless and divine. As I watch those planes climb into the sky, I know soon that will be me lifted into the air, and carried across the ocean. The same ocean my grandparents crossed decades ago when they came to America. The same ocean Nonna crossed forty years ago, when she left Mom alone to wander into that greenhouse, while she went back to Calabria.

Sitting next to my father, watching the planes rise so effortlessly into the air, I think about the difference between their crossings, and the one I'm about to make. I conjure up the image of Anthony Robbins, and hear his voice in my head, *know your outcome.* I see Jimmy Valvano at the *ESPY's—don't give up. Don't ever give up.* I feel Pop next to me, and think about how I was once only a twinkle in his eye; a dream he and Mom shared as they walked down the foggy Boardwalk arm in arm, talking aloud about having a son, and raising a family. And then it hits me. This isn't my first time on an airplane. There was that visit Mom made to Italy with Nonna, back in 1976. It was there she first realized she was pregnant with me. That means I flew with her across the ocean, a stowaway of sorts.

As my British Airways' flight begins to board, and I take my seat, I think of her. I think of Mom as the huge airliner races down the runway at dusk. I can feel the adrenaline. I sense the momentum. Soon, we'll be in the heavens. Soon, I'll be in Madrid. Just as the front tires leave the ground, I crane my neck to look out the window. An instant later we have left the earth, and begin to climb. My father was right; life is too short to fear the consequences. I will no longer be afraid. I will live undaunted, intrepid and inspired.

In honor of *Frankie the Voice*, and *Swing-Set Annie*, I will use the rest of my life as an opportunity to redeem his squandered talent, and her abusive childhood—and I will do so by "finding my voice." I want to discover who I truly am, and how I can best make an impact on those around me. Armed with this new revelation and desire, I know that I will do everything in my power, to be all that I can. But for now, as the autumn sky turns orange above Philadelphia, I think of Spain and smile to myself. I wonder what this trip will mean to me. I wonder who I will become.

Marina awaits me across the sea, as I lean back in my seat—the oldest of The Three Tooters—the one ready to fly away....

To connect with Francesco, visit his website:

www.francescogranieri.net

Made in the USA
Middletown, DE
22 September 2019